T0355556

RHETORICS OF DEMOCRACY IN THE AMERICAS

RHETORIC AND DEMOCRATIC DELIBERATION
VOLUME 25

EDITED BY CHERYL GLENN AND STEPHEN BROWNE
THE PENNSYLVANIA STATE UNIVERSITY

Co-founding Editor: J. Michael Hogan

Rhetoric and Democratic Deliberation focuses on the
interplay of public discourse, politics, and democratic action.
Engaging with diverse theoretical, cultural, and critical
perspectives, books published in this series offer fresh
perspectives on rhetoric as it relates to education, social
movements, and governments throughout the world.
A complete list of books in this series is located at the back
of this volume.

RHETORICS OF DEMOCRACY IN THE AMERICAS

EDITED BY ADRIANA ANGEL,
MICHAEL L. BUTTERWORTH,
AND NANCY R. GÓMEZ

The Pennsylvania State University Press | University Park, Pennsylvania

This volume is published with the generous support of the Center for Democratic Deliberation at The Pennsylvania State University.

Library of Congress Cataloging-in-Publication Data

Names: Angel, Adriana, 1981– editor. | Butterworth, Michael L., editor. | Gómez, Nancy R. (Nancy Regina), 1978– editor.
Title: Rhetorics of democracy in the Americas / edited by Adriana Angel, Michael L. Butterworth, and Nancy R. Gómez.
Other titles: Rhetoric and democratic deliberation ; v. 25.
Description: University Park, Pennsylvania : The Pennsylvania State University Press, [2021] | Series: Rhetoric and democratic deliberation ; volume 25 | Includes bibliographical references and index.
Summary: "A collection of essays examining the rhetorics that underlie democratic politics in Latin America and the United States"—Provided by publisher.
Identifiers: LCCN 2020057293 | ISBN 9780271089324 (hardback) | ISBN 9780271089317 (paper)
Subjects: LCSH: Democracy—Latin America. | Democracy—America. | Rhetoric—Political aspects—Latin America. | Rhetoric—Political aspects—America.
Classification: LCC JL966 .R49 2021 | DDC 321.8097—dc23
LC record available at https://lccn.loc.gov/2020057293

The Pennsylvania State University Press is a member of the Association of University Presses.

It is the policy of The Pennsylvania State University Press to use acid-free paper. Publications on uncoated stock satisfy the minimum requirements of American National Standard for Information Sciences—Permanence of Paper for Printed Library Material, ANSI Z39.48–1992.

CONTENTS

Acknowledgments | vii

Introduction: Rhetorics of Democracy in the Americas | 1
ADRIANA ANGEL, MICHAEL L. BUTTERWORTH, AND NANCY R. GÓMEZ

Part 1 **Questioning the Narratives of Democracy
Beyond the West**

1   The Democratic Hemisphere | 23
CHRISTA J. OLSON

2   A Strange Democracy: Rhetoric, Posthegemony,
and Latinamericanism | 39
JOSÉ CORTEZ

3   Draining the Democracy: Donald J. Trump
and Anti-Immigrant Rhetoric | 57
ALBERTO GONZÁLEZ, AMY N. HEUMAN, AND LINSAY M. CRAMER

4   Revisiting the Seeming Impossibility of Migrants
as Political Actors | 72
RENÉ AGUSTÍN DE LOS SANTOS

5   American Exceptionalism, Baseball Diplomacy, and
the Normalization of US-Cuban Relations | 88
MICHAEL L. BUTTERWORTH

Part 2 **Problematizing and Reconstructing Democracy
in Latin America**

6   Communicating About Corruption: Guatemalan Rhetorics
of Corruption | 107

ADRIANA ANGEL

7   Re/Tracing the Local Grassroots Women Activists' Crafting of Rhetorical
    Agency in Ciudad Juárez, Mexico | 125
    CLARA EUGENIA ROJAS BLANCO

8   The Peace Agreement and the Rhetoric of Religion in the Colombian
    Plebiscite: Religious Activism and Democracy | 143
    PAMELA FLORES AND NANCY R. GÓMEZ

9   People, Media, and Democracy in Brazil: Discourses About Lula's Oratory
    in the Brazilian Press | 160
    CARLOS PIOVEZANI

10 The Farewell Speech of Cristina Fernández de Kirchner | 180
    ALEJANDRA VITALE

11 Spectacular Crisis: Rhetorics of Representation in Venezuela | 196
    ABRAHAM ROMNEY

    Notes | 215

    List of Contributors | 257

    Index | 261

ACKNOWLEDGMENTS

Like many collaborations, ours began as a matter of luck. The three of us crossed paths through the School of Communication Studies at Ohio University. Coming from Manizales, Colombia, Adriana earned her master's degree in 2010 and doctorate in 2012 with support from a Fulbright Scholarship. Nancy, from Barranquilla, Colombia, was also awarded a Fulbright and completed her master's in 2012 and doctorate in 2015. Michael served as the school's director from 2013–17. Building on a relationship established by previous collaborations, we had several opportunities to develop programs that sought to bridge theoretical divides between the "North" and "South."

Our first effort was in Colombia, when Adriana helped organize the "Communication Dialogues between North and South" symposium in Manizales in April 2014. That event brought together scholars from Colombia, Chile, Puerto Rico, and the United States and led directly to Ohio University hosting the "Communication and Social Change" conference in September 2015. Nancy also organized two visits to the Universidad del Norte for the School of Communication Studies at Ohio. Each of these visits and events established or expanded relationships that continue at these institutions.

We also wanted to use these collaborations as a platform for research. We presented "Dialogues of Communication between North and South" at the 2015 meeting of the International Communication Association in San Juan, Puerto Rico. From there, we began conceptualizing a larger project, seeking advice from colleagues and friends who helped shape this book.

We are grateful for these opportunities—the friendships we have developed, the intellectual engagement during symposia, and the academic network and collaboration. We especially wish to thank everyone at Ohio University, Universidad de Manizales, and the Universidad del Norte for helping us build these relationships. We also wish to thank our current institutions, the Universidad de las Sabana, The University of Texas at Austin, and the Universidad del Norte, for their continued support. In addition, we wish to acknowledge the financial support for this book coming from Michael's appointment as the Governor Ann W. Richards Chair for the Texas Program in Sports and Media.

There are several individuals at these institutions and elsewhere who have contributed to our relationships and academic work. For their collaboration, advice, and support in various capacities, we want to acknowledge Roger Aden, Jesús Arroyave, Austin Babrow, Alejandro Barranquero, Ben Bates, Laura Black, Andrés Calle, Amy Chadwick, Devika Chawla, Lorna Jean Edmonds, Pamela Flores, Jessica González Herrera, Sonia Ivancic, Judith Yaross Lee, Luis González López, Belén Marco, Claudia Patricia Nieto Sanchez, Rafael Antonio Obregon Galvez, Kristen Okamoto, Christa Olson, René De los Santos, Camilo Perez, Kendall Phillips, Scott Titsworth, and Risa Whitson.

We also thank everyone involved in this project at Penn State University Press, including Brian Beer, Kendra Boileau, Jennifer Norton, Ryan Peterson, Alex Vose, and our two anonymous reviewers. They have been friendly, professional, and diligent at every stage of this process. We could not have asked for a better experience in helping to make this project a reality.

Adriana: I offer my thanks and gratitude to the School of Communication at Universidad de la Sabana for welcoming this long project and allowing me to continue working on it. I also want to thank Mike and Nancy for editing this book with me. I have learned a lot and enjoyed every moment of this journey. The dialogues between north and south start with conversations, projects, and friendships like ours. I am deeply thankful to all the authors who contributed to this book in order to encourage and strengthen the academic dialogues about communication across the Americas. I dedicate this work to my husband, Alvaro, and to my daughters, Elisa and Victoria.

Michael: As a rhetorical scholar of democracy who studies sport and politics, I would not have imagined working on a book focused on the Americas. So, I begin by thanking Adri and Nancy for their vision and commitment to this project, and for allowing me to be a part of it. The authors in this volume have been wonderful collaborators, and I am grateful for their scholarship and goodwill. I also want to acknowledge the institutional support I have enjoyed both at Ohio and my current home, The University of Texas at Austin. Both places have afforded me the opportunity to connect with others around the world and to pursue meaningful scholarship. Finally, I would like to thank my wife Gina, and children Emily and James, for their enduring understanding and support.

Nancy: I want to thank my children, Paula and Jose Alejandro, and Roberto, my partner in life. Thank you! Thanks to my coeditors, Michael and Adri, for their commitment and enthusiasm with the book. Also, I want to thanks the contributors to the book for believing in this project and inspiring me to (re) think democratic practices and navigate their possibilities and challenges in contemporary times in the Americas.

INTRODUCTION: RHETORICS OF DEMOCRACY IN THE AMERICAS

Adriana Angel, Michael L. Butterworth, and Nancy R. Gómez

In her review of the book *Rhetoric in South America*, edited by María Alejandra Vitale and Philippe-Joseph Salazar, Christa J. Olson acknowledges the common assumption that the rhetorical tradition is uniquely North American. As she writes, "Over the centuries during which rhetoricians in North and South America have ignored one another—or, rather, in which we in the North have claimed inheritance of *the* tradition—our scholarship has followed that supposedly single Tradition to rather different ends."[1] Of course, the book to which Olson responds is itself an indication that the borders between "north" and "south" are, and have been, shifting. Beyond the work of Vitale and Salazar, others have foregrounded the rhetorical *intersections* among and between the Americas.[2] In the words of Olson and René Agustín De los Santos, in their introduction to a special issue of *Rhetoric Society Quarterly*, the field should argue "for the richness of 'Latin' American rhetorical history on its own terms while also urging a wider notion of *Américan* rhetoric grounded in long histories of hemispheric interaction."[3] We take such interactions seriously, inspired by recent work and the efforts of other theorists to "uncouple the name of the [Latin American] subcontinent from the cartographic image we all have of it." In other words, this book endeavors to explore rhetorical practices among and between the communities of all the "Americas,"[4] with less investment in geographic boundaries and more investment in democratic culture.

The interest in expanding territorial and theoretical reach requires more than a simple declaration. We are far from the first set of critics who wish to redefine the boundaries of the field, after all. Indeed, we are stepping into existing conversations, at times overlapping and other times diverging, within rhetorical studies about related matters of borders, colonialism, and racial identity. As Boaventura de Sousa Santos contends, the very notions of "north" and "south" are themselves metaphors: "The global South is not a geographical concept, even though the great majority of its populations live in countries of the Southern hemisphere. The South is rather a metaphor for the human suffering caused by capitalism and colonialism on the global level, as well as for the resistance to overcoming or minimizing such suffering."[5] Writing more specifically about geographical borders, Robert DeChaine submits, "The doxastic, world-making function of the border signals its preeminence as a rhetorical mode of enactment. That is to say, borders are produced, defined, managed, contested, and altered through human symbolic practices." DeChaine is referring to the conventional borders of the nation-state, in particular the border between the United States and Mexico, and his edited collection evaluates the border's effect on "popular understandings and experiences of citizenship and identity in the United States today."[6]

The border between the United States and Mexico warrants critical attention, but it is far from the only location that shapes our understanding of such citizenship and identity. Bernadette Calafell and Fernando Delgado, for example, are invested in the political identities of Latina/o populations and they resist the homogenization of unique groups from distinct areas. As they explain, "Geographically situated Latina/o identities—each with their own sense of community and ethnicity—such as Chicanos in the southwest, Cuban-Americans in south Florida, and Boricuas in the northeast, complicate the pursuit of a singular Latino identity, community, ideology, or aesthetic."[7] Meanwhile, in his study of the Young Lords of New York, Darrel Wanzer-Serrano invites critical orientations from outside these geographical boundaries, noting, "I think it is possible and desirable to be guided chiefly by decoloniality and perspectives that emerge from the Global South."[8] This sentiment articulates well with de Sousa Santos's notion of the "epistemology of the South," in which he emphasizes that the "understanding of the world is much broader than the Western understanding of the world."[9]

This current and intense Latin American decolonial discourse resonates with our purpose of thinking locally about the rhetorics of democracy in the Americas. In other words, we want to contribute to the epistemic shift suggested by decolonial authors such as de Sousa Santos, Anibal Quijano, and Walter Mignolo,[10] and explore democracy through the voices and standpoints of Latin American authors who have themselves experienced the colonial, political, and social realities of the region. However, we cannot and do not want to claim that ours is a "pure" standpoint with no influence of

Eurocentric and hegemonic ideas and traditions. On the contrary, writing and reflecting on the Americas invites us to account for diverse authors, theories, and phenomena, even those from a Eurocentric tradition. We celebrate perspectives such as decoloniality, Afrocentricity, and Asiacentricity because of their strong critiques of the Eurocentric hegemonic production of knowledge and their invitation to epistemic decolonization.[11] We acknowledge that the transnationalization and globalization of knowledge give us the opportunity to listen to regional and alternative perspectives and to articulate them to hegemonic standpoints that have been more widely circulated.

The work of all of these scholars points specifically to the interests of this book, but we should acknowledge that they are also connected to a larger disciplinary focus on race. Lisa Flores has made the case for what she calls "racial rhetorical criticism, or rhetorical criticism that is reflective about and engages the persistence of racial oppression, logics, voices, and bodies that theorizes the very production of race as rhetorical."[12] Her project hails a range of scholars, including many who focus specifically on the construction of identities in and between the "Americas." Although our focus is not explicitly on race as an isolated category, we find inspiration in Flores's rhetorical attitude. Moreover, we share the sentiments of Michelle Colpean and Rebecca Dingo in their contribution to a forum on racial rhetorical criticism in *Communication and Critical/Cultural Studies.* In support of Flores, they caution against what might be termed academic tourism, or the tendency simply to add a reference or a case study from a "marginal" population and consider the work of inclusion to be done. Against this, they "call for white and Western scholars in particular to be attentive to the tricky politics of capitalizing on the struggles and domination of nonwhite and/or exoticized groups of the 'Global South' being used as 'interesting' case studies that do not substantially shift or decolonize dominant rhetorical scholarship and that may inadvertently serve to sustain the field's racist practices."[13]

We believe these commitments echo Olson's observation from above, and we contend that scholarship itself constitutes and acts on its own set of borders. Thus, in keeping with Wanzer-Serrano, we agree that *scholars must first alter the intellectual terrain from which we as critics and theorists speak and listen.*[14] It is our hope that this collection resists any tendency to "tour" different democratic terrains and that the individual voices of the scholars here may theorize a collective understanding of the "Americas" as inclusive and pluralistic. This theorizing opens pathways to Latin American rhetorical perspectives and democratic phenomena that rarely circulate in North America and that are often excluded when studying democracy. The transnational approach that this book offers can help scholars understand democracy beyond Eurocentric and US perspectives. The book also shows how rhetoric has been inherited, resignified, and reformulated in Latin America and how Latin American scholars coming from traditions such as linguistics, semiotics, discourse studies, and philosophy of language are doing "rhetorical studies" without using this label to name their work. Thus this book spotlights Latin America as a locus of articulation that also establishes dialogues with other authors and approaches around the world in order to understand the current challenges of democracy across the Americas and the role that rhetoric plays in those contexts.

Before we move forward, we would like to comment on two important matters: the discursive choices we make with respect to terms such as "Latina/o" and "Latinx" and our own scholarly positionality. First, we recognize that "Latinx" has increasingly become the preferred term in the academy in the United States. The virtue of the term is based, at least in part, on its inclusivity. However, as Karrieann Soto Vega and Karma Chávez explain, perhaps more important is its status as "an inherently interlocking category, overtly signaling attentiveness to coloniality, ethnicity and gender, and implicitly pointing to race and sexuality."[15] Nevertheless, Soto and Chávez also note that "Latinx" is not universally accepted, especially for those who prefer the distinction between Latina and Latino as it is gendered in Spanish. As Breny Mendoza suggests, "there is always something that is lost in the translation" in these concepts, and we want to preserve the distinctive meanings between languages as much as is possible.[16] Because this book works across the borders we have thus far described, accounting for territories within which it may not be the preferred term, we will not use "Latinx" to define this project. However, we respect the choices made by individual authors in this volume to use "Latinx" in specific contexts, and so readers will see the term in chapters 3 and 4.

Second, we believe it is important to state our own orientation to the subject matter of this book. Two of us are Latina scholars, from different cities in Colombia, who received their doctoral degrees at Ohio University in the United States. Both are scholars informed by an upbringing in South America and an enculturation to higher education in North America. The third among us is a white scholar from the United States. Although his expertise is in rhetoric and democratic theory, he cannot claim to be a scholar of Latin America in particular. Our overlapping histories at Ohio University have allowed us to establish friendships and a productive academic partnership. In 2014, faculty between the Universidad de Manizales and Ohio University gathered with other scholars from Central and South America for the symposium "Communication Dialogues Between North and South." Then, in 2015, Ohio hosted scholars from Colombia for a return symposium, "Communication and Social Change in the Americas." In between these two events, the three of us organized and presented a panel for the 2015 International Communication Association, called "Dialogues of Communication Between North and South." As these conversations developed, Ohio also engaged with Universidad Del Norte, leading to collaborations based on interests in health communication, intercultural communication, and political communication. Our original idea for this book emerged out of these scholarly activities and conversations, giving us now several years to have conceptualized its contribution to rhetorical studies. Moreover, our work together has taught us the value and richness of articulating our different identities, traditions, interests, and regions in order to overcome hegemonic interpretations of phenomena. We have taken advantage of our own unique positionalities to offer a dialogue where scholars with different backgrounds, contexts, and races reflect on the role of rhetoric in shaping democracy in the Americas.

Assessing Democracy in the Americas

While the scholarship cited above has contributed much to our understandings of citizenship and identity across the Americas, we aim to complement this work with a specific focus on democracy. Democracy, of course, is among the most vital concepts in rhetorical studies, and recent scholarship has been especially robust with respect to democratic deliberation and citizenship. Writing against the contemporary tendency to overemphasize the importance of voting, Josiah Ober maintains that democracy's original meaning points toward "the collective capacity of a public to make good things happen in the public realm."[17] Similarly, Octavio Paz notes that "the foundation of democracy is the belief in the ability of citizens to decide with freedom and responsibility on public matters."[18] How, then, does a public make good things happen or make decisions on public matters, if not through rhetoric? As David Timmerman and Todd McDorman suggest, "Democracy is impossible without the practice of public discourse and dialogue among citizens."[19] Rhetoric therefore requires the mutual engagement of citizens because, as Benedetto Fontana maintains, it "emerges, develops, and thrives under conditions of conflict, competition, and strife."[20] This suggests that, as much as references to elections and democratic institutions are instructive, we also must consider other modes of democratic citizenship, what Robert Asen refers to as "a mode of public engagement."[21] With this in mind, our aim is to account for democratic interventions in daily life across the Americas. This might lead us to examining "compensatory division" in the Occupy movement and its critique of Wall Street in New York City; it might focus on the emergence of "networked activism" in the Zapatista resistance in Chiapas, Mexico; or it might direct our attention to mass gatherings in opposition to the costly staging of the Olympic Games in Rio de Janeiro.[22] In such cases, we believe the voices of engaged citizens become the means by which we can consider democracy's promise.

As we enter the third decade of the twenty-first century, democracy's promise may appear in doubt. Indeed, although making sense of rhetoric and democracy's mutual dependence on each other is far from a new enterprise, it is worth taking stock of the contemporary moment. For example, when the Brazilian people elected Jair Bolsonaro as their next president, Western mainstream media reacted with worry and alarm. A *Financial Times* headline declared, "A Bolsonaro Victory Will Put Brazil's Democracy to the Test." Meanwhile, *The Atlantic* asked, "Can Brazil's Democracy Withstand Jair Bolsonaro?" and the *Washington Post* warned, "Democracy Is in Danger All over the World: Brazil Is Just the Latest Example."[23] What would prompt such reactions to the free election of a new president in the world's fourth-largest democracy? In short, defenders of democracy saw in Bolsonaro what they saw happening around the world: a resurgence of hyper-nationalism that, at best, could be called "populist" and, at worst, might be considered "fascist." Across Europe, North America, and South America, the legitimization of right-wing nationalism has increasingly been a cause for concern.[24]

Many of Brazil's neighbors, since the mid-2010s, have experienced what some call the "Latin American spring." Popular demonstrations in Mexico, Chile, Venezuela, Argentina, Bolivia, and Colombia have challenged governments with allegations of economic instability, corruption, and social inequality.[25] Late in 2019 in Bolivia, President Evo Morales resigned after thirteen years in office, a decision that came after the Organization of American States leveled accusations of electoral fraud. The new interim government has faced daily clashes between supporters of Morales accused of advocating a "socialism of the twenty-first century" and those who sought a political turn to the right.[26] Then, in Colombia, citizens organized national strikes (*para nacional*) to demonstrate opposition to President Iván Duque. Specifically, protestors expressed frustration with labor conditions, corruption, and lack of support for the peace agreements signed with the former Revolutionary Armed Forces of Colombia (FARC).[27]

In the United States, meanwhile, commentators have declared a "crisis of democracy" with growing frequency. In a widely publicized essay, former US senator, secretary of state, and presidential nominee Hillary Rodham Clinton warned, "Our democratic institutions are under siege." Specifically identifying President Donald Trump as the cause, Clinton pointed to the US government's failure to provide adequate hurricane relief in Puerto Rico, cruelty in its immigration policy, attacks on a free press, and corrupt relations with Russia.[28] Yet as troubling as the Trump administration's actions have been, we should avoid the temptation to reduce all democratic limitations to him and his associates. Indeed, various factors—from the idiosyncratic mechanism of the electoral college to legacies of racialized capitalism—have fueled growing doubts about the legitimacy of democratic elections and government.[29]

Beyond the United States, the nations across the western hemisphere face similar doubts, as citizens grow weary of ongoing corruption, gridlock, and instability prompted by global tensions. Of Bolsonaro's election in Brazil, the *New York Times* acknowledges, "in a country traumatized by violent crime, his iron-fisted approach to law and order has appealed to voters in traditionally left-wing strongholds."[30] Meanwhile, newly elected Mexican president Andrés Manuel López Obrador capitalized on similar sentiments. As former Mexican ambassador to the United States Arturo Sarukhan expressed in the *Washington Post*, "Fed up with politics and politicians as usual and driven by the tone-deafness and hubris of the three mainstream political parties, Mexicans chose someone to kick the legs out from under the table instead of simply resetting the dinnerware."[31] In Colombia, before the national strikes revealed dissatisfaction with Iván Duque, voters elected him in part due to outrage over the previous administration's negotiations with the FARC, which included "guarantees of softer sentencing for rebel leaders and guaranteed seats in congress."[32]

Of the thirty-four countries of North, Central, and South America, Cuba is the only one that currently does not have some version of democratic government. Yet nearly every one of these nations faces some form of the disquiet described above. Even the relative tranquility of Canadian politics has been interrupted by the "dramatic rise in the number of white nationalist and right-wing extremist groups operating in Canada."[33] In light of such widespread turmoil, it might be easy to lose faith in rhetoric's democratic potential. However, a longer view of recent decades reminds us that American nations have abolished dictatorships, ended internal armed conflicts, hosted radical left- and right-wing governments, embraced wars against terrorism, and experienced significant mobilization processes on behalf of the civil society. In other words, the relationship between rhetoric and democracy is both variable and contestable. As much as contemporary events can be discouraging, we believe that the promise of democracy still lies in modes of rhetorical engagement and action. Thus, we ask, how have these actions affected democratic culture? How has rhetoric facilitated or constrained efforts to expand democracy's reach? How can future rhetorical choices enhance the health of democracy?

Contrasting and Converging Histories

The Americas constitute a rich cultural, geographical, and theoretical terrain to study the intersections between rhetoric and democracy, not only because of the several challenges to implement and maintain democracy in the region, but especially because of the diversity found within and between the nations in the region. Democracy manifests differently across the hemisphere and various rhetorics underlie its history, characteristics, and challenges. Moreover, rhetorically, the United States has positioned itself as an advocate and guardian of democracy and has presented itself as the country called upon to implement—through distinct media and discourses—the democratic model across Central and South America.

A brief history and reflection of the current characteristics of democracy in the Americas may help us better understand the role of these intersections between rhetoric and democracy in the context of the different cases, situations, artifacts, and speeches analyzed throughout this book. This summary is necessarily incomplete, but it can contribute as a contextual frame of the rhetorical practices contained herein. The thirty-four nations we cited earlier have adopted democracy not only as a formal political model, but also as a set of micro-practices related to the active participation of their citizens. Even though the United States implemented democracy relatively rapidly, most countries in Latin America have struggled to define a political model and a system of governance. These struggles can be attributed both to European imperialist legacies manifest in colonialism, civil wars, militarism, and dictatorships and to the imperialism and interventionism of the United States.[34] Indeed, as we will show in the next brief historical account, the United States has significantly influenced Latin American political and development models over the last decades.

After gaining their independence from England, Spain, and Portugal, the countries of the western hemisphere strove to implement liberal political systems based on European constructs such as freedom and equality.[35] These principles have influenced the politics, economics, and even the daily life of the United States for centuries, but they have not had the same impact in nations to the south. Latin American countries followed, in the 1920s, a positivist wave in which the main goal was to achieve modernity.[36] As Paz explains, this goal was compromised from the beginning, as the standards of modernity were imposed by European and North American influences. In particular, the various attempts at social, economic, and political modernization have been burdened by the legacy of colonialism and Spanish heritage, leading many in Latin America to view modernity as "our goddess and our devil."[37] Nevertheless, this ideology was reproduced by intellectuals and politicians from the United States, and it led most of the countries of Central and South America to approach their societies as organic systems guided by scientific laws that, if well applied, would lead the peoples of the South to defeat the ignorance that kept them behind.[38]

During the 1950s, Latin American nations started looking for new models of development and, therefore, for original political and economic paths. The Cuban Revolution embraced a unique model of development in which socialism could be created through the implementation of guerrilla groups.[39] The revolution allowed Fidel Castro to replace the historical legitimacy of democracy with a revolutionary legitimacy and, in turn, constitute a bureaucratic dictatorship.[40] Other countries in Latin America adopted this kind of revolution in rural areas, through states, and supported by guerrillas in order to implement socialist models of development.[41] In response to this rise in socialism, US president John F. Kennedy created the Alliance for Progress to implement moderate reforms in the region and divert attention from socialism.

The 1960s and 1970s exhausted populism and developmentalism in the region.[42] These decades also revealed a set of political practices known as patrimonialism or clientelism that, by the hand of democratic and socialist governments (and even dictatorships), had an enormous impact in Latin America.[43] This system, inherited and learned during the Spanish and Portuguese colonial period, led politicians to govern the public realm as it if were private property, the bureaucracy to be based on personal relationships, and the state to present itself as the holder of wealth. This also resulted in a symbiotic relationship between entrepreneurs and the state in which the former has a clientelist relationship with the latter in order to obtain economic and political benefits.[44] This type of relation explains the magnitude of corruption in Latin America, an issue that will be addressed later.

By the 1980s and 1990s, agencies such as the World Bank and the International Monetary Fund promoted the implementation of neoliberalism in order to overcome the emergence of nationalism across Latin America. Neoliberal policies invited these countries to embrace privatization, liberalization, tax reforms, deregulation, and reduction of the state.[45] The reduction of the state that resulted from the so-called Washington Consensus considerably weakened Latin American democracies and led to numerous financial crises years after their implementation.[46] The vocabulary of neoliberalism provides an important anchor for this book, not because we believe it to be the only lens through which we can view democratic conditions but because it has had a disproportionate influence on the relationships between the United States and the other American nations. The origins of neoliberalism emerged as an economic experiment, theorized by Chicago School scholar Milton Friedman and deployed in South America in the early 1970s. That experiment emerged in the aftermath of a coup in Chile, orchestrated by Augusto Pinochet and "backed by US corporations, the CIA, and US Secretary of State Henry Kissinger."[47]

In the decades since, neoliberalism has become the hegemonic discourse among the nations of the democratic West.[48] As Wendy Brown defines it, neoliberalism is

> most commonly understood as enacting an ensemble of economic policies in accord with its root principle of affirming free markets. These include deregulation of industries and capital flows; radical reduction in welfare state provisions and protections for the vulnerable; privatized and outsourced public goods, ranging from education, parks, postal services, roads, and social welfare to prisons and militaries; replacement of progressive with regressive tax and tariff schemes; the end of wealth distribution as an economic or social-political policy; the conversion of every human need or desire into a profitable enterprise . . . ; and, most recently, the financialization of everything and the increasing dominance of finance capital over productive capital in the dynamics of the economy and everyday life.[49]

The influence of neoliberalism is by no means restricted to the Chilean "experiment." As Mark Goodale and Nancy Postero note in their introduction to the book *Neoliberalism, Interrupted*, studies of Latin America reveal "a spectrum of responses to what can be described as 'maturing neoliberalism,' from a Bolivian revolution that is framed as a formal rejection of neoliberalism to Colombia's deepening recommitment to the full suite of neoliberal social, political, and economic practices."[50] As neoliberal initiatives have matured, so, too, have organized efforts to resist "colonial heritages and similar postcolonial subjugation to global and economic and political powers."[51] In other words, neoliberalism—as both economic and rhetorical rationality—has fostered resentments and the capacity for social movements to emerge across the globe.

One such response since the 2000s has been a post-neoliberal trend that has emerged in Latin America.[52] Thus presidents focused on regulating markets and increasing public spending as a way to enlarge the state intervene in the economy and improve citizens' quality of life. Some media and scholars saw in this new turn to the left the emergence of a new socialism, hailed as the "socialism of the twenty-first century."[53] As we noted at the outset, despite the fact that most Latin American countries adopted leftist and left-center democracies in the early years of the new century, many of them have reverted to right-wing governments. Two cases stand out in this shift. First is Venezuela, a nation that for almost twenty years has implemented the so-called twenty-first-century socialism approach, and that has now brought about the increase of inflation to levels of more than 800 percent and the deterioration of Venezuelans' quality of life because of the shortage of food, medicine, medical attention, and educational services. Although elected through popular vote, the presidencies of both Hugo Chávez and Nicolás Maduro have weakened democratic practice and limited the promises of a new socialism. The election of a right-wing president in Chile constitutes the second recent case in Latin America that demonstrates the political movement back to the right. Following the presidency of socialist Michelle Bachelet, Chileans returned Sebastián Piñera to the office he had held from 2010 to 2014. Piñera's election signaled that the consolidation of left-wing government in South America that appeared to have taken hold in the early twenty-first century had given way to a right-wing resurgence. In the past few years, "conservatives have come to power in Argentina, Brazil and Paraguay, and Venezuela's 'Bolivarian Revolution' has come under severe pressure with anti-government protesters taking to the streets for months. The win by Piñera further consolidates that trend."[54]

Meanwhile, as challenges to neoliberalism ebb and flow in South America, the North—and, in particular, the United States—continues to emphasize neoliberal practices through commitments to privatization, international monetary control, and free trade. In the midst of controversies about border control, detaining immigrants and separating families, and building a border wall between the United States and Mexico, President Trump facilitated a renegotiation of the North American Free Trade Agreement (NAFTA). NAFTA, and other deals like it, has long been a representative target of anti-globalization activists and those who believe neoliberalism has exacerbated economic inequality. This offered the prospect of an unusual alliance between Trump and those on the far left; however, the new deal—called the United States–Mexico–Canada Agreement—includes only minimal changes to NAFTA.[55] Furthermore, despite Trump's unconventional presidency, US economic policy remains largely unaltered. Meanwhile, it is possible that Trump will affect the United States' global influence elsewhere, especially with respect to the military. Although still infatuated by military power, he has been unpredictable with defense policy, most dramatically symbolized by his sudden announcement of the United States' withdrawal of troops from Syria and his gamesmanship with Iran.[56] Such moves stand in contrast to the prevailing mindset of US leaders in the past four decades. Much more commonplace has been a worldview informed by American exceptionalism, through which military actions are deemed necessary and moral if and when the United States declares them to be so.[57]

The United States' aggressive and often belligerent approach to foreign policy and military intervention has led to growing criticism in the international community. The election of President Barack Obama ushered in an era of some renewed optimism, but even his more measured approach to global affairs retained US troops in Afghanistan and Iraq, and also increased the use of military drones.[58] The legacy of the "war on terror," especially the war in Iraq, has mitigated some of the United States' influence and even isolated it to a degree from its neighbors. As a result, despite neoliberal governments of their own, Mexico and Canada "have retained some degree of policy autonomy from the U.S. regime."[59] Canada is an especially interesting contemporary case, given the international popularity of Prime Minister Justin Trudeau. A political progressive in many ways, Trudeau is more nuanced than leaders such as George W. Bush and more diplomatic than Donald Trump. Yet the optimism with which many have greeted Trudeau has waned, in part because many on the political left have been disappointed by his stances on the environment and trade, while those on the political right have viewed him as ineffectual in foreign policy.[60] His reputation was further marred by the discovery of older photos showing him wearing "blackface," a controversy that did not prevent him from winning reelection in 2019 but may have contributed to his Liberal Party losing its legislative majority.[61]

Trudeau's fortunes aside, it is clear the United States still sets the agenda in North America and beyond. US leaders routinely invoke the nation's presumed exceptionalism, and it maintains enough economic and military leverage to dictate policy to many of its allies. Most centrally, the United States declares itself to be the world's leading example in democratic governance. Yet if the structure of democracy remains in place, what is to be made of democratic engagement among its citizens? The two-party system between Democrats and Republicans remains relatively stable, despite frequent criticisms that they both uphold the same general values.[62] Meanwhile, many citizens are cynical about politics and voter turnout is relatively unimpressive. In the 2016 presidential election, for example, only 55 percent of the voting-age population cast ballots.[63] US citizens tend to view government more favorably at the local level over the national, and they increasingly see issues in partisan terms.[64]

Despite contemporary challenges, citizens in the United States work within a long-established tradition of shared values rooted in classically liberal political principles, such as life, liberty, and the pursuit of happiness.[65] Accordingly, democracy in North America is often linked to an Anglo tradition rooted in the philosophy of John Locke, where reason and the protection of individual liberties is crucial.[66] While this amounts to a truncated genealogy of democracy in the United States, it is fair to conclude that these underlying values shape interpretations of democratic health in North America. And, although US ideology dictates the terms of engagement across the Americas, we also want to turn our attention to some of the principles shared in the South.

Latin America is not a homogeneous region and democracies in Central and South America have taken shape differently from nation to nation. However, it is possible to identify some common characteristics of Central and South America that, in turn, distinguish them from the United States and Canada. One such difference is a colonial heritage that, unlike the colonization in North America, reproduced the Iberian ethos of the Spanish and Portuguese colonizers. Following the ideas of Ignacio Walker and Jorge Carpizo, we observe that this Iberian ethos is evident in institutions and processes such as (1) the adoption of Catholicism and, along with it, a hierarchical and Thomistic thinking; (2) a clientelist, centralist, and elitist legal and political system inherited from the Spanish and Portuguese traditions; and (3) Spanish as the common official language of most Latin American countries (even though Brazilians speak Portuguese, it is easy for Spanish speakers to understand Portuguese and vice versa).[67] In addition, the notion of democracy in Latin America owes more to the influences of continental European theory, made most obvious in the philosophy of Jean-Jacques Rousseau. Whereas the Lockean tradition favors an emphasis on individual liberty, the Rousseauian tradition grants more attention to the collective.[68]

This common colonial heritage has influenced certain attributes of Latin American democracies: First, the fragmentation of weak political parties that coalesce around potential presidential figures and change their ideology in a pendulum movement according to the conveniences of the moment.[69] Second, the emergence of left-wing populisms that bring paternalistic and messianic leaders to power outside the rules of institutions and the legitimacy of political parties.[70] Third, the consolidation of electoral democracies—that is, democracies where participation is limited to electoral voting but lack mechanisms for citizen oversight, governance, and institutional strengthening. Fourth, a fragile and weak civil society that rarely organizes itself to pursue long-term social and political projects. Fifth, the increase of corruption as a consequence of patronage practices inherited from the colony and now transnationalized with globalization.[71] Sixth, the crisis of governance, which arises as a result of populist, plebiscite, and personalist democracies in which citizens have little confidence in institutions and accomplish several practices "outside" the frame of those institutions.[72] Finally, these are democracies defined by levels of poverty that, despite improvements in recent years, contend with problems of hunger, malnutrition, and illiteracy. Likewise, these are societies with significant levels of violence and gangs.[73]

Many of these features—both the attributes and limitations of democracy—will be featured in the analyses contained in this volume. Before turning to an overview of the chapters, we want to clarify three assumptions we have made as editors. First, we have oriented the book to identify the intersections of rhetoric and democracy as a means to interrogate the material conditions—that is, political, religious, economic, social—that shape the emergence of certain democratic rhetorics as well as the symbolic consequences of these rhetorics on concrete democratic processes. Consequently, we view democracy discursively, understanding it in terms of the rhetorical devices and ideas that both underlie and shape democratic processes across the Americas. Following scholars such as Russell Hanson, Robert Ivie, and Gerard Hauser,[74] we claim democracy is itself a rhetorical construction: the mere idea of democracy as a superior and ideal model requires rhetorical work and, therefore, the naturalization and incorporation of certain values and ideas associated to this political system throughout both the hemisphere and the world.

Second, we understand rhetoric, on the one hand, as an object to be studied, which means the studies in this book approach speeches, grass roots movements, and organizations as rhetorical exemplars of democratic practice in the Americas. On the other hand, we view rhetoric as a method/orientation and a theoretical invitation to consider how democracy is constituted rhetorically. In short, this project embraces a more constitutive than instrumental view of rhetoric. We consider rhetoric as a multifaceted phenomenon that works ideologically, mythologically, and ritualistically to constitute cultures and foster the construction of collective identities for social movements and activism in the Americas. At the same time, this standpoint leads us to study how certain rhetorics of democracy work as power devices that naturalize and institutionalize democracy at macropolitical and microsocial/cultural levels. With these ideas in mind, we concur with Lisa Flores, who suggests "that the art of rhetorical criticism is concerned with politics and publics, with cultural discourses and social meanings, with rhetors and audiences. Not merely observers, rhetorical critics are social actors, guided by our theoretical knowledge, our methodological skills, and our critical senses, who seek through our work to bring both insight and judgment."[75]

Third, the book makes every effort to capture democratic rhetorics across international borders. Ultimately, the examination of these diverse contexts will show and extend the field of rhetoric beyond the North American perspective where rhetoric is often confined. Thus this book is designed to cultivate conversations among and between the hemispheres, with the acknowledgment that limiting any conception of rhetoric to only "North" or "South" is politically problematic. This is why, to the extent possible, we have curated contributions from scholars across the Americas, including Argentina, Brazil, Colombia, Mexico, and the United States. In addition, our authors attend to other national contexts, including Cuba, Guatemala, and Venezuela. We cannot claim to be comprehensive, as there are certainly contexts and concerns we have not attended to in these chapters. However, we believe these studies collectively speak to previous calls in rhetorical studies to "offer a view of Américan rhetoric that acknowledges and attempts to account for the hemispheric complexities of symbolic action."[76]

Overview of Chapters

The chapters of the book recognize democratic ideals as irreducible to a single Western perspective and reflect the ways social minorities, both in North and South, question unique discourses that disguise the juxtaposition of difference. Thus the authors thoughtfully consider the fluidity and tensions of local, national, and global forces to deconstruct and construct democratic values, which are always in "becoming." In doing so, the chapters of the book engage in constructive dialogue to interrogate plural forms of democratic processes in the Americas not simply based on universalist approaches. The authors enter into the conversation that asks for the rhetorical modes of democratic culture and the new foundations to understand the transformations occurring in the region from the perspective of marginalized populations, such as immigrants, ethnic minorities, and victims of homophobia and racism.

The first section of the book, "Questioning Narratives of Democracy Beyond the West," navigates the possibilities of deconstructing metanarratives of democracy coming from the Western tradition while drawing attention to the multiplicity of voices of excluded groups to interrogate a single democratic framework in the Americas. In chapter 1, Christa Olson argues that democracy's rhetorical relationship with the material is thoroughly topographical, as appeals to the democratic hemisphere make democracy a state of nature native to the Americas. By sketching a map of democratic topography, Olson shows, through the work of different rhetors from the United States and Latin America, how land and the grounds for democratic rhetoric ultimately cannot be separated, setting up a presumption of natural democracy that was literally grounded in the western hemisphere.

José Cortez proposes in chapter 2, from the perspective of postnational rhetoric, a reevaluation of the concept of *topos* to highlight the complex understandings of democracy. Cortez's chapter depicts the impossibility of reproducing a single narrative of democracy in the United States and stresses the need to renew our meanings of democracy in the region rooted in the notion of *topos*. For Cortez, we are bearing witness to the emergence of a different regime of political signification in light of the breakdown of the nation-state form, which means democracy cannot be understood strictly from a single framework. In his chapter, Cortez examines how Mexicans appeal to the land with the language of democracy and points out the complexities of conflicting views that are present on the "topoi" ground to question a universal democratic framework in the Americas and create new meanings of cultural identity and citizenship in the hemisphere.

Turning to a specific scenario in the way minority groups challenge Western narratives, Alberto González, Amy N. Heuman, and Linsay M. Cramer address in chapter 3 how Donald Trump's essentializing rhetoric in controversies surrounding "the wall" along the US-Mexico border and NAFTA have made possible the emergence of counternarratives such as "draining the democracy"—a rhetorical play on Trump's claims to "draining the swamp" that symbolizes the political establishment in Washington, DC—to illustrate Latin American nations' incredulity toward the metanarrative of the democratic ideals of the United States. Their analysis then suggests several consequences for democratic politics, both within the United States and across the Americas.

René Agustín De los Santos emphasizes in chapter 4 the need to reconsider the significance of democratic values and citizenship in the United States, drawing attention to the case of Latin American migrants in the United States to examine contemporary forms of citizenship and to highlight the complexities of the binational rhetorics and rhetorical capacities of migrants living in the United States. In his chapter, De los Santos reminds us how migrants can often experience contemporary citizenship in conflicting ways that might legitimize the traditional notion of US citizenship or inspire other democratic ideals toward very different ends. His argument emphasizes the potential contradictory nature of contemporary migrant civil societies to resist metanarratives that reinforce the US or mono-national gaze of democracy.

In chapter 5, Michael L. Butterworth turns his attention to the ideological work of "American exceptionalism." Offering a critique of American exceptionalism as a foundational myth, Butterworth interrogates President Obama's efforts to normalize relations with Cuba through the idea of "baseball diplomacy," a rhetorical construct rooted in the notion of "democratic exceptionalism." By examining media reports about baseball diplomacy and analyzing their portrayals of American exceptionalism, he focuses on the ways that diplomatic efforts in and through baseball present American cultural identity. More critically, the chapter points to the limits of American exceptionalism, especially in light of growing doubts about United States' status as a democratic exemplar.

The second section of book, "Problematizing and Reconstructing Democracy in Latin America," moves out of the US context to interrogate how the intersections of rhetoric and democracy help rhetorical scholars examine the material conditions and the symbolic consequences of democratic processes in sociohistorical contexts in Latin America. In doing so, the authors of this group reflect on the material realities and democratic ideals that mobilize civil action toward very different political ends in the region. Each of the chapters of this section reflects on the possibilities of Latin American populations to understand democracy in their own terms and reality rather than allowing Western discourses to speak for them.

In chapter 6, Adriana Angel points to discourses on Guatemalan corruption to identify the vocabularies that different types of actors use to communicate about this phenomenon. She examines the notions of "fraud," "democracy," and "interventionism" as the three main terministic screens to demonstrate how understandings of corruption extend beyond the domain of politicians and include individuals' perceptions and symbolic action in everyday practices. One of the central contributions of Angel's chapter is to show the relationship between rhetoric and democracy in the specific context of corruption in Guatemala, a problem faced by all countries in the Americas. Angel's analysis attentively demonstrates how the central implication of corruption is its threat to democracy rather than other political, economic, social, and cultural consequences.

Clara Eugenia Rojas Blanco draws attention in chapter 7 to a group of political women activists in Ciudad Juárez and their political actions to gain political recognition as speaking subjects. Rojas approaches Mexican women activists by emphasizing their rhetorical agency as it relates to issues of power and its political and democratic implications. Her ethnographic inquiry offers a deep analysis of her conversations with local grassroots women activists in the discursive context of the emergence of civil deliberations to form civil spaces of deliberation underlined by the moral exigency of the feminicide in Ciudad Juárez.

In chapter 8, Pamela Flores and Nancy R. Gómez depict the complexities of considering human rights while considering religious beliefs untouchable in the context of the 2016 peace agreement in Colombia between the state and the FARC. In their chapter, the authors primarily focus on the use of gender ideology by opponents of the agreement, arguing that opponents were able to frame the discussion in terms that defined "gender ideology" as a threat to traditional religious norms and values. The chapter accentuates how conflicting views in the public sphere reveal the possibilities, contradictions, and limits of democratic ideals in Colombia. For Gómez and Flores, democracy might not be understood from universalist framework but always in a continuous contestation in which power is disputed between various political, religious, economic, and social forces.

Carlos Piovezani's analysis in chapter 9 demonstrates practices in Brazilian media that marginalize "popular" speech among the political elite. More specifically, Piovezani shows how depictions of former president Luiz Inácio Lula da Silva as unrefined serve conservative political efforts to define popular discourse as aggressive and foolish. Such portrayals are of particular concern because they are rooted in assumptions about the poor and disempowered populations in Brazil. Despite Lula's electoral successes, the negative images of him constructed by the media have facilitated the interests of the elite and delegitimized progressive social programs. Piovezani, therefore, invites readers to consider what becomes of "the people" when elite interests control narratives about democracy.

Presenting a critical analysis of the ways in which Cristina Fernández de Kirchner's ethos is constructed in her farewell address, Alejandra Vitale shows the multiplicity of narratives of democracy from Latin America in chapter 10. Vitale thoughtfully reflects on the implications of Fernández de Kirchner's farewell address for Argentina's democracy by legitimizing herself before her audience as a future opponent of Mauricio Macri rather than praising democracy and the popular vote in the tradition of presidential farewells. Vitale argues how Fernández depicts Macri as a potential traitor of Argentinian democracy while presenting herself as the nation's hope to realize democratic ideals when she returns once the four years of Mauricio Macri's presidency have run their course.

To conclude the book, Abraham Romney moves our attention in chapter 11 to examine the implication of the narrative of crisis in democracy in Venezuela. Romney navigates the rhetoric of the crisis under Nicolás Maduro, examining the legacy of the failed coup in 2002 that nearly ended Hugo Chávez's presidency. Romney's analysis of media representation of the more recent economic crisis under Maduro shows how both Maduro's government and its opposition reinforce the rhetoric of spectacle to frame events symbolically, connect them to a group's ideology, and drive community action. In contrast with the rhetoric of spectacle that perpetuates the spectacle's "real unreality," Romney explores how Venezuelans might create narratives of "everyday humanity" that can unite the country politically and resist facile representations from outsiders.

PART I

QUESTIONING THE NARRATIVES OF
DEMOCRACY BEYOND THE WEST

I

THE DEMOCRATIC HEMISPHERE

Christa J. Olson

Cultivators of the earth are the most virtuous and independent citizens.
—Thomas Jefferson, *Notes on the State of Virginia*

Land is alive and thinking and . . . humans and non-humans derive
agency through the extensions of these thoughts.
—Vanessa Watts, "Indigenous Place-Thought"

Place and territory have long been central to rhetorical theory, and rhetoricians have dealt repeatedly with democratic topoi and with democracy itself
as a topos.[1] In this chapter, however, I urge rhetorical studies beyond the
common places of the commonplace. I argue that, while democracy's rhetorical connection to the land is evocatively described by the part-metaphorical,
part-literal cast of rhetorical theory's favorite territorial concept, the topos
falls short in its ability to illuminate both democracy and land. It is genera-
tive to analyze democracy and land as inventional resources or "storehouses
of social energy."[2] But rhetorical studies ought also track how democracy
acquires and requires territory in ways that exceed the conventional frame of
the topos, especially its tendency to emphasize land as a concept more than
the land itself. Democracy's connection to land is deeply seated and often
simultaneously symbolic, historical, material, and relational.[3] As the epi-
graphs above and Indigenous communities' enduring decolonial struggles
remind us, social life is firmly rooted not only in common places but in the
ground.[4] Democracy's topography shapes democratic arguments and their

consequences; it births affects, relationships, and actions. This chapter maps the metaphorical and literal terrain of democracy in the American hemisphere and, in the process, asserts both democracy and rhetoric as earthy, muddy matters that resonate with but exceed existing topical theories.

For much of the modern era, America has been democracy's epicenter.[5] Uprooted from Greece and dug into new soil with the shovels of conquest, democracy colonized its environment. It became not only the defining American mode of governance but also so endemic to America that the soil itself could be imagined as its origin. Since then, democracy's hemispheric homeland has informed, constrained, and materialized arguments made about democracy both within the Americas and beyond. To trace that democratic topography, I follow the arguments it has authorized and the territorial claims made on it. I begin, though, by introducing this chapter's place-holding terms.

The rhetoricity of landscape has been well established.[6] Likewise, scholars have shown how land itself has rhetorical valence.[7] In this chapter, I introduce two territorial terms that further advance rhetorical studies' capacity to address land's rhetoricity. I treat here not only land but also the telluric and topography.

Telluric means "of the earth." While not a common word in English, in Spanish *lo telúrico* served as a key term for the mid-twentieth-century adherents of *tropicalismo*, an intellectual movement invested in the cultural potential of the American tropics.[8] *Tropicalismo* understood the character and potential of Latin America as grounded in its geospatial location. Human beings, governments, and arts were *telúrico*—of the earth. That framing had material as well as metaphorical consequences. *Lo telúrico* was a strategy of appeal and the foundation from which arguments emerged. I invoke that dual sense of the telluric in this chapter: its earthy tones appear in arguments made about democracy, and it grounds the very possibility of those arguments. As a framing concept, "the telluric" connects three primary ways that land informs democracy: arguments gain their power from appeals to common ground, territorial rights are often the object of democratic arguments, and physical places provide standing for those arguments.

The term "topography" serves a similar function, given its etymological link to both land and marking. However, where the telluric emphasizes origins, topography indexes land's ongoing action. It acknowledges that land shapes arguments. Though the suffix "-graphy" might suggest abstraction, my argument here emphasizes the land itself as a source of inscription. Linking land to inscription risks treating the land primarily in terms of language about it. But in this chapter, land is the agent, not the patient of marking. The land imprints its inhabitants, marking us. This assertion takes even further Caroline Gottschalk Druschke's admonition that "retaining a focus on the material aspects of the landscape—its creeks, rivers, and soils—along with its symbolic content—its existence as a concept—is critical to understanding its function as an inducement to action."[9] Traversing the topography of the democratic hemisphere reveals how the land itself—as material—induces action that is best understood as rhetorical.

That last step, returning to the rhetorical, is essential. My explanations of the telluric and topography have emphasized physical land, but land does not preexist rhetoric. They are simultaneous and co-constitutive. Rhetoricians have long been stuck with the dyad of the symbolic and the material, with Burke's division between symbolic action and nonsymbolic motion, but this chapter treats the elements of that dyad as so fundamentally intertwined that separating them inherently misshapes them. In this, I take a cue from recent trophic approaches to rhetoric that move beyond ecological metaphors and toward awareness of how matter and energy move together and move us.[10] Rhetoric and land, as Druschke—informed by Marisol de la Cadena and Eduardo Viveiros de Castro—notes, are always in equivocal relation.[11]

Noting rhetoric's equivocal work across multiple material, symbolic, and territorial contexts underscores that democracy's topography is constituted, not given. The practices of democracy in America are grounded *and* made. The claim that democracy is inextricably connected to land—and, more specifically, to American land—developed over time and emerged out of repeated acts of moving, mapping, and governing. It is a product of argument and occupation. The created aspects of that topography have also become natural and material over time. Asserted, disputed, and accepted, democracy has been so thoroughly pressed into its terrain that it has become the ground being mapped. This democratic grounding happened, at least in part, because democracy actually does require land. As I will show in the coming pages, the notion of a particularly democratic hemisphere is deeply connected to both colonial occupation and the decolonial land claims that refuse elite efforts to establish a democratic hemisphere in their own image.

Democracy's topos is muddied. It is always simultaneously material, symbolic, and practical. How any individual or group talks about democracy, lives it, and experiences it is, ultimately, all part of the topography. To do democracy is to be telluric. In this chapter, I bring democracy's telluric, topographical nature into focus by placing hortatory claims for the democratic hemisphere alongside struggles for land rights. I put the imaginaries and territories of elite white and criollo people in contact with the imaginaries and territories of the peoples they have colonized.[12] The democratic hemisphere, I suggest, emerges in the tectonic clash between them. There are commonplaces here, but settlers' appropriation of the common requires that rhetoricians understand the force of the land "otherwise."[13]

Land of Freedom and Independence

Athens was once the undisputed homeland of democracy, and the Greek polis is still dusted with democracy's romantic sediments. In the late eighteenth century, however, colonists shifted the democratic homestead west toward a "new" world where American liberty and rights were offered as stark contrasts with the monarchical "Old World." Over time, America gained place as the democratic hemisphere, the seat and soil of popular sovereignty. That political topography, rhetorically constructed yet telluric, has had substantial implications for argument and action, practice and place.

Of course, a "hemisphere" is more an idea than a geographic object. The earth does not come pre-sectioned into politically acceptable units, so Western settlers have divided it for ourselves. It is easy to recognize the rhetoricity of political mapping—the boundaries of nation-states, the names of cities. Hemispheres hide their rhetorical construction a bit more. Organized by continents, equators, and meridians, hemispheres may seem to be elements of physical reality. But, of course, meridians, continents, and equators are themselves partially imagined objects. Invoking the hemisphere gives a geological imprimatur to claims (and territories) that are thoroughly anthropogenic yet also thoroughly rooted in the land.

The "American hemisphere" is the perfect case study for this political formation of a geophysical unit. Separated from the other continents by vast oceans and readily captured more or less on its own in a two-dimensional view of the globe, America appears a naturally distinct object. Yet its division from other landmasses and presumed internal coherence are also constructed. After all, as the editors of this volume remind me, whether "America" is one continent or two depends on where you stand.[14] And, imagining an American *hemisphere* requires accepting the location of the prime meridian at Greenwich, England, in the "Old World." Likewise, though there is contiguous land all the way from Hudson's Bay to the Strait of Magellan, crossing it would require significant technological capacity. Land is as much a barrier to internal cohesion as are oceans; it simply makes different demands.[15] Finally, as my invocation of Hudson and Magellan signals, the shape of America is, ultimately, grounded in the history of violence and theft that began in Europe's fifteenth century. The western hemisphere, the American continent(s), and the "New World" are products of colonialism. They are lands of defense, slaughter, conquest, and reclamation.

Even more remarkable than the hemisphere's apparent geospatial naturalness is its acquired natural geopolitics. Over time, American territory has become coterminous with democracy—not just its site but its terroir. It has become a landmass defined by popular sovereignty not simply because of the human governments populating it but also—and sometimes more centrally—by virtue of the land itself. Indeed, assertions of telluric democracy appear as often in contexts bereft of popular rule as in those (nominally) embracing it. This presumption of democratic territory has been articulated with particular conviction by white elites in the United States who place the center of the democratic hemisphere always within their own nation-state. But rhetors in Latin America—especially criollo elites—have staked their own claims to telluric, topographical democracy. Colonized by the democratic hemisphere mapped out in the North, Latin Americans have cast shade on America's democratic territory, laid claim to it, and drawn it farther south.[16]

Even as elite rhetors have asserted the freedom-loving nature of their hemisphere, however, control of land has been foundational to the practice of settler colonial democracy in America. Policies requiring property for citizenship sit alongside land reform campaigns, Indigenous sovereignty claims, and the unfulfilled Reconstruction promise of forty acres. They all link the promise of equality, sovereignty, and opportunity to the land. Access to land rights has repeatedly reshaped the topography of the democratic hemisphere. But the metaphorical nature of democratic topoi has, simultaneously, underwritten democracy's limited application.

To map that circumscribed topography, this chapter begins with colonial racial science and James Monroe's 1823 "Doctrine" of hemispheric distinction. It then roughs in key sites from North and South. To close, it shifts from the telluric epideictic articulated primarily by elites to the decolonial actions that have echoed across the land since the time of conquest, putting the lie to elite protestations of hemispheric spirit and demonstrating the limits of topical understandings of democracy's territory. Elite appeals to the democratic hemisphere, I argue, repeatedly make democracy not a form of government or a way of life but a passive state of nature endemic to the Americas. Indigenous demands for land, in turn, make democratic land an active and thoroughly literal partner. Those competing notions of land and democracy have had distinct consequences for how people across the American continent(s) participate in actually existing (or nonexistent) democracy.[17]

Telluric Effects

From the moment that the landmass home to the Quechua, Mexica, Nishnaabeg, L'Nuk, and others became the "New World," territorial distinction has defined America. Early in the colonial era, rhetors on both sides of the Atlantic presumed that distance from Europe meant not only differences in flora and fauna, but also differences in lifeways. Those assertions continue to resonate today.

In political terms, colonial-era territorial distinction meant constraints on local authority, differential systems of taxation, and exclusion from decision making. Eager to keep power consolidated, Spanish monarchs limited positions in colonial administration to Spain-born Spanish men of "clean" blood. Britain, though it allowed colonists some self-rule, still limited its scope. As the eighteenth century passed, American-born criollos looked with distain at the *gauchupines* who held power over them and British settlers bristled at laws underscoring their subordinate status. Those senses of distinction grounded in physical distance and political control gave colonial difference environmental valence.

Not only was sheer distance a palpable marker of territorial division, but the racial (and racist) science of the sixteenth through eighteenth centuries grounded human difference in telluric influences. Some European scientists theorized that the American climate would eventually reduce "civilized" Europeans to "barbaric" Indians. Count Georges-Louis Leclerc Buffon argued in his *Histoire Naturelle* that the swampy climate of America led inevitably to degeneration, citing as evidence the continent's lack of large mammals and the rusticity of Native Americans. Later European thinkers extended Buffon's natural history to politics, arguing that the degenerative effects of the Americas would infect any species introduced into the continent—including humans. Abbé Guillaume Thomas-François Raynal and Abbé Cornelius dePauw each wrote best-selling treatises on the subject that influenced public opinion in Europe and provoked furious responses from the Americas. Perhaps most famously, Thomas Jefferson dedicated a large portion of his *Notes on the State of Virginia* to debunking the theory of degeneration and even tried to send Buffon a bull moose as counterevidence.[18] Using pen and brush, Spanish Americans likewise agitated against racial theories that would demean their climate, its produce, and themselves.[19] These American elites aligned themselves culturally and intellectually with Europe, but the push and pull of topographical difference increasingly informed a sense of necessary distinction from Europe. Though staunchly opposed to theories of degeneracy, if not to the racist hierarchies of caste and color that undergirded them, American settler elites developed a sense of American difference that was written in soil and climate and had significant consequences for the political future of their hemisphere.

Embracing the Democratic Hemisphere

In the early years of the nineteenth century, after the United States had achieved its independence and while Spain and Portugal's former colonies agitated for their own, the stakes of American distinction became particularly stark for elite settler rhetors. Working from sites of power—capital cities, church pulpits, and major public forums—they invoked democratic inevitability to authorize existing power or inaugurate new regimes. In the words of those rhetors from the United States and (to a lesser extent) Latin America, we find the most elaborated and consistent sense that democracy was more than a chosen political system; it was telluric in nature and topographically determinant.

The "Doctrine"—articulated in President James Monroe's seventh annual message to Congress, on December 2, 1823—imagines a hemispheric (rather than a specifically national) affinity for democracy.[20] Monroe's words are carefully circumscribed—cautious about committing the United States to military support for its neighbors and avoiding confrontation with European powers. Still, they assert an essential disconnection from Europe, one defined not only by the expanse of the Atlantic Ocean but also by character. President Monroe writes, "The political system of the [European] allied powers is essentially different . . . from that of America."[21] While he is initially focused on politics rather than territory, later portions of the doctrine invoke the continent itself to articulate America's political distinction. He asserts, "It is impossible that the allied powers should extend their political system to any portion of either [American] continent without endangering our peace and happiness."[22] Declaring that "the American continents, by the free and independent condition which they have assumed and maintain, are henceforth not to be considered as subjects for future colonization," Monroe metonymically offers the continents themselves as bastions of democracy.[23]

In Monroe's formulation, the democratic topography of the hemisphere remains latent. He emphasizes political differences and only obliquely makes the land a source for those innate differences. For Monroe, land is a topos more metaphorical than physical. Even so, his words present the continents themselves as free and independent, not just the people occupying them. Monroe's metonymy prepares the ground for future arguments planting the political particularity of the New World in American soil.

Twenty-five years later, Walt Whitman did just that. Famous lines from "Song of Myself" and "Poem of Many in One" make American character telluric, rooting it in rivers, rocks, and forests. They meld the human individuals central to Whitman's existentialism with the territory that nurtured them. Likewise, in an 1847 editorial, Whitman declared, "Hardly any evil which could be inflicted on the people of this hemisphere, and the cause of freedom all over the world, would be so great as the disunion of these States."[24] Monroe—and subsequent writers—often imagined the whole hemisphere to be laced with democratic potential. But, as Whitman explicitly asserts, they also understood the United States as the topographical center whose solidity was essential to freedom throughout the Americas.

South American appeals to democratic vision and practice were spottier in the early nineteenth century. Latin American governance was also—to white settler elites there and in the United States—more tainted by autocracy, racial mixture, and the numeric dominance of nonwhite peoples. Ironically, white and criollo elites understood native populations as obscuring America's democratic topography. Even so, it is notable that Monroe attributed a democratic nature to "our southern brethren" in his address.[25] Even in a moment when much of the southern continent remained under Iberian control and the region's independent governments were unevenly committed to democracy, Monroe saw the entire American hemisphere as fundamentally distinct from Europe's monarchical terroir. Whatever the present political topography of Latin America, Monroe asserted, it was tellurically democratic.

The most celebrated Latin American leader of the time shared both Monroe's skepticism and his assertion of American freedom. Simón Bolívar brought more pessimism to the matter than did his northern counterpart, and he reflected more honestly on the limits to his democratic inclinations. Elites in both North and South American circumscribed citizenship and land rights in order to retain white settler control over "popular" sovereignty. But where North Americans tended to bury that practice, elite men in Latin America frequently acknowledged their latent aristocracy. They wrote it into governing documents and reflected on the tensions it created in the spirit of the democratic hemisphere.

Bolívar encapsulates just this ambiguity in the distance between his 1815 "Carta de Jamaica" (Jamaican letter) and his 1826 "Address to the Constituent Congress" of Bolivia. Bolívar wrote his famous "Carta" during an early setback in the South American wars of independence. He was in political exile in Jamaica, and it would be another decade before Gran Colombia (present-day Venezuela, Colombia, and Ecuador) would achieve independence. Bolívar had seen Venezuela's initial independence efforts unraveled by disunity and what he deemed an excessive reliance on democratic values of tolerance and independence.[26]

In the "Carta," Bolívar was doubtful about the political future of South America. Adamant that independence from Spain would come, he nevertheless responded to his interlocutor's democratic inquiries with great caution. The need for independence and the fundamental separation between America and Europe were clear for Bolívar. "Success will crown our efforts because the destiny of America is irrevocably fixed," he declared, and "it would be easier to bring the two continents together than to reconcile the spirits and minds of the two countries."[27] Bolivar marked the distinction between Europe and America in territorial terms (they were as separate politically as their landmasses were physically). However, in 1815 Bolívar understood independence as something brought to the hemisphere, not endemic to it. American distinction was topographical but not (yet) telluric. Moreover, even if liberty was inevitable, Bolívar fretted about governance. Though republicanism may be the ideal form of government, he suggested, South America was not prepared for it. "It is . . . difficult," he wrote, "to predict the future lot of the New World, or to make definitive statements about its politics, or to make prophecies about the form of government it will adopt." Bolívar saw the leaders of the American continent as untethered from both the history of Europe and the land they occupied: "We, who preserve only the barest vestige of what we were formerly, and who are moreover neither Indians nor Europeans, but a race halfway between the legitimate owners of the land and the Spanish usurpers—in short, being Americans by birth and endowed with rights from Europe—find ourselves forced to defend these rights against the natives while maintaining our position in the land against the intrusion of the invaders."[28] Land and freedom were uncomfortably connected in this version of Bolívar's thought. If the criollo elites leading the wars of independence could have fully claimed the land, he implies, they might have made a telluric claim to freedom and republican leadership. Because they could not, their democratic efforts were hampered. "Although I aspire to a perfect government for my country," Bolívar lamented, "I can't persuade myself that the New World is ready at this time to be governed by a grand republic."[29]

Even so, aspects of the telluric democratic hemisphere infused Bolívar's thinking. He rejected the monarchical option, noting that "Americans, desirous of peace, sciences, art, commerce, and agriculture, would prefer republics to kingdoms."[30] Cognizant of that tension, he predicted difficult decades ahead: "The American provinces are involved in a struggle for emancipation, which will eventually succeed; a few will constitute themselves as conventional federal and centralized republics; almost inevitably the larger territories will establish monarchies, some so wretched that they will devour their natural and human resources in present and future revolutions, for it will be difficult to consolidate a great monarchy, impossible to maintain a great republic."[31]

Despite all that pessimism, Bolívar ended his letter with a note of hope, gesturing toward a future of popular government rooted in territorial destiny: "When we are at last strong, under the auspices of a liberal nation that lends us its protection, . . . then the arts and sciences that were born in the Orient and that brought enlightenment to Europe will fly to a free Colombia, which will nourish and shelter them."[32] Here, of course, those good gifts were external to America, having their roots ultimately in the Old World. The "auspices of a liberal nation" Bolívar invoked were those of England, after all, and not the always-problematic United States.

Ten years later, in 1826, with independence secured for most of Spanish America, Bolívar was invited to draft a constitution for his namesake republic. Far from popular democracy, Bolívar's "representative democracy" included an electoral college that mediated all major elections and a life term for the president, who would then appoint his successor. Even so, Bolívar's appeals to the nature and source of proper American government had by this time shifted to include the language of the democratic hemisphere. Before elite South Americans had nations to govern, democracy was an external practice and freedom a value brought from elsewhere. After independence, Bolívar planted freedom in American soil, carefully articulating its telluric source without placing excessive constraint on practice. In his address to the Constituent Assembly receiving his constitution, Bolívar declared, "From this day forward, freedom will be indestructible in America. Consider the wildness of this continent, which by its very nature expels monarchical rule: the very deserts invite independence." Rejecting recent, failed demagogues,

Bolívar asked, "Who will ever be able to found a monarchy in America, a land on fire with the brilliant flames of freedom that devour the planks used to build daises for kings?"[33] Bolivians need not fear the life term of their president, Bolívar explained, because the land itself would reject monarchical aspirations and the people would rise up to demand their natural sovereignty. In this, Bolívar echoed the leaders of Bolivian independence in their 1825 "Acta de Independencia." The "Acta" declared, "The world knows that, in the American continent, Alto Perú has been the altar on which the first blood of the free has been spilt and the land in which tyrants are buried."[34] It then justifies independence by contrasting Alto Peru's fecundity with the fallowness forced on it by Spanish rule. The land—as telluric producer and topographical site of freedom—authorized independence.

It is unlikely that either Bolívar or the Bolivian delegates who enacted his constitution were inspired by Monroe's assertions about America's democratic topography. Instead, we can see that confluence of early nineteenth-century claims for telluric, topographical American popular sovereignty as part of a larger narrative cultivated by Americans and Europeans throughout the hemisphere. The hotly contested natural philosophies of Buffon, Raynal, and dePauw were joined by parallel political philosophies linking region and governance. Montesquieu—a significant influence on Latin American political thought, including Bolívar's—argued in *The Spirit of Laws* that "the political and civil laws of each nation . . . should be in relation to the climate of each country, to the quality of its soil, to its situation and extent."[35] When de Tocqueville set out to explain the origins of democracy in the United States, he, too, presumed that political ideology was rooted in the land. Describing the early formation of authority in British America he noted, "Laws were made to establish a gradation of ranks; but it was soon found that the soil of America was entirely opposed to a territorial aristocracy."[36] De Tocqueville's reasoning was topographical: the agricultural conditions of the colonial territories did not lend themselves to massive landholding. A quick mental scan of US history and geography—even limited to that available to de Tocqueville himself—quickly reveals the factual shortcomings of his claim about landholding in the United States. Yet even as plantation slavery clearly rebuts de Tocqueville's assessment, his appeals to telluric democracy served to mediate that obvious disconnect. If the land itself birthed democratic inclinations, then nondemocratic features were incidental and democracy remained the natural American state.

Later nineteenth-century writers, from José Martí to Frederick Jackson Turner, extended appeals to the democratic hemisphere. Turner's famous frontier thesis rooted the character of the United States in its relation to land. Martí, for his part, sought to pull America southward, offering up "Our America" as a bulwark against the imperial behemoth of the North. Martí's understanding of the hemisphere's democracy remained thoroughly telluric, even if it emphasized movement over rootedness. When Donald Pease argues that Martí "distinguish[ed] democratic from nationalist identifications" through a notion of displacement that took the exile, nomad, and refugee as its model, he points to a more extensive and mobile notion of American democracy that is nevertheless grounded in the shaping power of a place—that is, America.[37]

In the mid-twentieth century, the *tropicalistas* likewise pulled the democratic hemisphere southward. They located Américan potential in the land and linked it with the god terms of democracy. Benjamín Carrión, in his "Cartas al Ecuador," argued that the tropics were "our physical reality. Our biological reality. Our economic reality. Our whole reality."[38] For Carrión, a geographic destiny rooted in *tropicalismo* called for a politics of freedom. The "highest expression" of "political *tropicalismo*" was "passion for liberty."[39] And Carrión's appeal to the land was not mere metaphor. He later explained, "By geography we must understand something real and living. Not the simple ordering of physical and political facts about the land and its regions but, primordially, an ordering of human criteria. . . . The climate and the land, above all."[40] That land and climate, for Carrión, gave rise to great American men whose thirst for liberty and sovereignty was unquenchable. Ecuador would become a "great small nation" by taming and cultivating its telluric democracy.

Whatever the ultimate inspiration for these appeals to democratic territory that cut across decades and national borders, their implications were wide-ranging. They set up a presumption of natural democracy that was literally grounded. This common sense about a democratic America provided the bedrock for arguments demanding greater freedom and the extension of democratic values; it also, paradoxically, relieved the pressures on democratic practice. Democracy became a fact of place as much as a matter of governance and civic life. As such, a telluric democratic spirit could persist even where actual democracy was lacking. While the democratic hemisphere appeared most often in hortatory contexts—energizing a demoralized populace, aggrandizing national influence, or forging ties among nation-states—it rarely served to extend liberty and equality to dispossessed or colonized populations. Instead, establishing democracy as native born, as inhabiting the rocks and soil, ultimately untethered the democratic nature of the hemisphere from the burden of enacting its values.

Claiming Land Rights

In "Democracy and Its Limitations," Ralph Cintrón emphasizes both democracy's open-ended availability as a universal positive and its many shortcomings in political practice.[41] Approaching democracy as telluric and topographical helps make sense of those simultaneous, contradictory aspects. When democracy infuses the ground we walk on, its actual practice can become superfluous. Anything enacted on that terrain is—by virtue of location—at least proto-democratic. Likewise, anything outside that territory can be dismissed as less authentically democratic. It is not a coincidence that Monroe imagined Europe as a uniformly monarchical "Old World" even when the democratic theories informing US political values had emerged out of Europe and the absolutist anciens régimes were under increasing popular pressure. Later invocations of the democratic hemisphere required even more adroit negotiations of their placed particularity, as when Carrión argued simultaneously for the particularity of Ecuador's telluric position and relied on a mixture of European and American heritage to establish its nature.[42]

Given that appeals to the hemisphere's natural liberty have often become substitutes for actual democratic practice, it should be no surprise that marginalized groups have been tactical and circumspect when linking appeals to the land with the language of democracy. Indigenous communities have occupied an especially complex position in this regard. They have appealed to a deep connection to land in order to authorize sovereignty claims, but they have also been denigrated by settlers for their proximity to the land.[43] Matters of land—telluric and topographical, territorial and resource-based, profoundly trophic—have been integral to Indigenous nations' responses to and practices of governance. These practices have frequently been fundamentally different from those engaged by white settlers, even at their most democratic. Here, especially, we see the limits of topoi as tools for understanding how land and rhetoric intertwine.

In the colonial context of America, Indigenous appeals to land and democracy have centered on territorial rights, sovereignty, and lifeways that depend on access to the land.[44] Such arguments emphasize not the inherent difference of American land from that of Europe, not the particular political structures the land calls forth, and not a partially metaphorical sense of land-as-invention, but a fundamental right of connected existence in which the land is a formative relation. Here, to apply Nishnaabeg scholar Leanne Betasamosake Simpson's insights on pedagogy to matters of rhetoric, we must recognize not "land-based [rhetorics]" but land *"become"* rhetoric and rhetoric become land.[45] These decolonial land claims—whether they refuse or engage the terms of democracy—rely on a literal relationship between freedom and the land, between land and life.

As Indigenous communities—both historical and contemporary—have appealed to land, they have strategically engaged the terms of the democratic hemisphere, picking up key orientations and manipulating them yet also refusing to cede control of its trophic rhetorical territory to colonizers. Indigenous claims to the land—where it is simultaneously the territory being contested, a participant in lifeways, and a physical place to stand—connect land itself to actually existing democracy via distinct epistemologies. For settlers in North and South America, that connection has often boiled down to the metaphorical and property-based implications of the common place as resource. For many Indigenous speakers, rhetoric and freedom are, instead, grounded in relationship to the land as a concrete source of refusal, resurgence, and resistance.[46]

When Emiliano Zapata released his "Plan de Ayala" in 1911, he invoked "effective suffrage" and other democratic rights as essential to his vision for a new Mexico.[47] Though land played a major role in the proposal, the land itself did not authorize popular sovereignty. Instead, Zapata imagined the land as the site on which despotic leaders had betrayed the people. That betrayal happened on the land and through the land; it also injured the land. The land, Zapata maintained, had been "despoiled. . . . Because lands, timber, and water are monopolized in a few hands."[48] In response, Zapata asserted, the many now claimed their right to the land. Their actions on the land, in order to gain land, also redeemed the land and returned a right relationship with land. They rebelled "in order that the pueblos and citizens of Mexico may obtain *ejidos*, colonies, and foundations for pueblos, or fields for sowing or laboring, and the Mexicans' lack of prosperity and well-being may improve in all and for all."[49] A sense of democratic land infuses this appeal to the good of the many over the ownership of the few. But in this case the land does not inspire sovereign individuals or reject monarchical governance—as it did in the arguments of elites—nor does the land serve as a metaphor for something larger. Instead, the democratic land of the "Plan de Ayala" is a foundation for common life. Its common place is not primarily a site for argument or a resource for invention, but a literal shared place. Despotic misappropriation of the land degrades it and the people. Access to land is a precursor to democracy and just governance. Democracy is not endemic to the soil, but the abuse of the soil nevertheless has consequences for democracy.

Some eighty years later, K'iche activist Rigoberta Menchú used her international platform to highlight centuries of "efforts to build up a real democracy" in America.[50] While her arguments for democracy relied on appeals to the land, the land's authorizing force was about community and redress rather than natural political ideology. Menchú invoked the "American continent" to unite an Indigenous hemisphere and acknowledge histories of violence, theft, and oppression. She dedicated her Nobel Prize "to those who are no longer alive to keep up the hope for a change in the situation in respect of poverty and marginalization of the Indians, of those who have been banished, of the helpless in Guatemala as well as in the entire American continent."[51] Pulling democracy out of its rocky rhetorical prison and into daily practice, she explained, would require ethical relationships with the land and among people. "Freedom for the Indians, wherever they may be in the American Continent or elsewhere in the world," would begin only when all people recognized "the European debt to the American indigenous people" and eradicated "those conditions of marginalization that condemned them to colonialism and exploitation."[52] The Indigenous peoples of America here stand alongside the land—colonized and exploited—and Menchú quickly transitions to link the exploitation of land and people: "The peculiarities of the vision of the Indian people are expressed according to the way in which they are related to each other. First, between human beings, though communication. Second, with the earth, as with our mother, because she gives us our lives and is not mere merchandise. Third, with nature, because we are an integral part of it, and not its owners."[53] Though Menchú tightly links land and the possibility for democracy, her democratic hemisphere is shaped by practice and relationship rather than preexisting nature. The land is a literal participant in rights. This strategy echoes in contemporary Indigenous movements across the hemisphere, from the Declaration of Quito and the Occupation of Alcatraz to Standing Rock.[54] As Gabriela Ríos explains, in Indigenous studies and for Indigenous rights movements, "colonial impact is seen most prominently as one having to do with territorial claims (e.g., to land, knowledge, representations, etc.) and, as such, as having to do with settler subjects and Indigenous subjects, even on a hemispheric or global level."[55] Repeatedly, Indigenous activists assert that democracy requires land, that the rights of the land are foundational, and that land constitutes all life-in-common. The land inspires, grounds, and is the source for human life. Literally. Western frames for the topos cannot quite grasp that.

Rights of the Land

The Organización Nacional de Aborígenes Independientes of Paraguay links "the ownership of land" and "access to all our rights" when they appeal to the Paraguayan government for redress.[56] Surveying the political efforts of

Andean Indigenous communities, anthropologist Bret Gustafson notes, "the plurinational project requires not fixing indigeneity within existing geopolitical lines, but decolonizing territory as a prerequisite for constitutive plurinationalism from the ground up."[57] Joy Harjo writes, "The land is a being who remembers everything."[58] The Organización Nacional Indígena de Colombia asserts, "For us, the land is sacred, is woman, we are part of her and she is part of us."[59] And David Choquhuanca, Bolivian foreign minister and member of the Aymara nation, declares, "We are beginning to imagine rights that go beyond human rights, rights that go beyond the rights of indigenous peoples, we are speaking of cosmic rights [that include all of nature]."[60] These statements, diverse in their focus and reflecting Indigenous perspectives gathered from across the hemisphere, assert democracy's topography in a way that challenges both the telluric democracy articulated by settler elites and rhetorical studies' reliance on the topos to understand rhetorical land. Resisting the elision of civic practice, they assert land rights as foundational to democratic life because land is at the center of all relations.[61] They position the land as an active participant in democracy and itself a subject of rights. In these land claims, we find a thoroughly trophic sense of the democratic hemisphere. If settler appeals to telluric democracy slide inexorably toward metaphor—toward democracy as topos—the decolonial arguments echoing across more than five hundred years center land as active, literal participant. In each context, democracy's topography remains weighty. Establishing and erasing borders, colonizing and reoccupying territory, privatizing and defending communal land all reshape the terrain of democracy. Land and the grounds for democratic rhetoric cannot be separated from each other. Just as Qwo-Li Driskill urges US- and Canada-based queer studies to "remember exactly on whose land it is built," Indigenous decolonial practices demand that rhetorical scholars, in our discussions of democracy, recognize and reenvision whose land we occupy and what territory we claim.[62]

2

A STRANGE DEMOCRACY: RHETORIC, POSTHEGEMONY, AND LATINAMERICANISM

José Cortez

The central argument of this chapter is that Latin American rhetorical and cultural thought has fundamentally misread the concept of politics into Latin America and, as such, has developed a conceptualization of democracy that subverts itself. The most immediate metaproject of Latinamericanism across the field of rhetoric has been to think of Latin American alternative modernities as exceptions (or, to think of Latin American rhetorical and political formations as exterior to, and exceptional from, Western modernity),[1] grounding a politics of resistance from the assumed consciousness of a non-Western, nonideological mestizo subject. It is widely presupposed, in other words, that the event of colonialism (the clash of Amerindian and European groups in the fifteenth century and the miscegenation that continues to unfold from it) produces an identity that is inherently resistant to what critics identify as the matrix of modernity/coloniality.[2] Critics identify this process of racial and cultural mixture as a form of hybridity unique to Latin America: *mestizaje*. And since mestizaje is the name for a locus of rhetorical invention grounded in mixture, grounded in the impurification of Western modernity, it is therefore assumed to be the proper name for a counterhegemonic rhetoric.

The problem with this metaproject, I contend, is that it establishes a false choice between a Eurocentric rhetoric and a mestiza rhetoric. Two very brief examples: Cristina Ramírez advances a reading of mestiza rhetorics as a subversive "decolonizing approach to identification outside of the dominant narrative of assimilation" that "breaks with the tired trope of well-known Euro- and malecentric stories."[3] In similar fashion, Damián Baca urges scholars to look for "rhetoric outside of the dominant and virtually exclusive

Greco-Latin canon"[4] and toward those "unique to Mesoamerica, México, . . . and the U.S./México borderlands, among other places within the Western Hemisphere."[5] The operational term in these texts is, of course, "outside." If, for Ramírez and Baca, the option is to decolonize rhetorical theory by replacing it in Latin America, then the operation reproduces a familiar problem: mestizaje cannot provide an alternative to Eurocentrism given that both operate within a field of politics as a state of exception.[6]

If rhetoricians are committed to pursuing the grounds of a democratic practice of critical thought, to a reflection on the grounds for democracy, and to asking after the conditions of possibility for thinking democracy in Latin America beyond a reduction of politics to a choice between states of exception, then it will be apposite to ask after an opening, or possibility irreducible to mere social democracy—or for that matter, to any epistemic machine. In response, this chapter advances a genealogy of two forms of Latinamericanist inquiry in rhetorical studies of democracy in Latin America, which Alberto Moreiras has identified as first- and second-order Latinamericanism. Whereas first-order, or identitarian, Latinamericanism amounts to "an epistemic machine in charge of representing the Latin American difference," a second order, which we might call in preliminary fashion a posthegemonic register of Latinamericanism, turns on a critical practice of tracing the absolute limits of first-order Latinamericanism as a means to prepare for a strange democracy—a democracy yet to arrive.[7]

From there, the chapter shifts its analysis to Guillermo Gómez-Peña's *Codex Espangliensis: From Columbus to the Border Patrol* to read a thought of democracy at the absolute limit of the false choice between Eurocentrism and mestizaje. I read in this text a confrontation with the problem established by the Latinamericanist reflection in rhetorical studies—a problem, as I have previously argued, that may ultimately amount to the reinstallation of hegemonic mediation under the guise of critical categories such as identity.[8] Whereas a good deal of scholarship continues to understand politics as a counterhegemonic process where agents develop commonplaces of resistance, as positive sites (topoi) of counterhegemonic cultural production, like mestizaje, from locations outside the reach of hegemony, Gómez-Peña's performance text produces a thought of politics as a non-nostalgic reflection on the loss of commonplace, and therefore, on politics at the absolute limits of identity. It is here, I contend, that one reads the trace of a strange democracy: a rupture in the epistemic machine from an atopic location yet to arrive.

The Decolonial Imaginary

I begin my analysis with a reading of the decolonial option, which I claim is one of the many forms of Latinamericanist inquiry to fall under the heading of first-order Latinamericanism. The decolonial option is a paradigm of critical thought that presupposes political community—democratic space itself—can be read as a self-contained, whole entity with no surplus parts. This problem can be summarized in Emma Pérez's widely cited *The Decolonial Imaginary: Writing Chicanas into History*, in which she advances the concept of the decolonial imaginary as a method of reading the silenced part of colonial history, the silenced Chicana voices that have been relegated to interstices of history by Western power/knowledge. As such, *The Decolonial Imaginary* turns on the articulation of a succinct counterhegemonic subjectivity outside of hegemonic mediation. The stakes of *The Decolonial Imaginary*, then, are to develop a thinking of politics "without the dialectical promise of a teleological history" via a nonhegemonic subject.[9]

Nevertheless, *The Decolonial Imaginary* remains ambivalent about the very interstice that it reads to be both interior and at the same time exterior to Eurocentric power/knowledge. In other words, for *The Decolonial Imaginary*, the topos of the interstice marks both the structural incompletion of history from its interstitial exclusion and the structural completion of history through its interior (that this gap, or structural incompletion, can be brought into the academy "without the dialectical promise of a teleological history"). Despite its claims to the contrary, *The Decolonial Imaginary* remains ambivalent about its most important postulate: that the interstice is the location of a nonhegemonic subject position *because* it is excluded from hegemonic mediation.

The Decolonial Imaginary hinges on a reading of a gap that can be filled with historical substance while at the very same time forcing the historical future to remain open to the future perfect tense—to a politics that will have arrived (in decolonized fashion) through the interstices of that which was always within colonial history itself. In the introduction of *The Decolonial Imaginary*, Pérez writes, "Foucault's methodology is useful to historians because archaeology seeks to uncover discursive practices by unmasking them. It is self-reflexive in intent, and it is in that self-reflection where coloniality is exposed. Through his own self-reflection, Foucault was undoing European history. . . . He concluded in *The Order of Things*, 'man is an invention of recent date. And one perhaps nearing its end.' In essence, he claimed that European white man would no longer be central to history and its interpretations."[10]

This passage establishes the first presupposition of the decolonial imaginary in explicit detail, a presupposition that will need to be rendered to
draw the stakes of this analytical practice into relief. Pérez reads discourse
as that which masks a subject. Analysis, therefore, amounts to the practice
of listening and recovering—of restituting a pure, unmediated subaltern
consciousness. The stakes of this practice, according to Pérez, are such that
we misinterpret the subaltern subject, and that this subject can and should
be restituted. *The Decolonial Imaginary* stakes its intervention, therefore, on
the grounds of meaning, which it claims are not located in Western power/
knowledge but in the authority of the subaltern subject itself.

Furthermore, *The Decolonial Imaginary* proceeds along a metaleptic articulation of postcoloniality, which does not designate a historical condition
after the end of colonization but a historiographical condition whereby previously functional political distinctions (friend/enemy, colonizer/colonized,
metropole/colony) have waned to the point of ambivalence. Postcoloniality
is therefore the name for what happens to political identities—to democracy itself—under the conditions of coloniality.[11] Thus it is only through the
representation of an irreducible gap between previously functional political
distinctions, through a not-quite-reformed colonial subject—the very ambivalent ideological kernel of coloniality itself—that a subaltern subject might
be read by an intellectual:

> The desire for a reformed, recognizable Other, *as a subject of difference
> that is almost the same, but not quite.* Which is to say, that the discourse of
> mimicry is constructed around an *ambivalence*; in order to be effective,
> mimicry must continually produce its slippage, its excess, its differ-
> ence. The authority of that mode of colonial discourse that I have called
> mimicry is therefore stricken by an indeterminacy: mimicry emerges
> as the representation of a difference that is itself a process of disavowal.
> Mimicry is, thus the sign of a double articulation; a complex strategy of
> reform, regulation and discipline, which "appropriates" the Other as it
> visualizes power. Mimicry is also the sign of the inappropriate, however,
> a difference or recalcitrance which coheres the dominant strategic func-
> tion of colonial power, intensifies surveillance, and poses an imminent
> threat to both "normalized" knowledges and disciplinary powers.[12]

The ambivalence of colonial discourse produces a slippage, a textual surplus between the demand of colonialism for reformed subjects and what
it desires in return: a reform only up to a certain threshold that if colonial

subjects were to pass through there would then be no way of distinguishing between the identities of, for example, English and Indian, or friend and enemy. This minimal gap between the demand and desire that constitutes the colonial subject, then, is the very moment of rhetorical invention that constitutes Englishness in the first place. I argue that the name for this unconscious surplus textuality, for the nonsubjective constitutive movement between poles that both binds and separates political community in the first place, is rhetoric, and furthermore, that the grounds of political meaning can only be located in the transactional movements of rhetorical invention.

Pérez, however, understands the interstice of history as an ontological gap that can be remedied by uncovering the silenced voice of the subaltern. The concept of the decolonial imaginary, then, serves as the method for this critical practice of restitution, and further, for deconstructing the "European and Euroamerican historical method," and for "going outside [this method] in order to come back with different kinds of inquiries."[13] "Traditional historiographical categories," Pérez argues, "questioned only from within for revision, have been built upon that which came before, and therefore have contributed to the colonial. The categories themselves are exclusive, in that they already deny and negate the voice of the other."[14] On the other hand, Pérez contends that the decolonial imaginary arises in the "interstitial gaps [that] interrupt the linear model of time, and it is in such locations that oppositional, subaltern histories can be found. Foucault's redefinition of archaeology, understood as a method, disrupts linear continuity to locate silences within the interstices. . . . I argue that these silences, when heard, become the negotiating spaces for the decolonizing subject. It is in a sense where third space agency is articulated. . . . This new category, the decolonial imaginary, can help us to rethink history in a way that makes Chicana/o agency transformative."[15]

The Decolonial Imaginary hinges on a conceptualization of alterity as a supplement to the category of history: both a negative part that was added to make history complete (the interstice *is* the antithesis that is the very condition of possibility for hegemonic synthesis) and the part added to replace history that was assumed to be already complete (that is, the interstice is assumed to be self-evident and, therefore, a positive element of history). The category of the decolonial imaginary—and the assumed positive subjectivity of the decolonial subject—is therefore mediated by the very absence that it attempts to supplement. Nevertheless, just like Western history, the decolonial imaginary is always inhabited by a certain lack that must produce alterity as a supplement. As such, because the decolonial imaginary merely reverses the grounds and authority of meaning from one location to another, from Western subject to non-Western subaltern subject, it reproduces the very logocentric edifice of power/knowledge that it claims to unseat.

The Posthegemonic Rupture

In *The Exhaustion of Difference: The Politics of Latin American Cultural Studies*, Alberto Moreiras defines two registers of Latinamericanist thought: first-order and second-order Latinamericanism. To begin with the latter, it presupposes and translates the identity/difference striae into a practice of critical thought for subjectivizing alterity into a politics of differential consciousness.[16] Pérez, for example, suggests that the topos of the interstice inaugurates an entirely new consciousness altogether, "issuing a 'new' postnationalist project in which *la nueva mestiza*, the mixed-race woman, is the privileged subject of an interstitial space that was formerly a nation, and is now without borders, without boundaries."[17] Mestizaje is proposed as the essence of bordered space, as the result of mixture, and as the very ontological process by which the category of the politics emerges. The interstice, now understood as the border itself, is understood to serve as a political gap in addition to its role as the historical gap. It should come as no surprise that Pérez grounds the figure of the border in the discourse of mestizaje, given that Pérez reads the category of new mestiza consciousness as the interstitial or borderlands consciousness from which to "write the 'other' without making the 'other' the same or placing the 'other' within the same."[18] Pérez wagers that the space of borderlands—or, rather, the consequences of mixture (supposedly the creation of smooth space) that borderlands exemplifies—"[introduces] the possibility of a postcolonial, postnational consciousness."[19] Now, the interstice becomes the site of the political—the site of hegemonic incomple-tion, which in her terms, signifies the condition of smooth, nonnationness brought about by mestizaje—in postnational times. This is a wager on the concept of politics in the *criollista* vein of transculturation, whereby cultural identity, understood as the result of mestizaje, is staged as the grounds for an active intervention in the restructuring of the public sphere.

Mestizo cultural identity has come to be thought of as the basis of demo-cratic freedom (from colonization, from nation-state hegemony, etc.) simply because it is assumed to be an impure, heterogeneous identity that impuri-fies any grounding of politics in racial purity. But this form of thought is itself a new form of purity. Gareth Williams demonstrates how this mode of identity thinking grounded nation-state hegemony—it constituted the very category of the people *itself* as a heterogeneous mixture around which to construct identities of resistance to the West and the North. In his reading of transculturation during the national-popular epoch in Latin America, Williams reads transculturation as two distinct but related registers: transculturation as the material condition of exchange obtaining within postcolonial conditions, and transculturation as a rhetoric of politics:

> If we distinguish between transculturation as a heterogeneous cultural ensemble and transculturation as a desire and an intellectual discourse; and if we do this as a means of viewing the thought of transculturation in relation to the formation of institutional structures, political identities, state apparatuses, and intellectual interventions into the public sphere (in relation to the notion of hegemony, in other words), then in transculturation we encounter not only the popular forms of self-expression and differential modes of collective self-definition but also an immensely powerful ideological machinery of which popular expressions of difference are often merely little more than an effect.

The threshold between these domains of transculturation not only corresponds to the antagonism that hegemony theory is supposed to describe (the formation of subjects from above [state] or change from below [people]); more important, it renders clear the problem inhabiting the core of intellectual desire—its indistinction from capitalist modernization in the region. If the category of the popular emerges as a material condition *and* an idea during a period in Latin America in which cultural elites were thinking about politics as a process of change from below (and as a means of integrating peasant classes into a national public sphere), then it's hard to imagine how the intellectual desire for popular incorporation from below can be said to operate beyond the state's calculation and mobilization of the people as the grounds of its own legitimation and reproduction. Or in Williams's words, by reflecting on transculturation in both registers "we can approach transculturation not merely as a positive culturalism but, more problematically, as a privileged discourse in the consolidation and often violent expansion of the Creole state's hegemony over national territories, populations, and classes."[20]

While *The Decolonial Imaginary* demonstrates the inadequacy of existing critical language for describing the shifting contemporary political terrain, it nevertheless "works as an instantiation of global agency, insofar as it ultimately wants to deliver its findings into some totality of allegedly neutral, universal knowledge of the world in all its differences and identities. Born out of an ideology of cultural difference, its fundamental thrust is to capture the Latin American difference in order to release it into the global epistemic grid."[21] What is really at stake with first-order Latinamericanism—via the production of a counteridentity that would serve as the marker of the ends of Western thinking—is the impassive maintenance of identity via difference. This is to say that *difference* actualizes for Pérez as substance, as an ontological formulation of A ≠ B. There is slippage, as I argued above, in the presupposed ground of the *does not equal*, a ground that, because it is presupposed, becomes the effaced logical kernel of the entire project. Pérez's categories—history, the West—are assumed to meet their finitude at a conceptual border, which prompts one to develop the following question: If the limits of the categories of the West and history are to be found in the terrain of the *does not equal*—in the maintenance of an inequality—what, then, is at stake in the maintenance of this difference? What would happen, in other words, if A = B?

Furthermore, this rhetoric of difference is itself irreducibly doubled, given that it is a project marked by the injunction to both draw the limit of the West, on the basis of difference, and at the same time, develop a project of constituting a new community around the maintenance of this difference. Is this not the very move that Pérez disavows with the proclamation of a postnational condition as the putative end of Western thought (writing the Other as the project of making the Other the same)? How can identity function as that which is both the grounds of legitimacy and illegitimacy? In short, it does this by turning politics into the game of friend versus enemy, drawn on an entirely arbitrary distinction between proper and improper identity.

Pérez is, of course, not the first to suggest, from reflection on the category of the border, that nation-state hegemony is experiencing a fundamental restructuring in the wake of globalization and that such an observation prompts questions about the possibility of reading culture in a historical moment defined by a crisis in hegemonic (nation-state) systems.[22] And, while critics agree that the form of nation-state hegemony in the region has experienced a fundamental shift in relation to globalization, they disagree on the effects such a shift has on the meaning of politics and possibilities for critical reflection in postnational times. In contrast to the decolonial program, there is another option that insists on the name of the non-All of democracy through a reading of the rhetorical grounds of a politics of knowledge production. This option goes by the name of *posthegemony*.

Alberto Moreiras forms this option with an aporia: "What is then the type of historical imagination that could warrant a reformulation of the project of critical reason as a properly politico-epistemological project? In other words, where can we find a force for intrasystemic irruption if the system has expanded in such a way that no productive notion of an outside is permitted?"[23]

To sketch an answer to this question is to reflect first on the role of critical reason in a context where "no productive notion of an outside is permitted." This "impossibility" to establish a view from the perspective of subalternity is infrastructural, for, as I argued above, given that rhetoric is the condition of possibility for hegemony that also restructures the entire hegemonic field when it emerges, textual surplus ceases to exist as such, and therefore would provide *only* the coordinates for hegemony's reinstallation on yet different terms. Subalternity is merely the subject effect of the differential movement conditioned by any rhetorical choice. It is the name for the condition of possibility of rhetoric: *differánce*. Recall the unacknowledged ambivalence that Pérez exhibited toward the interstice: the interstice became the name for the absence of historical substance, of which *la nueva mestiza* serves as supplement. If Latinamericanism in its first order relied on the conceptualization of the interstice in terms of its exceptionality, second-order Latinamericanism promotes the role of surplus to the condition of possibility for thinking the infrastructural transformation of hegemonic interpellation itself: "That is, no longer as the possibility of turning a dominated ideology into the dominant but rather as the possibility of thinking the outside of hegemony: posthegemonic thinking."[24] Posthegemony is an attempt to think publicity, public space itself, at the absolute limit of hegemonic interpellation, for what comes after the democratic rupture remains yet to arrive. Posthegemony is a rhetorical project that remains productive only as a permanent, affirmative critique of the negative.

The difference between first-order Latinamericanism's *outside* and the second order's *beyond* is subtle, but the latter points to the incongruence between the institutionalization of cultural politics and the site of subaltern excess always deferred: a given formation of sheer unreadability in a text that points to the incompletion of any form of intellectual practice, and therefore, the possibility of rethinking the relation of intellectual practice itself to the political. This structural incompletion is not an identity or consciousness but the residue of signification that interpellation will always fail to capture. By definition, hegemony is not only incomplete but it presupposes the lack of its own grounding, which is why signification and interpellation are phenomena in the first place.[25] Latinamericanism in its second order is an approach to the thinking of politics from the inevitable structural excess of the hegemony-subalternity relation itself. Posthegemony is a practice of asserting that politics can be thought beyond the incessant reduction of democracy to a false choice between Eurocentrism and mestizaje. The answer to Moreiras's question lies in determining the role of critical reason in a historical moment in which the university as a civic institution can no longer be said to operate outside economic law, which—as critics have noted—might have always been the telos of the nation-state.

Gareth Williams advances this line of investigation as he foregrounds the wane of the national-popular (national-revolutionary) after Latin America's insertion into globalized capital.[26] Analyzing "the even, incomplete, and ongoing passage from national to postnational cultural and political paradigms in Latin America,"[27] Williams argues that "transnationalization and the insertion of Latin American nations into global networks has ungrounded the nation-state and, alongside it, the transformational potential of the national-popular. It has brought the nation-state and the national-popular (Gramsci's 'nation-people') to their economic, institutional, and conceptual knees. Therefore, through increasing transnationalization, we are living the historical 'other side' of the national-popular; the (collapsed/collapsing) side of the people; the national-popular in its state of exhaustion and redistribution across regional and national frontiers."[28]

For Williams, the postnational does not signify the end of the nation-state form but its recombination in the wake of neoliberal development, which rendered a shift in hegemonic models in the region. Latin America's insertion into global circulation undermined the grounding and constitutive element of cultural and social hegemonies in discreetly bordered Latin American nations: the national/popular antagonism. Whereas hegemony, in the national/popular antagonism, functioned to enable the articulation of a universalizing national project through the constitution of distinct spatial exteriorities (with, for example, national frontiers), globalization set in motion a generalized spatial crisis—a generalized condition of the wane of previously functional topoi for emancipatory politics such as "the people."

Williams is not the first to give the name posthegemony to the wane of the national/popular period in Latin America. In "Civil Society, Consumption, and Governmentality in an Age of Global Restructuring," George Yúdice contends that the emergence of globalization corresponds with an erosion of the dialectical mediation of state and civil domains, which, he suggests, demonstrates a condition of new forms of hegemonic mediation and capital accumulation.[29] Yúdice conceives of this in the following terms: "Flexible accumulation, consumer culture, and the 'new world information order' are produced or distributed (made to flow) globally, to occupy the space of the nation, but are no longer 'motivated' by any essential connection to a state, as embodied, for example, in a 'national-popular' formation. Their motivations are both infra- and supranational. We might say that, from the purview of the national proscenium, a posthegemonic situation holds. That is, the 'compromise solution' that culture provided for Gramsci is not now one that pertains to the national level but to the local and transnational."[30]

Here, in opposition to Michael Hardt's conclusion in an article in the same issue of *Social Text*—"Not the State, but civil society has withered away!"[31]— Yúdice links the state/civil antagonism *together* as a hegemonic form that has come to be augmented by flexible accumulation. Yúdice suggests that flexible accumulation incites a shift in the relation of state sovereignty to global capital, a claim that reworks Antonio Gramsci's assumption that when the state is finally unseated or "reabsorbed" by the counterhegemonic force of civil society that "a sturdy structure of civil society [will be] at once revealed."[32] For Yúdice, then, posthegemony is the name for the condition in which flexible accumulation has taken its seat as the structure of civil society—a condition in which global capital, not the nation-state, saturates the field of social relations. The key phrase here—*flexible accumulation is made to flow*—signals a change in the nation-state's form. It is not that the border, for example, has been razed but that the very function of the border itself changes. If the concept of the border served as a threshold to spatial segmentation and restriction in disciplinary society, then perhaps the border serves as a threshold in which flexible accumulation is *made* (forced) to flow in control societies.[33] If this is the case, and the nature of the border has shifted in response to the restructuring of the nation-state, how is it possible that the interstitial border can serve as the site of any identitarian, counterhegemonic project?

What is at stake in the question of posthegemony is an "opening up of the political field to a certain form of unintelligibility," an alterity whose negativity signals only the incompletion of hegemony, but also, an opening to a narrative that will have never been overdetermined by institutionalized thought—to a locus of rhetorical invention, still, yet to arrive.[34] To return to Moreiras's question, then, is it possible to engage a thought of politics in such a way that no productive notion of an outside is permitted? If we understand Latinamericanism in its second register—that it to say, not merely as the management of the category of cultural practices contained within the landmass known as Latin America—it might be possible to answer this question by thinking of Latin America in the properly democratic sense: as a site of a negative singularity that cannot establish the grounds of any identity whatsoever. This "thinking of Latin America that thinks what thinking Latin

America destroys" would be properly rhetorical in the sense that it provides a means to trace democracy on the affirmation of the *chance* for a formation of political community hinging on that part that is always deferred and therefore impossible to incorporate.[35] In a formal sense, insofar as the sign "Latin America" signifies a surplus, Latinamericanist rhetoric becomes a critical enterprise that engages the imagination of democracy, for it becomes a reflection on the very problem of the proper account itself, and therefore undermines the logic of the false choice of Eurocentrism/mestizaje from which it withdraws.

A Strange Democracy

I can draw into relief the contours of such a reading by turning to Guillermo Gómez-Peña's performance art. Originally published in 1998 as a performance text—and later in 2000 as a trade book—*Codex Espangliensis: From Columbus to Border Patrol* narrates, if it can be said to do as much, the conquest of the Americas in reverse, recounting violent events from the constitutive encounter between European and Amerindian groups to the institutionalization of global capital in the North American Free Trade Agreement. *Codex* appears decisive in its narration of encounters at different borders, given that blood runs through nearly every page as a banal visual topos, and it appears that despite the direction in which one reads this historical fact— whether in forward or reverse, Europe to Latin America or Latin America to Europe, hegemonic or counterhegemonic—one cannot escape the violence that mediates cultural exchange. And, while the bulk of the text is focused on the reimagination of a cartography of domination in counterhegemonic fashion, it is the event of the encounter on which I focus.

Critics often read *Codex* through the prism of mestizaje. *Codex* could be read, as Damián Baca contends, as the hybrid result of the mixture of two previously existing forms of cultural production: "By fusing and embellishing Mesoamerican pictography into European inscription practices, Mestiz@ codex rhetorics promote a new dialectic, a new strategy of inventing and writing between worlds."[36] Additionally, Lisa Wolford describes Gómez-Peña's art as the production of "the Fourth World, it is a space that privileges hybridity and calls into question ascribed boundaries of identity and community, a realm in which binaristic conceptions of self and other collapse and implode."[37] It is perhaps valid to read *Codex Espangliensis* as the textual mode by which Gómez-Peña articulates a hybrid identity and the hybrid group identities of which he is a part—that is, as a mode of forming topoi, the textual spaces-in-common, commonplaces for establishing the account of a communal experience—to finally produce a level of intelligibility that would qualify them for inclusion into the categories of history, citizenship, and so on.

Additionally, for Franny Howes, "*Codex Espangliensis* is a massive act of memory, reaching into both American popular cultural imagery and indigenous imagery to invent a way to represent the ongoing struggles of colonialism in a way that is both new and old."[38] Kat Austin and Carlos-Urani Montiel read *Codex Espangliensis* as the product of hybridity—as evidence of the "Chicana/o mind" and the political space of the US-Mexico border, arguing that the "cultural negotiations and the distinct consciousness that emerges in their wake constitute the crucial components of a border identity that may provide the necessary threads for uniting a diverse community for the purpose of resistance."[39] Finally, in similar fashion, Cruz Medina reads the codex as a production of "the cultural mestizaje of border art and rhetoric."[40]

Critics read *Codex* as a formalization of a new hybrid, cultural identity from which to formalize a counterhegemonic program and imagine new modes of political community. These readings take the event of encounter as the inauguration of mixture—as the production of a new subject, and in turn, the production of a new form of politics. The event: the encounter between incommensurate groups; violent conquest. The mestizo subject (in its Latinamericanist first order): hybrid; subjectivity as the result of mixture. And yet what is exceptional about this subject is that which is external to it—the exceptional quality is not necessarily *of* the subject, but something that arrives and forcefully inaugurates it. Mestizo subjectivity's exceptionality is, as such, outside of it. If the distinguishing quality of the exceptional mestizo subject is hybridity, which comes about as a result of the encounter, then its value lies in the force of violence. The politics of mestizaje is grounded in a violence that it must reproduce as its condition of possibility. It is a politics of violence.

Still, the mestiza subject in the Latinamericanist first order is defined by an event outside it: a forceful violence. Whether this event occurs in forward or reverse, what is important here is the condition proceeding from the grounds of violence. The mestizo subject, when defined in a narrower sense of exceptionalism, is defined by a mixture grounded in violence. The first axiom of mestizo identification: the mestizo subject is constituted in an act of mixture grounded in the condition of violence. The second axiom of mestizo identity: "I mix therefore I am (the force of violence)." Gómez-Peña's counternarration of the event in reverse:

in 1492, an Aztec sailor
named Noctli Europzin Tezpoca
departed from the port of Minatitlan with a small flotilla of
wooden rafts.
3 months later
he discovered a new continent
& named it Europzin after himself.
in November 1512,
the omni-potent Aztecs
began the conquest of Europzin
in the name of thy father tezcatlipoca
lord of cross-cultural misconceptions[41]

It is possible, however, to interpret *Codex* in such a way as to interrupt the law of mestizaje by way of reading the irreducible gap between location and name that is baked into the concept of topos. Conquest is the founding event that sets hybridity in motion. It therefore inaugurates the mestizo subject. If this inauguration can be narrated in reverse—that is, applied to the opposite group—then one can reason that mestizaje can be dissociated from location. Perhaps it would be possible, then, to mark the mestizo subject in a generic sense—that of belonging to the category of different—as defined by its relationality, given that what defines the mestizo subject is an event that arrives and inaugurates a value of difference-from-_____. In other words, what one reads in *Codex* is the formation of the mestizo subject in Europe—truly, that Europeans, too, can be marked under the heading of mestizaje. Remember, the law of mestizaje states only the axiomatic mixture between European/Amerindian. Nowhere does it stipulate a location clause—that it can only occur in the landmass named Latin America. As such, what we have here is a Latinamericanism unmoored from the landmass of Latin America, to the degree that we witness the ambivalent and deferred nature of the category of topos. We now have a Latinamericanism in the most generic sense—a Latinamericanism at the absolute limits of identity.

I read in *Codex* a momentary loss of commonplace, a moment where the sign *Latin America* short-circuits itself. *Codex* narrates an impossible situation that would undermine the knowledge machine. As the text seems to suggest, the sign *Latin America* has been in circulation in different locations for quite a long time; indigenous bodies and objects have been placed on display as ethnographic data in museums and dioramas since 1493.[42] And, even if coloniality did not happen in reverse, and even if its reversal would be impossible, *Codex* nevertheless reveals the foundational ambivalence of the sign *Latin America*, which has always circulated value beyond the landmass the sign itself signifies. *Latin America* has always been marked as a constitutive exteriority, and as such, it is impossible to ground political community in the metaphysics of a mestizo subject. In this way, I contend that *Codex* provides the opportunity for reflection on what political activity means, understood in the precise definition that Jacques Rancière poses: as "whatever shifts a body from the place assigned to it or changes a place's destination." Political activity, he continues, is "a mode of expression that undoes the perceptible divisions of the police order by implementing a basically heterogeneous assumption, that of a part of those who have no part, an assumption that, at the end of the day, itself demonstrates the sheer contingency of the order, the equality of any speaking being with any other speaking being."[43] For Rancière, democracy is not the name for a mode of governmentality but, rather, the name for the rupture of social hegemonies that might pass themselves off as democracy. Rancière contends, "Any subjectification is a disidentification, removal from the naturalness of a place, the opening up of a subject space where anyone can be counted."[44] Perhaps the only way to read mestizaje in its properly democratic form is in this generic sense, which is to say, that mestizaje is democratic only when anyone at all can participate as a mestizo subject. Only then would hybridity become democratic, for it would articulate itself at the minimal gap of hegemony's closure where place is disarticulated from proper name. In such a reading, a minimal gap in the logic of hegemony is exposed: the impossibility of absolutely suturing proper place to proper name. This is the possibility for thinking about democracy in Latin America beyond the violence of exceptional mestizo subjectivity.

In an interview with Gómez-Peña, Eduardo Mendieta asks Gómez-Peña about the stakes of his work:

[MENDIETA] Are you suggesting that the discourses of difference have been already co-opted and have therefore become passé—even de rigueur and establishment—and thus perhaps suspect?
[GÓMEZ-PEÑA] The subjects of identity politics are passé. We are already installed in a postracist/postsexist society. They want sexy images of race and hybridity, but without the text. Unlike their multicultural or postcolonial predecessors, the new impresarios and self-proclaimed experts of Otherness are no longer interested in the tensions and clashes of cultures. They no longer wish to discuss issues of power and privilege. They know better. They don't want their neocolonial

positionality questioned by angry primitives and strident women. They suffer from the Vietnam syndrome of the cultural wars. Besides, what they really want is to market Otherness, not to understand it. What the impresarios of globalization want is mild salsa and tofu tamales. They want Zapatista supermodels, not "real" Zapatistas. They want Salma Hayek to play Frida Kahlo. They want "Livin' la Vida Loca" sung by Ricky Martin, not enacted by gang members. . . . In this respect, the pertinent question for performance artists is, How do we continue raising crucial issues without scaring our audiences or without facing deportation back to the margins? My answer, for the moment, is that we must mimic mainstream culture, and when the mirror is standing between them and us, reflecting their fantasies and desires, we break it in the audience's face. If parts of the mirror get in their eyes, that's their problem.[45]

To what does it refer to have race and hybridity without the text? That to which Slavoj Žižek refers in *The Puppet and the Dwarf* as the total rearticulation of politics without politics: "On today's market, we find a whole series of products deprived of their malignant property: coffee without caffeine, cream without fat, beer without alcohol."[46] Are the market and the decolonial not indistinct in offering a generalized form of flexible accumulation, which is to say, the consumption of identity without its malignancies (a Zapatista without the peasant, on the one hand, and a [hybrid] identity without difference, on the other)? What we have here is two sides of the same double injunction: if decoloniality is constituted by the injunction to both reduce and preserve alterity, with global capital we get the injunction to reduce and preserve the national frontiers that produce a forced migration of cultural forms. If globalized capital and decoloniality obtain as a false choice between two types of police should one not, instead, locate the moment that smashes the mirror and sends a shard into the eye? Could such a procedure shatter the topos of subjectivity where place is narrativized into a proper name? *Codex* prompts us to read both the subject and politics in a strange way, to read politics without commonplace.

I read the narration of the encounter in *Codex* as this critical mirror, the name for the minimal gap between place and name where one encounters a critique of the politics of the subject on the basis of its always-doubled articulation. There is a space that first-order Latinamericanism calls "politics" where place is narrativized into the topos of proper name, where the constitutive parts are accounted for and circulated based on the basis of encounter. But there is also an excessive remainder: the articulation of a name—unmoored from location—that cannot be sedimented into an epistemic machine. This is a politics of what Michel Foucault calls "atopics": the "loss of what is 'common' to place and name. Atopia."[47] It is in this sense that I read a trace of democracy, of an atopic rhetoric in *Codex*, given that its articulation of mestizaje in a universal sense short-circuits the logic of the subject on which first-order Latinamericanism is based.

If, as Moreiras claims, Latinamericanism conceives of itself as a form of antiglobalist intellectual practice through expressions of an irreducible geographical and critical distance from the global, and if the subjects and objects of study that it holds within its conceptual domain no longer reside on the other side of a set of neatly articulated national, cultural, and political borders—subjects and objects that were held to represent and demonstrate not only difference itself but the possibility for a locus of antiglobalist thought—in *Codex* one is confronted to think through the movement of this difference back into the Iberian metropole. In other words, if these subjects and objects were understood to represent differential identity because they were located beyond the reaches of the metropole, are we now to understand that they are no longer different, and therefore no longer representative of antiglobalist thought? No. On the contrary, in *Codex* one is confronted with a thinking of Latin American objects as that which "denarrativizes" the structural connection of history to logic (and of place to name) on the account of a miscount.[48] The moment of mis-encounter in *Codex* is the moment when mestizaje can be read democratically—that is, as *atopic*, removed from its placement as "natural" and "common" in Latin America.

As the moment of hegemonic failure in *Codex*, the denarrativization of the encounter event advances an *atopos*—a place not yet named, or a topos yet to arrive—whose translation into the conventional account of Latinamericanism would be impossible. It is on this deferred atopic terrain—rhetorical terrain proper, terrain yet to be common—that a moment of impossibility emerges. Žižek refers to this rupture as the preeminent democratic act: the eruption of a new mode of thought from which a previous regime was constituted. Mestizaje and democracy, both of which were previously accepted as familiar forms of accounting, open to the unthinkable, deferred part-of-no-part from a strange terrain that is entirely incommensurate with the previous form of thinking about public space. One might now be able to read the encounter event against itself—that is, against its first-order Latinamericanist conscription into service as the ground of politics—as a moment in *Codex* in which one witnesses "the struggle about the field of struggle itself," where the assertion that the encounter is always a miscount becomes an assertion that, as of yet, there exists no topos through which to mediate a new community based on identity.[49]

When we speak of Latin America as an object of analysis—when we reflect on Latin America with the goal of thinking how it could have always been, how it might yet still be, and might have always been otherwise—we produce the very referent as a sign-effect of that which the sign *Latin America* is intended to refer. To speak of rhetoric or democracy in Latin America, still, will place an impossible task: it will require the analyst read the text, whichever text, under the heading of an atopos: of a commonplace made uncommon, but also, of a proper name not yet sedimented. One cannot simply pretend to objectively report on "rhetoric in Latin America," to listen to the unmediated and pure-subaltern consciousness because subalternity is itself the rhetorical effect of a practice of reading the sign *Latin America*. Even as the decolonial option advances a claim on the presence of a subject, it can only achieve its utterance in a process of metaphorical substitutions and rhetorical inventions, shuttling movements between previously functional topoi like Eurocentrism/mestizaje. This atopic condition forecloses on the authority of any one rhetorical option, it is the space of a reading that remains undetermined, and it reveals the possibility of a future no knowledge machine could ever calculate and translate into a political program.

To speak of democracy in Latin America is to speak of the very rhetorical function that will always undermine the intellectual's ability to know: a strange democracy, yet to arrive.

3

DRAINING THE DEMOCRACY: DONALD J. TRUMP
AND ANTI-IMMIGRANT RHETORIC

Alberto González, Amy N. Heuman, and Linsay M. Cramer

In the US presidential election of 2016, there was no shortage of criticism over Democratic Party nominee Hillary Clinton's approach to Latin America. Her support of the North American Free Trade Agreement (NAFTA), her failure to condemn a 2009 coup against a progressive leader in Honduras, and her eagerness to facilitate the flow of global capital through privatization policies earned her reluctant support among many voters focused on US–Latin American relations.[1] At the same time, Clinton campaigned before Latinx audiences saying, "You are not intruders," and she promised comprehensive immigration reform that would provide a path to citizenship and "keep families together."[2] Whatever the reservations, voters were well aware of Clinton's positions from her years as US senator and secretary of state, and voters were also aware of the policies she was likely to promote as president.

Though Clinton won the popular vote by nearly three million ballots, Republican Party candidate Donald J. Trump prevailed in the electoral college and became the forty-fifth president of the United States. Over a year into Trump's first term, *Fortune* issued its Democracy Index that downgraded the United States from a "full" to a "flawed" democracy.[3] While *Fortune* pointed out that there had been a steady erosion of confidence in government, the downgrade came at a time when the prognosis for the health of democracy in the United States was particularly dire. Over a year into Trump's first term in office, labels such as "autocrat," "fascist," and "dictator" were commonly applied to describe the current occupant of the White House. In June 2018, longtime conservative commentator George F. Will told an audience to vote against Republicans in the fall midterm elections. In an editorial, he scolded congressional Republicans, writing that "by leaving dormant the powers inherent in their institution, they vitiate the Constitution's vital principle: the separation of powers."[4] Trump supporters have defended his unorthodox approach to the presidency by saying that he was elected to "shake up Washington" and "drain the swamp" of corrupt and ineffective politicians. In this chapter, we argue that, as a result of much of the Trump administration's rhetoric and many of its policies, something has indeed been drained, though perhaps not a swamp.

We document here what we have called elsewhere Trump's "new essentialism of racial logics."[5] These logics, expressed through the administration's rhetoric and policies on the border, migration, and citizenship, have produced a climate of fear in which Latin American refugees, immigrants, and DREAMers find themselves. We pay particular attention to how the administration employed this essentializing rhetoric in its discourse around "the wall" along the US-Mexico border and NAFTA, undermining democratic values of equality, inclusiveness, and justice. This dramatic shift in the discourse of the US government—namely, Trump's increasingly narrow depiction of Latin American identities through crude humor and negative stereotypes—has no doubt affected the image of America—indeed the very idea of America—particularly from the perspective Latin Americans. We employ here ideographic criticism as a way to show how <America> has taken on new associations centered on fear of Latin American immigrants and obsession with "border security."[6] Thus we argue that <America>, not a swamp, has been drained of democratic ideals and practices largely at the expense of relations with Latinx people and the issues that affect them, including the 2018 controversial and arguably inhumane separation of immigrant children from their parents at the US-Mexican border.[7] In addition, we argue that the dehumanizing, essentialist rhetoric of the Trump administration, combined with a white nationalist view of <America>, exposes the fragile quality of ideographs and the speed with which a key term can become a warrant for beliefs and actions that were suppressed but not eliminated.

In the latter part of the chapter, we describe the increasing resistance to Trump's essentializing rhetoric. Our analysis of the discourse on immigrants and immigration draws from events, tweets, and actions from the beginning of Trump's campaign for president in the summer of 2015 through the first year of his presidency. Because tensions were mounting regarding immigration and Latin American policy, we particularly focus on the summer of 2018. We conclude by offering three implications for Latin Americans as they look north to the drained democracy.

Trump's Anti-Immigrant Rhetoric

Josue David Cisneros observes that national borders are "physical and ideological." As such, deliberation about borders and national security serve to "demarcate identity and belonging" and invite redefinitions of who is valued and who is unwelcome. As political performance, rhetoric then "constitutes identity, incites emotions, and motivates actions."[8] To further illustrate these connections, scholars have illuminated the ways in which Latinx peoples residing in the United States and below the US southern border have been referenced as burdens, criminals, contaminants, and diseased within political discourses on national security.[9] Given this, we turn to ideographic criticism as a particularly powerful means of examining the rhetorical force of Trump's anti-immigrant and essentializing rhetoric and its implications for Latin American–US relations.

Michael Calvin McGee argues that certain terms can carry more meaning than claims can. For McGee, terms such as "rule of law" and "liberty" are rich in meaning in the collective American imagination.[10] People invoke these terms as if others have the same understanding of them; however, even though ideographs can vary in their articulation in political communication, their fundamental significance and the public commitment to them are unquestioned. The rhetorical critique of ideographs involves revealing their use in political language and analyzing their potential to "warrant action, excuse behavior, and garner assent."[11] Using the common representation of ideographs, we focus on how <America> and <Americans> rhetorically animate terms such as "immigrants," "border security," "the wall," and NAFTA. Given the vast scope of meanings contained within ideographs, they are inevitably contradictory (think "out of one, many" and "all men are created equal" in an era of slavery). Paradoxically, ideographs appear stable due to their use over time and the assumption of a common understanding of the term. But the Trump anti-immigrant campaign and administration rhetoric illustrate the malleability of ideographs. We argue that President Trump has quickly emptied the complex and contradictory aspects from the ideograph <America> by refocusing attention to aspects of <Americanism> that emphasize self-interest, centralization of wealth, white privilege, and unilateral action on the world stage. Affect is an element as well—fear of the brown Other.

An assertion that the United States is superior to all other nations would be ethnocentric. Yet discourses of <American> superiority are both traditional and current. References to the <American> Dream, <American> Ingenuity, <American> Exceptionalism, the <American> Way, or the <American>

Experiment, whether as myth or slogan, are ubiquitous features of political campaigns and policy justifications. It is commonplace to note that US citizens have appropriated for themselves the name "Americans" even as it also applies to the people across the South and North American continents. To call something "un-<American>" is perhaps the most undesirable and isolating judgment.

What we find remarkable is the transformation and normalization of the "accepted" <American> narrative to its ever-present-though-shadowy version. Trump's vision of a vulnerable <America> that must be protected from external identities and interests and whose own interests, as expressed in his "<America> First" slogan, can be achieved unconventionally (at best) and even unethically or illegally (at worst), propels a rhetoric that undermines international alliances and fosters nativism within the United States. Trump's anti-immigrant rhetoric follows familiar nativist dichotomies. Richard Pineda and Stacey Sowards summarize these dichotomies as follows: "One is either American or NOT, speaks English or does NOT, and should wave the flag of the U.S. and NOT another country's."[12] These dichotomies allow for a designation of an undesirable and dangerous other. Trump furthers this designation by employing tropes that are meant to reinforce disdain for struggling nations and incite fear and anger among the "real" <Americans> in the United States. In a bipartisan meeting at the White House with congressional leaders in January 2018, Trump asked, "Why are we having all these people from shithole countries come here?"[13] The Trump administration subsequently ordered an end to deportation protections for hundreds of thousands of Salvadorans and Haitians. The administration also ordered an end to special considerations for asylum-seekers fleeing domestic violence situations and gang violence in Central American countries.[14] To justify these actions, Trump draws from three key tropes regarding Latinx immigrants: economic cost to the US taxpayer, criminality, and disease.[15]

These three key representations of Latinx immigrants have been pervasive emblems throughout Trump's political career, beginning with the announcement of his candidacy for president in 2015 and continuing through 2018 (and beyond, though our discussion only covers this time period). For example, in a 2016 rally in Arizona, Trump stated that "illegal workers draw much more out from the system than they can ever possibly pay back" and that they "compete directly against vulnerable American workers."[16] In this depiction, immigrants are economic units who are best estimated through a cost/benefits analysis. The immigrants themselves have no humanity, no history, and no social context. Even in news stories that are favorable to immigrants, their economic worth is foregrounded. While much media attention is paid to the effects of immigration on individuals in border states, immigration policies extend beyond the border and influence much of the United States, including those in Midwestern states such as Ohio. For instance, the *Toledo Blade* featured a story about a small Ohio family farm that canceled its traditional strawberry crop due to a lack of farmworkers. Workers would be available through the H-2A visa program, but the associated costs of the program increased labor expenditures and thereby eliminated profit from sales of the crop.[17] While it is expected in a capital-driven society to view items (including human migration) as economic units, immigrants are particularly decontextualized from humane considerations. Associated with this economic narrowing of immigrant identity is the criminalization of immigrant activity.

In February 2017, the Department of Homeland Security founded Victims of Immigration Crime Engagement (VOICE), a hotline and resource website "to acknowledge and serve the needs of crime victims and their families who have been affected by crimes" committed by immigrants.[18] This website was established by one of the first executive orders signed by President Trump. In reference to Latin American countries, Trump is fond of saying that "they aren't sending their best" and identifies immigrants as human traffickers, drug dealers, and gang members. To make memorable a negative image of Latinx immigrants and Latinx people, Trump referred to Latino men as "bad hombres"[19] and launched an intense tirade against Garcia Zarate—an undocumented immigrant who was acquitted of murder charges in the death of Kate Steinle[20]—as examples of the deviant criminality at work among Latinx people. Amid the intense criticism of child separations, on June 22, 2018, Trump brought to the White House <Americans> who were victims of crimes committed by undocumented immigrants. Despite studies that show that undocumented and documented immigrants are much less likely to commit crimes than native-born citizens are, Trump emphasized the "death and destruction" that immigrants bring across the border.[21]

The disease metaphor also has been applied to describe immigration at the southern border. In 2014, Trump tweeted opposition to Operation United Assistance, a program initiated by President Obama to support countries in West Africa during the Ebola outbreak. Trump asserted that military personnel sent into the "Ebola infested areas of Africa" would bring the "plague" back to the United States. During the presidential campaign, Trump also tweeted his appreciation of Fox News "for shedding more light on diseases fr. porous border"; and in 2015, he chastised his primary opponent Senator Ted Cruz for neglecting to mention "all the infectious diseases they brought to US." In 2018, Trump referred to sanctuary cities (that is, municipalities that refuse to cooperate with Immigration and Customs Enforcement raids and immigrant detentions) as a "crime infested and breeding concept." In Z. Byron Wolf's reporting of Trump's tweet, he noted that in the "fear of immigrants from certain countries 'breeding' has been a staple of nativist thought for hundreds of years. The 'breeding' fear has been affixed to Jews from Eastern Europe, Catholics from Ireland and Italy, Chinese and, now, Latinos, Filipinos, Africans and Haitians. . . . 'Breeding' as a concept has an animalistic connotation. Dogs and horses are bred. So his use of it is, at best, dehumanizing to the immigrants he appears to be referring to."[22] In June 2018, Trump blamed the Democratic Party for supporting crime and allowing "illegal immigrants, no matter how bad they may be, to pour into and infest our Country." Infestation is a key term for Trump. It can refer to the spread of disease or it can be a metaphor that names the inclusion of an immigrant population. For immigrants from the South, simply having children is an infestation. In Trump's anti-immigrant rhetoric, any foreign inclusion is an infestation, a viral invasion, or a danger to the <American> body. Trump's anti-immigrant rhetoric is not constrained by these three tropes.[23]

A rhetoric of absolutism also helps to explain policy implementation. In early April 2018, US attorney general Jeff Sessions announced a "zero tolerance" policy directed toward individuals seeking immigration across the southern border. Anyone seeking to enter the United States (including asylum-seekers who were turned away at a port of entry and forced to enter elsewhere, hence illegally) would be committing a misdemeanor crime and subject to prosecution.[24] The result of this new policy was the apprehension of approximately 2,300 minors who were separated from their parents or guardians—or "child smugglers" in the administration's parlance—for an indefinite period. Kirstjen Nielsen, secretary of the Department of Homeland Security (DHS), stated in a White House press conference that children could not remain "at large" as their parents were detained. The resulting public outrage over the family separations and the government's apparent inability to reunite families created a public relations nightmare for the Trump-Sessions-Nielsen nexus. The attention paid to this and other actions, such as the administration's announcement to eliminate the Deferred Action for Childhood Arrivals (DACA) program in 2017, reinforced for racially marginalized individuals and their allies the racialized qualities of policies that were poorly planned and meant primarily to punish and deter immigrants. By late June 2018, the administration was not only asking for military bases to offer housing to detained minors, it was also requesting that the DHS develop a database to track separated and detained children for eventual reunification with their parents.

The irony of the "zero tolerance" debacle was that the State Department in early 2017 had outlined to Trump an approach for US influence in Central America that included support for economy, public safety, and governance.[25] The Trump administration apparently ignored this report that addressed the root causes of northern migrations. Where the State Department saw a population in danger, the Trump administration saw a dangerous population. As problematic as previous US interventions have been in Central and South America, the abdication of leadership in the name of <America> First proved to be a mistake in this case. In the next two subsections, we examine the vulnerabilities to democratic ideals and conventions created by Trump's policies toward Latin America and Latinx bodies.

The Wall

Dana Cloud argues that powerful visual images interplay with "verbal ideographic slogans, making abstractions . . . concrete."[26] The slogan, "Make <America> Great Again" is propelled in audience chants of "Build the wall!" at Trump rallies. National pride and security are realized in images of wall prototypes, US soldiers being deployed to South Texas, and barbed-wire additions to existing portions of the border wall. In this discourse, <America> is under siege. Demo notes that this depiction establishes "the erosion of U.S. sovereignty as the defining warrant of immigration restriction" policies.[27] Trump's wall materializes the commitment to a secure <America> and allows him to attempt to bypass legislative and judicial processes.

Meeting with state Republican leaders in Texas, President Trump remarked, "I'm the builder president. Remember that."[28] He has used his real estate background to generate confidence in his ability to construct grand structures such as a two-thousand-mile-long, thirty-foot-high wall along the southern border. Under the rationale of national security, the wall is a simple idea that appeals to many. On March 19, 2018, Trump examined prototypes near San Diego, California, that were built at a cost of between $2 million and $4 million.[29] So insistent was Trump about moving forward with building a wall, he threatened a government shutdown if Congress did not allocate $25 billion by the end of the fiscal year in September 2018.[30] A deadlock ensued that resulted in the longest partial government shutdown in US history.

Trump and his surrogates are fond of saying that he has "absolute authority" in many domains; however, some proposals from the Trump administration seem to show a lack awareness of the separation of powers or a disregard for this principle. For example, when Congress allocated only a small portion of the 2018 budget to the border wall (mostly for maintenance of existing fencing), Trump floated the idea of moving funds from the $700 billion allocation for military spending. The president seemed not to be aware that such changes to the budget (for 2018 or 2019 fiscal years) would require amendments and the involvement of lawmakers. Similarly, Trump tweeted that increasing the number of immigration judges "is not the way to go" and that "people must simply be stopped at the border and told that they cannot come into the U.S. illegally."[31] Trump failed to recognize that immigrants have rights to due process; he assumed that as president he could waive such due process requirements. In his mind, apparently, protecting <America> excuses these oversights.

Mexico's foreign minister Luis Videgaray called the proposed construction of the border wall "an unfriendly, hostile act."[32] The unilateral decision changed the relationship between two partners whose economies are highly interdependent and is likely responsible for growing nationalism in Mexico. The wall reversed the identity of the United States as "a nation of immigrants" that upholds the democratic ideals of inclusion and due process and reinforced the notion of the United States as being under increasingly authoritarian rule.

NAFTA

Trump signaled his intent to shed multinational partnership models early in his term by withdrawing from the Trans-Pacific Partnership Agreement.[33] Subsequently, the United States withdrew from the Paris Agreement (more commonly known as the Paris Climate Accord) in June 2017. Although the United States cannot formally leave the agreement until 2020, it has since maintained a muted presence in ongoing climate protection negotiations.[34] The United States also withdrew from the seven-nation Joint Comprehensive Plan of Action (commonly known as the Iran Deal) under which Iran pledged to stop nuclear arms production in exchange for the removal of economic sanctions.[35] Finally, in June 2018, Trump refused to endorse the G7 Summit Communique (after arriving late to and leaving early from the Summit in Canada hosted by Prime Minister Justin Trudeau) that outlined economic, educational, and environmental initiatives.[36]

As a candidate and as president, Trump expressed harsh opinions regarding another multinational partnership, NAFTA. "We are in the NAFTA (worst trade deal ever made) negotiation process with Mexico and Canada," Trump tweeted. "Both being very difficult, may have to terminate?"[37] Building on trade agreements with Canada, the trilateral agreement including the United States and Mexico took effect in 1994, during the Clinton administration. NAFTA reduced or eliminated tariffs and allowed for less regulated commerce among the three countries. Trump claimed that the agreement created trade deficits with the other two partners. Labor unions had long opposed the deal, arguing that it would make it easier for US companies to move manufacturing jobs to Mexico, where wages were significantly lower.

Our goal here is not a consideration of the economic pros and cons of NAFTA. Instead, we suggest that the NAFTA renegotiations have become a de facto element of Trump's anti-immigrant policy. In January 2018, Trump tweeted that "the Wall will be paid for, directly or indirectly, or through longer term reimbursement, by Mexico."[38] When it became apparent that the Mexican government was not going to equivocate on its vocal opposition to the wall, and when fiscal conservatives in the House of Representatives balked at the $25 billion price tag, the Trump administration had to begin exploring creative ways to be able to claim that Mexico was paying for it. In June 2018, Trump announced that he wanted to restructure the renegotiations such that the United States would negotiate with Mexico and Canada separately.[39] Negotiating a trilateral agreement in separate bilateral meetings sounds odd unless the objective is to end up with very separate agreements. This model would allow Trump to push Mexico on immigration. In another tweet, Trump revealed the strong connection between the NAFTA and immigration policy. In April he tweeted, "Mexico . . . must stop people from going through Mexico and into the UNITED STATES. We may make this a condition of the new NAFTA Agreement."[40] In the summer of 2019, Trump threatened to impose tariffs on Mexican goods if Mexico did not do more to stop the flow of refugees and migrants from passing through on the way to the United States. In this anti-immigrant discourse, the flow of Mexican commerce becomes associated with the "open border" flow of asylum-seekers and immigrants from Mexico and Central America. Furthermore, protecting <America> means creating new trade "walls" or barriers that reflect a failure to view trade policy between the United States and Mexico holistically or to consider the interdependent economies among the United States, Mexico, and Canada. It is highly ironic that many business sectors, such as agriculture (which is seeing major losses in revenue due to a lack of migrant labor and new tariffs), may experience further disadvantages if Mexico were to concede on a topic such as the wall in return for other perks. Given all these unfolding dynamics, from the campaign trail to Trump's first years of presidency, we turn to the vernacular responses of pro-immigrant rights rhetoric, which reached a climax in the summer of 2018, as a response to Trump's <America>.

Vernacular Responses to Anti-Immigrant Rhetoric

In mid-June 2018, vernacular responses in opposition to Trump's <America> were particularly striking. These vernacular responses—primarily in the form of locally based and organized demonstrations and rallies—are important to note because they are animated by key democratic components of the "accepted" <American> narrative, namely, free speech and freedom of assembly. Public outrage ensued over the exposure and subsequent media coverage of tent cities and child detention centers for undocumented youth who had been separated from their families. On Father's Day, June 17, hundreds descended on Tornillo, Texas—the site of a tent city on federal land housing undocumented immigrant children—at the border crossing near El Paso.[41] Protesters expressed outrage at the Trump administration's zero tolerance policy leading to the separation of families. Former secretary of Housing and Urban Development and political leader Julián Castro stated, "This is an issue about what is right and what is wrong," and California secretary of state Alex Padilla asserted, "Detaining children, taking little babies away from their mommies and their daddies, is not who we are as Americans. The rest of the world needs to be reminded of that. We need to be reminded of that."[42] Other leaders included activist Dolores Huerta, Will Hurd, Veronica Escobar, and US Senate candidate Beto O'Rourke, who spearheaded the march. In the days that followed, these protests spurred dissent across the nation from McAllen and Brownsville, Texas, to New York City and Washington, DC.

In the wake of this national exposure and public protest of child detention sites—referred to as "tender age" facilities by the Trump administration—at least eight states ended their cooperation with a White House initiative to send National Guard troops to secure the border.[43] Governors of these states cited their disagreement with policies that separated families as reasons for recalling or withholding their troops. Additionally, on June 20, 2018, four major airlines each refused to fly immigrant children separated from their parents by the federal government under Trump's zero tolerance policy.[44]

American, Frontier, Southwest, and United Airlines each conveyed that the policy ran counter to their corporate goals of connecting people; they claimed they had no evidence that they had transported children under the policy but were very clear about their refusal to do so. American Airlines took the lead by issuing a statement indicating that the separation policy was not aligned with the airline's values. They noted, "We have no desire to be associated with separating families, or worse, to profit from it. . . . We have every expectation the government will comply with our request and we thank them for doing so."[45] Numerous corporations, organizations, and political groups have followed suit. For example, the Organization of American States, comprising thirty-four nations, has called for Trump to return children to their parents and reunite families as soon as possible.[46]

As the pressure mounted for the Trump administration, it declared an end to child- and family-separation policies. Yet in the six days that followed a presidential executive order to rectify the crisis, only six children were reunited with their parents. In late June of 2018, a federal judge in San Diego set a thirty-day deadline for reuniting parents and children, and an approximately fifteen-day deadline for very young kids, as a means of spurring the Trump administration into swift movement.[47]

More recently, calls for the dissolution of Immigration and Customs Enforcement (ICE), one of the many federal agencies created after the 9/11 attacks, have gained momentum. On June 19, 2018, a group of approximately one hundred protesters took to the streets of Manhattan, chanting "Abolish ICE." Later that day, about ten to fifteen demonstrators confronted DHS secretary Kirstjen Nielsen at a Mexican restaurant in Washington, DC.[48] They called for an end to the separation of migrant families at the border that resulted from the Trump administration's immigration policies, shouting "Shame!" and "End family separation!" One man yelled out, "How dare you spend your evening here eating dinner as you're complicit in the separation and deportation of over ten thousand children separated from their parents? How can you enjoy a Mexican dinner as you're deporting and imprisoning tens of thousands of people who come here seeking asylum in the United States? We call on you to end family separation and abolish ICE!" As the protest accelerated the protesters then chanted, "Abolish ICE!" bringing the notion of ICE as a dysfunctional agency into mainstream discourse. Earlier that same day, Alexandria Ocasio-Cortez won the Democratic primary in New York's Fourteenth Congressional District after campaigning on the agency's abolishment. Days later, New York's Kirsten Gillibrand became the first US senator to announce her support for eliminating the agency.[49] Just hours later, New York mayor Bill de Blasio told WNYC Radio's Brian Lehrer, "ICE's time has come and gone."[50]

On June 30, 2018, nearly seven hundred "Families Belong Together" rallies took place across the United States to protest Trump's zero tolerance policy and ICE. By April 2019, Nielsen resigned as DHS secretary. After mass protests against police bias and brutality and demonstrations for gender equality after Trump's election, lawmakers in eighteen states introduced bills that would limit civil resistance.[51] First Amendment freedoms were being undermined at a time when Trump tweeted that journalists were the "enemy of the people."[52] The consolidation of executive branch authority continues.

Reflections on Immigration in <America>

By the summer of 2018, emotions over Trump's immigration statements and policies reached a fever pitch. As outlined above, administration officials were being run out of casual leisure establishments by frustrated citizens and immigrant rights protesters. New rounds of discussion on public discourse and civility erupted on radio and cable news shows. As thousands of children who had been separated from their parents spent the summer in hastily erected tent cities and many in facilities far from the border, political victimhood was claimed on all sides. But as columnist Michelle Goldberg notes about the flash disruptions, "It's less a result in the breakdown of civility than a breakdown of democracy."[53] At the time of this writing, the Supreme Court upheld Trump's order to ban immigrants from a certain subset of countries. The vote was 5–4, with Trump-nominated justice Neil Gorsuch—who occupies a seat that Senate Republicans blocked Obama from appointing—siding with the conservative justices.

In May 2018, US ambassador to Mexico Roberta Jacobsen, whose career in the State Department focused on Latin America, resigned over concerns with the tone and direction of Trump's policies regarding the border wall and NAFTA. Earlier in 2018, the US ambassador to Panama also resigned due to disagreement with Trump's perspective on Latin America. In the new administration, communication with Mexico and other countries now filtered through Jared Kushner, the president's son-in-law and adviser.[54]

In this chapter, we have described how Trump's core essentialisms work to dehumanize immigrants and undermine key US democratic values such as governmental checks and balances, due process, a free press, and inclusivity. In Trump's essentialist logic, brown bodies present a negative return to the economy; they are criminal and diseased, not <American>; they are undeserving "invaders" who are "rushing" the border and threatening <America>. By applying the ideographs <America> and <American> in key slogans, he allows essentialist and stereotypical notions to gain greater acceptance. The judiciary is fine when it agrees with the administration and biased when it does not. The press peddles "fake news" when investigative journalism uncovers conflicts of interest, corrupt behavior, and false or contradictory statements.

What is noteworthy about the essentialist turn is the pace of change in recharacterizing <America>. Only three years had elapsed between when Trump announced his candidacy for president and when US soldiers were deployed to string barbed wire along the southern border. While many opposed this new/old view of <America> (after all, the Democrats regained control of the House of Representatives in the fall 2018 midterm elections), no one can deny the clarity of what <America> now means to Trump and his supporters.

What does the draining of US democracy—Trump's version of <America>— hold for democratic-leaning states in Latin America? Based on our analysis of the application of <America> in negotiations over NAFTA and funding the Mexico-US border wall, we offer the following three conclusions to observers of Latin American–US relations.

First, stereotypes matter. Trump is most likely to harbor the most negative stereotype about Latin American people and their particular government. What is that stereotype? How can it be countered? Trump and the Department of Homeland Security reflexively link immigrants and Latin Americans to MS-13—the violent gang *of US origin* that now terrorizes El Salvador, other Central American regions, and also operates in the United States.[55] The Trump administration's essentialist rhetoric views all nations south of the US border monolithically and negatively. There is no expression of curiosity about the history of nations, their cultures, or their distinctive environments. There is no difference between Buenos Aires, Argentina, and Bogotá, Colombia— they are stereotyped as one negative identity. In December 2018, at the G20 Summit in Buenos Aries, Trump walked away from his host, President Mauricio Macri, saying to an aide "Get me out of here."[56] This action seemed to summarize Trump's discomfort with and lack of interest in Latin America.

Second, the history of partnerships and common South and North American interests no longer matters for this administration. The conventional observation that Trump is a transactional president is true. Only the present matters. Preexisting doctrines and strategies can be revoked with a tweet. Previous treaties, traditional arrangements, various wrongs (past US interventions or the annoyances of previous Latin American authoritarian leaders) are largely erased. The United States no longer casts itself as a moral leader or example. Relations are beginning anew. Latin American leaders are in a position to focus on specific issues and do not have to worry about deep context. The Trump administration will either not know or not care.

There will be no coherent US strategy toward Central and South America, since that would be seen as "globalism" and therefore not in <America's> interest. Effects will outweigh causes—should a humanitarian crisis occur along the Mexico-US border, or in Central or South America, US reaction will likely be determined by whatever leverage the United States may extract (threatening to withhold previously committed aid in return for some unrelated goal, for example). Intervention and/or agreements between Latin American nations and other nations such as Russia and China will have no principled reaction from the United States. It is likely that a free press in any Latin American nation will be seen as a deterrent to US relations. Journalism is not likely to be protected or proclaimed as a value in democracy, and the administration is not likely to advocate for protections for journalists.

Finally, images of power matter. Trump is enamored with pomp and circumstance. He was so impressed with the Bastille Day military parade on his visit to France in July 2017 that he ordered the Pentagon to stage a similar parade in Washington, DC. (After considerable review, the parade was subsequently canceled.) Trump saw images of North Korean dictator Kim Jong-un wearing binoculars surrounded by military personnel and being revered by an adoring public; soon thereafter he attended a summit in Singapore with, in Trump's words, the "talented" "Chairman Kim."[57] The summit reinforced our first insight above: history no longer matters. Given this, how can presentations of authority, culture, and affluence direct Trump administration attention to trade arrangements such as the reformulation of NAFTA to the USMCA (the new United States–Mexico–Canada Agreement) or other support that benefits the national agenda?

Related to the authoritarian and transactional preferences of the Trump administration, countries no longer have to account to the United States for human rights violations. On June 19, 2018, the United States withdrew from the United Nations Human Rights Council. The putative reason was that the Council had failed to prevent human rights abuses and that it was biased toward Israel. But the withdrawal came a day after the United Nations had called the US treatment of immigrants on the southern border "unconscionable."[58] The United States has no moral high ground from which to lecture or condescend to Latin American nations. The favored strategy would be to focus on the fairness of the deal, not necessarily its goodness, and not to allow the introduction of human rights issues. This may seem to contradict the democratic impulse, but if the deal itself is in the service of a participatory and inclusive agenda, a greater good will be accomplished.

Further, limitations on democratic reforms through the imprisonment of opposition leaders and journalists in Latin American countries are not likely to be of concern to the Trump administration. The murder of *Washington Post* journalist Jamal Khashoggi in October 2018, in the Saudi Arabian consulate in Turkey, provided that lesson. After Trump's dissembling on holding the Saudi crown prince accountable, *Washington Post* publisher and CEO Fred Ryan called Trump's response to the murder as "a betrayal of long-established American values of respect for human rights and the expectation of trust and honesty in our strategic relationships."[59] Latin American nations that seek to strengthen democratic institutions must look to one another to build new coalitions and alliances in the absence of US leadership.

Most political observers in the United States agree that the Republican-led nomination process for Supreme Court justice Neil Gorsuch was "rigged" against an Obama appointment to advantage Trump. When the Court subsequently ruled in favor of the Trump travel ban, the president publicly thanked GOP Senate leader Mitch McConnell.[60] The irony, of course, is that many elections *are* rigged via GOP gerrymandering of voting districts, and outcomes are influenced by sophisticated foreign intervention in US elections. Trump and his surrogates always claim the underdog position, eliminating common understandings of the ways that marginalized individuals, like Latinx peoples in the United States, are actually systemically disadvantaged. Hence, a Latin American leader who claims such an underdog position (like the political leader Juan Guaidó in Venezuela) might gain an unexpected advantage when negotiating a deal that benefits a key democratic goal or perhaps a more strategic limited objective.

The draining of democracy in the United States may pose interesting opportunities for democratic- and socialist-leaning nations in Latin America. In the Trump administration, given the treatment toward North Korea, Russia, and other nations, it is obvious that more authoritarian regimes would now have a more sympathetic reception. What the United States has illustrated for the world is that seemingly absolute democratic ideals and structures are vulnerable. The nexus of executive ambition, legislative acquiescence, and judicial manipulation is resulting in a transformation of the social order that will have hemispherical and global consequences.

4

REVISITING THE SEEMING IMPOSSIBILITY
OF MIGRANTS AS POLITICAL ACTORS

René Agustín De los Santos

For US-based Mexican hometown associations (HTAs), 2006 was the culmination of a decades-long battle to reassess and rearticulate *lo mexicano* (Mexican-ness) and Mexican citizenship from their status for Mexican citizens living abroad. For the first time ever, *Mexicanos en el extranjero* would be able to vote in a Mexican presidential election. This right came on the heels of securing both dual-citizenship rights (granted in 1997) and absentee voting privileges for Mexicans abroad (granted in 2005).

While certain aspects of this public (yet not highly *publicized*, at least not in US mainstream media) civic and political activism were new, others were not. Mexican HTA political activism did not emerge out of thin air, as responses to exigencies found exclusive to the local national scene of US political and rhetorical culture. Nor were their arguments grounded in the concept of lives lived between two worlds—*ni de aquí, ni de allá*, belonging nowhere. Their rhetorics resist easy classification, asking us to reassess what it means to behave in public spaces and in public ways.

These rhetorics offer evidence of a robust yet largely unknown Mexican migrant civil society that has existed for over a century in the United States.[1] Mexican HTAs are thus examples of how migrant civil society's binational rhetorical lives challenge some of the basic assumptions embodied in our theories of rhetoric and democracy: What does it mean to behave publicly? What and how does it mean to inhabit a public, democratic space? Who, when, and how can individuals participate publicly? Where, when, and how does a *public* begin and end? Where does citizenship, and our ability to act and interact as citizens, begin and end?

This chapter makes a simple assertion that aims to have far-reaching consequences for studies of rhetoric and democracy: while it may be possible to study "American" rhetorical citizenship, and other forms of political participation, without attending to the rich rhetorical histories of migrants in the United States, doing so would be woefully misguided. I use Chicago's Mexican HTA political activism during 2006 as evidence to support my assertion.

For Rebecca Vonderlack-Navarro and William Sites, Chicago HTA activism during 2006 offers a specific challenge to "the often artificial analytic divisions between domestic immigrant politics and diaspora reincorporation politics.[2] As they argue, these artificial divisions perpetuate the ongoing erasure of Latin American migrant civil society in the United States, a tendency that makes it "difficult to recognize and analyze the dynamics that are specific to migrant collective action when the foreign-born are subsumed into US ethnic and racial categories."[3]

Moreover, this activism counters the prevailing belief in the so-called crisis of citizenship that understands: (1) citizenship as referring only to membership in a singular political community; (2) that global processes ranging from the "hyper-mobility of capital and people to the introduction and use of universal rights" has exposed the limits of citizenship as a viable political reality;[4] and (3) that migrants are "always already" excluded from citizenship's possibilities.[5] Instead, following Luis Guarnizo, the rhetorics of Mexican HTAs display a vivid example of how contemporary citizenship—as well as contemporary rhetoric *in* society—has been reconfigured as fluid ("as opposed to 'established'"), multiscalar (as opposed to singularly scaled) realities related to different aspects (that is, local, translocal, national, regional, supranational, transnational) of life.[6]

In other words, despite its supposed impending demise or irrelevancy, citizenship remains a key mechanism of state governance whose "overlapping scales of excluding, controlling, and ruling dialectally intercept with new ways of belonging, participating, and resisting."[7] Increasingly, these "dialectic relations are expressed by the exercise of substantial citizenship rights (including mobility) by people who have been nominally barred from having any formal rights."[8] While migrants are "often socio-politically excluded in the North, many are nevertheless included by states of origin (e.g., via dual and multiple citizenships), which seek to maintain the loyalty of their diaspora."[9] In short, the rhetorics of Chicago's Mexican HTAs highlights an exercise of citizenship rights by groups and a public (that is, migrants and migrant civil society) that have long been overlooked or unknown by rhetoric scholars in the United States.

However, such an assertion requires more than a leap of imagination; it requires a profound shift in our orientations. Such a shift means viewing migrants seriously as political actors. What is called for are new theoretical and methodological orientations whose starting points consider migrants both as citizens *of some place*, who are able to act rhetorically as fluid, multiscalar actors, as well as rhetorical actors who often simultaneously engage politically with both their nations of residence and birth.

This chapter, then, focuses on the year 2006 and HTA rhetorics in order to remark on the limitations that dominant mononational orientations have for our understanding of contemporary rhetoric in society and its democratic (im)possibilities. These observations are followed by an analysis of a Chicago HTA leader's reflection of this crucial moment in Mexican migrant civil society in the United States. While this analysis is not meant to be exhaustive, it does aim to push our collective gaze beyond our mononational tendencies to the point where the rhetorical histories of migrant civil societies and their sending nations rub uncomfortably but productively against our own mononationalistic tendencies.[10] In what follows, a brief sketch of the context faced by Chicago's Mexican HTAs prepares the way for the subsequent analysis.

The Context

Most accounts of the political and rhetorical activities by US Mexican (and other Latin American) migrants and their supporters during 2006 focus on the March 25 Los Angeles demonstration (better known as La Gran Marcha). Such a move implicitly places the political exigencies created by the 2005 anti-immigrant "Sensenbrenner Bill" and the localized national scene of US politics as the primary, and often only, rhetorical reality faced by these groups.[11]

While a useful starting point, such accounts only capture the US side of a much larger binational reality faced by these migrants in 2006. Instead of focusing on La Gran Marcha—which, at best, situates migrant civil society as an often silent (even *silenced*) element of a much larger coalition of intersecting national interests largely organized and led by others—a turn instead to the long history of Mexican HTAs in the United States offers a more nuanced, complex picture.

A compelling portrait is offered by Chicago's HTAs, some of the old-est and (arguably) most powerful migrant-led organizations in the United States. Largely unknown outside their immediate communities, Chicago's HTAs are linked to the long history of Mexican hometown associations in the United States that originated in the late nineteenth and early twentieth cen-turies. HTAs "are widely recognized as important forms of first-generation Mexican immigrant civic and political participation at the grass-roots level."[12] Possessing strong binational institutional structures, Chicago HTAs have long been active in "sustaining transnational ties through participation in cultural, infrastructural and political activities in Mexico while fostering important *paisano* network and kinship connections in the United States.[13]

Their power and growth during the late 1990s and early 2000s should not be overlooked. As a Chicago HTA leader reminisced, "[Migrants] participate [in an HTA] because it is a form, a mechanism of mental hygiene in order to escape the oppression and the lack of participation in this [US] society."[14]

In recognizing the key role played by HTAs, we are reminded that the Sensenbrenner Bill was not the only or primary exigence driving the political and rhetorical activities of Mexican migrant civil society in 2006—at least not at first. A bigger exigence was found in that year's Mexican presidential election when, for the first time, Mexicans living abroad would be able to cast a vote for president.

This right to vote would be put to the test in one of the most highly con-tested presidential elections in the nation's history.[15] Sensing the potential impact that their vote could have, Chicago HTAs were very active in organiz-ing absentee voter registration drives. To accomplish such tasks, they drew on a vast network of institutional and legal structures found in both nations, as well as other binational formal and informal associations constructed over decades. The Mexican government funded binational television and radio ad campaigns. Leading presidential candidates, including Andrés Manuel López Obrador, made campaign stops in cities such as Chicago and Los Angeles.

As Xóchitl Bada notes, the Sensenbrenner Bill's passing in 2005 thus caught Mexican HTAs by surprise. The bill passed "while many HTAs and other Mexican political groups were preparing to register voters for the fol-lowing year's Mexican presidential elections." However, this did not unnerve them, as "they understood the importance of orchestrating an immediate response to [the bill] despite their busy workload with the Mexican election campaign."[16] For the first time in their histories, Mexican HTAs moved to expand their historically Mexican-centric political orientation toward a truly binational articulation with both Mexico *and* the United States.

Rhetorics of Citizenship

A productive avenue for exploring how Mexican HTAs challenge some of our basic assumptions found in our current theories of rhetoric and democracy is to look at Josue David Cisneros's overview of recent rhetorical scholarship on citizenship. As he correctly points out, "A voluminous body of literature on citizenship exists within rhetorical studies." For Cisneros, rhetorical scholars have "generally studied [citizenship] according to its so-called what, where, who, and how."[17] These four approaches thus provide the framework he would use to write his review. In what follows, I provide an overview of these four approaches as outlined by Cisneros with an eye toward the strengths and weaknesses they reveal about dominant mononational orientations found in these areas of rhetorical scholarship.

As Cisneros outlines, approaches that emphasize the "what" of citizenship "focus on how a type of rhetoric characterizes, instantiates or best secures citizenship." These approaches are concerned with the deliberative and discursive forms of "civic engagement as tools to invigorate democratic citizenship."[18] For Christian Kock and Lisa Villadsen, rhetorical citizenship acts as a frame that "asks us to appreciate [that] how we 'do' citizenship discursively and the way we talk about society are both constitutive and influential on what civic society is and how it develops." An umbrella term, "rhetorical citizenship" draws from what Robert Asen and Dan Brouwer call "modalities of public engagement" that are "fluid, multimodal, and quotidian enactments of citizenship in a multiple public sphere," where democracy is seen "more as a guiding light than a set of institutions or specific acts." Thus, to take rhetorical citizenship as a conceptual frame requires less a "focus on what a particular utterance is like, or how effective it is, but more on how suited it is to contribute to constructive civic interaction."[19] Robert Asen's discourse theory of citizenship reorients matters by turning to the "how" of citizenship. In his approach, which emphasizes practice over the more normative views of citizenship furthered by scholars like Kock and Villadsen, "the creativity and agency of citizenship enactment" is highlighted.[20]

For Cisneros, Linda Bosniak's scholarship emphasizes the "'where' of citizenship, the boundaries of belonging." In Bosniak's articulation of citizenship, borders and the bordering of citizenship function as threshold matters that work internally as well as externally. Key for Cisneros is how Bosniak underscores that questions of borders are endemic to citizenship: "rhetorics of citizenship also serve to draw borders and construct the 'alien' in legal and cultural terms."[21]

The fourth and final approach, the "who" of citizenship, addresses most explicitly the parameters of who can participate in the performance of citizenship. However, what distinguishes this approach is not simply its descriptive nature, but its attempt to expand the parameters of who can participate or perform rhetorics of citizenships. From Belinda Stillion Southard's work on the National Woman's Party campaign for women's suffrage, to Cisneros's own development of a cosmopolitan vernacular notion of citizenship that "challenges the preeminence of race, legality, culture, and single-state national identity,"[22] much of this scholarship emphasizes how alternative perspectives on citizenship serve as examples for how marginalized groups confront dominant forms of citizenship and assert political agency.

A key thread in this approach has been to offer a structural critique of citizenship itself. Hector Amaya's central argument in *Citizenship Excess: Latinos/as, Media, and the Nation*, for instance, "is that nation-state citizenship is irreparably rooted in exclusion, racism, and colonialism because excess is its structural precondition."[23] For her part, Ana Ribero offers a similar conclusion: citizenship "cannot truly be decolonized." As Ribero laments, "Regardless of their juridical citizenship status, bodies of color are often not understood as normative citizens within the national imaginary and their performances of citizenship are not read as such by their audience."[24]

A major goal of this research thread, then, is not to find a solution with or against citizenship qua citizenship—a move that puts them at odds with Southard and Cisneros, who both suggest the need to challenge the normative status of citizenship while also working toward its rehabilitation. Rather, Amaya and Ribero call for other forms of conceptualizing community that move beyond citizenship's exclusionary underpinnings.

The Rhetorics of Mexican Civil Society in the United States

While these four approaches as a whole have expanded, even challenged dominant and classical notions of citizenship, especially in its "normative form of political subjectivity and community membership,"[25] Chicago's migrant civil society casts a long shadow on this literature. By ignoring migrant civil societies in places like Chicago, this scholarship has missed opportunities to fully treat the breadth of its concepts, especially for how migrants as individuals, and as part of larger migrant communities, have affected theories and practices of rhetoric and democracy.

I use the analysis of an interview of an HTA leader to reflect on what attending to the rhetorics of migrant civil society can tell us about rhetoric and democracy in the present and their possible futures. This analysis thus aims to provide an outline of the kind of reorientation necessary for future studies of rhetoric and democracy.

This interview comes from Vonderlack-Navarro and Sites's sociological study of the 2006 marches in Chicago, which was a combination of archival, interview, and ethnographic data. As they argue, this data, "when examined through a historical lens, enable them to shed light on how the efforts by various government leaders to develop migrant associations as vehicles for their own purposes tended, over time, to enhance these organizations' efforts to become a unified—and eventually contentious—political actor."[26] I take both their studies further by applying a rhetorical lens to their work.

The binational rhetorical work undertaken by Chicago's HTAs during this period underscores that for migrant civil society, rhetoric and democracy (broadly conceived) are not necessarily concepts, practices, or (im)possibilities that begin or end at borders. Neither are they gained nor lost when immigrating to new places. For these groups—and arguably for some, many, most (?) other immigrant groups—participation in the political life of Mexico or the United States is not a zero-sum choice between here *or* there.

For instance, when faced with the threat of the Sensenbrenner Bill, Chicago's HTA leadership crafted responses that began from their lived experiences as both Mexican binational political actors *and* marginalized foreign nationals living in the United States. For Chicago's HTA leadership this double consciousness was arguably new. Importantly, the threat posed by Sensenbrenner motivated a radical rethinking of their long history of strict Mexico-centered political engagement. The following interview passage captures this shift:

> We were going with the vote of the Mexicans [i.e., in Mexico]. But when we became aware of the fiasco, of the lack of people [living in the United States] with electoral credentials, there was great disenchantment and all of that hope we had of being able to have major political weight in Mexico [disappeared]. So then it grabbed our attention: Mexico is very far from here, many kilometers. Here is where we are, here is where we are living, and they are at the point of passing a law that is going to make you a criminal—and you continue thinking about voting in Mexico's next elections?[27]

Important to highlight here is that this new binational political consciousness was *first* given shape and meaning through Mexico's own ongoing political drama and Mexico's political history, not despite them. That is, it was their direct articulation with Mexican political life as active political actors that grounded how Chicago HTAs came to understand their need to engage publicly with political life in the United States as never before.

This leader's assessment of Mexico's presidential election, especially for how it might ensure a bright future of "major political weight" for *mexicanos residents en el extranjero* (Mexican citizens living in the United States), is not hopeful. There is a sense of resignation (a "great disenchantment"), perhaps even a hint of bitterness, that a decade of direct political engagement in Mexico has been for naught, at least for this issue. However, rather than leading to political disengagement, Mexico's political "fiasco" suddenly (it "grabbed our attention") made him and others aware of how events in front of them, in their place of residence, directly affected them.

What is rhetorically noteworthy here is how this "great disenchantment" led this leader to conclude that not only was "Mexico [geographically] very far from here," but it was also very politically remote as well. In part, this sentiment suggests a recognition that geographical distances may, in fact, possess important political constraints and (im)possibilities that could not be overcome simply or solely through absentee voting. Missing is the use of the inclusive first-person plural pronoun "we" that one might expect. Instead, the phrase he does use—"the Mexicans"—appears to imply a differentiating between an *us* here (Mexicans in the United States) and a *they* ("the Mexicans") living over there. At least for the moment, this distance appears to be an irreconcilable position.

But there is also an implied sense that even as he and others suffered a "great disenchantment," their political activism in Mexico has given them the tools and ways of thinking that can help them address the current exigencies of US immigrant politics. That is, these words are not from someone who is in awe or fearful of politics in the United States. There is a sense of *desafió* (defiance) in these words that suggests that this HTA leader believes the moment is not too big for Mexican migrant civil society to tackle, for "here is where we are, here is where we are living." We are thus faced with a political actor who, if not outright engaging with two national contexts, at least appears to be making sense of his own political positionality from an awareness of his status as being here *and* there.

This sense of *desafió* carries over throughout the interview. In a key passage, the HTA leader reflects on what this new binational awareness meant for him and other HTA members:

There used to be this conception that, well, the question of immigration reform and all that, we should leave it for the gringos to do. [But] in
Washington there are people speaking who are not migrants, someone
else is speaking for us. I believe it is important that the migrants . . .
we are the ones who should speak for us about topics that affect us.
The Mexican Americans don't have problems with [legal] papers, they
don't have problems of documentation and migratory status. We are
the Mexicans. We are the ones that should be speaking for our own
people, for our own members.[28]

In this passage, the interviewee turns explicitly toward the US context, but
it is a move grounded in experiences of a politically active *mexicano residente
en el extrajero*.

Furthermore, this reflection reinforces this interviewee's newfound
awareness of his and his group's potential as binational political actors. His
tone is direct, even confrontational. It possesses impatience with unnamed
individuals—possibly Mexican Americans and "gringos"—and their "conceptions" of immigration reform. For instance, Mexican Americans cannot
adequately speak for his community, for they "don't have problems with
[legal] papers, they don't have problems of documentation and migratory
status." There are (at least) two premises undergirding this argument. On
the one hand, it is an argument grounded on an unstated yet implied belief
that Mexican HTA political activities in Mexico provide Mexican migrant civil
society with the political "know-how" that Mexican Americans simply do not
and cannot ever have.

On the other hand, it is also an argument premised on the different legal
status that both communities (Mexican and Mexican American) possess in
the United States. It is the implied protection of *legality* versus the uncertainty of having "problems of documentation" that makes Mexican Americans incapable of fully speaking "about topics that affect" Mexican migrant
civil society. Both of these points assume an implied binational political
and rhetorical knowledge base that is not available or accessible to Mexican
Americans. Drawn from such presuppositions, then, it becomes obvious
that only "we"—not Mexican Americans or "gringos"—"should be speaking
for our own people, for our own members" in this political moment.

What we see here, then, is a binationally oriented rhetoric that does not
necessarily seek inclusion into or exclusion from US civic society, at least not
in the ways or terms often desired by many US Latinx rhetorical scholars.[29]
Nor is it a rhetoric aiming to expand dominant notions of US citizenship

with a Mexican-scented infusion. Rather, it is an outright embrace of concepts and realities like the *nation, migrant-ness,* and *citizenship* in a manner different than what current rhetorical scholarship often describes.

Importantly, it is a rhetoric that appears to draw great rhetorical strength—its *energeia*—from its connection to, as well as its knowledge of, Mexico's long legal, economic, rhetorical, and political history. This is a complex, robust history with its own topoi, theories, and modes of argumentation that Mexican Americans and others do not know and cannot fully access. Finally, it is a rhetoric that possess knowledge and experience of what the phrase "we are the Mexicans" means (or could mean, or cannot mean)—not just in a discursive or performative sense, but also in its governmental bureaucratic (im)possibilities.

In this sense, then, the phrase "we are the Mexicans" comes to possess a binational rhetorical force not often visible in studies of Mexican immigrant rhetorical culture that possesses strict allegiance to US-focused topics and concerns. On the one hand, this phrase denotes a Mexican binational, nationalist rhetoric, whose origins and raison d'être draw as much from its connections to Mexico as from the United States. Second, the phrase is also a rhetoric that appears to understand migrant-ness as always already in possession of some sort of political agency despite or in fact because of its marginalized political status in the United States.

In both cases, *lo mexicano* as a political and national reality—and embodied in realities like citizenship—greatly matters. To be a Mexican citizen in the United States is not simply performative; more important, it is what Guarnizo describes as a multiscalar reality (that is, local, translocal, national, regional, supranational, transnational) that moves with people even as they migrate to new places. I return to this point in the conclusion.

As a whole, such an argument is a complicated rhetorical position for this interviewee to take. Such a move can easily backfire. It can appear arrogant, even shortsighted. For instance, it could be argued that this rhetoric, by rejecting that others should "speak for us," is not only a rejection of the more visible and recognized Mexican American, Chicanx, and/or Latinx worldviews—ones that "[don't] have problems with papers"—but also a rejection of any present and future collaboration with others. Thus, rather than help eliminate the historical cleavage between HTAs and US-focused immigrant organizations, such a position could be perceived as extenuating these differences.

Together, events in Mexico and the United States gave Mexican migrants a belief in their greater ability and right to make demands on both nations. For instance, the Mexican government could no longer justifiably ignore the growing political demands and influence of its diaspora. Just as HTAs acted quickly, pushing for greater political rights in Mexico, the Mexican state also quickly moved to increase its reach and influence with its diaspora through a variety of formal legal and political institutional structures (for example, the Tres por Uno program and the Program for Mexican Communities Abroad). These newer structures built on, expanded, and eased the transformation of HTAs from Mexico-oriented organizations to broader binationally focused organizations that could take advantage of the binational political and rhetorical possibilities presented by events like the passage of the Sensenbrenner Bill. This transformation would only increase the political stature and clout of HTAs, as well as the benefits for possessing membership in the organization.

Some of the explicit benefits of HTA membership can be found in another key passage of this HTA leader's interview: "[Migrants] participate [in an HTA] because it is a form, a mechanism of mental hygiene in order to escape the oppression and the lack of participation in this [US] society. . . . When you go to the real world . . . everyone tries to ignore you. They try to ignore your rights and you are a second-class citizen. [Yet from] the moment the *diputados* [Mexican officials] come and they listen to you and respect you, you [begin to] have a certain amount of respect for what you represent as a collective mind."[30] Rhetorically, such beliefs are important, for they do not reveal a passive or a politically neophyte population; rather, they showcase binationally politically and rhetorically savvy actors who are aware of how their supposed marginalized status—both here *and* there—may actually function as powerful political and rhetorical resources.

This passage, in particular, suggests that contra many rhetorical scholars of transnationalism and citizenship, Mexican migrants were not stateless, but were actually thinking and behaving as Mexican citizens inside the United States. This articulation between migrant and sending nation was as much the migrants' own doing as it was the moment the *diputados* came, listened, and respected them.

As this passage further implies, this political confidence was not simply an effect of language, but, extending Kock and Villadsen, also effects of "enactments"[31]—for example, *diputados* physically "coming" to "listen," to show "respect"—that were as formal and highly institutionalized across national borders as they were discursive. For this HTA leader these acts meant something (that is, they bestowed "respect") for the individual as well as for the "collective mind" in the "real world."

This reminds us that citizenship—and its rhetorical and democratic possibilities—is not something that stops at borders, but rather *moves* with people. As the above passage suggests, citizenship's movement across political borders exhibits dual liberating and controlling tendencies that can inspire new forms of political organization or can wreak havoc on a migrant population. Additionally, just as citizenship's movement can potentially weaken a nation's connection to its diaspora, Mexico's actual political reality underscores what Guarnizo describes as the increasingly multiscale (that is, local, translocal, national, regional, supranational, transnational) reach of the nation-state into all areas of public and private life.[32]

Just as migrant populations can make demands on their home country, sending nations are also increasingly making demands on their diaspora. Thus, rather than decreasing in influence, migrants cannot fully escape citizenship's or the sending nation's multiscale reach. In some circumstances this can be useful, but in others they may be harmful. These multiscale realities especially challenge newer theories of rhetorical citizenship—like Cisneros's cosmopolitan vernacularism—that aim to theorize "forms of subjectivity [and belonging] that can operate outside the bounds of the nation-state" and nation-state citizenship.[33] This is an intriguing point to highlight since it hints at the reality that even the seemingly most insignificant migrant is always already imbricated to his or her nation at a variety of scales or contact points that cannot be easily escaped, transformed, or surmounted. And yet this multiscalarity can also create spaces from which to speak and act that were not available to such migrants if they still lived in their nation of birth. As this interview also signals, many members of Mexican migrant civil society also want to behave as Mexican citizens outside their country— not just for the political clout that it gives them back home, but also for the potential rhetorical and political force Mexican citizenship might offer in the United States.

The What, How, Where, and Who of the Rhetorics
of Citizenship Revisited

The above interview contains an outline of what would emerge as a new multiscalar political orientation subsequently by Chicago's HTAs. Taken together, these passages complicate what political participation both inside and outside one's own nation might entail, and what such participation can tell us about rhetoric and democracy in contemporary society. To address some of these implications, I return to the questions I posed at the beginning of this chapter.[34]

If the rhetorics of migrant civil societies are fundamental for understanding current and future issues related to rhetoric and democracy, what, then, can we learn from them? On the one hand, we learn that Mexican migrants, individually, and Mexican migrant civil society are not stateless nomads, as rhetorical scholarship often directly or indirectly seems to suggest about this and other migrant populations. While it is true that not every Mexican migrant enjoys the full benefits of being a Mexican citizen abroad, it does not follow that these communities are legal, organizational, political, and rhetorical blank slates.

Rather, Mexican migrants and migrant-led organizations have long used their rhetorical and political experiences in Mexico and as Mexicans residing in the United States to ground their rhetorical and political engagements in both nations. Such work has benefitted from sophisticated organizational structures that Mexicans have built over decades in places of both birth and residence. Importantly and ironically, many Mexican migrants have learned how to be Mexican citizens from their engagements as *mexicanos residentes en el extrajero*.[35]

Consequently, even if the rhetorics of Mexican civil society are not highly publicized in the US mainstream or are ignored in US rhetorical scholarship, it also does not mean these rhetorics are not *public* in nature. The rhetorics of HTAs are highly public and *publicized—en español* (and increasingly in English)—to a wide audience of mostly recent and first-generation Mexican migrants. Their rhetorics engage a sense of the public and publicness that remain invisible only if we believe that citizenship refers solely to membership in a singular political community or that it is an assemblage or hodgepodge of diverse and discrete "types" (for example, cosmopolitan or urban).[36]

Rather, as the HTA leader's interview hints, because Mexican citizenship operates at multiple scales, it also travels along with migrants to their new places of residence. It may exert ever greater modes of governmental control on these populations but it can also offer migrants new modes of agency, resistance, and negotiation they have never possessed before. Thus, instead of conceiving of contemporary citizenship as a totally new version of citizenship, we should see it as a sort of synthesis of the long history of citizenship that we inherit from ancient Greece.

Moreover, the mobility—the *where*—of citizenship effects not just how and when citizenship matters, but also for *whom* it matters. For instance, *where* citizenship is enacted can elicit different responses by the nation-state. A Mexican living in Mexico might be ignored by the powers that be. That same Mexican citizen, now living in Chicago, might suddenly be inundated by requests from

Mexican politicians to come "listen to you . . . for what you represent as a collective mind."[37] Living in Chicago thus bestows a different, even better value (at least for this person) on Mexican citizenship than what it would possess for this same person in Mexico. This different value is as much a product of its geographical location—its scale—as it is a product of discourse.

This example suggests that a migrant's or migrant civil society's geographical location can influence how the nation-state can and wishes to interact with them. This ability is as much determined by the politics of the receiving nation (for example, the United States) as by the articulated needs of the sending nation (for example, Mexico) toward its diaspora.

In another sense, this example of migrant civil society exposes the limits of the *public*, as often understood in rhetorical studies. Under the multiscalar realities revealed here, where, when, and how does a public begin and end? An easy yet ultimately unsatisfactory answer would be to contend that it is everywhere and thus nowhere, a byproduct of the multiscale nature of contemporary citizenship. However, given this evidence, it is perhaps more responsible to contend that a public is a living symbolic and material practice that emerges and just as quickly can dissipate as individual or communal interests shift and adjust.

But even this stance overlooks and negates the enduring power of *institutions* (for example, legal, economic, trade, governmental) to shape and define public interests and practices. The Mexican government, for instance, was highly motivated in establishing and maintaining durable institutional articulations with US Mexican migrant civil society that would resist the vagaries of shifting interests and motivations—so, too, was the United States government; but so, too, were Mexican HTAs, who themselves were not just well organized but also well *institutionalized*. This suggests, then, that it is not enough to create a mass movement, but that there exists the real necessity of similarly creating durable institutions and institutional structures that can facilitate the rhetorical actions of migrant-led organizations across overlapping multiscalar realities.

At the very least, attention to how migrants undertake this and other similar work underscores the rhetorical complexity and difficulty of what it means to be in a public, democratic space and be doing public civic things in the twenty-first century.[38] These attempts also remind us that citizenship remains an important, if not key mechanism through which migrants and migrant civil society pursue such tasks.

In the broadest sense, then, this interview reveals that such questions are enriched by theoretical orientations—such as the one developed in this chapter—whose starting points view migrants not as society's perpetual stateless outsiders, but rather as citizens of *some place* able to act rhetorically within arenas of life (for example, local, regional, national, transnational) that are no longer strictly confined to the physical boundaries of a nation.

Migrants therefore underscore that citizenship is best understood not as an assemblage of diverse and discrete "types" of citizenships, nor as a hodge-podge of monoscalar citizenships (for example, global or urban), but rather as a "'multilevel membership' related to different scales (that is, local, translocal, national, regional, supranational, transnational)" of a person's and community's political and rhetorical life.[39] Such an understanding of citizenship reveals dynamic aspects of citizenship, democratic participation, and publicness long denied or deemed impossible for migrants. Conversely—ironically perhaps—citizenship's "multilevel membership" also hints at mechanisms that nation-states use to exert greater political and legal control on both its diaspora and remaining-at-home citizens from greater distances and at diverse scales.

Finally, the interview provides evidence in support of the following key observation made by Guarnizo vis-à-vis citizenship: that the multiscalar nature of contemporary citizenship "subverts one of the central tenets of classical citizenship: namely, that citizens are settled residents."[40] As this HTA leader's interview underscores, people move and their citizenship (often? sometimes?) moves with them. Our theories of rhetoric and democracy must begin tracing such movement and its nuances.

Closing Thoughts

At the very least, the rhetorics of migrant civil society compel us to rethink our loci of enunciations.[41] As scholars and activists, it matters where our scholarly interventions begin and toward what they are oriented. Do our theoretical and political orientations lead toward perpetuating the erasure of marginalized groups or does our research "do right by them"? Increasingly for topics and issues related to rhetoric and democracy, we can no longer address such questions without also acknowledging and embracing perspectives that are multiscalar and multinational in scope and nature.

All of this argues that the so-called crisis of citizenship is anything but. For migrants, especially, citizenship promises not just cultural, economic, or discursive connections to the home nation. As the 2006 rhetorics of HTAs reveal, citizenship remains a powerful multiscalar mechanism for making political, social, legal, and economic demands on two nations, often simultaneously. Increasingly, Mexican governments (at the local, state, and federal level) have had to publicly engage with Mexicans abroad in order to meet their demands as *mexicanos residentes en el extrajero*, but also as Mexican citizens who possess direct, often lengthy structural, political, economic, and legal ties to the multiple scales (local, translocal, national, regional, supranational, transnational) of the nation.

From a rhetorical standpoint, these rhetorics compel us to rethink how we understand, evaluate, and theorize basic concepts around rhetoric and democracy. Often our scholarship has a tendency to view migrants as peripheral to these conversations. This outsider status has rightfully led some scholars (for example, Amaya, Cisneros, DeChaine, and Ribero) to challenge such views, broadly reminding us that a nation's civic imaginary comprises its excluded "Others" as much as citizen alike.

Nonetheless, because these challenges primarily speak *about* and *for* these populations, even this work inadvertently reinscribes migrants to the periphery. Fundamentally, these arguments are premised on a "belief that rights associated with citizenship are geographically bounded to the scale of the polity, whether it is a city, a region, a nation, or an empire, and in relation to people's emplacement and displacement."[42] This "geography of rights," Guarnizo further notes, "assumes that the subjects endowed with these rights are localized inhabitants rather than mobile subjects."[43] In this sense, then, theories of hybridity or cosmopolitanism offer a way out of this conundrum.

But this way out comes at a cost. This move signals a turn from structural, legal, historical—and ultimately rhetorical—analyses of citizenship, toward an overly deterministic insistence on the performative, the local, and the particular. However, as Guarnizo further reminds us, "international borders and territories do exist and are enforced, no matter how porous they may be."[44] Scale matters not just from an epistemic, subjective perspective. It is also an ontological reality.

Thus rather than search for solutions that aim to overcome democracy's and citizenship's limitations, we may do more right by first understanding migrants' own efforts to "exercise agency [through] finding access to the right legal/institutional articulations in a world where overlapping multi-scalar constructions are increasingly part of the social fabric."[45] Rhetorical studies is especially primed to contribute to this multiscalar orientation toward rhetoric and democracy.

We live in worlds that move; our scholarship must move with them.

5

AMERICAN EXCEPTIONALISM, BASEBALL DIPLOMACY, AND THE NORMALIZATION OF US-CUBAN RELATIONS

Michael L. Butterworth

At the start of the 2018 Major League Baseball (MLB) season in the United States, nearly 30 percent of players identified as Hispanic or Latino.[1] Among these players are some of the brightest stars in the game, including Venezuelan-born Jose Altuve and Cuban-born Yasiel Puig. Beyond their considerable talents, Altuve and Puig also represent different iterations of American mythology. Altuve's popularity derives both from his ability and his likeability; he is characterized in the *Washington Post* by "his boundless energy, lightning speed and fierce yet joyous competitiveness."[2] His energy, work ethic, and positive attitude are attributes that articulate nicely with ideal portrayals of the American Dream, upholding Altuve as an exemplar of opportunities uniquely to be found in the United States. MLB has long celebrated the game's role in welcoming immigrants and affirming the purportedly distinct virtues of the nation.[3] In the past half century, this narrative has increasingly focused on players coming from Latin America, at times converging with larger national discourses about immigration (especially with respect to Mexico, which often stands in for all of Latin America in immigration discourse in the United States). Although Latino players are now some of the most successful and popular in the sport, this has not inoculated them from bigotry and stereotypical portrayals in the media. In particular, they are often characterized as passionate, hot tempered, and undisciplined—all traits frequently attributed to Puig.[4]

Former MLB player Juan Samuel, a native of the Dominican Republic, once famously explained how Latino players envisioned their path to the majors by stating, "You don't walk off the island. You hit."[5] This declaration neatly summarizes a style of play—aggressive, passionate, *flamboyant*—that is often stereotypically juxtaposed against commonly accepted standards of major league play—disciplined, measured, *respectful*. Few players have spotlighted this tension so well as Yasiel Puig, whose boisterous approach to the game has been complicated by lapses in focus, speeding tickets, and altercations with teammates and fans.[6] All at once, Puig appears to represent both the great promise of the American Dream and the fears many in the United States have about immigrants, especially those from Latin America. US attitudes and policies toward Latino immigrants have long been problematic, and in recent years national discourses have become increasingly suspicious and hostile.[7] Within this larger discourse that often treats Latino peoples homogeneously, there are more particular issues with respect to US relations with Cuba.

In many ways, Yasiel Puig's journey to the majors symbolizes the promise of democracy and the ongoing conflict between the United States and Cuba. Scott Eden's 2014 *ESPN The Magazine* feature "No One Walks Off the Island" explicitly invokes Samuel's famous phrase as it recounts Puig's struggle to defect from Cuba. Also detailed by *Los Angeles Magazine*'s Jesse Katz, Puig's story includes multiple failed attempts to leave the island, smugglers, kidnappers, extortion, murder, and, of course, a $42 million contract with the Dodgers.[8] Although some of the details are sketchy and rely on marginally credible sources, it is clear that Puig faced considerable risks to make his way to the United States. Similar to the story of the late José Fernández, whose death in 2016 revived the accounts of his multiple efforts to defect,[9] Puig's journey dramatizes the ongoing tensions between the United States and Cuba, tensions that have been variously provoked or soothed by baseball.

Space here prevents an extended discussion of the troubled relationship between the United States and Cuba, but it is important to note that baseball has been central to the two nations since at least the 1860s. In the United States, baseball was being hailed as the "national game" or "national pastime" as early as 1856.[10] In Cuba, the game's emerging popularity in the 1860s allowed it to become an overt threat to Spanish colonial rule as early as 1873. As Louis Perez describes, "Baseball carried a political subtext that served both to form, and to give form to, Cuban discontent. That increasing numbers of Cubans were turning away from the national pastime of the bullfight to take up baseball offended Spanish sensibilities and aroused Spanish suspicions."[11] Using baseball as a symbol of resistance against colonial rule aligned Cubans with Americans who viewed the sport as uniquely representative of democracy. By the time of the Spanish-American War and the turn of the twentieth century, MLB was embarking on world tours to trumpet American exceptionalism across the globe and inventing a mythology of baseball's origins that claimed it to be a distinctly American creation.[12]

In the first half of the twentieth century, Cubans and Americans enjoyed a robust relationship through baseball. Cuban barnstorming teams entertained fans throughout the United States, Cuban-born players represented early challenges to MLB's segregation, and MLB even located a successful minor league team in Havana. Circumstances changed significantly when Fidel Castro assumed power in 1959 and, by 1961, baseball in Cuba was deprofessionalized and the channels to the United States were closed. In the subsequent half century, Cuba built one of the most successful international sports programs in the world and the United States defined the Soviet ally as one of the most strategic fronts in the Cold War. In this context, baseball commonly served propagandistic and diplomatic purposes.

Late in the presidency of Barack Obama, the United States declared its intentions to restore its diplomatic relationship with Cuba. In December 2014 Obama announced, "We will end an outdated approach that for decades has failed to advance our interests, and instead we will begin to normalize relations between our two countries."[13] By October 2016, despite vocal criticism from Republican officials and anti-Cuban activists, the administration affirmed an attitude of "positive engagement" and nullified "key aspects of the fifty-five-year-old economic embargo that, to date, the Republican-controlled Congress has refused to lift."[14] In between these announcements, the president attended an exhibition baseball game during a trip to Havana. Several media reports characterized the event as an example of "baseball diplomacy," suggesting that the game could play a meaningful role in the new relationship between the nations.

In the remainder of this chapter, I want to take up the idea of baseball diplomacy as a rhetorical construct. Underlying the notion are assumptions about democracy and global politics, many of which are rooted in familiar discourses of American exceptionalism. These discourses are both central to historical political rhetoric in the United States and to competing visions of the nation's role in contemporary political affairs. Obama's normalization efforts have been largely reversed under President Donald Trump, and these two most recent US presidents offer a striking contrast that spotlights the challenges to democracy featured in this book. Before attending to these challenges, I first want to review the notion of American exceptionalism and then examine the Obama presidency through the lens of what Robert Ivie and Oscar Giner call "democratic exceptionalism."[15] This leads to a discussion of baseball diplomacy and the specific efforts of the Obama administration in

Cuba. In the conclusion, I address the prospects of baseball diplomacy and the normalization of relations in Cuba, both of which must now be understood in the context of the Donald Trump presidency.

From American to Democratic Exceptionalism

The term "American exceptionalism" itself reflects the insular nature of political rhetoric in the United States, as it clearly claims "American" at the expense of the rest of the hemisphere. As the introduction of this volume explains, "America" and "American" are complicated constructs, and part of this book's challenge is to disrupt the commonplace use of them to stand in only for the United States. Despite the chauvinism embedded in the term, I will feature it here because it expresses a particular rhetorical tradition that largely characterizes the political culture of the United States. Expressions of American exceptionalism date back to well before the nation's independence. Scholars suggest that the most influential early iteration of this mythology is found in colonist John Winthrop's 1630 sermon in which he referenced Jesus's Sermon on the Mount to declare the American continent a "shining city upon a hill."[16] This imagery has more recently been a defining feature of American presidential discourse, with prominent references from both John F. Kennedy and Ronald Reagan.[17] Beyond this particular metaphor, "primary themes of American exceptionalism consist of U.S. presidential invocations that overtly mention the United States as being a single exception to the international community."[18]

Presidents are not the only ones to suggest the United States is an "exception." Perhaps most influential in this regard is Alexis de Tocqueville, who wrote in *Democracy in America*, "The American position is, therefore, entirely exceptional and it is quite possible that no democratic nation will ever be similarly placed."[19] Based on this observation from 1840, Seymour Lipset deems Tocqueville to be "the initiator of the writings on American exceptionalism." He also clarifies that exceptionalism marks the United States as *different* but not necessarily *better* than other nations.[20] Nevertheless, prevailing discourse in the United States claims for the nation an inherent superiority. In the words of David Weiss and Jason Edwards, "Champions of American exceptionalism hold that because of its national credo, historical evolution, and unique origins, America is a special nation with a special role—possibly ordained by God—to play in human history."[21]

Earlier in the nation's history, the rhetoric of exceptionalism primarily helped Americans fashion an identity distinct from the "Old World" in

Europe. By the time the United States became a global power, however, it began to serve as a justification for foreign policy and attitudes toward the rest of the world. David Zarefsky explains that various events in the early days of the US republic—such as the successful revolution and the expansion of US territory—helped cement the belief that Americans had been singled out by God himself. From this view, "the statement that Americans are God's chosen became not the *conclusion* of a conditional argument aiming to motivate [Americans], but the *premise* of a pragmatic argument aiming to license [them]."[22] Although such a perspective has provided American citizens with an assurance that the United States is always a force for good in the world, the moral certitude that follows from being God's chosen nation has allowed Americans to accept a range of actions across the globe that otherwise would have undermined the nation's authority. This tension has become increasingly relevant in the years since World War II, during which the Cold War led the United States to justify military interventions abroad and domestic inequalities at home in order to counter the threat of communism. As Donald Pease argues, "The cold war state fantasy of American exceptionalism enabled U.S. citizens to experience their national community as coherently regulated through the disavowal of its inherent transgression as exceptions required to counteract the Soviet threat."[23]

The Cold War is especially relevant to understanding the United States' relationship with Cuba. Fidel Castro's allegiance to the Soviet Union made him an immediate threat, leading to the spectacular failure by the United States in the Bay of Pigs incident in 1961. Just two years later, perhaps the most dramatic standoff of the Cold War played out during the Cuban Missile Crisis, a moment that confirmed both the fragility of US-Soviet relations and Cuba's strategic importance. In between these moments, US officials passed the 1961 Foreign Assistance Act and enforced an embargo of Cuba the following year.[24] Anti-Cuban sentiment was grounded in the larger resistance to communism, and the embargo and Cold War–based policies remained standard practice for the United States well after the fall of the Soviet Union. Meanwhile, there has long been tension over the presence of the US naval base at Guantanamo Bay in Cuba, an issue that became more pronounced when the George W. Bush administration established a controversial prison camp there in 2002.

The arc of the Cold War, with Cuba serving as an important reference point, helps explain shifting perceptions of American exceptionalism. Although US citizens appeared able to reconcile the nation's mythology with its questionable actions, others objected to smaller-scale interventions—such as covert sponsorship of military coups in the Third World or the exercise of influence in the United Nations or World Bank—and large-scale military ventures—such as the war in Vietnam. Near the end of the twentieth century, declarations such as President Bill Clinton's, that "America stands alone as the world's indispensable nation," were met with equal parts praise and scorn.[25] Global distrust of American exceptionalism then peaked in the early twenty-first century, as the US-led "war on terror" further eroded the nation's standing and left many feeling hostile toward a nation largely perceived as an international bully.[26]

If the Bush presidency and the excesses of the "war on terror" represented something of a breaking point, then many found promise in the election of Barack Obama that a new rhetorical course could be charted. Indeed, rhetorical critics were eager to embrace the Obama presidency, both because of the new president's oratorical skills and the shift in tone he brought to the office. For Robert Ivie and Oscar Giner, this shift was grounded in a sense of humility and egalitarianism, as well as a message "conveyed as much by his rhetorical manner as by explicit articulations of what might be termed democratic exceptionalism."[27] Jason Edwards contends that the early stages of the Obama presidency were framed explicitly by this notion, pointing out that "the Obama administration pursued three rhetorical strategies—using the language of contrition, using the language of partnership, and leading by example—to carry forward this democratic exceptionalist ethos."[28] Jay Childers, meanwhile, highlights a contrast with the Bush administration, suggesting that Obama's embrace of nuance and willingness to accept that conflict in politics is unavoidable demonstrate a healthier, agonistic conception of democracy. As he concludes, "This shared humanity was the necessary component for getting people with very different worldviews and belief systems to struggle together as democratic citizens without demonizing one another as enemies."[29]

The move away from a traditional rhetoric of American exceptionalism toward an ideal of democratic exceptionalism was met by at least two challenges. First, as Obama settled into the presidency, real-world contingencies caused him to reflect on the United States' role in the world. This happened during the president's first year in office, when he was awarded the Nobel Peace Prize in 2009. Although critics wondered how someone could receive such an award with a minimal track record, supporters saw in the moment an affirmation of Obama's rhetorical aspirations—he was being recognized for an ability to move the nation (and the world) away from the belligerence of George W. Bush. Nevertheless, in his acceptance speech Obama had to wrestle with the realities of war and the role of the United States in mediating global conflict. As Robert Terrill argues, "The resulting text is a curious affair. A common observation was that, for a speech given on the occasion of accepting a prize for peace, it actually has quite a lot to say about war." For Terrill, Obama navigated this paradox by offering "a thoroughly rhetorical understanding of war and peace; it is governed by the practical judgment that rhetorical training has always been meant to foster, and it is coupled fundamentally to a particular style of speech."[30] This does not amount to an endorsement, necessarily, but it does suggest the president was able to capture the nuances of a "just war." Ivie and Giner are less charitable. In their genealogy of war culture in the United States, they suggest the speech revealed that Obama's democratic exceptionalism had been eclipsed by a retreat to conventional American war rhetoric. "War culture prevailed," they argue. "The president affirmed that the Nobel Peace Prize was a symbol of 'our highest aspirations' to 'bend history in the direction of justice.' Toward this end, he assumed the title 'Commander in Chief' of a nation 'at war' and made 'just war' the measure of his actions."[31]

Later in his presidency, Obama further raised eyebrows when he explicitly invoked American exceptionalism in a speech arguing in favor of US military action in Syria. The nation's willingness to protect its own people as well as those around the world is what "makes America different. That's what makes us exceptional," the president asserted.[32] Obama's language was criticized by Russian president Vladimir Putin, who cautioned, "It is extremely dangerous to encourage people to see themselves as exceptional, whatever the motivation."[33] Although most in the West would dismiss Putin simply because he is Russian, his commentary nevertheless tweaked concerns about American justifications for war.

While those sympathetic to Obama struggled with the tension between war and peace, his more obvious political critics presented a second challenge to the president by openly lamenting his abandonment of a stalwart American myth. His early speeches spoke to the pride all people feel for their own nations, to the extent that some observers felt he undermined America's rightful claim to greatness.[34] As the 2016 US presidential election cycle began, Obama's efforts at rhetorical nuance were framed as signs of weakness. Former vice president Dick Cheney charged, "We are not just one more nation, one more indistinguishable entity on the world stage. We have been essential to the preservation and progress of freedom, and those who lead us in the years ahead must remind us . . . of the special role we play. Neither they nor we should ever forget that we are, in fact, exceptional."[35] Meanwhile, the entire candidacy of eventual winner Donald Trump was predicated on the slogan "Make America Great Again," a less-than-subtle accusation that, under the Obama administration, the nation's reputation had faltered.

The election of Trump further calls into question the viability of democratic exceptionalism, and it clearly has implications for the United States' relationship with nations across the Americas, including Cuba. No reasonable assessment of his campaign can dismiss the overt appeals to racism and xenophobia that have unleashed renewed white nationalist sentiments in the United States.[36] Building on recent manifestations of discourses about immigrants that depict them as invaders or contaminants,[37] Trump sparked fears of criminality and violence. Perhaps most notably, his 2015 speech announcing his candidacy exploited these fears: "When Mexico sends its people, they're not sending their best. . . . They're sending people that have lots of problems, and they're bringing those problems with us. They're bringing drugs. They're bringing crime. They're rapists. And some, I assume, are good people. . . . It's coming from more than Mexico. It's coming from all over South and Latin America, and it's coming probably— probably—from the Middle East."[38] Trump's xenophobia led critics to conclude his vision to be a "racist and populist variant of traditional American exceptionalism."[39]

As president, Trump has shown little inclination to temper his attitudes about immigrants and immigration policy. Yet it is more complicated than simply declaring a resurgence of exceptionalist rhetoric. Rather, Trump's belligerence and hostility toward anything he believes not to be in the United States' interests reflect a shift in emphasis or even an outright decline of American exceptionalism. In expressing the sense that the nation has for too long shouldered the burdens of other nations around the world,[40] Trump has both asserted the supremacy of the United States and diminished its sense of mission. As Stephen Wertheim summarizes, "Donald Trump does not speak the language of American exceptionalism. Trump . . . assigns no providential role to the United States and locates it far from the vanguard of world history."[41] Moreover, Jason Edwards specifies the economic focus of Trump's exceptionalism at the expense of the nation's mythic aspirations, noting "Trump redefined American exceptionalism by emphasizing the source of its uniqueness and superiority were material principles instead of ideational ones. U.S. presidents have traditionally represented its exceptionalism by calling upon the power of its ideals and institutions. . . . Throughout the campaign, his rhetoric focused on how reforming U.S. policy on trade, immigration, international engagement, and democracy promotion would be a means to deliver the material gains it had lost because of previous presidential administrations."[42]

In other words, the Trump administration embraces exceptionalism only to the extent that it affords the United States the right to do as it pleases in international affairs and thus sharply reverses the course of the Obama presidency. Although this shift has consequences for Obama's normalization efforts, it is nevertheless worth examining the previous administration's initiative as well as the consequences of both administrations' policies on MLB and Cuban baseball players.

Identification and "Baseball Diplomacy"

In his study of Obama's more democratic rhetoric, Edwards notes with surprise the president's emphasis on relations across Latin America. As he observes, "Obama's pledge of equitability in US-Latin American relations was unusual, remarkable, and potentially groundbreaking. For over two hundred years, presidents and politicians have constructed the Western Hemisphere as America's backyard; a place for the United States to play and do what it wants with it. This backyard mentality has created a paternal tone in US-Latin American relations."[43] Indeed, official US attitudes about the western hemisphere have long been dominated by the 1823 Monroe Doctrine and Theodore Roosevelt's Corollary issued nearly a century later, both of which serve as testaments to American exceptionalism. Of the Roosevelt Corollary, Christa Olson asserts, "Its paternalistic imperialism, its assertion of U.S. prerogative, and its assumption of cultural superiority are blatant and have been remarkably influential on subsequent policy."[44] Throughout the twentieth century, the United States has intervened repeatedly in Central and South America, often sponsoring covert military action and orchestrating economic policy. Indeed, any understanding of contemporary politics throughout the Americas must account for US efforts to shape various economies in its own neoliberal vision.[45]

The influence of Roosevelt brings us back to baseball and Cuba. The turn of the twentieth century was marked by the growing influence of the United States in global affairs, and sport played a prominent role asserting the nation's professed virtues.[46] In the case of Cuba, the United States saw the end of the Spanish-American War as an opportunity solidify its standing in the region. As a result, "Baseball's possible functions began entering into U.S. policy calculations, and Americans began using it to promote political order and social control."[47] In subsequent decades, MLB owners saw Cuba as a fertile ground for scouting talent. Even as the league operated with its "gentle-man's agreement" that prohibited players of color, some owners skirted this policy by signing light-skinned Cubans.[48] This practice provided a precedent for MLB's relationships with nations in Latin America. After Fidel Castro became Cuba's prime minister in 1959, MLB strengthened relationships with other countries, most notably the Dominican Republic. In the years since, the influx of players from Latin America has transformed the league.

In many ways, the interest in Latin talent reinforces other exploitive practices in the region. Although it is possible MLB's global interests are sincere, there is also a well-established history in which the league has repli-cated the nation's efforts to control Latin American nations and extract their resources. Players are signed at absurdly young ages, funneled through acad-emies sponsored by the major league franchises, and often given minimal mentorship or support.[49] In the specific case of Cuba, Castro had viewed sport as an extension of the revolution. He created the National Institute of Sport, Physical Education, and Recreation (INDER) and, much like leaders in the United States, used events such as the Olympic Games as platforms for asserting national virtues. Meanwhile, he relegated baseball to amateur status and sought to create an elite domestic league and dominant inter-national team. As Peter Bjarkman explains, "Baseball was . . . seen by the Maximum Leader as an instrument of revolutionary politics—a means to build revolutionary spirit at home and to construct ongoing (and headline-grabbing) international propaganda triumphs abroad."[50]

On the one hand, Castro's efforts were inarguably successful, as Cuban athletes thrived in the Olympics and the national baseball team dominated global competition for decades. On the other hand, rising tensions between Cuba and the United States meant that baseball was a potent political symbol that more often served the interests of those competing for power than it did the players themselves. Yet given baseball's stature in both nations, it occu-pies a unique space for possible connections and reconciliation.

International sporting events are commonly celebrated as opportunities to put aside political differences and affirm a shared sense of humanity. This is the premise that underlies large-scale events such as the Olympic Games as well as smaller-scale exchanges and exhibitions. Although it is easy enough to describe the ways sport is inherently political, there is nevertheless appeal in the idea that a friendly competition could help transcend more substan-tive divisions. It is also a reminder that sport is a fundamentally rhetorical institution; that is, "it is a constitutive site in which [sociopolitical] issues are communicated."[51] More important, it is a site that depends on the gathering of people, a means for communal engagement and contestation.[52] From this view, it is easy to see why so many see sport as a mechanism for engaging with conflict and division.

This cooperative spirit is reflected in the concept of "sports diplomacy," which has been relevant since the advent of sport itself. As Stuart Murray describes, "The institutions of sport and diplomacy are global in scope and nature and, working in tandem, they can disseminate positive values such as mutual respect, comity, discipline, tolerance, and compassion amongst both established and acrimonious diplomatic relationships." At the same time, the blurring of sport and politics makes some observers uncomfortable, fearing that the dirty business of politics might spoil the allegedly pure pursuits of sport.[53] Murray draws on Hedley Bull's definition of diplomacy itself— "the conduct of relations between sovereign states with standing in world politics by official agents and by peaceful means"[54]—to note a post–Cold War shift to forms of "public diplomacy," including sports diplomacy. In other words, although diplomatic efforts through sport are not new, the frequency and visibility of such efforts *are* new (or, at least, recent). According to Murray, government officials are increasingly aware of sport's ubiquity and symbolic power, and they are therefore eager to leverage its soft power potential for larger foreign policy aims.

Over the years, leaders in both Cuba and the United States have looked to baseball to compensate for some of the political divisions between the two nations. This was especially the case in the 1970s, when MLB attempted to organize exhibitions that could be understood as examples of "baseball diplomacy." Justin Turner details how leaders were inspired by the success of the "ping-pong diplomacy" that symbolized improved relations between the United States and China. Similar efforts in Cuba were seen as opportunities to improve that relationship and allow for greater American influences on the island. Some proposals were thwarted by State Department officials, others by MLB leaders. As Turner summarizes, "Political considerations overwhelmed baseball diplomacy, complicated the planning, and ultimately prevented a notable change in U.S.-Cuba relations."[55]

It took another two decades before the two nations reached an agreement for a baseball exhibition. In the intervening years, the Soviet Union collapsed and Cuba's economy followed suit. This led to substantial challenges for the domestic baseball league, and opened the door for a wave of defections by players seeking opportunities in MLB. Throughout the 1990s, eighty players defected to the United States, leading Cuban officials to loosen domestic restrictions and allow some of its players to sign with leagues in other nations (not including the United States). Between the US embargo of Cuba and MLB policies, Cuban defectors could maximize their opportunities if they first established residency in another country and then declared free agency. The influx of talent generated media attention and sparked interest in a new source of (cheap) Latin labor.[56] It also led to an underground industry in which "agents" facilitated defections and helped players sign with major league teams. Most representative of this phenomenon was Joe Cubas, whose media accounts helped reinforce familiar narratives of American exceptionalism and the American Dream. As Afsheen Nomai and George Dionisopoulos assert, "The stories which comprise this narrative present anecdotal evidence which reifies the tenets of the materialist mythos of the American Dream: the 'rags-to-riches' story that America is a land of boundless freedom and economic opportunity. The promise and the glory of the mythical America presented in the Cubas Narrative is made even more dramatic through a juxtaposition against a vilified Communist Cuba."[57]

Depicting baseball in exceptionalist terms certainly helps Americans identify with one another, but it does little to help them identify with Cubans. Not surprisingly, then, the next major effort at baseball diplomacy fell victim to the historical antagonisms between the United States and Cuba. After complicated negotiations, in 1999 MLB's Baltimore Orioles played the Cuban national team in Havana before hosting a return game a few days later in Baltimore. The Orioles won a narrow victory in the first game, but the Cuban team subsequently dominated their major league opponents on American soil. In an atmosphere marked by political symbolism and vocal protests, the game did little to advance US interests. As Turner concludes:

> For Cuba, baseball diplomacy had been an unqualified success. After the Cuban players proved they could contend with the American professionals in a close loss in Havana, they embarrassed the Orioles in Baltimore, reaffirming Cuba's reputation as a global leader in baseball. Furthermore, despite speculation leading up to the second game, no major defections occurred during the trip. . . . For many Americans, baseball diplomacy was defined by the embarrassing Orioles performance in Baltimore and the joyous Cuban victory celebration. If the series was indeed a contest of "us vs. them," the United States suffered a humiliating defeat.[58]

Part of the problem with the 1999 effort lay in the degree to which baseball diplomacy specifically mirrored US diplomatic strategy generally. In short,

American officials too often have relied on what Joseph Nye has called "soft power," emphasizing symbolic (rather than militaristic) means of persuasion to win over its adversaries.[59] As Craig Hayden explains, "Much of what counts as U.S. public diplomacy since the Cold War outside of exchange programs reflects an implicit assumption that exposing foreign audiences to U.S. values will illuminate a shared identification with U.S. motives and policies."[60] In other words, rather than seeking to engage with Cuba on terms of mutual respect, the United States has continued the exceptionalist practices that have defined its rhetorical stance since the end of the Spanish-American War.

Against this backdrop, President Obama's intention of normalizing relations with Cuba is all the more remarkable. Despite his inconsistent interpretations of American exceptionalism, Obama's approach to Cuba appears to model the democratic exceptionalism identified by Ivie and Giner. As Daniel Añorve suggests, "President Obama seems to understand that engagement is the key to spread American values in Cuba rather than the isolation of the island."[61] More than the announcement in 2014, Obama loosened the grip of the US embargo through new regulations enacted in 2016. Along with the material changes, the policy shift is significant for the attitude of identification it implies. Significantly, "the new presidential directive mandates positive engagement, as opposed to perpetual hostility, as the *modus operandi* of future US policy toward Cuba."[62] To demonstrate this attitude, the president traveled to Havana for an exhibition game between the Tampa Bay Rays and the Cuban national team on March 21, 2016.

Media accounts immediately seized on the idea of "baseball diplomacy" to describe the president's visit. According to the *USA Today*, "There was certainly a festive atmosphere about this Obama family outing. But it was also part of Obama's broader strategy for people-to-people engagement on the formerly isolated island. Call it baseball diplomacy." Contrasting the game with other events connected to his visit, *The Guardian* noted that "Obama stayed on to give television interviews and clearly seemed content to let baseball diplomacy do the work of détente that more stagey press conferences and speeches have struggled at times this week to convey." Meanwhile, *Sports Illustrated* claimed the visit "signals a new era," even if it did not mean an immediate end to the decades-long embargo.[63]

Even as many criticized Obama's posture toward Cuba and his decision to attend the game despite a terrorist bombing in Brussels the same day, most of the accounts of the contest were positive. As the president himself noted in an ESPN interview conducted during the game, "Ultimately, what this game's about is goodwill and the recognition that people are people, but we can't forget that there are some larger stakes involved in this. . . . I've said this before, that's the power of baseball. That's the power of sports. It can change attitudes sometimes in ways that a politician can never change, that a speech can't change." Meanwhile, MLB's Joe Torre confirmed implicitly that key to the effort was baseball's capacity for identification, stating "When I came here, I was curious and anticipated something really positive, but this is so much more than that. And I want to really be grateful to President Obama for making this possible. . . . I think the two countries, the one thing they agree on for sure is how much they love the game."[64]

Such optimistic accounts demonstrate the rhetorical promise of baseball diplomacy. If, indeed, baseball enables an equitable exchange between the two nations, then perhaps it can soften the legacy of American exceptionalism. Unfortunately, there is reason for skepticism, especially given the interests of MLB. As the *St. Louis Post-Dispatch* reported, "Baseball has sought to play a role in bridging the diplomatic ties between the two nations. Last December, Major League Baseball and the players' union dispatched several active players, including Cuban defectors Brayan Pena and José Abreu, on a goodwill mission to the island to begin fostering a better relation between the country's baseball organizations."[65]

Such an interest is not based on benevolence. Rather, MLB recognizes that normalized relations with Cuba have enormous implications for the labor market. MLB commissioner Rob Manfred confirmed in 2015 that the league was in communication with the Obama administration, stating "We are in conversations with the [US] government about Cuba. Cuba is a great market for us in two ways. Obviously it's a great talent market. [And] it's a country where baseball is embedded in the culture."[66] Meanwhile, the *Washington Post* summarized the potential of Obama's direction: "President Obama's move to normalize relations between the United States and Cuba will resonate through baseball. The trickle of dazzling talent that already flows from the baseball-crazed island could turn into a geyser, a stream of available players that would force Major League Baseball to frame and police how teams acquire Cuban players. The political thaw would also eliminate the dangerous back channels of defection. The impact on the sport could be immense and, in the words of one team official, 'drastic.'"[67] Eliminating the dangers associated with defection would indisputably be a positive development. However, the larger rhetorical justification in terms of an expanding labor pool is a troubling retreat to American exceptionalism. As Añorve warns, "The heart of the matter is that many of the voices in favor of using baseball as a diplomatic tool, are based on a speech in which the beneficiaries would be only the MLB and the Cuban baseball players."[68] Indeed, there is considerable risk that individual stories of Cuban players coming to MLB would be framed as exemplars of the American Dream, all made possible because of the nation's exceptionalism.

Diplomatic Promise or America First?

When Barack Obama announced his plans to normalize relations with Cuba, it is unlikely he foresaw the election of Donald Trump. Quite suddenly, the reconsideration of American exceptionalism symbolized by Obama was swept aside in favor of the "America First" doctrine of Trump. In the case of Cuba, Trump labeled Obama's initiative a "terrible and misguided deal" as he rescinded several components installed by his predecessor. Although the initial reversal was far from total, Latinos both in the United States and across Latin America quickly expressed intensified fears about harassment, deportation, and reductions in humanitarian aid.[69]

Meanwhile, MLB followed Obama's lead and, in late 2018, agreed with the MLB Players Association on a new policy regarding players from Cuba seeking entry to the United States. In brief, the policy was designed to mirror the pathway available to players from Asia—especially Japan, South Korea, and Taiwan—and therefore "eliminate the dangerous trafficking that had gone on for decades."[70] The deal included the cooperation of the Cuban Baseball Federation, which then released a list of thirty-four players who would become eligible to sign with MLB without having to defect.[71] This announcement represented the most dramatic evidence of the change made possible by the Obama normalization efforts. However, any optimism it may have prompted was short-lived.

In April 2019, the Trump administration "abruptly ended a deal between Major League Baseball and the Cuban Baseball Federation that had eased the path for players to compete in the United States without defecting from their country." According to national security adviser John Bolton, the official reason for rescinding the policy was the belief that Cuba was using its players as pawns in the effort to support the regime of Nicolás Maduro in Venezuela.[72] MLB officials had expected Trump to maintain the policy, and members of the Obama administration were immediately critical of the change in direction. As deputy national security adviser to Obama, Benjamin Rhodes had taken the lead on the Cuban baseball policy. He called the new administration's reversal "an indefensible, cruel and pointless decision that they've made that will be ending the lives of Cuban baseball players and achieve nothing beyond appeasing hard-line factions in Florida."[73] Players, too, expressed concern. Cuban-born Aroldis Chapman, for example, lamented, "The biggest impact is going to be the guys who are back in Cuba. For me and a lot of our fellow Cuban players who have already established ourselves here in this country, we're fortunate enough to have our families here. It really doesn't affect us here. We've been lucky."[74]

Looking ahead, it is unclear what Trump's ascendancy will mean for Cuban baseball players. MLB, which had cooperated willingly with President Obama, has appeared to change course. Perhaps out of a pragmatic need to work with the new president or, more cynically, out of a primary concern for securing access to a valuable labor pool, the league has hired a lobbying firm with significant connections to Trump. Presumably, lobbyist Brian Ballard is invested in "issues related to combating human trafficking," an aspiration that would be supported by anyone committed to democratic rights. His sincerity is dubious, however, given his role as an influential fundraiser during the Trump campaign in 2016.[75] Whether Ballard is a surprise ally for Cuban mobility remains to be seen, but the MLB's status in Cuba is at best murky.

Less ambiguous are the implications for democratic exceptionalism. The promise of Obama's normalization policy has been erased by an emphatic and nationalistic Trumpian rebuke. "Diplomacy" itself seems now to be a foreign concept, and the current administration sees little value in the nuances of "soft power." Yet even before Trump's election, there was reason to be cautious about the use of baseball to foster identification between the two nations. Surely Barack Obama's sincere engagement with the people of Cuba and his considerable charm positively reframed a historically antagonistic relationship. At the same time, MLB's investment in diplomacy as a means of simply enhancing its access to Latino labor too clearly bears the traces of the imperialistic and exceptionalist rhetoric of the past, perhaps evidenced by the quick recalculation and decision to hire a pro-Trump lobbyist.

In Murray's discussion of sports diplomacy, he worries that the inherently competitive characteristics of sport may limit its diplomatic potential. As he writes, "International sport can bring people together but it can also foster distance from the 'other' by encouraging nationalism through flag-waving, national anthems, and exhortations to patriotism on and off the proverbial pitch."[76] Such limitations are made more or less relevant by the state actors who deploy sports diplomacy as a tool of foreign policy. In the case of baseball between the United States and Cuba, Murray's concern manifests in the Trump administration's retreat into highly nationalistic and exclusionary rhetoric. Thus there may be good reason to be optimistic that baseball diplomacy may yield positive engagement under a regime guided by the democratic exceptionalism of the Obama presidency. Its prospects are decidedly less encouraging under the "America First" logic of Trump. For scholars of rhetoric and democracy, then, this case points both to the potential of sport as a diplomatic tool and its limited utility when leaders refuse to play by the rules of the democratic game. As the United States walks back the diplomatic steps taken with Cuba during the Obama administration, Cuban baseball players find themselves in much the same place they did previously. Once again, for those who wish to follow the lead of MLB stars like José Fernández and Yasiel Puig, they face a dangerous and precarious journey to the United States. Similarly, the pathway to democratic engagement between the United States and Cuba remains fraught with obstacles and uncertainty.

PART 2

PROBLEMATIZING AND RECONSTRUCTING DEMOCRACY IN LATIN AMERICA

6

COMMUNICATING ABOUT CORRUPTION:
GUATEMALAN RHETORICS OF CORRUPTION

Adriana Angel

On April 25, 2015, thirty thousand people gathered in Plaza de la Constitución (Constitution Square) in the capital city of Guatemala. Blowing whistles, banging pots and pans, and releasing blue and white balloons into the sky, they called for the resignation of President Otto Pérez and Vice President Roxanna Baldetti, both of whom had been implicated in a serious corruption case and recently denounced by judicial authorities. For the first time since the days of dictatorship and internal conflict, Guatemalan protesters were not killed or imprisoned for marching and protesting against the political class.[1] For four and a half months, every Saturday, youth, workers, indigenous people, and citizens marched toward the Plaza de la Constitución to demand the truth about recent corruption cases. The peaceful demonstrations, along with the judicial investigations, prompted the resignation of both the vice president in May and the president in September. Unlike protests in many Latin American countries, the Guatemalan citizens' protests against corruption were surprisingly influential, especially considering that Central and South American countries have some of the world's most corrupt cities.[2]

The Guatemalan protests—and their outcomes—constitute an intriguing phenomenon of study for scholars from disciplines as diverse as communication, political science, sociology, public deliberation, and social justice, among many others. The protests have drawn attention to a scarcely studied country in a little addressed region, Central America. Based on a rhetorical cluster analysis, this chapter strives to enrich communication scholarship on Guatemala—and Latin America in general—in relation to the serious social phenomenon of corruption.[3] More specifically, by examining several discourses concerning the recent Guatemalan cases of corruption, a rhetorical analysis shows the relationship among three main terministic screens that cluster around corruption: fraud, democracy, and interventionism. Although I address the specific case of Guatemala, these findings could be extrapolated to other regions of the world because I develop a broad understanding of the role of rhetoric in communicating corruption. The general purpose of this chapter consists of showing the relationship between rhetoric and democracy in the specific context of corruption, a problem faced by all countries in the Americas.

For this chapter, I aimed to assemble a collection of representative discourses on Guatemalan corruption that would allow me to identify the vocabularies that different types of actors use to communicate about this phenomenon. As I will describe later, in fulfilling this aim, I found that discourses on corruption entail three different levels of abstraction—concrete, intermediate, and abstract—that explain how corruption is communicated and internalized. I argue that challenging corruption accordingly requires identifying the vocabularies and narratives of corruption so that existing programs of action might be deconstructed and revised. I unpack this argument by first summarizing the recent corruption cases that prompted the resignation of the president and vice president of Guatemala. I then outline the concepts associated with rhetoric and corruption as well as the general guidelines of rhetorical cluster analysis. Next, I examine fraud, democracy, and interventionism as the three main terministic screens that cluster around corruption. Finally, I discuss the implications of these findings in relation to the rhetorical nature of corruption and the programs of action that the clusters spur. The discussion of these implications leads me to offer recommendations for addressing the fight against corruption more generally.

Corruption in Guatemala

"La Línea" (the Line) was the name that Guatemalan citizens used to refer to the corruption case implicating the involvement of their president and vice president during 2015. Guatemalan senior customs officials created a parallel payment schedule for custom duties to allow certain businesses to pay lower customs in exchange for bribes. This network of corrupt officials gave the businessmen "a line," that is, a designated telephone number for negotiating lower payments. On April 14, 2015, a UN-backed anti-impunity agency called the Comisión Internacional contra la Impunidad en Guatemala (International Commission Against Corruption in Guatemala; CICIG in Spanish) disclosed more than sixty thousand wiretaps, some of which indirectly implicated government ministers, the vice president, and the president and turned them into suspects of corruption.[4] A week later, on Saturday, April 25, thirty thousand citizens peacefully went to the main square of the city to request the resignation of several high-ranking government officials.[5] Two weeks later, twenty state officials were arrested, and the vice president resigned from office.

The demonstrations lasted ten weeks. Every Saturday, people gathered at Plaza de la Constitución to pray, play, sing, and protest against corruption. Meanwhile, the Guatemalan Public Prosecutor's Office and the CICIG continued denouncing more corruption cases in addition to the multimillion-dollar customs fraud scheme. On May 20, the heads of the Guatemalan Central Bank and the Social Security Institute were imprisoned because of another serious case involving the supply of low-quality devices to hemodialysis patients with kidney failure.[6] On June 24, the prosecutor and the CICIG denounced a network of high police officials who had established million-dollar contracts with ghost companies to maintain police cars and police stations—repairs that the officers performed themselves or that were never performed at all.

Although citizens' protests continued as subsequent cases of corruption were denounced, the Guatemalan president, Otto Pérez, refused to resign, in an effort to reaffirm his innocence. However, on August 25, the public prosecutor formally began to prosecute Pérez, prompting him to resign from office on September 2. The next day, after attending the first hearing of his trial, Pérez was imprisoned to prevent him from fleeing the country. Two months later, comedian-turned-politician Jimmy Morales was elected president of Guatemala as an act of citizens rejecting the traditional political parties.

At the time of this writing, a judge in Guatemala ruled that Pérez will stand trial in preventive prison for his alleged role in La Línea. Baldetti, on the other hand, is still standing trial for the same case, but she has already been sentenced to fifteen years in jail for another case of corruption related to the embezzlement of millions of dollars from a state fund set up to decontaminate Lake Amatitlán in south-central Guatemala. The United States has also asked for her extradition because of drug-trafficking charges. At the same time, thousands of Guatemalans have come back to the streets to protest the newly elected president Morales after he was accused of corruption. In August 2017, CICIG requested that Morales's immunity be lifted—as had happened with Pérez—so that judicial authorities could investigate alleged funding irregularities during this presidential campaign in 2015. Despite his promises to tackle corruption and impunity, Morales is currently facing charges of corruption while he insists on eliminating CICIG because the institution limits the freedom and sovereignty of his country.

Rhetoric and Corruption

Communication about and action against corruption require rhetorical work to reify a phenomenon that is otherwise blurred, cultural, and subjective. Corruption has no single definition because its meaning derives from the cultural context in which it occurs.[7] Thus what is considered an act of corruption varies by region and time period. Corruption in Latin America is related to practices such as patrimonialism and clientelism, inherited and learned during the Spanish and Portuguese colonial period. These practices have led politicians to govern the public realm as if it were private property and have led citizens to look for the opportunities to take advantage of the state and, specifically, of social and economic capital to access more economic or political power.[8]

Nonetheless, the lack of consensus about its definition has not prevented the creation of typologies and classifications of corruption. In relation to its scope and magnitude, Vargas claims that corruption may be black (high-impact corrupt practices), gray (medium-scale practices), or white (commonly accepted practices).[9] The naturalization and typification of corruption in Central and South America explains why white practices are commonly accepted and reproduced there, while the same practices could be considered as gray or black corruption in other regions of the world. Citizens have made of these practices normal habits that do not frighten or even draw the attention of others. For example, paying small bribes to avoid a traffic ticket or lying in a court are white practices in the Latin American context, but can be considered gray in other societies.

In terms of the agent committing the act, the literature distinguishes among political, state, private, and nongovernmental agents, depending on the type of outcome. Corruption may also be economic when agents seek monetary benefits, whereas it may be political when they endeavor to increase their symbolic, social, or political capital.[10] Beyond these classifications, no consensus exists regarding the causes of corruption: while behavioral approaches emphasize individual factors and behaviors, neoclassical approaches underscore social and structural factors.[11] Likewise, no consensus exists concerning the relationship between political regimes and economic models, on the one hand, and corruption, on the other hand.[12]

The competition among multiple analytical approaches to corruption is productive for the use of rhetoric, which is understood in this chapter in a Burkean sense of using words to form attitudes that prompt individuals to perform particular actions.[13] I focus here on a constitutive perspective in which rhetoric is invitational because it implies the identification of speakers with textual positions that help them to share some points of view, ideas, or even vocabularies. More than a deliberative action that speakers use to manipulate audiences, rhetoric involves the use of language as a common ground for perceiving and understanding the world. This approach to rhetoric highlights a symbolic dimension of rhetoric that has been seldom considered in Latin America, where the studies of texts and discourses have followed the structuralist roots of European semioticians and discourse analysts.

We should consider that, in addition to the lack of academic consensus on the understanding of corruption, the very nature of the corrupt act invites the use of rhetoric, as corruption implies the communication of a situation that must be hidden or denied by the agent performing the act yet is denounced by the judicial authorities or media professionals who publicize the act. Both the agent involved in corruption and their accusers must establish solid accounts that are contradictory, however, because they refer to a hidden event whose existence may never be corroborated, given the interests of the agents and the high levels of impunity. In the scientific field, the rhetorical device for establishing "facts," "evidence," and "proofs" becomes an essential discursive tool to substantiate competing accounts of corruption in a context of uncertainty.

Although the symbolic dimension of corruption constitutes a crucial field of study, communication scholars have focused on the media coverage of corruption and, more specifically, on the types of corruption scandals,[14] the trivialization of information,[15] the mediatization of justice,[16] and the politics of shame.[17] Another branch of the literature focuses on creating public systems of information that grant citizens access to public data so that they can monitor the transparency of the proceedings of public administration officials.[18]

While this study contributes to understanding the role of traditional and new media in representing corruption, it is nevertheless important to embrace a more symbolic approach to corruption that focuses on the language that social agents use to discuss this phenomenon and, subsequently, on the programs of action—to use Burke's terminology—that the language promotes. Adopting this approach, Angel and Bates analyze how six different understandings of Colombian corruption (namely, illegal action, decay, irregular practice, unethical behavior, piñata, and normal practice) engender distinct and somehow contradictory actions linked to changes in Colombian legislation, culture, and education.[19] Similarly, in this chapter I analyze the rhetorical representation of Guatemalan corruption to identify programs of action that underlie this phenomenon. However, unlike the Colombian study where several terministic screens of corruption coexist making this a polysemic practice of diverse understandings, the Guatemalan case—as I will describe later—shows that one terministic screen prevails among politicians, citizens, and the media and this screen carries with it an elaborated narrative about the causes and consequences of this corruption.

Accessing Terministic Screens of Guatemalan Corruption

As soon as the CICIG and the judicial authorities denounced the first cases of corruption, Guatemalan media engaged in permanent coverage of the events. The media interviewed the president, vice president, judicial authorities, and citizens from different social groups. To understand how these agents understand corruption, I performed a rhetorical cluster analysis to identify the terministic screens of corruption used by the main politicians involved in corruption cases and by representatives of Guatemalan civil society. I selected twelve discourses that were broadcast over Guatemalan radio and television and that directly involved these various agents in conversation.[20] These discourses comprised lengthy interviews and debates. The broadcasts spanned the period from the CICIG denunciation of the customs fraud scheme in May 2015 to the resignation of the president in September 2015. I selected this time because it encompasses the first denunciation of corruption declared by judicial authorities, the citizens' mobilizations, and the resignation and incarceration of the president. This period also enabled me to analyze how agents transformed their discourses according to the nature of the investigations and citizen pressure.

Once I identified and became familiar with several media pieces, I decided to examine those in which different types of agents explain corruption in depth. Thus I assembled a collection of twelve media discourses. Regarding the political agents, I analyzed six discourses involving both the president and vice president, as these officers were suspected of participating in the customs fraud and were at least aware of the other corruption cases. Regarding members of civil society, I studied six discourses involving judicial authorities as well as youth, civic actors, farmers, and indigenous leaders, as these people were both organizers of and participants in the crowded demonstrations against corruption. Because of the challenges of accessing and interviewing them, I analyzed their mass-mediated discourses broadcast on one radio station (Sonora) and two television channels (Guatevisión and Canal Antigua). These three media channels are the most consumed and well-reputed outlets (Multivex 2015).[21] They also afforded significant visibility and coverage of all types of agents.

After selecting and transcribing these discourses (constituting more than 150 pages), I performed a rhetorical cluster analysis that led me to identify the main terministic screens representing Guatemalan corruption. These screens, as Burke explains, comprise the vocabularies and terminologies through which individuals perceive the world.[22] Terms do not work in an isolated manner; rather, they cluster in groups, thus producing terministic screens that create frames of interpretation. Cluster analysis allows researchers to examine the subjects that cluster around other subjects and, in this case, to explore the clusters of terms that Guatemalans use to communicate about corruption. These clusters reveal not only the ways in which different speakers understand corruption but also the motives that lead speakers to normalize, anormalize, and act against corruption.

I performed a rhetorical cluster analysis by following the four classic steps of this methodology.[23] I first established corruption as the a priori term that would guide the subsequent search for other terms that cluster around it. I then identified clusters of terms that agents use to define, describe, or refer to corruption. As Lynch explains, these terms "appear in the same context as the key term and rank them according to frequency of appearance and the intensity or power of the term."[24] Through a close reading of the discourses, I inferred the wider discourses to which these clusters of terms belong and broke down the rhetorical elements shaping the corruption discourses. Finally, I identified the subjacent motives underlying the generation of every cluster of terms to suggest subjacent programs of action on behalf of different types of agents. According to Burke, these motives are not psychological intentions but frames of interpretation that lead to specific programs of action—that is, to specific ways to act.

After performing this analysis, I found that both politicians and citizens understand and communicate corruption by using three main terministic screens: fraud, democracy, and interventionism. In addition, they use three rhetorical devices to defend themselves from or accuse others of corruption: accreditation, accusation of third parties, and use of evidence. Finally, the programs of action against corruption associated with the discourses of both

types of agents (that is, politicians and citizens) entail strategically transforming the Guatemalan system so that politicians cannot abuse it. The next
section explains how all these elements together establish a particular way of
communicating about corruption.

The Vocabularies of Corruption

As mentioned, three main terministic screens cluster around corruption:
fraud, democracy, and interventionism. The fraud cluster is used to define
and comprehend corruption, the democracy cluster is used to describe the
consequences of corruption, and the interventionism cluster is used to signify the US intervention in a Guatemalan soft coup. The fraud cluster also
includes one subcluster, system, which is employed to describe the cause of
corruption. The narrative associated with these clusters might be specified as
follows: (1) corruption is a type of fraud that the Guatemalan system permits;
(2) corruption threatens democracy and therefore threatens the viability of
the country; and (3) the denunciation and representation of the most recent
cases of corruption in Guatemala are the result of US interventionist strategies. Remarkably, the first two clusters correspond to the vocabularies and
narratives of the two types of agents studied. Politicians and citizens approach
corruption as fraud and identify a threat to democracy in this practice. The
third cluster, interventionism, corresponds to a particular rhetoric of the
Guatemalan president to explain the role of the United States in Guatemala.
Unlike other studies that have found different and polysemic understandings of corruption among the same type of agents,[25] the discourses analyzed
here are consistent with one another in that the terminologies and narratives
clearly fit one cluster of corruption as fraud.

According to the speakers, fraud might be understood as abuse that
individuals commit for personal benefit. Corruption is considered neither a
problem of values spurring individuals to act unethically nor a strong legal
offense; rather, it is regarded as an abuse that individuals commit to reap
the potential benefits of the Guatemalan system. These benefits often result
from gaps in the legal code or access to information. In other words, agents
represent corruption as an invitation built into the system, thus minimizing
the responsibility of the person involved in the corrupt act. Additionally, considering the system (rather than the person) as the element motivating corruption imputes the cause of corruption to a blurred and abstract agent that
is not directly accountable. The following excerpt from a quotation by former

Guatemalan vice president Roxanna Baldetti illustrates this idea: "Although governments change, the system we have is no longer useful. Here, we could elect a bishop as the president, and nothing would happen. That bishop could not control all the corruption we have because what we need to do is to change the system."[26]

Citizens also embrace this standpoint. For example, Cruz, a young Guatemalan citizen, claims that "corruption is embedded in the different institutions of the Guatemalan state. We need reforms on the Tax Administration Office, the electoral law, the political parties, and the Prosecutor's Office."[27] Although citizens use the term "system" to explain how corruption has invaded all Guatemalan institutions, designating the system as the cause of corruption allows politicians such as the former vice president to defend herself from the accusation of complicity in the case of La Línea (i.e., it is the system's fault, not hers). In both cases, however, the focus of corruption is the structure of a system that encourages abusive behavior, which, in turn, is blurred because it does not have the severe connotations of violating the law or being unethical. Abuse is an exaggeration or overreach of a privilege that is originally or to a lesser extent permissible and legitimate.

The consequences of committing such fraud generate a second cluster of terms that aggregate around the term "democracy." Politicians and citizens focus their discourses on the damage that corruption might cause to the Guatemalan democracy. Unlike other cases of corruption, which offer detailed accounts of the acts of corruption in which agents are involved or that they have witnessed, my analysis shows that agents invest considerable time in highlighting the consequences of specific corrupt acts. The following claim by the Guatemalan citizen Merlyn Torres exemplifies this investment in relation to the future of the country: "It is like Guatemala is waking up! Now we can believe in justice regardless of whether it is justice brought by CICIG. This is a great step so that the country can move forward."[28] Former president Otto Pérez similarly asserts, "I invite you all to respect the due legal process. Unfortunately, this is a situation that I have to face, and I will face it respecting the legal processes. But the most important thing right now is to unify all efforts for Guatemala to succeed. We need to build the Guatemala that we all want, a country with justice, peace, security, and a decent life for all Guatemalans. . . . This is something I've always carried in my heart: to defend our country's democracy."[29] I observed a concern for democracy throughout all discourses featuring all types of agents. Surprisingly, politicians' and citizens' discourses do not focus on the economic, cultural, and social consequences of corruption; rather, they focus on a more abstract implication related to preserving the democratic system. This wide-spread concern for democracy is sensible, considering that the Guatemalan democracy is merely thirty years old. The need to maintain the Guatemalan democracy is justified by the following terms that contribute to this cluster: "safeguard," "break," "defend," and "support" democracy. Protecting the democracy will avoid a "throwback" or "reversal" of the country so that it maintains "viability." The allusion to democracy might also be considered a resource for agents implicated in corruption to divert the discourse from corruption to democracy.

In relation to both clusters, fraud and democracy, politicians and citizens alike claim that Guatemala might be a viable country after legislative changes make the law more rigorous and the judicial system more severe. Both actors argue that these legislative changes would consolidate democracy and reduce Guatemala's risk of corruption. President Pérez, for example, claims it as follows: "Of course, now our successors will have to make those [legislative] changes so that these transformations become consolidated. This requires the Congress to make changes in several laws so that Guatemala becomes a viable country, a country that has all it needs to face the twenty-first century."[30]

The relationship between clusters demonstrates that corruption is an attribute of a legal system rather than a culture that must be changed. It also reinforces the idea that the central and almost the only consequence of corruption is its threat to democracy rather than other political, economic, social, and cultural implications of corruption.

Unlike this democracy cluster that focuses on the main consequence of corruption, a third cluster, called interventionism, focuses on the possible causes of corruption. As mentioned above, although Guatemalan judicial authorities denounced the government's involvement in the scandal of La Línea since April 2015, President Otto Pérez refused to resign until September, once the public prosecutor formally began his prosecution. The rhetorical analysis shows how these two moments—before and after the resignation—underlie two different discourses about his responsibility in Guatemalan corruption. Before his resignation, Pérez focused on denying his participation in any case of corruption, and after his resignation, his discourses focus on assigning the responsibility for corruption to third parties.

Thus, while the president was in office, his discourse emphasized his lack of knowledge concerning the corruption cases in which he is suspected of being involved. After resigning, however, Pérez transformed his discourse and began accusing the United States of implementing interventionist strategies in Guatemala to wage a soft coup and remove him from office. In the context of

Pérez's resignation, the interventionism cluster emerges as a way to accuse the United States of encouraging a Guatemalan soft coup that enables the North American country to achieve its geostrategic objectives in Central America.

To this cluster belongs terms such as "strategy," "enforcement," "imposition," "geostrategic interest," "soft coup," "intervention," and "national interests." The following excerpt illustrates the general narrative of the cluster: "It is unacceptable that the United States strives to use an intervention strategy in Guatemala to tell us what to do and to break our democracy. If some sectors of the international community and some sectors within our country don't consider our political class valuable, they must first put aside their own interests and pay attention to the people of Guatemala."[31]

After being placed in prison to prevent his escape, Pérez transformed his discourse and ceased explaining the course of corrupt events, including his participation therein. Instead, he began blaming the United States for initially associating him with corruption. Thus the focus of Pérez's discourses is no longer himself, but the United States. Hence, the primary topic of discussion changes from corruption to American interventionism, in effect prompting the media to focus on the possible US geostrategic interests in Guatemala. Finally, with the introduction of the interventionism cluster, Pérez reinforces the democracy cluster because he presents the former as a threat to the latter and as a more serious threat than corruption itself. It is important to note that, unlike the other two clusters, the interventionism cluster is mostly communicated by Pérez and Baldetti and not by other citizens. I cannot confidently conclude that they did not agree with the idea of foreign intervention in Guatemala but did not communicate it directly in the media studied here.

Although other cluster analyses typically discuss the term "agon" found across several discourses on a specific topic, a particular agon that contradicts corruption was not found. Agons, as Burke explains, are terms that contradict and work in contraposition to others—in this case, in contraposition to corruption. While justice seems to function as an agon term, speakers rhetorically construct this notion as the "punishment" that corrupt individuals receive or as the "path to discover the truth" about corrupt acts. The fact that agents embrace a tenuous and weak definition of corruption explains the difficulty of finding an agon that directly opposes corruption. This fact also explains why Burke's classification of frames of acceptance and rejection are difficult to establish here: outside of a specific context, all agents reject corruption. When accused of corruption, however, they rhetorically find a way to reject corruption while presenting a credible account of the reasons why their alleged actions are not corrupt as such.

Defending Oneself from and Accusing Others of Corruption

Speakers use three rhetorical devices to defend themselves from or accuse others of corruption: accreditation, accusation, and the use of evidence. The accreditation of both the president and vice president as public servants is the first such device. Following Jonathan Potter,[32] I consider this accreditation to be a rhetorical device that allows speakers to construct a particular persona that places them in a textual position enabling them to project particular rhetorical images about themselves. To defend themselves from the accusations, these politicians configure their personas as servants and patriots who desire "the best for the country"[33] and who "don't mind making one last sacrifice for Guatemala to move forward."[34] As national servants, they claim and insist on their willingness to "face justice" and to cooperate with all legal proceedings until the judicial authorities "discover and prove" their innocence. Their insistence on respecting the law and submitting to due legal process rhetorically allies them with the law rather than with corruption.

Citizens undermine these politicians' claims to be honest individuals and rhetorically configure them as "abusers" of their political power. As one professor describes it, "These politicians act that way because they can do it and because things have always been done in such a way; this is the political culture of our country, and it has become worse over the last few years; it is a problem of our culture!"[35] This representation corresponds with citizens' understanding of corruption as an abuse of power. Citizens refer to their former president and vice president not as thieves, liars, or criminals but as individuals who, exploiting their political capacities, benefited from the Guatemalan system. At different times, citizens claim that their loss of trust in politicians is a main consequence of this abuse. Politicians see in the delay of elections the main implication of this abuse, whereas citizens see these acts as compromising public trust.

Notably, citizen representations of politicians vary depending on the type of citizen. Most citizens, however, construct the politicians' persona by characterizing them with traits that they would not associate with themselves. In particular, they depict politicians as corrupt individuals who abuse their political privileges. By contrast, scholars contend that Guatemalans as a group have naturalized corruption to an extent that the latter now characterizes Guatemalan culture.

A second, less frequently used device is the accusation of third parties in order to attribute responsibility to others. To defend themselves from the accusations of corruption, the president and vice president blame others—namely, the entrepreneurs—for participating in cases such as La Línea because they were the ones who accepted bribes in order to obtain lower customs. In the words of the president, "Entrepreneurs are responsible for corrupting the country. They have been behind the acts of corruption of this country, and the worst thing is that these entrepreneurs are still doing the things that they are accustomed to doing for many years."[36] Thus the president changes his positionality and speaks from the standpoint of a victim who has been falsely accused of participating in corrupt acts rather than speaking from the standpoint of blame or suspicion.

As the multitudinous demonstrations show, citizens also undermine this positionality because they consider the politicians responsible and accountable for the acts of corruption in the country. The citizens also request changes to the system so that other politicians do not commit the same mistakes. Citizens, however, use the same rhetorical device of accusing third parties of the problems of corruption in their country. As noted, insofar as citizens position themselves as victims of corruption and thus not as active agents contributing to it, they accentuate the prominence of black corruption. In other words, they rhetorically reproduce the idea that only the high-impact corrupt practices of high-ranking government officials qualify as corruption. As indexes and studies importantly show,[37] both black and white corruption occur in Guatemala. However, the civic and political agents studied here focus their discourses solely on black corruption, which tends to release citizens from any responsibility and give politicians the opportunity to blame big businesses.

The reference to evidence constitutes the third rhetorical device whereby speakers accuse others of and defend themselves against claims of corruption. The use of evidence contributes to building the factuality of accounts and helps speakers to construct a quality of out-there-ness in their discourses. For this study, the president and vice president often claim that no strong evidence exists tying them to corruption. When asked about the thousands of wiretaps that mention pseudonyms possibly referring to them, politicians defend themselves by discrediting the institutions that present the evidence and by questioning the objectivity of the interpretation of that evidence. For example, when asked by a Radio Sonora journalist about her involvement in cases of corruption, Baldetti answered strongly: "Bring me solid evidence to the table, and I will believe you, but I won't allow you to come here with lies. If you work for a serious radio station, then show proof about what you are saying because I won't play that game for a pamphlet or a radio program of lies."[38]

Clearly, agents use evidence either to enhance or undermine the factuality of a statement of corruption by deleting or adding elements concerning

contexts, opinions about institutions, and qualifications about agents. Likewise, citizens refer to facts, evidence, and proof to support their call for the
president's resignation. CICIG (the UN-backed anti-impunity commission),
for example, is presented by citizens as the "heroes" that "finally brought
justice to Guatemala" and "proved what was really happened" while being
discredited by the president as a symbol of US interventionism and interference that incited a soft coup to overthrow the Guatemalan president.

Discourses of corruption might be considered an interplay between accusers and accused in which the following actions occur: (1) the same evidence
is rhetorically read in different ways; (2) institutions that provide evidence
are questioned or exalted; and (3) evidence is normalized and anormalized
after being placed in a context in which it is intentionally minimized or maxi-
mized. Thus speakers must use rhetorical tactics in addressing the evidence
to help them defend themselves from accusations or accuse others of corruption. As corrupt acts must be hidden and denied, the reference to evidence
becomes a point of contention to be rhetorically managed.

Actions Against Corruption

Rather than being evaluative, the rhetorical analysis performed here was
epistemic.[39] Following Richard Weaver, I maintain that "every utterance is
an attempt to make others see the world in a particular way and to accept
the values implicit in that point of view."[40] By additionally considering Potter's perspective on methodological relativism, my analytical emphasis was
exclusively rhetorical in that I did not aim to ascertain the factual accuracy
of the corruption cases studied here. That is, my goal was not to discern
guilt, innocence, responsibility, or even the "true" magnitude of corruption
in Guatemala, but to analyze how corruption is rhetorically constructed such
that the phenomenon of corruption might be deconstructed. Thus, because
I approached rhetoric as a device of power—instead of a tool of truth—I
endeavored to analyze how the use of language referring to corruption gen-
erates particular attitudes and actions toward this phenomenon. The way in
which agents communicate about corruption explains how they act for or
against it. Such communication also helps us understand its naturalization,
normalization, and anormalization.

Designating corruption as a fraudulent action implies transforming the
system that permits corruption. Although responsibility for abuse is shared
by the abuser and the structure permitting it, the Guatemalan discourses

analyzed here attribute the majority of responsibility to the system. Rhetorically, the notion of a system is constructed in a blurred and ambiguous manner as it relates to gaps in law, historical problems of the country, or malfunctioning of organizations. Although we can deduce that the transformation of this system—and, therefore, the reduction of corruption—requires several legislative reforms and the restructuring of organizations, this transformation is rhetorically too ambiguous, particularly considering the role of the individuals who enable the system to function. Thus the programs of action that adopt a terministic screen of corruption as a type of fraud are too general and abstract, as they advocate a broad transformation of an entity of an elusive nature. I analyze some consequences of this phenomenon below.

Three Discursive Levels of Corruption

The discussion presented above leads me to claim that discourses of corruption in Guatemala work at three levels: concrete, intermediate, and abstract. At the concrete level, discourses involve specific events within a broader episode of corruption. For instance, individuals discuss how the CICIG denounced wiretaps, which made the president a suspect of corruption. Alternatively, the former vice president informs citizens how she learned about the investigations against her while she was in South Korea. At the intermediate level are more elaborated accounts in which individuals construct narratives about broad episodes of corruption. For example, politicians, citizens, or journalists explain how La Línea worked and discuss the role of the president in the customs fraud scheme, as the journalist Paola Hurtado briefly shows here when asking the CICIG commissioner, Iván Velázquez, about the case of La Línea: "Good evening, Mr. Commissioner. From the historic April 16 and over the last weeks the CICIG has shown, along with the Public Ministry, a series of cases in which different entities of the state and different actors have operated as structures or networks that used public funds and resources to defraud or to take advantage of the state. What has this entity done in order to trigger the resignation of the vice president? How would you describe all this that we are experiencing?"[41] At the abstract level are general accounts of corruption that reflect attitudes and motives related to corruption and, therefore, programs of action against it. For instance, citizens claim that the recent corruption scandals form part of their everyday life or argue that demonstrations are required to change the political system.

To some extent, these three discursive levels correspond with Burke's classification of positive, dialectical, and ultimate terms, as the levels reflect an increasing degree of abstraction that moves from a reference to concrete, tangible events (positive terms) to ideas about corruption (dialectical terms) to, finally, a set of principles and naturalized terministic screens of corruption (ultimate terms).[42] Unlike Burke's understanding of these terms, however, my understanding emphasizes not only the terms but also the sets of terms that construct broader accounts or narratives in relation to concrete and broad episodes of corruption, as well as abstract ideas about corruption.

Notably, this increasing abstraction does not correspond to a progressive time frame, as if to imply that these levels occurred sequentially: the concrete, intermediate, and abstract levels can influence one another in several ways. For instance, a general attitude of distrust related to the idea that most politicians tend to be corrupt (an idea pertaining to the abstract level) might influence a specific narrative of corruption in which politicians are accused of abusing the system in relation to a particular episode (an accusation pertaining to the intermediate level). In other words, the three levels need not follow a temporal sequence; they may occur synchronously.

These three discursive levels of corruption might also anchor specific terministic screens that cluster around them. In specific relation to the Guatemalan case examined here, we can note that the fraud cluster operates particularly at the intermediate level—that is, in the narratives of both government officials and citizens who explain the corrupt acts in terms of an abuse committed by or because of the system. The democracy and interventionism clusters, by contrast, operate mostly at the abstract level.

Conclusions and Recommendations

Through the rhetorical cluster analysis of several discourses concerning Guatemalan corruption, I suggest that fraud, interventionism, and democracy function as the main terministic screens through which Guatemalans reference, understand, and motivate their actions in response to the recent episodes of corruption in their country. Both senior government officials and citizens understand corruption as an abuse arising primarily from the system, which ultimately affects the young and fragile Guatemalan democracy. The metanarrative that underlies and groups together these three clusters states that corruption is a type of fraud that the Guatemalan system permits, one that threatens democracy and the viability of the country and whose public denunciation is the result of US interventionist strategies. Through rhetorical devices such as accreditation, accusation of third parties, and use of evidence, both politicians and citizens reproduce this narrative and communicate each cluster while defending themselves from or accusing others of corruption.

My chief goal was to explore the main terministic screens whereby Guatemalans understand and motivate their actions against corruption. I aimed to provide theoretical and practical conclusions to assist efforts to challenge corruption not only in Guatemala but also in other Latin American countries. First, I recommend that civic agents and politicians who lead actions and campaigns against corruption should identify the vocabularies used by particular groups or the broader society to communicate about corruption. As demonstrated in the case of Guatemala, the exploration of these vocabularies can identify the programs of action underlying the terministic screens. For example, conceptualizing corruption as an ethical problem orients programs of action toward a moral and educative path, whereas framing corruption as an illegal action encourages the development of programs that seek to change the legislative system. Based on the discursive typology of corruption suggested above, acting first on the concrete and intermediate levels would enable transformation at the abstract level, where the motives and ideologies of corruption reside.

Reducing and acting against the harmful material consequences of corruption may entail identifying and transforming the vocabularies that individuals use to communicate about this phenomenon. This transformation of vocabularies will lead to the transformation of terministic screens and, consequently, of the corresponding programs of action. I am not defending a radical standpoint according to which all material transformations must be accomplished at a symbolic level.[43] Rather, I assert that actions against corruption must be taken both at a material level (for example, judicial investigations, incarcerations, and economic redistribution) and at a symbolic level (for example, transforming vocabularies and programs of action, language, and culture). Because targeting both levels requires time and effort, I argue that societies could start addressing the levels simultaneously.

Second, I recommend that actors including the media, civic agents, politicians, and national or international organizations involved in leading actions and campaigns against corruption address the issue of white corruption. As demonstrated in the case of Guatemala, communication about corruption tends to focus on black corruption—that is, on the practices of high-ranking politicians. Initiating discussion about white corruption will nuance and deepen the understanding of corruption by highlighting other actors, practices and, therefore, terministic screens involved in producing this phenomenon. That is, through the discussion of white corruption, ordinary citizens and commonly illegitimate practices will inform and thus broaden the spectrum of analysis of and action against corruption. Thus the understanding of corruption will extend beyond the domain of politicians attempting large thefts and swindles to include more ordinary practices and agents.

Third, I recommend thinking through other possible and nonnormative ways to approach the relationship between corruption and democracy. As stated above, there is no consensus concerning the relationship between political regimes and corruption, which means that some studies show that corruption tends to increase in dictatorial regimes, while others prove that democracies are more prone to face corruption. We should consider the possibility that corruption is inherent to all types of political regimes so far known. We can work at the material and symbolic levels to reduce it and we can also denaturalize white corruption; however, we could also study to what extent and with what consequences our systems of government call or somehow invite corruption as a part of their desired and unwanted effects.

Undoubtedly, additional studies of corruption are needed to help reduce the incidence of this phenomenon. I identify the need for further research on the communication of corruption to discern the extent to which corruption is a cultural and communicative phenomenon that may respond to intervention at a symbolic level. Moreover, to improve existing understanding of the rhetoric of corruption, I suggest that future studies embrace a transnational rhetorical perspective, which would allow researchers to explore the programs of actions underlying different terministic screens of corruption worldwide and, more important, to analyze how those programs are accomplished.

7

RE/TRACING THE LOCAL GRASSROOTS WOMEN ACTIVISTS' CRAFTING OF RHETORICAL AGENCY IN CIUDAD JUÁREZ, MEXICO

Clara Eugenia Rojas Blanco

The moral exigency generated by the public disclosure of the murders of young women and girls in Ciudad Juárez, Mexico (1994–2001), produced an overarching social and political contingency where the murdered bodies wrought the sign of the *feminicides* as the ultimate manifestation of gender violence[1] in a community with an already long history of multifaceted violence.[2] Moreover, the feminicides and the injustice surrounding them simultaneously produced multiple rhetorical situations at local, national, and international levels, which in turn constructed a range of rhetors, texts, and audiences. Most of the texts were centered on the exposure of the misogynists' trace on victims' bodies, the mothers' *dolorismo*, the unjust construction of the "double life" of the victims, low-income women in the community, and the government's negligence and impunity.[3]

For more than ten years (1998–2011), uncountable texts (videos, blogs, movies, academic, and newspaper articles) surrounding the feminicides in Ciudad Juárez were created during this overt and public crisis by national and international feminist scholars in several languages, mainly in English. Today, due to an apparent national and international silence in regard to the feminicide tragedy in Ciudad Juárez, it seems that everything has been said and discussed. This silence, evident since 2005, was publicly noticeable because the feminist activists' rhetorical agency during the public manifestations, characterized mainly by agonistic protests, has subsided.[4] Although the official silencing of the feminicides called for an urgent and necessary feminist social and political interruption, when the public events stopped it seemed that the struggle to move the women's rights agenda had ended.

But to understand silence solely as the absence of sound and public visibility through media prevents us from appreciating that the feminicide crisis had produced a discursive displacement where culture, gender, gender violence, feminicides, and overall the women's rights agenda became the part of the form and substance of the local civil deliberations.

In fact, there is no silence regarding women's human rights; there are different political voices struggling to maintain the exposure of gender violence in the community. At the local level, justice is pending; most of the murders are unresolved, and young women and girls continue to disappear. Local women activists are managing the feminicide crisis and advancing their struggle for social justice as political agents, networking with other civil associations in the community and participating in civil deliberations. They have created their own spaces and positioned a women-centered agenda as part of the Movimiento Amplio de Mujeres de Ciudad Juárez (Women's Collective Movement of Ciudad Juárez). Furthermore, local women activists have established connections with other movements in Latin America, such as Red de Feminismos Comunitarios de Latinoamerica (Latin American Network of Communitarian Feminisms). But most important, many of these individuals moved from being community-based grassroots activists to becoming political activists involved in civil deliberations concerned with the construction of women-centered public policies.

For the past fifteen years, I have been documenting the process of a possible local feminist consciousness as it relates to rhetorical agency, understood as persuasive language or symbolic action.[5] During the public protests (1998–2004), I documented a preliminary account in my doctoral research.[6] Overall, I claimed that, based solely on the public protests, local activists did not have the rhetorical agency necessary to construct counterhegemonic discursive practices.[7] As I have revisited my findings, I realized that by focusing solely on the public protests, I failed to see that the feminist rhetoric surrounding the public confrontations demanding justice had unintentionally constructed an "us and them" relation of power between feminist activists who made the calls and local community-based grassroots women activists.[8] As I recall, during those years, many, if not all, local grassroots women activists did not self-identify as feminists; rather, they identified as human rights advocates. Many of these young women were already active participants in the Comunidades Eclesiales de Base (Base Ecclesial Communities; hereafter referred to as CEBs). Their long-standing knowledge related to the living conditions of women in the impoverished sectors of the community was basically ignored. They were not recognized as epistemic subjects, and their rhetorical agency was not audible or visible outside their close-knit barrios.

In this case, I privilege Verónica Corchado's and Sandra Ramírez's stories because I have witnessed their struggle to gain political recognition as speaking and epistemic subjects in Juárez. In 2012 they created their own civil society association, called Colectiva Comunidad, Arte y Equidad (Community, Art, and Equality Collective). In January 2016 Verónica Corchado was named as director of the Instituto Municipal de las Mujeres de Ciudad Juárez (Women's Municipal Institute of Ciudad Juárez),[9] and Sandra Ramírez is currently the organization's main coordinator of research and social projects. Verónica Corchado was proposed to the municipal administration by the Movimiento Amplio de Mujeres de Ciudad Juárez (Women's Collective Movement of Ciudad Juárez).[10]

Also, I wish to clarify that Verónica and Sandra are not token subalterns; they do not represent the lost voice of the Juarense female subalterns. On the contrary, I consider them organic intellectuals who are currently politically visible in the local circuits of civil deliberations. Furthermore, they are aware of the notion of rhetorical agency and how it relates to their political voice and activism—that is, their recognition as *sujetas hablantes* (speaking subjects) locally and nationally.[11] Here I emphasize Gayatri Spivak's notion of the organic intellectual. She argues that "quite often the remarkable organic intellectuals who become spokespersons for subalternity are taken as token subalterns. . . . The effort involved in those singular figures becoming intellectuals is completely undone in their positioning as 'the' subaltern. . . . The effort required for the subaltern to enter into organic intellectuality is ignored by our desire to have our cake and eat it too: that we can continue to be as we were, and yet be in touch with the speaking subaltern."[12]

In this essay, I argue that over a span of twenty years, a group of local political women activists were able to gain political recognition as speaking and epistemic subjects by crafting their rhetorical agency based on their situated knowledge as community-based grassroots activists. As part of a wider research project, I mainly use an abductive methodological approach in order to explain my participants' contextual creation of rhetorical agency.[13] I do not part from explicit theories of rhetoric or communication to analyze my data, nor am I trying to illustrate other theoretical perspectives. Nevertheless, I use theoretical underpinnings or concepts that helped me understand my research within a wider discussion related to rhetorical agency as symbolic action, connecting to issues of power and political recognition. I understand the risk of weakening my academic voice by privileging Verónica and Sandra's narratives over my interpretation, but it is a risk I decided to take in order to highlight other ways of knowing and doing.[14]

Likewise, my perspective is framed by Juarense society's multifaceted effort to form civil spaces of deliberation underlined by the moral exigency of the feminicides, within the evident complicity of the government. My discussion proceeds as follows. First, I briefly describe the discursive context of the emergence of civil deliberations, where local grassroots women activists realized that the women-centered public policy agenda had been left out, and how they began to organize and network to create women-centered civil organizations. Second, I introduce my theoretical considerations on rhetorical or discursive agency as it relates to epistemic agency, power, and gender. Third, I offer a succinct analysis of a series of conversations with Verónica and Sandra centered on their rhetorical agency construction. I center my analysis on their experience within several interlocking rhetorical spaces that, I believe, unintentionally contributed in the construction of their current political agency. I do this by writing and translating succinct excerpts of conversations (due to space limitations) where I privilege their accounts related to rhetorical and epistemic agency, power, and gender.

Emergence of Civil Deliberations

In Ciudad Juárez, violence in general was/is a social concern, but the feminicides, and the social injustice surrounding them, exposed the living conditions of the victims and their families, as well as those of large sectors of impoverished people dwelling in the outskirts of the city. Nonprofit civil society organizations, civil associations, human rights coalitions, local scholars, and others began to organize wider support to demand attention from the federal government. Local and national scholars exposed the social injustice evident in low salaries, lack of infrastructure, transportation, education, and health, among many other ailments suffered by wide sectors of the community, who mainly worked for the maquiladora industries.[15] Accordingly, the massive national migration due to the availability of jobs in the maquiladora sector had deprived the city; it had been abandoned by the state and federal government.[16]

In 2001, the Consejo Ciudadano por una Agenda Social (Citizens' Assembly for a Social Agenda) was created with the participation of more than thirty-five local nonprofit civil organizations and associations,[17] which represented a wide spectrum of Juarense civil society.[18] The main objective of these forums was to create a public policy agenda that privileged Juárez as the point of departure. Salient in this process were the voices of several grassroots women activists, notable in their participation as they engaged in a rhetorical struggle to forward a women-centered human rights agenda. Even though the feminicides were present in the local social imaginary, the organizers of the deliberation forums, all of them men, resisted the inclusion of a women-centered public policy in the Juárez Agenda: most of the participants considered the feminicides, and gender violence in general, to be causally related to poverty and social injustice. Overall, because the gender lens continued to be absent, local women activists had to continue their struggle for women's rights, but this time within civil deliberation spaces. By this time, the murders were beginning to be recognized, by local grassroots women activists, as gendered crimes. They were continually active in gender sensibilization workshops, which contributed to raising awareness of gender equality. Their understanding of human rights advocacy began to shift to a more comprehensive approach to women-centered agendas. In this sense, the gender lens offered them the language to articulate their experience as community caretakers, and in this process they understood the political limitation of being constructed solely by that label and not as political activists.

Moreover, and despite the fact that the organizers in these spaces always began by stating that all the participants (men and women) had the same opportunity to participate, in practice each one of these organizations was/ is constituted, in Lorraine Code's terms, as a "rhetorical gendered space,"[19] tacitly informed by the production of power relations that structure and limit the kinds of utterances that can be voiced within them with a reasonable expectation of uptake and "choral support."[20] And since reaching consensus was the main rhetorical strategy within most of these organizations, those who were recognized as having more political, economic, social, or cultural capital were the ones who usually ended up establishing the agenda. Nonetheless, participants (women and men) in these organizations are not naïve about it; they usually explain this process as follows: *quientienemás saliva tragamás pinole* (those who have more saliva swallow more *pinole*).[21] So, those who knew they were "democratically" excluded through consensus, in this case women grassroots activists, could either accept their subordinated inclusion or create separate spaces. They decided to create their own woman-centered spaces; in this process, some of them became political activists and constructed their own rhetorical agency.

Theoretical Considerations

Social crises, such as the feminicides in Ciudad Juárez, produce political conjunctures that are key rhetorical situations that unveil who speaks, who listens, and who is silenced in the process. Today, I understand that the exposure of a social tragedy produces multiple rhetorical situations, where contradictions become visible, and where normalization processes can be exposed and productively contested.[22] However, being publicly visible does not necessarily mean being politically recognized or respected as speaking or epistemic subjects. So, it is pertinent to explain how at a given social contingency or contradiction not everybody speaks, not everybody listens, and not everybody cares.

It is not enough to claim that certain subject positions were taken up, but it is also necessary to explain the ideological and material mechanisms that made it possible for some, and impossible for others. There is a need to open a rhetorical critical optic to expose and analyze how individuals are discursively persuaded to occupy or to reinforce certain subject positions, or to be socially constructed within positions of subordination. According to Lawrence Grossberg, "Questions of agency involve the possibilities of action as interventions into the processes by which reality is continually being transformed and power enacted. That is, in Marx's terms, the problem of agency is the problem of understanding how people make history in conditions not of their own making. Who gets to make history?"[23] Rhetorical agency encompasses the capability to act by using persuasive language or symbolic actions to be recognized as a subject; it depends on subjective actions of social and political recognition. But it also involves the capability of networking, moving, and belonging to locations of political activity and power to have a part in political decision making. In this sense, the culturally available subject positions can work both as passages and barriers because they rely on ever-changing identities subjected to processes of negotiation, appropriation, resistance, or opposition.

In these terms, Karlyn Kohrs Campbell argues that rhetorical agency is communal, social, cooperative, and participatory, but also simultaneously constituted and constrained by the material and symbolic elements of context and culture.[24] Furthermore, she asserts, "Rhetorical agency refers to the capacity to act, that is, to have the capacity to act, to have competence to speak or write in a way that will be recognized or heeded by others in the community. Such competency permits entry into ongoing cultural conversations and the sine qua non of public participation, much less resistance as a counter-public. . . . It is learned through trial and error under the guidance of a mentor that emerges ideally as the ability to respond well and appropriately to the contingencies of circumstances."[25] Notwithstanding, Campbell asserts that authors/rhetors are materially limited, linguistically constrained, historically situated subjects; at the same time, they are "inventors" in the rhetorical sense, articulators who link past and present, and find means to express those strata that connect psyche, society, and world; these forms of feeling encapsulate moments in time. In this sense, agency is invention, including, however temporary, personae, subject positions, and collectivities.[26]

As mentioned above, rhetorical agency is part of a crafting process dependent on the productivity of power and authority that are implicit in all rhetorical situations. In this sense, for deauthorized rhetors, agency is clearly related to their ability or capability to engage with the hierarchal structures of power; to enter in the circuit of political and social recognition. For those who are recognized as naturally capable of moving and speaking in diverse cultural and social milieus, rhetorical agency is embodied, based on symbolic power, on the degree of cultural, social, and economic capital with which they grow up.[27] In this sense, Pierre Bourdieu clarifies that practical linguistic competence is not limited to the capacity to produce or generate grammatical utterances, "but *also* on the capacity to make oneself heard, believed, obeyed, and so on. . . . Those who speak must insure that they are entitled to speak in the circumstances, and those who listen must recognize that those who speak are worthy of attention."[28]

If we take a closer look at the rhetorical agency formation within the daily lives of marginalized groups, Lorraine Code's concept of "rhetorical gendered spaces" gives us the theoretical and investigative depth to analyze pragmatically the moral-political implications of how knowledge is produced and circulated through rhetorical agency, as situated knowledge.[29] Here we are able to see how rhetorical agency is part of our daily negotiation, opposition, and appropriation of the strategies of hierarchal structures of power.

Lorraine Code incorporates metaphors concerned with the notion of location such as territories, mappings, and positionings where resources are unevenly available; subjectivities are variously enacted; and identities are constructed and continuously reconstructed. However, hierarchies of power and privilege always contribute to shape these processes, sometimes by creating receptive friendly environments, at other times deauthorized speakers/rhetors (low-income women) can come across oppositional or indifferent publics. She conceives of "rhetorical gendered spaces" as

fictive but not fanciful or fixed locations, whose—tacit, rarely spoken—
territorial imperatives structure and limit the kinds of utterances that can
be voiced within them with a reasonable expectation of uptake and "choral support": an expectation of being heard, understood, taken seriously
. . . daily lives, structures, and circumstances where "concrete" moral and
epistemic agents are engaged in deliberations that matter to them. . . .
It centers on the structural implications of granting and withholding
acknowledgement or recognition within complex and perplexing situations. . . . The tacit social knowledge and territorial imperatives that structure and restrict how knowledge and experiences can be voiced.[30]

Interlocking Rhetorical Gendered Spaces

In this section, I represent Verónica and Sandra's process of discursive or
rhetorical formation.[31] For reasons of limitations of length, I arranged and
analyzed their narratives according to their experience in each rhetorical
space. Their experiences were by no means linear, nor were our conversations; it was a process of going back and forth to what they remembered
and what I was able to recall from those years. This was clear during the
transcription due to redundancies and approximate dates. Departing from
the description of their account of the location or place where they were born
and raised, I analyze a series of conversation excerpts, where I follow their
narratives as these relate to their rhetorical agency.

Verónica and Sandra grew up in one of the most impoverished sectors of the city. They were in their early twenties and late teens, respectively, when the feminicides were publicly exposed. The dissemination of
the injustice surrounding the feminicides was a breaking point for them
to recognize themselves as gendered subjects—which in turn was the start
of their critical stance within several of the rhetorical spaces where they
participated. I am aware that there are many local grassroots women activists whose stories have not been heard; however, in this case, my concern
was/is solely related to the local women's discursive or rhetorical agency formation, within the context of political or public communal participation and
civil deliberation. I consider Verónica and Sandra as examples of ongoing
struggles to surpass their position as deauthorized speakers/rhetors due to
their upbringing in a low-income social position, in Lorraine Code's terms.

After their participation in the CEBs, their involvement in other spaces,
especially from 1994 to the present day, appears interlocked or overlapped

because they participated concurrently in several spaces, such as: (1) CASA Promoción Juvenil (CASA Youth Promotion); (2) Consejo Ciudadano por una Agenda Social (Citizens' Assembly for a Social Agenda); (3) Movimiento Pacto por la Cultura (Pact for Culture Movement); (4) Colectiva Comunidad, Arte y Equidad AC (Community, Art, and Equality Collective); (5) Red Mesa de Mujeres de Ciudad Juárez (Women's Table Network of Ciudad Juárez); and (6) Movimiento Amplio de Mujeres de Ciudad Juárez (Women's Collective Movement of Ciudad Juárez).

Base Ecclesial Communities

The CEBs were instituted formally in Ciudad Juárez during the mid-to-late 1980s on the premises of several Catholic churches, mostly located in low-income sectors on the west side of Ciudad Juárez. These groups were formed under the influence of the Latin American proposal of liberation theology, where the "poor" became the central actors to promote change in their barrios or neighborhoods. The presence of liberation theology in Juárez was manifested through the teaching of nuns and priests who lived in low-income Juárez neighborhoods in the late 1970s. The groups' development was centered on the rational process of "see, think, and act." Many of the local grass-roots activists, both men and women, were influenced by liberation theology as the basis for their current political engagement. This theology was an articulation between Christian theology and a Marxist socioeconomic perspective concerned with the liberation of "the poor."[32] One of the main characteristics of this movement is the construction of a profound class consciousness among those who were formed in these communities.[33] In this sense, they not only recognized themselves as "being poor," but they became aware that their marginalized position was social and political, due to the unequal distribution of resources, and not due to divine destiny. The young people took part as social promoters, and their participation was voluntary; most of them, like Verónica and Sandra, worked for the maquiladora industry.

According to Verónica, the CEBs were empowering in many ways, but they disempowered her in terms of gender. She minimizes her experience as a maquiladora worker as merely an economic necessity, but not a significant personal experience. In her words:

> I worked in the maquiladora as soon as I finished secondary school [i.e., when she was fifteen years old]. We all had to work there, we had

no other options. . . . My life, as a teenager and a young woman, was empowered by my involvement in the CEBs (1986–93). The premise of liberation theology forced me to become conscious of my surroundings; to think about how to change it. We thought about change always as a group.

I believe that the CEBs gave me a strong platform to construct my sense of security as a speaking subject [*sujeta hablante*] and the idea that we could never stop learning creative ways to convince others to be part of our communities. Speaking and listening to other young people also gave me a sense of solidarity with others by working in groups in different ministries of the church, which had extensions in the barrios. I also gained a profound knowledge of needs and desires of the low-income communities where I lived; their desires, their fears, what made them happy or sad, but also about violence related to drugs, male and female prostitution, health, and mental health, and so on.

Similarly, Sandra believes that the CEBs "saved" her. She claims that being able to get away from domestic violence and creating an alternative place of refuge and belonging gave her a sense of empowerment. She also talks about gang-related violence, territories, and the symbolic power of the CEBs to open those territories:

As I remember . . . I began to work in the maquiladora when I was about fifteen years old. There, I made a lot of friends who, like me, lived on the outskirts of the city. I was one of those young women who every Friday, after work, went out to dance in the Av. Juárez. Remember the authorities were saying that the murdered young girls were "loose" in that they were out dancing and drinking on Friday nights after work in the maquiladora? Well, I was one of them!

The place where I was born was one of the poorest and most violent places in Juárez. During the 80s and most of the 90s, the west side of city was divided by gang territories. Nobody could cross the line between territories. Like it or not, if you lived in one side you were part of the territory, especially if you were a young woman, you belonged to the territory—and also because we could not just physically fight our way in and out.

That is why I still believe that the CEBs saved me and many others; we had the opportunity for mobility within and outside those territories. Besides, I and many others had a place to belong. From there, I had the opportunity to meet and work with other people in other barrios. Almost all gang members participated in the activities promoted by the CEBs in their barrios [e.g., football and basketball games]. This interaction eventually opened up the territories.

We read and discussed the theology of liberation as it related to the "church of the poor"—in other words, to us. This gave us a strong class consciousness. It became clear to us that we were poor because of social injustice; part of an unjust system . . . but there was a point when *some of us* felt that the church was limiting our options by promoting the idea that it was our faith that moved us to work to better our barrios and for the poor, and not our will to overcome our situation.

It was because I understood why we were poor that I was unsatisfied with myself and my situation, not only economically but also emotionally. I thought education was my way out.

Verónica and Sandra's narratives show a process of self-recognition as agents as they recall how, through the CEBs, they felt empowered; they gained the ability to use persuasive language or symbolic action, by learning creative ways *to convince others* to be part of their ecclesial community. Accordingly, their acquisition of persuasive strategies through the teaching of the theology of liberation, also gave them courage and ability to transgress, physically and symbolically, their domestic realm (family), and their immediate barrio (territory), by interacting with youngsters from other barrios or gang territories. Moreover, throughout our conversation, both of them insisted on how their gaining class consciousness was influential on how they thought and act to the present day. In acquiring class consciousness, they became critical thinkers toward hierarchal relations of power. This process becomes clear when they became aware that the church was symbolically restricting their options "by promoting the idea that it was our faith that moved us to work to better our barrios and for the poor, and not our will to overcome our situation." In short, their participation in the CEBs gave then a strong platform to become aware of their capability to think, create, write, and speak—in other words, to use language persuasively, not solely in linguistic terms. Moreover, they became capable of moving and interacting with diverse persons and groups; at first, solely within low-income sectors of the west side of the city, but later with many other local civil associations.

CASA Promoción Juvenil AC

CASA, as it is known locally, has changed its name to Centro de Asesoría y Promoción Juvenil AC (Youth Promotion and Advising Center).[34] It is a non-profit civil association, which is constituted legally and formally by a board committee. The Almada family are socially recognized as the main promoters of this organization. CASA is no longer supervised (openly) by the Catholic Church, but it is characterized by the same method of liberation theology, although informed by Paulo Freire's critical pedagogy. It is widely supported by secular individuals and associations from the civil society at large. Moreover, CASA organized the Citizens' Assembly for a Social Agenda in 2001, work in which both Verónica and Sandra participated.

Verónica was one of the founders; she participated for seventeen years as a grant proposal writer, designer, social promoter, and instructor of youth programs. Sandra was hired in 1999 as an instructor in literacy and sports youth programs. In this case, I privilege Verónica's voice because, I believe, she summarizes the learning experience of most of the grassroots activists who participated in CASA, according to my conversations with other social promoters in the organization. Verónica claims:

> In CASA, I learned about critical pedagogy, which was an enriching experience for me, because for the first time I recognized myself as knower; I began to value my own knowledge. I realized that experience accounted for knowledge. But as I remember, we only used it as a pedagogic tool, not to think about our situation as women in society, like many other women did.
>
> Nevertheless, working in this association opened another world for me because CASA was part of a wider network of civil organizations, not necessarily grassroots. It received support and contributions from many other sectors in the local civil society, such as academic support from local and regional artists, intellectuals, and researchers.
>
> CASA was a wider platform of mobility, where I met, talked with, and learned from people from diverse sectors, which I had never done. I never felt intimidated to speak—even though I was in many ways disadvantaged. I received recognition for my work, my ideas, and my proposals, from people I could never had imagined. I felt that people, besides my base community, listened to me. I began to recognize that I knew things about my community they did not know and were useful to others.

In this case, Verónica emphasizes critical pedagogy as a breakthrough to recognize herself as a "knower"; she recognizes knowledge and social recognition as power. Not only that, she realizes that local grassroots activists had an exclusive, long-standing knowledge that other civil organizations did not have—specifically, a profound knowledge of the economic, health, education, and emotional needs and desires of the people who lived in low-income sectors of the city. In CASA, as social promoters, Verónica and Sandra showed they had the capability to use language persuasively through speech, writing, proposals for at-risk youth programs, and PowerPoint presentations, among other texts. But most of all, they were able to attract their audiences' attention; others were listening.

The Citizens' Assembly for a Social Agenda

According to Verónica and Sandra, the Citizens' Assembly for a Social Agenda was a threshold for their development as political activists outside their grassroots CEB activism. In the beginning they were part of the organizing process, but as employees of CASA they were not allowed to take part in the deliberations. Notwithstanding, their position within the assembly gave them the occasion to listen and speak to people from other nonprofit organizations, academic institutions, and civil associations.

They recall that the first meetings were centered on creating different discussion tables to address the abandonment of the government related to social justice and widespread violence in the community as a whole. More than thirty-five local organizations participated, plus people from local research centers and universities. Verónica explains that the issue of social justice for women was never addressed, and the organizers never accepted the urgent need to talk about gender violence, or the urgent need to create a woman-centered agenda. This was in 2001, when the public protests surrounding the feminicides were ongoing; more victims were being found.

In these terms, Sandra claims that it was clear that the organizers had a male-centered agenda. Although some of them informally agreed that the prevention of gender violence had to appear in the agenda, it was never discussed—they just ignored it. She says, "Those who had more experience in public speaking, mainly men, were the ones who geared the agenda away from a discussion of gender or gender violence. They generated a deliberation centered on the urgency of thinking on social development as the main problem in the city, without a gender lens. They did not think a gender lens was necessary, and sadly most of the local organizations, including CEBs (all headed by women), agreed."

Furthermore, Verónica explains that even though they, as CASA employees, could not take part in the discussions, they saw how several grassroots women groups organized a discussion table, known as *mesa de mujeres* (not yet a formal organization). In these first discussions, they could not get others (either men or women) to accept that there had to be a women-centered discussion table, so they became part of the social equality table in a vacuum of social injustice issues. The discussions to organize the tables took two years. Once the tables were established, in 2003, the Citizens' Assembly became a formal civil association. In 2003, the *mesa de mujeres* group abandoned the assembly. They decided instead to form Red Mesa de Mujeres de Ciudad Juárez, a civil association, coordinated—to date—by Imelda Marrufo, a local lawyer. These women had the knowledge to discuss through a gender lens, and were capable of promoting the local women's human rights agenda. They were eventually recognized as speaking subjects by other associations, including the victims' mother-centered associations. In other civil deliberations, Red Mesa de Mujeres was able to position gender violence and the feminicides as part of the Juárez Agenda.

Verónica and Sandra continued to work in CASA until Verónica was fired. Verónica says that on October 30, 2007, she was dismissed from CASA. She claims, "That was the moment when I broke from the socially constrained position as a community-based activist, I now recognized myself as a political activist." Sandra also left her job in CASA; she says, "When we left CASA we had already networked with other groups in civil society. We were no longer limited by community-based activism, we could freely form links with other sectors in the city, not under the 'protection' of the church. So, we became active participants of the Movimiento Pacto por la Cultura [Pact for Culture Movement] group for several years."

The Pact for Culture Movement was initiated by local artists and scholars, whose main agenda was centered on promoting, as a central part in de Juárez Agenda, art as a human right. They created a movement that revalued and promoted local, affordable artistic events, as well as the local production of music, painting, poetry, and theater, among many other artistic activities, throughout the city. They broke the local elitist notion of difference between high and low culture. According to Sandra:

> Through this movement we had the opportunity to travel to different cities in Mexico, mainly to Mexico City. We met a lot of people (both men

and women) dedicated to the production and teaching of many types of artistic expressions. We became aware that art was a human right! We met other women groups working in community-based art projects.

So, by the time the Citizens' Assembly finished the Juárez Agenda, both of us had recognized our social knowledge acquired through community-based grassroots activism. We had no problem speaking to others about our projects or writing grant proposals. But art as a human right became central to our political activism.

Eventually, the Pacto group dissolved, because it had to officially become a civil association to have access to resources, and most of them did not want to do that. That is when Verónica and I decided to form our own civil association: Colectiva Comunidad, Arte, y Equidad AC [Community, Art, and Equality Collective]. Our main financed projects are La Promesa, Colectivarte, and the women's writing group and book titled *Mi Vida en Juárez* [My Life in Juárez].[35]

Verónica agrees, stating:

> In general, I think our interaction as listeners and organizers in the Citizen's Assembly opens the entire new world for many of us, especially for community-based women activists. We were able to meet other women and men who were also trying to do something about gender violence, poverty, political corruption, and negligence, among many other issues.
>
> In this process, we as Colectiva Comunidad, Arte, y Equidad AC became part of the Women's Table Network of Ciudad Juárez and the Women's Collective Movement of Cd. Juárez. We realized that most of the civil organizations in Juárez were led by women. We decided to organize and become a political force. If not, our women-centered demands related to women's health, child protection, labor rights, migration, gender violence, and discrimination, among many other issues, would be constantly erased as unimportant.

Sandra talks about the need for community-based women activists to become political agents and to connect to a wider civil society. She claims, "All community-based organizations have the vision of community building, but they do not incorporate the political perspective in the sense of networking with other actors in the city. We continue to work with a community-based philosophy, but the difference is that we no longer understand community solely as barrio or neighborhood; the city is our community. Sometimes places are too small, because you do not find what you are looking for, so you move and connect with others in other places; that also offers you other ways of doing, seeing, and living."

Final Discussion

In this chapter, I sought to share the struggle for recognition as speaking and epistemic subjects of two well-known women activists in Juárez. I consider them part of a wide group of organic intellectuals in Ciudad Juárez who were formed in the CEBs during the early 1980s and 1990s and who are currently heading most of the local civil organizations. Furthermore, I have argued that in a span of twenty years, a group of local political women activists were able to gain social and political recognition as speaking and epistemic subjects by crafting their rhetorical agency based on their situated knowledge of community-based grassroots activism. Throughout this text, my main goal was to show that rhetorical agency was/is part of a crafting process always contingently and contextually changing. With this, I am not implying that the grassroots women activists acted through "free will"; they wrought their rhetorical agency within structurally constrained symbolic and material conditions. In these terms, their choices were always limited by the sociocultural context in which the discourse of gender and class circulates.[36]

In this sense, it obvious that Verónica and Sandra have developed the capability to produce persuasive texts through speech, writing, and art production, in diverse rhetorical spaces. But how did they do it in adverse social, economic, and political conditions? What did they have to negotiate in confronting class and gender structural limitations? In short, how did they become authorized speakers/rhetors? It was through a long process of learning how to craft their rhetorical agency based on the means of persuasion contextually available to and useful for them. They were able to create meaningful texts to—following Campbell's notion of "rhetors as inventors" and "agency as invention"—rearticulate their past experiences and subject position as community-based grassroots activists to the discursive circles of civil deliberation through the creation of a political personae closely related to the formation of women-centered collectivities.

As I have listened to several stories of grassroots women activists in Ciudad Juárez, besides those of Verónica and Sandra, I see a long communal story of conscious, ongoing learning and transgressing of symbolic and material constraints. In this sense, they have been resignifying their discursive or rhetorical practices, which have symbolically erased them as speaking and epistemic subjects, due mainly to social constructions of gender and class. Moreover, they have surpassed some of the material constraints, which are directly concerned with economic resources, such as basic needs, access to education, and transportation, among others.

By inviting them to recall their interactions within specific rhetorical gendered spaces, they and I were able to understand how they specifically constructed their ability to use language persuasively based on their situated knowledge. As I understand it, they crafted their current rhetorical agency through a long-standing process of mobility, networking, communal learning, and acting toward the improvement of the impoverished sectors in the city. Nevertheless, they place much importance on critical thinking in terms of being able to recognize the structures of hierarchal relations of power in order to construct their texts. They insist on consciousness raising in terms of class through the teachings of liberation theology during their participation as voluntary social promoters in the CEBs. They recognize the power of knowledge in that they—former and current grassroots, community-based activists—have knowledge concerning the needs and desires of those who live in low-income sectors of the community that others do not have. Their rhetorical agency is underlined by this knowledge.

For instance, Verónica and Sandra claim that during their participation in the Pact for Culture Movement they confirmed their idea that local art production and distribution was elitist, but they did not know that art was also a human right. They learned about the relationship between art and human rights in the Global Campus of Human Rights; art offers many other ways to express thoughts and feelings. By networking with other art production groups throughout Mexico, they understood the rhetorical or persuasive potential of art as symbolic action, besides speech and writing, to promote human rights. Based on this, they created their civil organization, the Community, Art, and Equality Collective. (The story of this collective, and the rhetorical analysis of each one of the texts and activities produced therein, are still pending.)

Moreover, similar to how Verónica and Sandra understand class consciousness, they refer to gender consciousness as an analytical way of seeing women's social, economic, and cultural circumstances. They claim that gender can only be acquired through knowledge—that is, studying and learning to better understand how and why violence and discrimination works against women, mainly "poor women." For instance, Sandra says that it helps her understand how gendered relations of power are built between

men and women, among men, and among women, based on the devalua-
tion of the feminine as less worthy. According to her, this knowledge was/is
useful to construct projects that consider women's rights, needs, and desires.
Both Verónica and Sandra claim that critical thinking, class, and gender consciousness is the basis to understand and expose the productivity of power
relations, and thereby to act accordingly to expose social injustice. Moreover,
the crafting of their rhetorical agency has always been informed by their
long-standing situated knowledge as community-based, grassroots activists,
and by their yearning to promote change and social justice for women living
in impoverished areas.

It is also necessary to say that rhetorical agency is part of their daily lives—
their daily negotiation, opposition, and appropriation of the strategies and
tactics of hierarchal structures of power. But the existence of the grassroots
activists' rhetorical agency was symbolically erased; it was politically and
publicly recognized in the contingency of the feminicides. Thereby, rhetorical agency is not something that is "owned" solely by those in power; rather,
it is contextually created. It is never not self-evident, but closely articulated by
historically situated individuals.

Overall, as a feminist scholar informed by the feminist critique of language as a social institution, I place a lot of importance on how we, as feminists, albeit unintentionally, uncritically reproduce and re-create relations of
power among women, on the basis of socially constructed notions of knowledge as it relates to subject positions of class, gender, sex, race, and others.
I recognize the potential of feminist rhetorical agency to interrupt the patriarchal structure, as it was exhibited during the public protests surrounding
the injustice of the feminicides. However, I see how it can be limiting if
we, as feminists, do not have the agency to network with grassroots activists
or have the disposition to listen and learn from them. This is why I think
there is a need to promote a self-critical feminist consciousness (including
in academia) to network with local grassroots women activists with the willingness to recognize their capability and ability to craft agency under limited
material and symbolic conditions. I also believe that the rhetorical agency
needed to be able to organize public calls in order to expose and confront the
patriarchal structure requires not only the gender lens as an argumentative
tool to expose sexism, but the spontaneous creativity and the critical edge of
a feminist consciousness.

8

THE PEACE AGREEMENT AND THE RHETORIC OF RELIGION IN THE COLOMBIAN PLEBISCITE: RELIGIOUS ACTIVISM AND DEMOCRACY

Pamela Flores and Nancy R. Gómez

In Colombia, there are 8,376,463 victims of the armed conflict; these are enough reasons to work for a country in peace.

—Juan Manuel Santos, president of Colombia (2010–18)

In every country and in every age, the priest has been hostile to liberty. He is always in alliance with the despot, abetting his abuses in return for protection to his own.

—Thomas Jefferson, letter to Horatio G. Spafford, March 17, 1814

On October 2, 2016, after four years of debate, the Colombian government invited the people to participate in a plebiscite to approve or disapprove the peace agreement between the state and the Colombian Armed Revolutionary Forces (Fuerzas Armadas Revolucionarias de Colombia; hereafter FARC). Inspired by the principle of popular sovereignty, the definition of a plebiscite according to the Constitutional Court in Colombia is "the pronouncement that the ruler asks the people about a fundamental decision for the life of the state and society."[1] The FARC is the oldest guerrilla organization in Latin America, and the armed conflict between them and the government lasted for more than fifty years, leaving millions of victims among a displaced population, assassinations, and missing persons.

Previous attempts to achieve peace with this guerrilla organization were unsuccessful, and the four years of negotiation between the government and the FARC faced the permanent opposition of the Centro Democrático Movement. This created pessimism and distrust among the population. As a consequence, even though the result had enormous importance for the future of the country, only 37 percent of the potential voters cast a ballot. This shows the deficiencies in political education in Colombia and the fact that most people did not realize what was at stake. The difference in the number of votes between the two groups was very narrow. "No" voters won with 50.23 percent of the votes, edging out the 49.76 percent who voted "Yes."[2]

However, even if the numbers were similar, the attitudes were very different. No voters were, mostly, an active religious citizenship, led by sacred beliefs and by the conviction that the agreement would destroy the nation. Different Christian churches united under one goal and created a unique body of believers to fight against evil and corruption. Consequently, winning became a sort of crusade characterized by religious emotions and supernatural fears. On the other hand, many potential Yes voters were skeptical about the real consequences of the agreement and did not feel the results would bring great changes to Colombia. For example, Sergio Fajardo, former governor of Antioquia and one of the candidates in the presidential election of 2018, affirmed that there was a lack of educational strategies about the agreement. As a result, most people were not aware of the real consequences of the peace dialogues, and many supporters of the agreement did not vote on the plebiscite.

In contrast with the apathy of many supporters, the rhetoric of religion fueled opponents, and they became the central focus during and after the campaign. Religious rhetoric has a decisive impact on political campaigns, in Colombia and throughout the Americas.[3] In this case, opponents believed that the agreement was leading Colombia to destruction; thus religious voters continued fighting even after they had won the plebiscite. The results showed that they were a powerful political force.

This chapter examines the implications of religion in a democracy, viewing as a case study the No campaign created by the opponents of the 2016 peace agreement. The chapter argues that the plebiscite's opponents used religious rhetoric to persuade voters that the agreement contradicted God's will and that its approval would lead automatically to the imposition of the so-called gender ideology.

"Gender ideology" or "ideology of gender" is a term used by some religious groups, who believe that granting equal rights to women or LGBT groups is unacceptable since it entails danger to society. It is a term created by US-based conservative Catholics,[4] and it is widely accepted by other religious groups who argue that contemporary gender theories have the potential to destroy the traditional family. For these groups, nonheterosexual conditions and practices are not *normal*, and neither women nor the LGBT community should have the same political, social, and economic rights that the Constitution grants to male citizens.[5] In the case of LGBT communities, demands such as the right to adopt children, to inherit property, to receive a pension from a spouse, or to show affection in public spaces, are inadmissible. As Judith Butler states, "Gender ideology is taken as a 'diabolical ideology' . . . because they see gender diversity as a historically contingent 'social construction' that is imposed on the divinely mandated natural distinction between the sexes. And while it is true that gender theorists generally reject the idea that gender is determined by the sex assigned at birth, the account of social construction as a willful destruction of a God-given reality misconstrues the field of gender studies and the notion of social construction in inflammatory and consequential ways."[6] From Butler's perspective, to fight "gender ideology" is simply to fight against freedom, and against the right all individuals should have to live with their given or chosen gender without discrimination and fear.

Appeals to gender ideology serve usually to justify discrimination and to maintain exclusion. In Poland, "Catholic bishops launched a campaign against gender ideology that was quickly taken up by socially conservative activists, groups, and politicians."[7] In Argentina, despite liberal regulations concerning gay marriage and transsexual surgery, the Senate defeated the law to approve voluntary abortion since "the Catholic church has an enormous influence in Latin America," according to Dr. Germán Cardoso.[8] What was new in the Colombian case was for opponents to identify the imposition of gender ideology with participation in the government of a new political party created by former the FARC members, who were not interested at all in the promotion of the rights of LGBT communities. Thus, in the Colombian context, the opponents of the agreement referred to gender ideology in the same terms accepted by all monotheist religions: as a pernicious teaching that aims to impose homosexual practices and affect heteronormative values in Colombian society.

We examine here the rhetoric of the No campaign through the model of classical sophistic rhetoric, or "the art which seeks to capture in opportune moments that which is appropriate and attempts to suggest that which is possible."[9] In particular, we argue that opponents made the false claim that the agreement's ultimate goal was to advance gender ideology and under-mine the moral values of Colombian families. Using a full range of classi-cal rhetorical devices—*apatê, pathos, kairos, prepon, dynaton*—they exploited cultural fears and relied on opportunistic timing to define the agreement as negative for the nation. As Susan Jarratt explains, for the sophists, "not only was it essential to judge the circumstances obtaining at the moment of an oration, its *kairos*, but even more essential was the orator/alien's understand-ing of the local *nomoi*: community-specific customs and laws."[10] Leaders of the No campaign were aware that movements asking for rights for the LGBT community presented a challenge to traditional religious groups, and they took advantage of that situation to create in the minds of voters the idea that the agreement would entail the imposition of gender ideology.

In the first part of the analysis, we study the construction and transmission of the narrative to create the idea that the agreement will impose gender ideol-ogy in Colombia. To achieve this aim, the No campaign used a variety of rhe-torical figures compelling religious groups to become an essential part of their cause. Politicians and pastors, as expert rhetors, knew that illusion or *apatê* is "inherent to *logos*,"[11] and they used *logos* to create a "reality" coherent with their purposes. We then discuss how religious leaders created an emotional triad (fear, anger, disgust) that led people to political activism. The use of emo-tions to achieve persuasion or *pathos* has been a traditional rhetorical strategy since the time of the sophists. As George A. Kennedy establishes, Gorgias was aware that a soul could experience a particular feeling depending on the words. In the case of the agreement, the emotional triad reinforced a previous emotional community, and the leaders took advantage of these emotions to create an army of believers. The whole community united around the need to prevent the agreement, and the campaign became an offering to God to save society from evil. This contributed to hiding the actual interests and fears regarding the agreement and prevented thinking about fundamental aspects such as the fate of the victims, the recovery of lands taken with violence from their legal owners, and the need to create a political arena where differences are accepted. Finally, we draw some conclusions on the inclusion of religion in the public sphere and the differences between ethics and religion.

Rhetoric as art means that it "does not strive for cognitive certitude, the affirmation of logic, or the articulation of universals."[12] Likewise, neo-sophistic perspectives state that "rhetoric may be viewed not as a matter of giving effec-tiveness to truth but of creating truth."[13] However, if we are inquiring about the implications of the rhetoric of religion for democracy, we are obliged to ask axiological questions even if we agree with the sophists that reality is not represented, but constructed with words or *logos*.[14] With a grounding in the sophists, this chapter embraces the contemporary interest in classical rhetoric to interrogate how reality, democracy, and participation are constructed.[15] Does this construction have an ethical responsibility? Should the rhetoric of religion have such an impact on the public sphere? Is it possible to respect human rights while considering religious beliefs untouchable and maintaining unequal relationships among groups? In short, is religion compatible with a democratic public sphere?

Gender Ideology and Communism: A Strange Couple

The topic of gender ideology became a serious issue for conservatives since President Santos appointed Gina Parody, in August 2014, as minister of education. Instead of considering her political experience, religious groups focused on the fact that Parody is a lesbian. They argued that the minister of education should be a model for students, and that a member of the LGBT community could not communicate moral values to children and young people. Due to this, the minister received constant disapproval from groups defending traditional conceptions of sexuality.

The link between norms for sexual behavior and monotheistic religions is widely studied. Monotheistic religions give precise rules to control sexual practices among believers. Erika Pluhar and colleagues, for example, demonstrate the relation between sexual practices such as premarital sexual intercourse or the use of condoms, and religious beliefs and such practices among college students.[16] Amy Adamczyk and Brittany Hayes explore the differences in extramarital sexual practices between the different major religions of the world.[17] In relation to the recognition of sexual diversity and the implementation of politics giving rights to LGBT communities, all monotheistic religious groups agree that it is unacceptable. For example, an article published by the *Economist* describes how British Muslim parents oppose the teaching of LGBT lessons in primary school to children, contradicting British public policy of respecting gender diversity.[18] The fact that religious values are deeply rooted in culture explains why political campaigns promoted to prevent radical changes in society usually take advantage of the differences between public policies and religious beliefs concerning sexual practices.[19]

Following this line of judgment, on August 2016 Parody was accused of trying to impose gender ideology in schools through a fake school primer that showed explicit homosexual images drawn by Belgian artist Tom Bouden.

The diffusion of these images through social media created a huge commotion, and conservative groups in several Colombian cities protested against the minister. As shown in the video, "What is the mess with the Ministry of Education primers,"[20] while Parody was trying to explain that the images belong to the comic created by Bouden, another primer appeared to ignite the debate. The purpose of this book, published by the Ministry of Education, UNICEF, and the United Nations Development Programme, was to comply with ruling T478 of the Constitutional Court, which ordered a revision of school regulations to ensure respect and a safe environment for all sexual orientations. The controversy was so big that the government withdrew the primers, and traditional groups imposed their views.

In September, a month before the plebiscite, Parody joined the Yes campaign. This move proved costly to advocates of the agreement, as opponents seized on her support. The presence of Parody in the campaign gave reasons to traditional religious groups to argue the existence of a bond between the agreement and the normalization of homosexuality. Street pamphlets from the No campaign appeared, stating "Colombia is in danger of falling under the control of a communist dictatorship and the imminent passage of a gender ideology."[21] The presence of the minister of education in the Yes campaign unwittingly contributed to the creation of a narrative that identified the peace agreement with the imposition of gender ideology. The attempts to clarify or argue were largely ineffective, since the agreement's opponents had found a powerful narrative to summon religious groups to fight: the idea that admitting the FARC members into mainstream society would bring the immediate imposition of nonheterosexual perspectives and practices in Colombia. Many adults that had remained indifferent during the long debate became active opponents to save their families and protect their children.

Rhetorical Resources to Create an Illusion or *Apatê*

The No campaign thus attracted voters in Christian and evangelical groups because the political opponents to the agreement transformed the political discussion into a religious issue, and convinced these groups that the approval of the agreement would destroy the traditional family's very foundations since it would impose in Colombia so-called gender ideology.

To describe the rhetorical resources used by the agreement's antagonists to attract conservative religious groups, and how they used them as essential pieces of their media campaign, we examine media discourses showing the fallacies that allowed the opponents to impose such a narrative. In the sophistic tradition, Nola Heidlebaugh points out that the notion of *apatê* might be equivalent to "trick, fraud, deceit."[22] The sophists' use of *apatê* reminds us that one function of language is to create illusions, transmit reality, and produce effects. We find similar tactics in the narrative of the opponents to the agreement.

Since the beginning of the dialogues with the FARC, the opponents repeated that the government "was delivering the country to the guerrillas."[23] On September 26, 2016, the government, the FARC, and representatives of different organizations including the victims of the conflict, met in the Caribbean city of Cartagena to sign the agreement. While the ceremony was taking place, Pastor Miguel Arrázola, leader of Ríos de Vida (Rivers of Life), a powerful religious congregation in the city, cried, "They are delivering the country to the devil."[24] The first claim (delivering the country to the guerrillas) might be a *non sequitur*, but it keeps the discussion on political grounds. Arrázola's claim not only establishes a false analogy (guerrilla equals devil) but moves the discussion to the religious arena. Taking the debate to the religious realm was one the reasons for No campaign's success. The use of rhetoric served to divert the arguments to unrelated issues (*ignoratio elenchi*), such as gender ideology, a tangential topic during the dialogues.

Although opponents used gender ideology to fight against the agreement, they did not want to be accused of promoting exclusion or violence against sexual minorities. On September 19, 2016, a journalist asked Alejandro Ordoñez, a former attorney and one of the agreement's main opponents, "Are you homophobic?" Ordoñez answered, "No. I am not homophobic. Homosexuals have rights that must be protected and respected; for example, they cannot be prosecuted due to their sexual orientation. However, they cannot have legal rights as they [supporters of gender ideology] have granted to them."[25] In other words, "Homosexuals have rights, but they do not have rights." Instead of clarifying these types of statements, antagonists of the agreement used expressions such "natural reality," "good families," and "good citizens"[26] to justify their opposition to the so-called gender ideology. In this sense, Ordoñez explained that if we have "good families" (meaning heterosexual families) we will have "good citizens," making use of *aposiopesis*, a rhetorical device in which an idea is left unsaid for empathic effect or because the conclusion is too obvious.

Conservative families believed that the agreement, with its putative support of LGBT rights, would lead to the privileging of homosexual families. Shortly, these sexual minorities would endanger the very foundations of the traditional family. Thus, in order "to have a society without corruption," Colombians must preserve families' right to educate their children in what they called a "free environment," a metaphor for a society in which Christian values prevail and there is no place for the LGBT community. Free, as opposed to enchained, may be associated with a world liberated from sin in contrast to a world immersed in evil. Pastor Arrázola summarized this idea when he stated, "Gender ideology is the spawn of Satan,"[27] an effective metaphor to terrify the audience.

Through repetition, the narrative shifted from politics to religion and from discourse to action. For example, a WhatsApp message released during the campaign warned that, according to point 82 of the General Agreement to end the armed conflict signed in Havana, gender ideology that became public policy would become a supra-constitutional norm, meaning that it would be irremovable. Consequently, before it became "irremovable," all Christian churches must act. The WhatsApp message added, "No Catholic can vote or support a candidate, nor policies that violate Christian morality. The agreement includes gender ideology. I think it is clear what a Christian and a Catholic must do."[28] Though this conclusion follows from a false premise, for religious audiences the message was clear: if you follow Christian principles, you cannot accept gender ideology. Moreover, if you do not accept gender ideology, you must work to prevent its imposition. In other words, the peace agreement must be stopped, meaning that the moral duty of citizens is to vote against it.

Although such arguments were very convincing for these religious audiences, some faith groups still maintained that they should support the agreement. To attract those groups as well and to persuade them to change their minds, religious leaders frequently used *apagoresis*, a figure of speech designed to inhibit someone from doing something, usually exaggerating the negative consequences of the action. To prevent voting in support of the agreement, they used strong words such as "destroy," "misrepresent," "purge," or "colonize" to warn that Christian families would lose control over the education of their children if gender ideology became a state policy. As Cardinal Ruben Salazar claimed, "We reject the implementation of gender ideology in education in Colombia because it is a destructive ideology; it destroys the human being, and it removes the fundamental principles of the complementary relationship between male and female."[29]

The appeal to authority or *argumentum ad verecundiam* was frequent during the campaign. Appeals to God himself were often made, making use of an authority that no one is entitled to discuss or question. For example, a few days before the plebiscite, Colombian soccer player Daniel Torres, who plays on a Spanish team, sent a message to President Santos stating that the agreement would bring no good to the nation, because "Jesus Christ is neither in the center of your government nor in the center of the negotiations."[30] In another case, a member of a Christian church posted the following: "My opinion is not mine, but the opinion of the Almighty God, so I do not aspire to be understood by those who do not love God nor have put their hope in His Son Jesus Christ. But if you are a child of God, take your Bible, ask the Holy Spirit to guide you, and with His help we will see in the Bible why saying No to this peace is what God wants."[31]

It is also important to consider that the No campaign sent a unified message directed by the Centro Democrático movement. In contrast, the Yes campaign had a variety of sources, with contradictory messages generated by diverse movements and ideologies. As *Revista Semana* explains, "While the No campaign followed in a unified way the directives of Uribismo, the Yes campaign was scattered. This is due to a political reason: while only the Centro Democrático Movement defended the No, seventeen parties and social movements defended the Yes with little unification. Cambio Radical supported Yes within certain conditions; Gustavo Petro supported Yes with a Constitutive General Assembly; Polo Democrático was supportive with opposition; and the Conservatives supported it reluctantly. Meanwhile, Green Party, Liberals and the U Party were unconditional."[32] In other words, while the supporters were divided, the message from the opponents was consistently communicated, which was a fundamental reason for the success of the No campaign.

Creating a Strong Emotional Community: The Power of *Pathos*

A second strategy used by the opponents of the agreement was to appeal to the emotions of religious voters, and the effectiveness of this approach is well known. As Barbara Rosenwein states, people who "have a common stake, interests, values, and goals" create an emotional community, which implies shared "vocabulary and ways of thinking."[33] In addition, since this "common 'discourse' has a controlling function, a disciplining function,"[34] emotional communities are frequently created to produce specific outcomes in social, political, or religious debates. Many politicians and religious leaders are well trained to take advantage of rhetorical devices to evoke emotions that lead people to specific actions.

Among the different emotions used by political or religious leaders to create emotional communities, fear is especially convenient. In the various Christian traditions, fear is good since it is "the proper response to the tumult of unwanted thoughts"; however, "unsupported by virtue, fear is a liability."[35] Consequently, fear of something can be understood as proof that the one who experiences fear is the righteous one, the virtuous. In other words, those who do not experience fear are not responding rightly to unwanted thoughts and to sinful acts. Because "fear often concerns the most immediate future,"[36] it is particularly useful for preventing unwanted results in the realm of politics.

Fear is a powerful strategy for creating a strong emotional community. An appeal to fear claims that a "specific outcome in political elections will bring in the immediate future the prevalence of a feared out-group." However, fear is not an isolated emotion, since only extreme fear is paralyzing. We experience it when we perceive the threat as undefeatable. If the threat seems controllable, on the other hand, fear is usually followed by anger, and when directed toward a group previously defined as "unwanted," it is usually accompanied by disgust. Thus this triad of emotions—fear, anger, and disgust—requires blocking the threat or undesired outcome. In the rhetoric of religion, the feeling of being on the right side strengthens this triad. In the case we are analyzing, fear, anger, and disgust were experienced as positive emotions directed to protect the most important asset of society: the family. The agreement's opponents experienced fear, anger, and disgust as positive emotions directed to protect the most important asset of society: the family. For many religious groups, the family is the basic unit of society, and to protect the nation and its citizens we must protect the family first. For many Christians, this is a central idea in the book of Genesis, since God established the family via covenants and later the nation via a new covenant.[37] Thus, what is homosexuality but the most terrifying threat to the preeminence of the traditional family, the covenants, and the nation?

It is important to remember that "implicit in the idea of a Covenant is the idea not just of obedience or disobedience to that Covenant, but also of obedience or disobedience to a rival Covenant."[38] In this case, the "rival Covenant" is the peace agreement with the FARC, which entails a turn in the political conditions of the nation. Since in the imaginary of Colombian people there is a link between family and nation founded on religious grounds, the triad of fear, anger, and disgust easily became indignation, and indignation became action. Therefore, telling the most conservative Christian followers that the approval of the peace agreement would impose the so-called gender ideology became a powerful motivation to vote No. Thus voting No became a religious duty, directed to preserve the family and the nation, instead of a political decision. The stress on the dangers of homosexuality became a rhetorical motive, a form of mystification that hid the real concerns of the agreement's opponents. Thus, while the opponents of the peace agreement were quietly discussing the political and economic implications of the treaty, Christian groups were shouting, singing, and warning people in the streets and in the media about the war they had to fight. This war, as one Christian journalist wrote, was not against the FARC or the president. It was a war against "the rulers of the darkness of this century; spiritual hosts of evil that dominate culture and collective thinking and create cultural lies such as gender ideology or communist ideology."[39] This appeal to evil as an abstract force instantiated in homosexuals and guerrillas, two very different groups that, due to the powerful rhetorical devices used by the conservative organizations, became one. Meanwhile, debates on the distribution of land, the reparations owed to peasants, the need to open investigations on the processes related to the acquisition of land, the victims of violence, all vanished behind "hosts of evil," and the different Christian groups emerged as one compact, unified, unbreakable, emotional community to prevent the agreement.

For these groups, the wrath of God won. Those opposing God had to be defeated in order to save the nation. This is why the discourse of forgiveness promoted by the government was unacceptable to these groups. The act of forgiveness is only adequate and tolerable when maintaining the social order. Otherwise, it entails chaos. In religious terms, the "kingdom of darkness" is the space of disorder, and leaving this realm requires punishment as a path toward redemption. On the opposite side, the space of "order" leads to reward, a payment received for following the covenant.[40] To forgive would have meant leading the nation into chaos.

As Kenneth Burke states, "Our ideas of the natural order can be infused by our ideas of the socio-political orders."[41] The presumed natural order is, in this case, the traditional family: mother, father, sons and/or daughters. The imposition of the so-called gender ideology, the admission that gender is a sociocultural construction, would undermine the very foundations of this order, where our deepest emotions are rooted. This way, fear of chaos, anger for the harm that could be inflicted on our loved ones, and disgust for a sinful act, all become unified.

For this reason, we suggest that the defenders of the plebiscite made a mistake when they opposed forgiveness over wrath. In this particular case, it was not possible to build an emotional community based on forgiveness since this feeling could not be associated with justice. Forgiveness, in this case, would have been the result of weakness and indulgence with sin. On the contrary, fear, anger, and disgust expressed virtue, and the righteous cannot remain impassive in the face of sin. It was the wrathful God of the Old Testament against the merciful God of the New Testament. And the former won.

The legal link between family and private property implies that undermining the family is equivalent to destroying the rules that support the nation. As conservative British philosopher Roger Scruton points out, "Home is the place where private property accumulates, and so overreaches itself, becoming transformed into something shared. . . . Here everything important is 'ours.' . . . It is for some such reason that conservatives have seen the family and private property as institutions which stand or fall together. The family has its life in the home, and the home demands property for its establishment."[42] However, there is no need to communicate this fear. There is no need to express rage for losing privileges. Keeping the discourse in the realm of religion divides the opposing groups into the virtuous and the wicked. The real oppositions disappear. In other words, if obeying God and defeating those opposed to God results in a reward, then those who commit disobedience must receive a punishment. This is why the entire No campaign previous to the plebiscite was offered as an oblation.

An Oblation . . . for What?

Leading the people into "the possible" (*dynaton*), instead of confining them to "the actual," proved to be a powerful instrument to influence the results of the plebiscite. Thus, since "the actual" was the effort made by the government to destroy the covenant Colombian people have with God, "the possible" was the result of the offerings that good people could make to God. In the book of Leviticus, the third book of the Pentateuch, there is a detailed description of the rituals and laws regarding offerings. As the book describes, there are different types of offerings, all having in common the purpose of maintaining the relationship between God and humanity. Among the various types, oblations have special meanings since they are not directed to redeem sin or guilt, but to keep the covenant with God: "And every oblation of your meat offering shall you season with salt; neither shall you suffer the salt of the covenant of your God to be lacking from your meat offering: with all your offerings you shall offer salt" (2:13). Salt is "an emblem of incorruption and purity, as well as of a perpetual covenant," stressing the validity of the pact beyond historical situations.[43]

Thus the No campaign became for the pastors and their followers an offering directed to maintain the covenant with God so that the nation does not follow into the dark. The use of political resources such as marches, manifestations, videos, and newspaper ads; the conversion of altars into political arenas; the combination of readings from the Bible with antigovernment discourses, all created a religious community that decided to transform fear, rage, and disgust into an act of love for the Creator. Thus this offering did not have the purpose of redeeming the sinners or praying for forgiveness. As an oblation, it was the kind of offering conceived as a "pleasant Smell to the Lord" (Lev. 1:19).

In the speech given by Pastor Eduardo Cañas prior to the plebiscite, he called for disobedience to the government, stating that in the Acts of the Apostles we learn that Peter and John disobeyed the orders given to them by the government because they had to obey God. While people were clapping, the pastor read, "They called them in again and commanded them not to speak or teach at all in the name of Jesus. But Peter and John replied, 'Which is right in God's eyes: to listen to you, or to him? You be the judges! As for us, we cannot help speaking about what we have seen and heard.'"[44]

Deliberately, they defined themselves as outlaws. If the Yes campaign did win, they would not have to obey. Disobedience is, in this case, a tribute to God, showing that human law falls under divine law. The timeless validity of the covenant with God cannot be ignored by the agreement, which is earthly as opposed to heavenly, and temporal as opposed to eternal. Obedience to the covenant implies a reward. This is why these groups were sure that victory would be theirs. As Pastor Cañas said a few days before the plebiscite, "I am raising an active church here in Colombia. We prayed for the family. We prayed for schools, we prayed for the primers, and that's why we marched. And it happened that the president retracted. So, now, I believe that something is going to make God as a product of this cry."[45]

Kairos, Prepon, and Dynaton: The Results of the Clamor

These religious groups thought they won because the Lord heard their clamor. Even though the margin was small, they could claim that they had attained victory. As John Poulakos states, "What compels a rhetor to speak is a sense of urgency. Under normal circumstances, that is . . . [when] things are 'under control,' there is no pressing need to speak . . . [since] ideas have their place in time."[46] Rhetorically considered, they felt that they had spoken in the right time (*kairos*), meaning that the No campaign was developed at the precise period when it was required to achieve positive results. *Kairos*, as Heidlebaugh states, implies "the rhetor must find what to say by surrendering himself to the conditions of the logos offered up by the moment."[47] These religious groups adjusted their speeches using an appropriate tone and structure at the right time.

Nevertheless, ideas must comport not only to the occasion but also to the audience. This is what the sophists called propriety or *to prepon*: the quality that makes speech adequate to a certain audience. Both notions (*kairos* and *to prepon*) are concerned with the rhetor's response; however, as Poulakos explains, the former is concerned with the when, while the latter has to do with the ways ideas are expressed. The intense clapping, the shouting, the words of approval, all these manifestations during the speeches demonstrated that the words spoken by the pastors were those the audiences expected to hear. Since appropriateness and timeliness have to do more with feelings than with prescribed rules, this shared emotion, this "active church," was easily mobilized to become a political force.

"We won, we won; no one makes fun of God," cried Pastor Arrázola.[48] He posted the video a few minutes after the government released the results of the plebiscite and, with the confidence of being on the right side, meaning from a religious standpoint to be *the righteous*, he shared that President Santos is the antichrist.[49] The confirmation of being on the right side gave these groups a new strength. This helps explain why, after the victory, they did not dissolve as a political entity. It also reveals why they were ready to negotiate with the government. Unlike the political parties that used them to prevent the agreement, their main concern was to prevent the imposition of gender ideology. Thus, during the negotiation process, they did not discuss any clause in the agreement that could open the door to the acceptance of a constitutional definition of the family different from the traditional concept. These groups were even able to force the government to omit from the agreement the expression "gender/sex," eliminating any possibility of admitting differences between these two terms, and avoiding any risk of accepting more than the two "natural" genders. As Cynthia Enloe argues, "Anything that passes for natural, inevitable, inherent, traditional, or biological has been *made* . . . the masculinized peace negotiations, the romantic marriage, the all-male Joint Chiefs of Staff."[50] However, they became so powerful after defeating the government that the idea that what we call natural or inherent is a social construction was eliminated from the discussions.

Even though religious groups were worried about gender ideology in Colombia, the truth is that the definition of "gender perspective" in the documents mainly referred to the rights of women. As the agreement stated, "Gender perspective means recognition of the equality of rights between men and women, and of the special circumstances of each one, especially of women regardless of their marital status, life cycle, and family or community relations, as a subject of rights and of special constitutional protection."[51] This is why, when conservatives had to explain how gender ideology was present in the agreement, they argued that it was included surreptitiously, and that it was their duty to read very carefully and "purge" the document, as Ordoñez expressed.[52]

To prove their arguments, the No campaign managed to find expressions that they believed reinforced gender ideology or prepared the way for the normalization of nonheterosexual behaviors in Colombian society. Since they considered their religious doctrines to be in conflict with the language of the agreement, they made sure that the rights of LGBT communities remained absent from the final document.[53]

However, the real victory was not in the changes they introduced in the documents. Their victory lies in the fact that they assured themselves chairs in the National Council for Reconciliation and Coexistence. In addition, since they are divided into four different groups (churches, religious confessions, organizations based on faith, and religious organizations), they acquired several positions in the Council to guarantee their influence on the decision.[54] In other words, they ensured that "they will actively participate in the construction of peace."[55]

Poulakos states that once rhetors know that their discourse conforms to time and audience, they move "toward the suggestion of the possible or *dynaton*."[56] He continues, "The starting point for the articulation of the possible is the ontological assumption that the main driving forces in man's life are his desires, especially the desire to be other and to be elsewhere."[57] This fact, according to Poulakos, shows a great difference between sophistic and Aristotelian rhetoric: Aristotle "privileges the world of actuality" while the sophists prefer "the world of possibility."[58] In the case of religion, the realm of possibility is always directed toward God. To be Other means to be more virtuous, and to be elsewhere means to achieve what is beyond Earth—that is to say, Heaven. The result of the clamor was to define what is *good* from a religious perspective, which to the No campaigners meant denying rights to the LGBT community and diminishing the rights of women to avoid the gender perspective.

Religion in the Political Arena: A Backlash or a Social Breakthrough?

The results of the Colombian plebiscite show how dangerous the influence of religious beliefs in political decisions may be, and how easily church leaders can take advantage of the rhetoric of religion to achieve their aims. Religious leaders are often great rhetoricians. Their discourses may, in many occasions, show love or compassion for others; however, when moving toward the possible, religious groups tend to imagine a world where many groups, usually associated with evil, are necessarily excluded, suppressed, or stigmatized.

For this reason, we cannot agree with Poulakos when he states, "To the extent that style is seen primarily as an aesthetical issue, the question of its inferiority or superiority to content, essentially an axiological question, becomes secondary."[59] On the contrary, style, "as an aesthetical issue," is a fundamental part of the content since no aesthetic is neutral. Moreover, as this particular case demonstrates, beauty cannot be present in a discourse that promotes fear, hate, and prejudice.

The strength of a public sphere lies in the capacity of citizens to debate and argue based on facts, and on the ability to modify traditions that discriminate against others. Since any religion is a set of undeniable *truths*, religious principles and ideas cannot be discussed. This is why democracy and religious principles may be incompatible. As this case study illustrates, religious rhetoric is frequently used to maintain unequal relationships among groups, and religious systems too often serve to legitimate and maintain differences instead of opening a path toward equality.

In this sense, the opponents of the agreement framed the notion of "good Colombian citizens" based on religious codes to depict LGBT communities as a hazard to the foundations of the traditional family and democracy. Consequently, in the context of the plebiscite, homosexuals were represented as a minority group with too limited a set of legal and civil rights to be involved in decision making on matters that affect the entire country. Through the "good" citizen notion, the opponents connected citizenship status with the institutionalization of heterosexual individuals.[60]

For these reasons, the growing presence of religion in the public sphere serves as a backlash to laicism. It could be considered a social breakthrough, but it is a conservative reaction against democratic principles and equality. As Génica Mazzoldi, Irina Cuesta, and Eduardo Álvarez state, "Let us not lose sight of the fact that, through unfounded arguments about the inclusion of the gender approach in the final agreement, significant results have been achieved: first, attracting mass votes for the No; and, second, opening the door to a reversal of the legal advances backed by the Constitutional Court."[61] Research published by *Revista Semana* on July 1, 2017, shows that there is a close relationship between religious beliefs and attitudes toward the peace process in Colombia. While 49 percent of atheists have a positive attitude, only 37 percent of the Catholic population and 29 percent of evangelicals think the process is good for the nation.[62]

The fact is that Colombia is not a laic state, since Article 19 of the Constitution describes the Republic of Colombia as a "state with religious freedom" and with "equality for all religions."[63] It is a country where the Constitution "guarantees the participation of (all religions) in the achievement of common good."[64] Under this constitutional principle, religious groups are entitled to worship in public and to intervene in political issues concerning their religious beliefs. This creates a constant contradiction between those who work to give rights to groups traditionally excluded and those who want to maintain marginalization due to traditional beliefs founded on unquestionable truths.

If Christian groups want to exercise their right to participate in the public sphere, they should practice solidarity with the most vulnerable citizens. During the debate, the victims—those who had directly suffered the consequences of the war, those who had lost their families and their homes—should have been at the center of the agenda. However, their voices, as well as their hope to end the conflict, remained silenced. The International Committee of the Red Cross remembered this concern on several occasions.[65] Thus, although the aim of the agreement was forgiveness and reconciliation, religious rhetoric centered the discussion on virtue against sin, truth against error, salvation against catastrophe, and redemption through punishment. This convinced voters that the approval of the agreement would represent a triumph of the forces of evil and a recognition of the power of the devil himself governing the nation and making the laws.

The use of this kind of language shows that it is almost impossible to translate secular reasons to religious motivations as well as the difficulties of constructing a public sphere where religious groups recognize that all men and women deserve the same protection from the law. Democracy requires ethical citizens. While religion implies following prescribed rules and avoiding discussions, ethics entails personal responsibility and critical thinking. The question remains open: What limits should religion have in a democratic public sphere to preserve equality and avoid discrimination?

9

PEOPLE, MEDIA, AND DEMOCRACY IN BRAZIL: DISCOURSES ABOUT LULA'S ORATORY IN THE BRAZILIAN PRESS

Carlos Piovezani

Mainstream media in Brazil have often approached the oratorical performance of political leaders based on dichotomies such as nature/culture,
body/soul, and barbarism/civilization, which have been directly or indirectly
related to other dichotomies, such as orality/writing, voice/speech, and
grammar mistake / language correction. This perspective has been developed even more extensively when the intention is to evaluate the language
performance of subjects belonging to or originating from popular classes.
There is in such a posture a certain mechanism that can be explained as follows: the oral performance of the "proletarian" in the subject's public speech
is judged by the written performance of the "bourgeois" media. This explanation, in turn, is consistent with another representation, which is strongly
anchored in the Brazilian public's imaginary: the "civilized metropolis" versus the "savage colony."[1]

The distinctions between sound (animal) and language (human) and
between orality and writing have played an important role in the construction of hierarchies and in the distribution of awards and punishments to oratorical practices in Brazilian society. The influence of these distinctions can
be observed in other areas where the conflicts between classes, races, genders, ages, and so on take place. Besides its economic, political, and social
advantages, the first element of each of these pairs enjoys the privilege of
"graphic reason," which enables them to downgrade the second elements as
no more than their lives and the sound of their voices.[2]

Unequal and conservative societies consolidate forms of disparaging the
political proposals that claim their transformation. Means of expression of

those belonging to these societies are as well the object of discrimination. With even greater reason, such means of disparagement are radicalized when it comes to attacks on public speeches that combine political proposals to defend pro-people causes and their materialization in popular means of expression. The speeches of former president Luiz Inácio Lula da Silva—commonly referred to as "Lula"—carry some traits of those discourses and material forms of expressions within themselves, which have surely been noticed by right-wing opinion leaders in the traditional Brazilian press. This chapter examines the Brazilian media's discourses about Lula's oral performances from 1989 to 2012.[3] It is widely assumed by mainstream Brazilian media that Lula carries in his speeches the Brazilian poor people's language, body, and voice. I argue that it is precisely for this reason that the media focus on and critique his speech.

Can an effective democratic regime coexist with discourses that depreciate and delegitimize popular causes and the rhetorical performances of "the people"? In order to answer this question, and taking into account the political and social context of Brazil, it will be necessary to discuss the following questions: What do the Brazilian media state about Lula's public speeches as a presidential candidate, as a president, and then as a former president? And how are those media's utterances formulated? To address these questions, this chapter is based on a rhetorical history of the discourses. This method describes linguistic forms and relates them to the historical and social conditions of discourse production in Brazil and also connects them to the ideological positions of the individuals who interact in these conditions. From this perspective, my analysis seeks to answer this question, posed in the words of Michel Foucault: "How is it that one particular statement appeared rather than another?"[4] I will analyze a range of utterances extracted from texts produced by the Brazilians' principal newspapers, *Folha de São Paulo* and *O Estado de São Paulo*, and by the their principal magazines, *Veja* and *Época*. In addition to these conservative Brazilian media outlets, I also include the progressive magazine *Carta Capital*.

Lula had a childhood and a youth lived in poverty. In his adult life, he was a worker and a trade unionist. He became visible in the Brazilian political scene in 1970, which allowed him to find his way to the National Congress. Later on, in 2002, after three defeats and facing fierce political and media opposition, he won the presidential election. These accomplishments, as well as his 80 percent approval rating at the end of his presidency, suggest a path opened by democratic movements in Brazil. However, the severe criticisms of his style and his popular performances of speech by mainstream media point to a hatred for democracy that persists in an unjust and unequal Brazilian society.

The Historical Discrimination Against Popular Speech in Brazil

As Arlette Farge states, "Always reduced to its presumed vulnerable condition and aggressed for its supposed rustic and rude accents, the people's voice is mistreated by the job market; it is diminished and considered a sign of danger." However, such a treatment is not always and necessarily performed in identical ways. Prior to its performance, there are variations that reveal both the historical assumptions made about the popular voice and a tenacious continuity of the belittlement directed at that voice. Farge adds, "The elites fear [the popular voice] and read the instant revelation of daily problems in its rhythm, intonations, and tonicities," whereas "the least well-intentioned fustigate it as they label it tactless and animalistic." Finally, since the French Revolution, "some leaders have believed that it is necessary to correct and to control it." In any case, and despite all of its changes, "popular language seems to permanently scratch the ears of the literate population."[5]

In France, before and after the eighteenth century but also at other times and places, the stigmas of deformity and violence have usually been attributed to the people's voice, whereas other equally contemptible characterizations, such as touchiness, naiveté, and ferocity, have been applied to the popular understanding of language.[6] The power and the range of these judgments are so broad and consistent that they have crossed spatial and chronological barriers, although they have surely been affected by considerable changes since ancient times, including the period of the European journey to the Americas. Moreover, the discursive construction of the vices of language, behavior, and character of the subjects belonging to a particular community or social group involves direct or indirect attribution of certain virtues to others regarded as different or strange. In this case, the converse is certainly true.

A quick analysis of what the Romans called *eloquentia popularis* contributes to the comprehension of this two-way belittling process—transferences of the illiterate speaker's distortions to the popular communities' vices, and identifications of the latter with the former—and its update in the texts about Lula's public speech produced by the Brazilian press. In Cicero's work, the expression *eloquentia popularis*, as well as its synonyms *oratio popularis, exercitatione et consuetudine dicendi populari et forensi, popularis dictio, populare dicendi genus,* and *locuti populariter,* refer to the following conception: "Those who talk to the people tend to use a particular style."[7] According to Jean-Michel David, the Ciceronian texts present two distinct oratorical qualities: "That of the words *suavis-lepidus-urbanus-elegans,* and that of the words *acer-vehemens-acerbus-asper.*"[8] After presenting these two opposite directions, David adds, "Vehement speakers are, beforehand, the *popular ones* or those who play the role of accusers," and as such make use of pathetical strategies to gain popular support. On the other hand, "elegant speakers tend to be the opponents of *popular* speakers."[9]

Popular speech is related to the aggressiveness of the speaker's language, body, and voice and to the unpleasant effect it produces with the listeners belonging to the elites:

> The *eloquentia popularis* is defined as a force, a strong energy, and an angry oratory that mobilizes what was considered anger or hatred in the speaker's gesturing when it states simple utterances in the discourse. This kind of eloquence designates the physical impressions that those discourses would trigger, as its elocution could come high-pitched, in its strongest sonorous power. Therefore, such discourses would indicate the aggressiveness of those who uttered them, but they would also provoke the irritation and the disruption experienced by those who listen to and criticize them. However, this vocabulary involves, as well, some qualities of the oratorical behavior *popularis* as *turbulentus,* and mostly, as *furor* and *audacia.* . . . In brief, the criteria used to define such style highlight the violence of the oratorical expression and gesturing as its main characteristic.[10]

The speakers of the *eloquentia popularis* were often discredited by its so-called lack of *urbanitas.* As reported by David, this concept is quite difficult to comprehend, because it is constituted by a whole range of semantic values. In any case, it referred to what was common in Rome: *urbani* designated the people from the city. However, it likewise referred to the Roman language and style, which the unfortunate non-Roman inhabitants of the peninsula were deeply lacking. Their first and main mistake was the inability to pronounce words in Latin.[11] In short, the mistakes in orality, voice, and grammar were and would continue to be objects of depreciation among members of the elite, urban, and privileged class.

In the city, there was a particularly Roman pronunciation that was formed by nuances insensible and inaccessible to those who had not been living in

Rome since their childhood. It was the accent that defined legitimate Latin. The belief was that, although they had been living in Rome for a long time, non-Romans could not assimilate all of Latin's idioms and intonations. Making one of these linguistic or prosodic mistakes then became a way to be identified as a foreigner. As David explains, this aspect became a crucial trait in the obstacles imposed on the promotion and integration of citizens, because it was simultaneously unbearable and insuperable: the sound of their voices operated the distinction.[12]

It would be a mistake to think that the stigmas of violence and deformity attributed to the language, the body, and the voice of public speech in Rome during the first century could not cross the boundaries of space and time and thus come to contemporary Brazil.[13] Indeed, the popular public discourse was invented by members of the aristocracy, yet suffered strong condemnations simply because it addresses the people. In modern and contemporary democratic eras, after the emergence and consolidation of the notion of popular sovereignty, we have witnessed the emergence of populist discourses, which simulate defenses of popular causes and oratorical performances that pretend to mimic popular speech. However, we also have witnessed the rise of groups and subjects of "the people" on the political scene. Both the simulated popular speeches and the authentic popular public speeches have been, although at different levels and by distinct means, the object of an elitist understanding of language characterized by disdain and condemnation. Therefore, it has created a regime of understanding that, by giving greater attention to the "unpleasant" means and forms of speech, makes broad room for the delegitimization of what people say—that is, of the "contents" of legitimate popular claims and complaints.

Consequently, the benefits of freedom of speech provided by the democratic state are not applied equally to all speakers of a language community, since prejudice and discrimination against popular means of expression are present in contexts frequently conceived as the most favorable spaces for dialogue and rational communication in the public sphere: democracy in ancient Greece, the republic in Rome, the Enlightenment in Europe, and so on.[14] Put differently, in the historical and, to some extent, idealized experiences involving the progress of freedom of speech, the belittlement of popular speech and popular understanding of language, and the delegitimization to which they are subjected, reflect a continuity of censorship by other means. Even the field of rhetoric itself, classified by Nietzsche as "an essentially republican art,"[15] is replete with condemnations of popular speech.[16] Based on *mutatis mutandis*, one may conclude that this is the story in Brazil during recent chapters of its history, more precisely in the period that followed the end of the civilian-military dictatorship, from 1964 to 1985. Shortly after the end of the Brazilian military regime, the president was elected indirectly by the National Congress of Brazil. Starting only in 1989 was the president chosen through a direct election.

On that occasion, Luiz Inácio Lula da Silva, who had been a factory worker, a union leader, and a congressman in the Brazilian Chamber of Deputies, became a candidate. This happened again in the elections of 1994 and 1998, when he was defeated, and in those of 2002 and 2006, when he was victorious. The period that began in 1985 is commonly called "the democratic openness," which implies the idea that the borders and prohibitions imposed on freedom of speech had been abolished. Nevertheless, it does not mean that the public sphere was ready to accept, without restriction or discrimination, the people's voice or the words of those who had presented themselves as the people's voice. As a result, the opposite happened: the national importance and visibility of someone like Lula coming from a miserable socioeconomic class—who did not possess the characteristics and the level of formal education required for the intended post—and the growing possibility he would win the elections dramatically increased the production of discriminatory discourses and attitudes.

The naturalization of those acts of discrimination gained an unprecedented reach and power as they started to be produced and broadcast by the major Brazilian media. In fact, prejudice and intolerance do not emerge spontaneously or from the intrinsic limitations of their victims. As the subsequent discourse analysis shows, persistent class conflicts and other relations of power produced within a society are materialized through ideologies. In turn, ideologies are materialized through practices in which discourse plays an important role, considering its close relation to the whole process of ideological materialization. The history of social conflicts will then be reflected in the texts they produce and, more important, will materialize in these texts in the very instant of their production.

The corpus of utterances that I present in the following sections demonstrates that, because of Lula's connection to popular classes and union positions, his oratorical performance has always been a fruitful target for derogatory and delegitimizing judgment. Discourses and actions that discredit public speeches marked by popular traits, as well as the popular understanding of those and other public speeches, go beyond the long-term history and the spatial barriers of institutional and epistemological fields and are still omnipresent in contemporary Brazil.

Language, Body, and Voice in the Media: Lula as a Candidate

In this section, I transcribe a set of utterances extracted from texts published in two of the main communication vehicles of the traditional Brazilian media, *Folha de São Paulo* and *Veja*, which are, respectively, the newspaper and the weekly magazine with the largest circulation in Brazil. These texts were formulated under similar conditions of production—namely, the context of elections for the presidency of the republic. Although Lula's oratorical performances have consistently been subject to discrimination, it is possible to observe that the discourses of depreciation of his public speech were even more intensely and extensively produced in the 1989 election. For this reason, I will limit my attention to some texts that were published in that electoral context. Before turning to the analysis of this discourse, I begin with some representative passages from a text published in *Folha de São Paulo* on November 30, 1989, that I have translated for illustration purposes:

> Lula's political advertising last night tried to contain its aggressiveness to a certain extent. It went back to attacking Fernando Collor, but it also made room for a discourse in which Lula tried to get closer to the middle class. The objective was to escape from the rhetoric of the factory gate and to calm down the voters who are frightened by the radicalism shown in the first round of the election.[17]

> As in other debates, Lula slipped on the vernacular. The candidate left some questions with no answers, as when one interviewer asked if he would coerce the opposition in case it reacted against his government. In other words, he made use of catchphrases to fustigate his opponent.[18]

> It is true that Lula is still weaker than Brizola and has only one third of Fernando Collor de Mello's electorate. However, the concrete matter at the current stage of the campaign is that the PT candidate, with his peasant beard, his Pancho Villa belly, and his verbal agreement mistakes, has got the chance, at least in principle, to occupy the official residence of the commander in chief, pompously wearing a tux and granted the constitutional right to make it happen, even though his leftist views might shock all of those who will have to treat him as the president of the republic. Scary! . . . Lula is campaigning with the appetite of those who want to get there . . . and he says, in his deep and raspy voice, that he intends to make a government that benefits the poor and harms the rich.[19]

Many people that watched the debate were amused by Lula's grammar slips. The candidate distorted some verbal tenses, replaced the adverb *menos* [less] with *menas*,[20] and even created a new expression—*a promessa de gatos e sapatos* [the promise of cats and shoes]. With a restricted vocabulary, he made use of his quick thinking and of short, colloquial and easy-to-understand sentences. . . . Lula gave a passionate speech to more than ten thousand people in front of the city hall using one of his most prominent strategies—the aggressive and popular language.[21]

Lula's oratory is repeatedly evaluated as aggressive. When this is not the case, it is defined as a fictitious attempt "to contain its aggressiveness *to a certain extent.*" Similarly, his proposals regarding the middle class are presented as attempts to bring Lula closer to this group—that is, as a strategy of social manipulation. On the other hand, in his "rhetoric of the factory gate"—an expression that clearly displays the writer's elitist judgment—"the radicalism" and the voters' "frightened" state are perceived as real and evident practices, conditions, and phenomena. The phrases determined by definite articles—"*the* objective," "*the* rhetoric of the factory gate," "*the* radicalism," and "*the* voters who are frightened" (in this last example, there is, as well, the evidence of the voters' mood, which is expressed by the adjective "frightened"—used in the reduced form of a restrictive adjective clause)—are constructs that produce the evidence found in each of those elements.

Another central opposition underlying the comments about Lula throughout his public life resides in his supposed dualistic nature. He would be a two-faced individual: he is violent and radical, expressing his cunning or his weakness, but he is also calm and polite, expressing his efforts to simulate or dissimulate what he really is with the intention to please the general public. Thus, from the perspective of the enunciator from the hegemonic media, Lula has two faces, one characterized by violence and the other by dialogue, just like a Brazilian ruined Janus of the worst kind. The media simply do not treat other Brazilian politicians in the same manner.

Lula's oratory and language are characterized as both aggressive and distorted. When the media focus on what they classify as language problems, the candidate's mistakes are described as regular occurrences: "As in other debates, Lula slipped on the vernacular." The supposed repetition of grammar mistakes in Lula's oratory is referred to with contemptuous irony, which can be observed in the use of the colloquial, suggestive, and sarcastic expression "slipped." Moreover, his performance is classified as making use of another rhetorical strategy: he leaves some questions without answers, which would reveal his precarious knowledge. It was repeatedly stated that Lula was not "prepared" for the post of president—that is, the media indirectly referred to the fact that Lula was not properly educated—and that he would use "catch-phrases" to answer other questions during the electoral debate.

If the use of such resources testifies in itself against the speaker, using them "to fustigate his opponent" becomes even more serious. It is not by chance that the enunciator asserts that one of the questions left with no answer was precisely the one that asked "if he would coerce the opposition in case it reacted against his government." In this instance, Lula's silence relates to his cunning, his radicalism, and his aggressiveness, thus producing the effect of confirming a quite known, but unconfessed, posture.

The utterances about the candidate's oratorical performance produced from the discursive position of the Brazilian traditional media tend to be even more shocking and offensive. This happens, for instance, when Lula's profile is presented by the magazine *Veja* through a clearly prejudiced and discriminatory perception of his language, his body, and his voice: "the PT candidate, with his peasant beard, his Pancho Villa belly, and his verbal agreement mistakes" and "his deep and raspy voice." In another *Veja* text, it is still affirmed by the following: "a bearded worker who speaks Portuguese wrongly and has a missing little finger in his left hand . . . although he makes use of his erroneous grammar and doesn't have the elegance."[22] The rawness and cruelty of such expressions demonstrate how *Veja* regards those who convey real or imaginary traits that connect them to popular classes, in general, and how it regards Lula, in particular.

Performances that could be taken as demonstrations of his great assets or linguistic and oratorical abilities—"he asks questions that Collor's electorate can understand," "his language is comprehended by such groups," "he made use of colloquial and easy-to-understand sentences," and "a passionate speech"[23]—as well as his presence of mind ("his quick thinking") and his sense of context, which has always been a great rhetorical matter (we might think of the ancient Greek rhetoricians and the concept of *kairos*), become signs of weakness or deception, or are considerably reduced in relation to the lengthy, aggressive criticism of what precedes or succeeds them. Besides the offensive expressions formerly mentioned, there are some others with a similar tone: "Lula's grammar slips," "his most prominent strategies—the aggressive and popular language," and "a restricted vocabulary." In other words, "passionate speech" is paraphrased by "aggressive and popular language." The same derogatory discursive device is used in each element that could be related to some euphoric value in his language performance. After all, the shadows of accusation against the two-faced subject keep haunting Lula the candidate.

The supposed evidence of Lula's aggressive speeches, his deformed language, and his dualistic nature, as well as of his nonidentification with the bourgeois habitus of voice, behavior, and clothing, is presented through vehement and sometimes offensive and hostile formulations. The hypothetical amusement that "many people" felt and the consecutive laughs motivated by "Lula's grammar slips," as well as his invented expressions, lead to the grave and harsh tone produced by the media in which they are contextually framed—"the candidate distorted some verbal tenses, replaced the adverb *menos* with *menas*"; "a restricted vocabulary"; "his most prominent strategies—the aggressive and popular language"—and by the statements already mentioned consolidated through interdiscourse, that is, in the commonly said and repeated expressions in society, many of which reflect perceptions about the deficiencies and inelegances of poor people's language and behavior.

However, prejudice and discrimination are not only made of declared aggressiveness. They can take another shape and, as such, count on the strength of certain politeness: the discursive impact of what is discreetly or humorously suggested will produce diverse effects according to their relation to different ideological fields. Hence, enunciators can create distance and social distinction between themselves and listeners without being explicitly aggressive. On the one hand, there is the enunciator's group of distinguished people; on the other, there is Lula and other subjects belonging to popular classes, with their impolite, ridiculous, and inappropriate expressions and habits. This can be observed, among others, in the following excerpt: "PT pays homage to the French Revolution and launches its sonorous motto: the 'Lulalá.' In fact, the Lulalá is becoming more and more stylish: it wears a tie, shouts *ulalá*, and his goal is a metallurgical industry. It only needs to learn the piano."[24]

Lula as President

I begin this section with a fragment published in the newspaper *O Estado de São Paulo* because it is emblematic of the ways privileged voices marginalized Lula's public speech. As this publication corresponds with Lula's election as president of Brazil, it seems that aggressive portrayals of his oratorical performances may have diminished. However, this did not alter the fact that his means of expression continued to be the target of violent attacks. This extended passage by Gilberto de Mello Kujawski is representative:

Lula's "wrong" speech is not an isolated phenomenon without consequences. His "stupid words" carry the "ordinary thinking," that in turn ends in "irrelevant acts." Language abnormalities condition the banality of thought and the irrelevance of acts of a formless government. If everything were restricted to Lula's grammar mistakes, it would be easy to forgive him. But those mistakes do not only display the rupture of academic language rules; they reveal something much more serious—the simplicity of ideas, inadequate to the complexity of government problems; and the ineffectiveness of conduct, limited to irrelevant, that is, palliative measures. Some foolhardy people will say that, as a people's representative, Lula has the right, even the obligation, to speak wrongly. That is the point where the doubt resides. Does Lula really speak the people's language? Does speaking the people's language mean speaking wrongly? . . . What does Lula do then? In order to look like a people's representative, he merely mistreats his language, omitting the s,[25] violating the syntax, forcing agreement mistakes, as if it were enough to "kindly speak the Brazilian Portuguese." In brief, Lula forges a mockery of popular language, which is quite different from both the formal language patterns and the legitimate uses of popular speech. Lula's speech degenerates into a scary Frankenstein. People also distort language, but they do it with innocence. In Lula's distorted speech, there is everything, but not innocence.[26]

This text initially highlights what is presented as its main objective, which is to establish a relationship between the critique of appearance—that is, what is said about Lula—and the critique of something considered even more serious: the president's thoughts and actions. Mello Kujawski explicitly assumes that he had been inspired by a text of Dora Kramer titled "In the Name of the Law of Least Effort," published in *O Estadão* on January 26, 2005.[27] The repetition of truisms, arguments, and prejudices in both texts derives from an absolute ideological identification with the same conservative discourse. Kramer and Kujawski state that there is a populist attitude in Lula's deliberate option to speak "wrongly," and they report a malicious effect caused by a "companionship that disqualifies language." Such an effect would convince the less-educated people that an oratory constructed by "stupid words" and that "mistreats . . . language, omitting the s, violating the syntax, forcing agreement mistakes" would be not only suitable but also rewarding.

The interpretations about the relationships between what exists and occurs within ourselves and what is revealed through our bodies and gestures, such as in our voice modulations and facial expressions, are constant and crystallized. This happens because of the restricted knowledge we have of the fact that our interpretations are intimately related to hegemonic discourses. Moreover, based on the studies of Carlo Ginzburg, it is known that this kind of articulation between the outer zone of the body and its sensitive signals—those we can see, hear, touch, and experience—and the inner zone of human feelings—our inner space that consists of what proceeds in our hearts, minds, and souls—is constantly present in different historical contexts.[28] Such a relationship between the outer and inner zones of the subject is likely to have become an anthropological matter regarding the interpretations we usually construct about one another.[29]

Supported by consolidated views of how people think and feel, the text in focus delegitimizes Lula's speech and consequently his aptitude to think reasonably and to make decisions, producing the effect that its intention is essentially to discuss his oratorical performance. Consequently, the critique could become more credible and more relevant, as it would not be difficult to guide the readers of O Estadão through a discursive process anchored in the following dichotomies: outer/inner, form/content, language/thought, acts/words, and so on. Although this motto, "Whatever is well conceived is well said," establishes the need of previous elaboration of what is uttered in public, it contributes to the idea that expressions not clearly stated relate to confused thinking, as well as the idea that language "mistakes" refer either to cognitive deficiencies or lack of complexity. This argument corroborates the view that the criticism produced by the Brazilian press is certainly directed at Lula's oratory, but it is also aimed at a more damaging and meaningful target: the plans and actions of the Workers' Party government.

In addition, the author's tone throughout the text is markedly violent. Usually associated with Lula's oratory, aggressiveness is now firmly and clearly present in Kujawski's formulations: "stupid words" relate to "ordinary thinking" and "irrelevant acts." The words chosen to produce this offensive belittlement of someone's oratorical performance leave no doubts about the author's intent. Here, the strength of prejudice plays a decisive role, because the popular traits of Lula's oratory are classified with regard to a hegemonic conception of language—that is, they are presented as mistakes. This supposed evidence, in its turn, aims at producing the effect that the president's thoughts and actions are similarly distorted, and that his truisms and irrelevances are not innocuous. In other words, the bad language and behavioral examples given by Lula are related to equally or even more damaging consequences in his governmental decisions and actions.

Kujawski suggests that the popular characteristics of Lula's speech would be a trick or mark of his populism, or even a simulation of the popular condition that intends to achieve personal gain. Moreover, in both Kujawski's and Kramer's texts, we can easily identify, together with the emphasis and violence of their formulations, a considerable degree of irony in their judgments of Lula's oratorical performance and character: "a ruthless populism," "a partnership that disqualifies the language," "violating Portuguese, without saving almost any sentences," "language abnormalities," "the banality of thought," "the irrelevance of acts of a formless government," "ridiculous," "Lula forges a mockery of popular language," "Lula's speech degenerates into a scary Frankenstein," and "in Lula's distorted speech, there is everything, but not innocence."

Finally, it is necessary to highlight an equally perverse complacence in this conservative and intolerant discourse. This is certainly a true attitude of the elites and the great Brazilian media, as it reflects what Michel de Certeau calls the "beauty of the dead."[30] As Kujawski continues, "I know that popular language, in its informality, has irreplaceable flavors and is vividly expressive, either in the population's plebeian version or in the *caipira* [rural] or the *sertanejo* [northeast] versions."[31] The popular actions and demonstrations are considered beautiful in cases where they appear to be inoffensive. Such a beauty will continue to be recognized while those actions and demonstrations are restricted to particular contexts of entertainment. According to an elitist and folkloric conception, the people's voice might be graceful and enchanting if it is embalmed, exotic, and innocuous—that is, if it is properly static or exclusively cheerful along the borders imposed by entertaining spectacles. In the public sphere of national politics, such a perspective seeks to prevent people from speaking, even if their expression is roughly materialized in indirect ways. It gains visibility through the voice of a representative that no longer belongs to the dominated group of plebeians and proletarians, but that still carries in their speech the marks of a social class that continues and has never stopped being a fruitful target.

Lula as Former President

Lula was the president of Brazil from January 2003 to December 2006, and again from January 2007 to December 2010. In October 2011, he announced that he had throat cancer. After the release of this news, many texts were published about the risks this disease presented to his voice and, by extension, to his role in the Brazilian public life. Lula's illness and its possible consequences were topics for conversation in several areas and social groups. The threats to his voice were the subject of daily conversations, messages on social networks on the Internet, debates among health professionals, and comments from politics, news, and media reports.[32] After the announcement of his cure, the subject did not immediately leave the journalistic field. It was in this context that the following text was published, in which the use and characteristics of Lula's language, body, and voice in his public speech were still subject to aggressive attacks:

> The president who has committed the most blunders in the history of Brazil usually stole the show when he opened his mouth. His raspy voice with Portuguese mistakes and his soccer metaphors and popular jokes connected him to the masses, as he played the acclaimed union leader or the peace-and-love Lulinha. Brazil has had other lively speakers who used to express themselves vigorously in writing as well. Lula does not. He performs an oral leadership. Most Brazilians do not master the written word. In such a country, voice is overrated as a symbolic capital. Lula has always spoken too much.[33]

The partial recognition of Lula's eloquence and communicative abilities—"he usually stole the show when he opened his mouth"—follows what is presented as a true, serious, and evident fact: "The president who has committed the most blunders in the history of Brazil." The ex-president's popularity, which is intimately connected to his oratorical talents, is also recognized in order to be more effectively questioned and delegitimized. This happens because his "connection to the mass" is produced through a voice and a speech full of mistakes and distortions, an assumption that resumes all prejudices commonly related to the mass: "his raspy voice with Portuguese mistakes and his soccer metaphors and popular jokes." As usual, Lula's duplicity and vehement performance, which would be seen as typical traits of the "enthusiastic speakers" of *eloquentia popularis*, are omnipresent and highlighted with an open and aggressive irony: "as he played the acclaimed union leader or the peace-and-love Lulinha." In sum, Lula's rhetorical competence is reduced to a series of language distortions that question, delegitimize, and transform it into the opposite of what any legitimate aptitude is supposed to be.

Furthermore, it is necessary to explain that both language models play their role in the fundamental opposition that we inherited from both old and modern conceptions, found in the classic Greek philosophy and in the Enlightenment: on the one side, we can see writing, letters and the literate, reading, the world of ideas, and the autonomy of soul and reason; on the other side, we can see orality, the voice, and the illiterate, speaking and listening, the sensitive world, the imprisonment of the body, and emotive manipulation. The relationship between the supposedly exclusive oral leadership and the masses that can merely count on its deficient understanding could not be declared in a more explicit, prejudiced, and intolerant manner. In order to do so, the mechanism used promotes an invariable movement from appearance to essence, from expressions to content, and so forth. Thus the "blunders" are perceived as such because of the evidence constructed around the "raspy voice" and the speech full of "Portuguese mistakes and his soccer metaphors and popular jokes." Regarding their connection to blunders, mistakes, ignorance, and cheapness, the masses could not be more attracted by elements other than those that impregnate its supposed essence. As I have pointed out, concerning the public sphere and the national political scenario, any word that comes from the people or from one of its representatives—who carries popular traits in his body and voice—is considered an intemperance: "Lula has always spoken too much."

Lula in the Progressive Media

Despite the changes in his social place and condition, the judgments that depreciated and delegitimized the things Lula said and his way of saying them remained constant. The vehicles of the Brazilian conservative media usually undertook the depreciations and delegitimizations of what had been or was said by Lula through offenses attributed to his means of expression. Without great variations, this has occurred at least since he was a candidate for the presidency of the republic, continued to occur during his presidential term, and remained after the end of his presidency, even at particularly sensitive moments, such as the moment of his illness. Would these critiques of Lula's public speech occur in progressive press texts in Brazil on the eve of the twenty-first century? In order to try to answer that question, once again I reproduce an excerpt published in a magazine in Brazil—*Carta Capital*, which is considered progressive—and then analyze the text. The context is once again electoral, as this was the second time that Lula was one of the main candidates for the Brazilian presidency:

There is no way to classify as elegant a man who projects his belly while sitting to the point of nearly removing his shirt buttons. Lula's opponents do not consider his manners and language mistakes as a handicap. They actually fear looking like dandies. . . . If your anti-Lula character follows Fernando Henrique's manners, you understand that an anti-Lula subject must speak, present himself, and behave in a better way than the PT candidate does. He does not perform the standard behavior expected from a presidential candidate: he is so excessively frank as to eat a *buchada de bode* [goat intestine] and say that he liked it, his speech is more intelligent than astute, and he puts all *s*'s and *r*'s in the right places. These personal virtues would be regarded, throughout the campaign, as weaknesses. However, the surveys have been demonstrating an opposite phenomenon. There are people who even call him gorgeous.[34]

As I have stated, the prejudice against popular speech and popular understanding of public speech crosses the barriers of time, space, and knowledge. Its strength and range can even extend to different ideological positions. If it is evident that this prejudice is not performed here in the same frequency and intensity as it is in the conservative media, it is also true that the contempt for certain traits of popular speech is not completely absent in this example of progressive discourse. This is exactly what we can perceive in this extract from *Carta Capital*.

In fact, the target of the journalist is the invention of an ideal and idealized opponent to beat Lula in all presidential elections. Despite the explicit kindness and support devoted to Lula, his body, language, and other traits frequently associated with popular manners are clearly diminished: "there is no way to classify as elegant a man who projects his belly while sitting to the point of nearly removing his shirt buttons"; "his language mistakes"; "an anti-Lula subject must speak, present himself, and behave in a better way than the PT candidate does." In addition, the author of the text seems not to support or even to refuse the mechanism of outer/inner, form/content, and so on—Fernando Henrique Cardoso "puts all *s*'s and *r*'s in the right places," but this is not a reason for him to be considered better than Lula in that context. He is the anti-Lula: although he "speaks, presents himself and behaves in a better way than the PT candidate does," he must be regarded as the candidate who is not engaged with popular demands, progressive ideas, and so on. However, it does not eliminate the fact that Lula's manners and habits continue to be defined as language mistakes and inelegant performances.

The effects of humor and softness, the attenuation of prejudice, and the distance of the author of the text in relation to what is uttered, which are produced both by lexical choices and by delocutive enunciations, do not prevent the spread and maintenance of the discrimination against popular forms, habits, and means of expression. To a certain extent, the opposite might happen as these effects deliberately enhance the repetition of prejudice. At this point, there is no innocence or remorse concerning the discrimination produced, because the disdain for the people's traits, the hidden interests, and the hostility of ideological opponents are considerably more accepted than they used to be. In any case, in the progressive press, the prejudices are much rarer and much more attenuated than those found in the vehicles of the conservative media.

Final Remarks

It is a sure thing that Lula's public speech has always been related to linguistic ineptitude. Sometimes, it has been even connected to a nearly absolute linguistic inability, as if his speech was no more than a sum of mistakes ("violating Portuguese, without saving almost any sentences"; "language abnormalities") and, as such, could be defined with regards to his crude means of expression. The judgmental classifications of Lula's oratorical performance belittle not only his language but also his body and voice, as these elements become targets of the media's disdain and of its explicit and degrading attacks. Furthermore, it is repeatedly stated that Lula's language is aggressive; or, when he deviates from being emphatic or assertive and chooses to speak more softly, making room for dialogue, that Lula is a two-faced subject. From a conservative ideological standpoint, the enunciators of the traditional media label "radical" the speaker who speaks for better life conditions on behalf of the working and popular classes, and they call "two-faced" the speaker who seeks to negotiate and to cool down the resistances to his issues.

Except for Lula's objective to please the whole Brazilian population—workers and businessmen, poor, rich, and middle-class people—the other characteristics attributed to his oratorical performances tend to point to the same direction: the diminishment of human speech to the condition of a sound of nature; the reduction of the *logos* to the *phoné*; the reduction of the *vox*—namely, the language directed and devoted to the Other —to *rumor* and to a sonorous and bestial confusion. Thus, the strength of Lula's speech is considerably weakened for a substantial part of the population—that is to say, not only those belonging to the elite and middle classes, which are mainly the readers of the press analyzed in this study, but also those belonging to the popular classes. All of them share the dominant linguistic imaginary, according to which Lula's speech is full of errors. Such an imaginary is based on a contradiction that it deletes: economically, socially, and culturally underprivileged people usually see their own speech as more distant from the standard language, while those belonging to privileged classes of society usually believe that their own speech corresponds completely to a supposed linguistic ideal.[35] Because the Brazilian press directly draws the attention of its readers to Lula's "incorrect" speech and, in doing this, helps indirectly to draw the attention of those who are not its readers to Lula's speech as well, it weakens the importance of what he says and consequently the policies his government establishes.

If such propositions have been targeted by the reactionary rhetoric,[36] it could be presumed that others marked by traits connected to poor people, which aim to promote some transformative power and some views detached from folkloric ideas, are more likely to be addressed. The passage for a few centuries and the crossing of an ocean transformed, but did not eliminate, the elitist offensives. With regard to the discrimination of the Brazilian media against Lula's oratorical performance, it is possible to assert that we are not far from the resources and strategies of belittlement of the *eloquentia popularis* as they were used toward the end of the Roman republic. This disparagement of speeches with popular echoes and roughly directed to ordinary people has been produced by the accusation of its lack of *urbanitas* at least from Cicero's time onward.

However, we cannot state that nothing has changed between old Rome and contemporary Brazil, a period that comprises the French, American, and Russian revolutions and some political and social achievements resulting from uncountable and painful struggles in the Brazilian context. Nevertheless, the stigmas associated with popular speech and its speakers demonstrate the continued marginalization of the nonelite class. Moreover, the attribution of these stigmas has strength and reach from other long-term ideas that, as stated above, are sufficiently powerful to cross barriers of space and time. It does not mean, though, that the discrimination against people's voice and/or representatives, especially against those who carry popular traits in their own performances and behaviors, and the discrimination against the popular understanding of public speech, are identical in their forms and content.

Among the changes in the discourses about popular speech and popular understanding from the second part of the nineteenth century onward, it is required to highlight the emergence of a new place for the people's voice and perception, as well as a certain tendency to dissimulate or to moderate the prejudices directed toward ordinary people through more implied formulations. This general tendency, however, does not prevent the reiteration of all kinds of discrimination (implicit and explicit ones). In opposition, it makes room for important changes regarding the effects produced by more violent acts of discrimination. Otherwise, the possibility for reactions like this one—"The language used by Luiz Inácio Lula da Silva is the people's language, the one people understand,"[37] which still does not have a significant reach—would be practically null. On the other hand, the judgments of popular language, in general, and of people's public demonstrations, in particular, continue to be hegemonic, which can also be observed in the judgments of Lula's speech.[38]

Based on a series of texts produced by the Brazilian traditional media, one might observe that the popular traits in the speeches of the most popular politicians in Brazilian history have always been targets of depreciation and harsh judgment. Speculation that extremely unequal societies multiply and consolidate mechanisms to silence and reduce discourses that argue for their transformation and the means of expression of those they diminish and exclude is confirmed both by our long-term history and by recent circumstances in Brazil. These strategies are spread and intensified through some conservative practices when they focus on public speeches, practices in which the discourses rooted in popular claims are materialized in expressive forms and resources used by subjects originating from poor and marginalized communities.

It is evident that the obstacles imposed on Brazil's development have been greatly influenced by the power of conservative ideologies, which are managed and empowered by their elites and upper middle classes. These ideologies comprise discourses and practices, and are paradoxically disseminated among those who are their main targets and the most affected by this dissemination. All progressive social programs proposed or implemented in Brazil will be immediately targeted by such ideologies and by their discourses and practices, because those programs directly point to their deconstruction. This is what happens, as well, to popular speech and popular means of expression, which are profoundly marginalized.

One of the darkest effects of the condemnations of Lula's oratorical performance is precisely the discrimination and delegitimization of popular voices and popular understandings. Therefore, politics and psychology might become inextricably connected: the certainty of a positive judgment of one's language performance produces a confident subject; negative judgments, on the other hand, which follow timid and unconfident behaviors, often produce silence and the absence of or at least a substantial inability for liberating citizen projects. In electing the privileged and diminishing the marginalized, by means of discriminations and delegitimizations rooted in popular expressions, the media's intention is to condemn the voice by which people express themselves and make their imperative claims and struggles visible.

10

THE FAREWELL SPEECH OF
CRISTINA FERNÁNDEZ DE KIRCHNER

Alejandra Vitale

The political discourse of former Argentine president Cristina Fernández de Kirchner has aroused great interest among researchers in Argentina.[1] Well known for her controversial oratory and her prodigious memory (she never reads any of her speeches), Fernández de Kirchner has been an innovator in the genres of presidential rhetoric. She has exploited established genres, such as the presidential address to the nation, in new ways and has introduced new ones, such as her "courtyard speeches" and her farewell speech.[2]

On December 9, 2015, a day before Argentina's new president-elect Mauricio Macri took office as leader of a center-right coalition called "Cambiemos,"[3] Cristina Fernández de Kirchner spoke to a crowd of supporters in Plaza de Mayo in her last public address as president. The speech can be considered within the genre of the farewell discourse, and unlike the United States where valedictory speeches are commonplace, it was without precedent in Argentina.[4] In fact, never before in Argentina had an outgoing president given a public speech in which explicit reference was made to the end of his or her presidency and the arrival of a new administration.

Bearing this fact in mind, this chapter examines the ways in which Cristina Fernández de Kirchner's ethos is constructed in her farewell address. It starts from the argument that her speech is primarily intended to prepare the audience for her return once the four years of Mauricio Macri's presidency have run their course, rather than to praise democracy and the popular vote in the tradition of the presidential farewell in the United States.[5] Indeed, her speech does not give priority to the epideictic dimension of praising shared values as a rite of passage confirming democratic continuity. Instead, it adopts a polemical attitude toward Macri and his followers, a confrontational position that was characteristic of her previous political oratory.[6] By exalting the alleged achievements of the Kirchners' twelve years in government (her husband, Néstor Kirchner, who died in 2010, was president for one period between 2003 and 2007, and she herself was president for two consecutive four-year terms from 2007 to 2015), and by implying at the same time that Macri would betray the ordinary citizens who had elected him, she thus presents herself implicitly as someone who will have to be president again in order to repair the mistakes Macri will inevitably make.

This chapter begins, then, by summarizing the political context in Argentina. Next, it presents the main authors and methods used for studying political discourse in Argentina. After that, it analyzes Fernández de Kirchner's farewell address before presenting some conclusions.

Kirchnerism and the Shift to the Right with Macri's Government

Kirchnerismo is the political movement founded by Néstor Kirchner and carried forward by Cristina Fernández de Kirchner. During the first years of the new millennium, Argentina experienced significant socioeconomic turmoil. The legislative elections of October 2001 made clear that the country was also entering an acute crisis of political representation. Forty-four percent of the electorate submitted a null ballot, a protest ballot, or failed to return a ballot at all, making for an anomalously large group of nonvoters in this country where suffrage is compulsory.[7]

At that time, Fernando de la Rúa of the Alliance for Work, Justice and Education (ALIANZA) had held the Argentine presidency for two years of a four-year term.[8] The recession, unemployment, and impoverishment of the population; the effects of neoliberal policies inherited from the administration of President Carlos Menem during the 1990s; the ALIANZA government's own failings; and the discontent of citizens with the political class as a whole crystallized in late December 2001 in *cacerolazos* (mass displays of pot-banging), supermarket robberies, looting, and popular assemblies under the slogan *¡Que se vayan todos!* (Throw them all out!).

In the face of this turmoil, Fernando de la Rúa resigned on December 20, 2001, and the executive office underwent a period of significant instability until the elections of 2003 brought Néstor Kirchner to power under the banner of the Front for Victory Party.[9] Kirchner's ascension led to the weakening of political parties across Argentina, deinstitutionalization, and the emergence of a centralized leadership that did not consult with peers—a strong-willed, populist, "cult of personality" model with Néstor Kirchner at its head.[10]

Kirchner established his ability to govern based on an "image grounded in popular representation that was sustained through a direct relationship with the masses" at a time when the existing party structures displayed a markedly fluid state.[11] His tenure was marked positively by the restructuring of external debt, a growing economy, a reduction of homelessness and poverty, and the recomposition of a Supreme Court discredited since the government of Carlos Menem. Moreover, the Kirchner administration repealed the Obediencia Debida and Punto Final laws, which allowed legal cases against participants in the National Reorganization Process (PRN, better known in the United States as the "Dirty War").[12]

Cristina Fernández de Kirchner took office as president in 2007 after Néstor Kirchner's four-year term. Although he still maintained a high popularity rating and could aspire to a second term, his wife was the candidate. This was interpreted by Aboy Carlés as a "scheme of alternate succession between spouses" that could ensure their hold on the presidential chair indefinitely so long as they could muster enough votes to ensure their reelection.[13] But the death of Néstor Kirchner in 2010 thwarted the couple's plan.

As Marisella Svampa explains,[14] Fernández de Kirchner's government was marked by a conflict with Argentina's farmers in 2008, almost as soon as she took office. The confrontation originated in an increase in taxes on agricultural exports, which rose from 35 to 44 percent. For the first time ever, the farmers' revolt united large organizations (including the traditional Sociedad Rural Argentina, which represents the biggest landowners) and representatives of small and medium producers (Federación Agraria Argentina). The latter set up roadblocks, agricultural strikes, and lockouts, which left the country on the brink of shortages for a hundred days. In this connection, the government achieved the active support of a broad group of progressive intellectuals and academics called Carta Abierta (Open Letter), who interpreted the farmers' strike as an attempt to overthrow the government and came out "in defense of the country's institutions."

The government recovered the political initiative in 2009 with the Audiovisual Communication Services Law, which brought it into direct confrontation with the multimedia group Clarín (which had benefited from Kirchner's policies before the farmers' strike). The new law aroused enthusiastic support among many journalists, artists, and teachers, who until then had tacitly supported the Kirchners—or at least had not opposed them.

As has happened at other periods in Argentina's history, polarization around an isolated conflict developed into a broader political divide in the country. At the same time, the Kirchners widened their political base to include young people. Small youth organizations such as La Cámpora (founded by Máximo Kirchner, Néstor and Cristina Kirchner's son) grew rapidly. The governments of Cristina Fernández de Kirchner undertook a series of active nationwide policies, including the new Audiovisual Communication Services Law, the Equal Marriage Law (which allows same sex marriages), the nationalization of the social security system, and the Universal Child Allowance.[15]

Gabriel Vommaro describes the triumph of the Cambiemos (Let's Change) alliance in the 2015 presidential elections that brought Mauricio Macri to power as a shift from a center-left to a center-right government via the ballot box.[16] For Sergio Morresi, Macri's government is pro-market and right-wing, but with a self-avowed commitment to democracy and a post-ideological position "beyond left and right" and in favor of efficiency.[17]

Political Discourse Analysis in Argentina

The analysis of political discourse in Argentina frequently focuses on the rhetorical notion of ethos, as revisited by Dominique Maingueneau and Ruth Amossy.[18] For Maingueneau, the ethos of both written and oral texts includes a tone and a character, seen as a bundle of stereotyped psychological traits.

In relation to the way the speaker's image is constructed discursively, Maingueneau lays the way open to a semiological approach to ethos. Indeed, his proposals suggest a semiological-discursive construction of ethos. This includes a verbal and a nonverbal component. The verbal component is made up of linguistic elements and paralinguistic elements; the nonverbal component consists of kinesics, proxemics, and dress. This semiological approach conceives of ethos as a dynamic structure that results from interactions between and among diverse semiotic systems. Amossy's approach to analyzing ethos, or the images speakers construct in their discourse, is also important and leads us to consider the enunciative dimension, especially the use of "we" and the register used in public speaking.

Significantly, studies on political discourse recover the notion of pathos, which is intertwined with that of ethos. Thus Christian Plantin distinguishes between "spoken" pathos, where speakers explicitly express their emotions, and "manifested" pathos, where emotions are aroused by diverse resources, such as rhetorical figures and the use of words from the lexical field of emotions.[19] However, to explore the use of emotions in political discourse, we must return to Amossy, who incorporates traditional rhetorical figures into discourse analysis, especially those related to repetition and to the question of how emotions are aroused.

Another key author in Argentina for analyzing political discourse is Eliseo Verón. Verón argues that politicians design their discourse for a heterogeneous audience consisting of three different kinds of interlocutors: the pro-addressee, the para-addressee, and the counter-addressee. The pro-addressee is the partisan voter who shares the same beliefs as the speaker; the para-addressee responds to the indecisive voter in parliamentary democracies, the voter who must be persuaded and to whom the argument is directed; and the counter-addressee is a supporter of the speaker's opponent with whom the speaker polemicizes.[20]

Ethos and Conflict

Karlyn Kohrs Campbell and Kathleen Hall Jamieson argue that without a farewell speech, the transition to a new government would become abrupt.[21] Accordingly, this genre of presidential rhetoric symbolizes the closure and end of a period of government. This symbolic process also helps citizens adjust to the new role and status of their former leader. In this sense, the fact that farewell speeches are delivered at some time between the election and the inauguration of a new incoming president is of fundamental importance. This time interval is characterized by the fact that the president retains authority but is less likely to be motivated by party political considerations than by the national interest. The unusual way in which Cristina Fernández de Kirchner chose to hand over the presidency, however, neutralized the symbolic function of the traditional farewell speech as developed in the United States. In fact, partisan passions played a leading role in her address. Using an integrated "rhetorical arsenal," different rhetorical figures will be analyzed, such as the pronoun "we" and an enthymeme, among others. These political passions were linked to a confrontational ethos that presented Fernández de Kirchner as a victim of the new government itself.

However, increased antagonism toward a political adversary does not necessarily represent a risk for the democratic system in Argentina. Comparing the Chilean and Argentine electorates, Elizabet Gerber points out that

Argentineans are very critical, argue a lot, and expect others to do the same.[22] In this way, democracy in Argentina is marked by a political culture in which controversy is not frowned upon.

As José Natanson explains, Kirchnerism presented itself from the very beginning as a tough form of opposition to Macri's government.[23] In this way, it differed from other sectors of Peronism, such as Sergio Massa's Frente Renovador, which were more moderate. After the election, the Peronist movement was severely weakened by its defeat. Indeed, deep divisions began to show almost as soon as Macri's victory was announced. For the first time in thirty years, Peronism had simultaneously lost control of the national government, the province of Buenos Aires, and the Autonomous City of Buenos Aires—that is to say, the three most important administrations in Argentina, with all this implied in terms of budget, organizational resources, officialdom, and so on. However, in addition, it was defeated in provinces it had governed for two decades, such as Jujuy; it lost half a dozen municipalities in the Metropolitan Area of Buenos Aires, each with population as large as some provinces, and it lost in all the large towns and cities.

Cristina Fernández de Kirchner's hardline opposition to Mauricio Macri's government, already present in her farewell speech, was ratified in statements by the former Supreme Court justice and current member of the Inter-American Court of Human Rights, Eugenio Zaffaroni, a man loyal to the Kirchners. Zaffaroni said in a radio interview, "I would like Macri's government gone as soon as possible."[24] He also stated publicly, "I do not want it to happen, but something similar to 2001 could happen." In a country like Argentina, where several presidents have been forced to leave office early because of acute economic and political crises, Zaffaroni's words were interpreted as "encouraging crime" and an "incitement to collective violence," giving rise to a legal complaint against him.[25]

In Argentina, the transfer of power occurs in an inauguration ceremony in which the outgoing president hands the president-elect the attributes of power—the presidential sash and the baton of command. A confrontation developed between Fernández de Kirchner and the president-elect, Mauricio Macri, regarding the place where the transfer should take place. Since Argentina's return to democracy in 1983 after the last military dictatorship (1976–83), presidents-elect had been sworn in before the Legislative Assembly gathered in the National Congress and then driven to the Government House (known as Casa Rosada) to receive the attributes of power. However, Néstor Kirchner changed this custom when he became president in 2003: he received the presidential sash and baton in the National Congress after taking the oath there. Fernández de Kirchner repeated this arrangement introduced by her husband in both her presidential terms, and her intention was to hand over the presidential attributes to Mauricio Macri in the Congress. But the outgoing president's political party had a majority in the Congress and Macri suspected that militants were planning to disrupt the ceremony with heckling and slogan-chanting. He wanted her to hold the inauguration ceremony at the Casa Rosada. When she refused, Macri filed an appeal to judicial power, which was accepted. Rumors had spread that Kirchnerist organizations would harass and insult Macri supporters during the ceremony, and it was unclear who would have command over the police during the event. Judge Maria Servini de Cubría granted an injunction to Macri and his running mate, Gabriela Michetti, stating that Fernández de Kirchner's term of office ended at midnight on December 10. The provisional president of the Senate, who belonged to the same party as Macri, assumed the presidency for twelve hours and gave him the presidential sash and baton at the Government House.

Standing on a stage set up in front of the Casa Rosada and facing a crowd of supporters and sympathizers, Fernández de Kirchner began her farewell address at 8:00 p.m. on December 9. Her clothes had a clearly symbolic meaning. In fact, she wore a close-fitting white dress trimmed with lace and transparencies, the same color and style as the dress she wore for her first inaugural speech in 2007.[26] In this way, her farewell to the presidency hinted at the beginning of her first term in office and, perhaps, suggested a new beginning. Moreover, white is the traditional color of bridal dresses in Argentina and thus a symbol of womanliness, a quality that Fernández de Kirchner exploited in her fight with Macri over where she would hand over the presidential sash and baton. Referring to a telephone conversation with Macri, Fernández de Kirchner claimed he had shouted at her and "the person at the other end of the line sounded quite different from the way he comes across in the media and even the person I've had conversations with, so much so that at one point I had to remind him that beyond our offices, he is a man and I am a woman, and I did not deserve to be treated as I was."[27]

Fernández de Kirchner's farewell speech refers very critically to the judge's ruling that her presidency must end at midnight on December 10. This can be seen very clearly in the rhetorical use she makes of an analogy based on the pumpkin motif from the popular tale "Cinderella": "Look, I cannot talk much because at twelve I will turn into a pumpkin, so don't make me talk a lot. At zero hours," and "That's why and to finish . . . because they are turning me into a pumpkin, seriously."[28]

The explanation "seriously" expresses an irony that seeks to achieve a humorous effect. This attempt at humor influences the construction of the ethos of the president as the victim of a court action sponsored by Macri while at the same time placing her in a position of superiority from which she is able to laugh at her own predicament. Similarly, Fernández de Kirchner argues, this time in a more confrontational tone:

> I want to tell all of you that if after these intense twelve and a half years with all the hegemonic media against [me] and after these twelve and a half years with the main national and international economic and financial corporations against [me], if after twelve and a half years of persecutions and permanent harassment, of what I call the Judicial Party, if after all that, of so many spokes in the wheel, of so many successful and unsuccessful attempts to destabilize [my government], if after so many attacks, persecutions, defamations and slanders we can be here, accounting to the people, I imagine that if we have done so many things for Argentines with so many things against us, how many [things] can be done by those who have all these factors in [their] favor.[29]

In this excerpt, Fernández de Kirchner takes as counter-addressees—that is to say, as supporters of her opponent with whom she polemicizes—the media, national and international corporations, and the judiciary, whom she blames for "so many successful and unsuccessful attempts to destabilize [my government]." The term she uses in Spanish is *golpe destituyente*, literally an "overthrowing coup," which implicitly equates her counter-addressees or political opponents with the military who staged the *golpe de Estado*, or coup d'état, in 1976. In this way, she constructs a victim ethos for herself. The emphatic tone is created mainly by two rhetorical figures—anaphora and amplification, both of which reinforce this ethos. Through anaphora she emphasizes the notion of twelve and a half years of suffering, and through amplification, she highlights the bad things her enemies have done to her: "attacks, persecutions, libel, and slander."

Anaphora consists of repeating expressions at the beginning of several sentences or verses, and amplification consists of enhancing and developing a theme by presenting the ideas in different guises or from different points of view.[30] With both figures, Fernández de Kirchner also seeks to emphasize that both she and—more generally—the three Kirchner administrations that governed for twelve years were victims of sectors she implicitly depicts as undemocratic. In this regard, it is worth remembering that on March 11,

2008, shortly after beginning her first term as president, she announced an increase in soybean and sunflower export taxes. The action, known as "Resolution 125," was immediately rejected by the four agricultural sector employers' organizations in Argentina, which declared an agricultural lockout the following day. The conflict lasted several months, until President Fernández de Kirchner sent a bill on grain export taxes to the National Congress on June 17 in order to enhance the legitimacy of the measure. Finally, on July 17, the Senate rejected the bill. The mass media, which opposed Resolution 125, confronted Fernández de Kirchner's government on another issue that divided public opinion. This was the passing of the Law on Audiovisual Communication Services in August 2009 after intense parliamentary and judicial debates. The law especially hurt the Clarín Group, which was forced to give up its television licenses, and led it to assume a tougher stance against Fernández de Kirchner's government.

On a slightly different note, the extract in question includes an enthymeme that starts from the implicit premise that the more support a president receives from influential and powerful sections of society, the more he or she is able to do.[31] Thus Macri, who supposedly has the support of the rich and powerful, will be able to do many things once he is in office. With this enthymeme, the outgoing president suggests that her audience should have high expectations of Macri's presidency and that if he fails to live up to them, they will be entitled to feel dissatisfied. In connection with these expectations, she implies that they will not be satisfied, since she states, "You must also know that tomorrow's world is a difficult world because international [commodity] prices have fallen."

Regarding the precautionary measure (i.e., the court injunction) preventing her from making decisions starting the first minute of December 10 until noon that same day, and in connection with what in a negative way she calls the "Judicial Party," Fernández de Kirchner adds, "The truth is that I have seen many precautionary measures, against the Media Law, against executive decrees, but I can assure you that never in my whole life [did I expect that] I would see a precautionary president—for twelve hours—in my country."[32]

With these words, Fernández de Kirchner expresses her surprise at and criticism of the federal judge's decision to end her mandate at midnight on December 10 and appoint an interim president for twelve hours until Macri assumes office. Following the same line of confrontational ethos, Fernández de Kirchner again uses irony against the president-elect: "So next time, besides [voting for] president, we will have to vote for a provisional president, too, in the ballot."

The use of terms evoking a coup d'état and the ethos that Fernández de Kirchner constructs for herself as the victim of a judicial maneuver preventing her from making executive decisions after midnight is part of an overall strategy that seeks to convince the audience that Mauricio Macri is a president who does not respect institutions. The ethos of victim is strengthened by the use of pathos: "I was hurt and I had a hard time seeing a president for whom no one had voted in a judicial sentence. . . . I was hurt, I confess I was hurt as an Argentine, none of us deserved this, no Argentine deserved this."

Fernández de Kirchner uses what Plantin calls "expressed emotion" (*l'émotion dite*) through which she explicitly expresses her feelings—"I was hurt"—while the pathos is increased by anaphora thanks to the use of repetition.[33] In front of a crowd of supporters chanting "Indicted! Indicted!" in reference to a criminal prosecution in which Macri himself was the accused, Fernández de Kirchner says:

> Look, I want to say something about what you are saying, I want to tell you that with this state of affairs, all Argentines are, in a sense, on parole and the truth [is] that I had the hope, I had the dream that somehow it would be understood how important it is for a people, for a democracy, that really—beyond political differences—even in the antipodes, the most important thing is to show respect for the will of the people, which is not limited to the last election, the will of the people that was also expressed—four years ago—when you chose us. The will of the people must always be respected.[34]

The audience's cries of "Indicted! Indicted!" clearly express their approval of, and agreement with, the speaker's criticisms of Macri and in this sense can be considered instances of what rhetoricians call *acclamatio*.[35] Fernández de Kirchner, in turn, uses a strategy that is well known in political discourse, at least in Argentina, which consists of taking the words of the audience and feeding them back into her own speech ("I want to say something about what you are saying"). The negative image projected by Macri's audience allows Fernández de Kirchner to continue with her criticism of the president-elect.

Fernández de Kirchner thus attacks Macri as a privileged counteraddressee, implying that if Argentina does not enjoy full freedom, it is because of Macri. The fact that he sought an injunction preventing her from making decisions after midnight on December 10 shows that he does not respect democracy or the will of the people. Hence, she states, "I hope for an

uncensored Argentina, I hope for an Argentina without repression," implying that both problems may possibly arise with the Macri government. At
the same time, she implicitly accuses the president-elect of not respecting
the Constitution, stating that "violating the Constitution and putting in a
president by decree or by a court ruling is not a banal issue, it's a bit thicker."

In contrast to the way she constructs Macri, Fernández de Kirchner builds
a democratic ethos for herself as a person who respects the Constitution and
the will of the people. In this sense, she does not limit herself in her farewell speech to the polemical and victim ethos; she also identifies an epideictic
dimension that praises core values, uniting the Argentine community beyond
its political differences. In fact, Fernández de Kirchner lays claim to a series
of democratic values when she says, "The most important thing is to show
respect for the will of the people" or "the right of the people to speak out for
and against each government, because that is the essence of democracy."

However, the overall purpose of her speech is to confront Macri and position herself as the person who will return to the presidency to correct the
mistakes that, she claims, the new president-elect will inevitably make. To
this end, Fernández de Kirchner refers to the alleged achievements of her
own governments and expresses her wish that these achievements will continue during the Macri government:

> But I also hope that we can enjoy, that all Argentines can enjoy the social
> gains, economic progress, the successes that workers, shopkeepers,
> entrepreneurs, intellectuals, artists, scientists have had in Argentina,
> where in the last quarter we have come [down] to 5.4 percent unem-
> ployment, a historic record. I aspire that in addition to many more
> schools, that in addition to more hospitals, that in addition to more
> [university] faculties, more students, more laboratories, more vaccines,
> more increases, more pensions, more collective bargaining negotia-
> tions, more factories, more businesses, more companies—I aspire that
> in addition to all this you will have the same freedom of expression as
> you have had as never before in the past twelve and a half years.

In expressing this desire that the achievements of her government should
continue during Macri's administration, Fernández de Kirchner suggests
that the opposite may actually happen. Following this train of thought, she
also suggests that Macri is going to betray the popular vote when she says
to her audience, "When each one of you, each of those forty-two million
Argentines feels that those in whom he trusted and deposited his vote, have

betrayed him, let him take up his banner and know that he is the leader of his destiny and the builder of his life."[36]

By representing ordinary citizens as creators of their own destiny, she also implies that, if or when Macri betrays them, they will be able to remedy this betrayal by voting for her again. This is the position she takes in her farewell address. Hence, Fernández de Kirchner makes the following statement, in which she promises always to listen to the ordinary citizens of Argentina: "I want to tell you that I have also listened to you, I listen to you and I will always listen to you."

In contrast to the betrayal she predicts at the hands of Macri, Fernández de Kirchner constructs herself as a head of state who can look ordinary citizens in the eye—that is to say, she has kept her word, she has not betrayed anybody, and she has nothing to hide:

> We can look the Mothers, the Grandmothers of Plaza de Mayo, HIJOS, in the eye, for we responded to the historical demand for memory, truth, and justice;[37] we can look the workers in the eye to tell them that we never betrayed them, to tell them that they always had free collective bargaining, that we never demanded from them any social pact on wages; we can look scientists in the eye, those who came back and those who stayed to lend a hand, and tell them that we have recognized their rights, their income, their knowledge as no one had ever done before; we can look press workers in the eye and tell them that they never had the freedom they had during our government even to libel [us] in some cases, to slander [us] in others, and many [could] also say what they think. . . . We can also look shopkeepers, businesspeople, and producers in the eye, people who were bankrupt in 2003 or who did not exist either as businesspeople or as shopkeepers, and who today have businesses and shops.

Through the anaphora created by repeating the phrase "we can look [them] in the eye," Fernández de Kirchner introduces the achievements of her government as they affect the various sectors of society. When using the first-person plural, she includes herself in a group, "we Kirchnerites," that confronts "them," the followers of Mauricio Macri. "They" are to be held accountable, and she offers "them" her own government as a model to follow: "But they also have an immense responsibility"; "I ask all of them to also act in the same way from now on. They have the responsibility toward society to act in the same way."

However, Fernández de Kirchner, in referring to voters who may feel "betrayed" either now or at a later date, implies that "they" will not fulfill their responsibilities or act in the same way as "we" have done. In this confrontation between "us" and "them," she also takes it for granted that "they" are neither mature nor patriotic: "We have an obligation to be more mature. Do you know why? Because we love the country deeply, we believe in the people, we believe in what we have done; and because we believe in what we have done, we have to have a positive attitude to stop those things from being destroyed."

What Fernández de Kirchner's words imply is that Macri and his followers, unlike "us," do not believe in the people and may destroy everything the Kirchnerists have accomplished. In this way, she closes her farewell speech by building a future in which she will be a champion of the people: "Thank you for so much happiness, thank you for so much joy, thank you for so much love, I love you, I carry you always in my heart, and [I want you to] know that always I will be with you." In this epilogue, pathos predominates—a pathos created by the repetition present in anaphora and parallelism, and by words from the lexical field of emotions.[38]

Conversational Tone and Informal Register

The ethos of Cristina Fernández de Kirchner is also constructed through a conversational tone, familiar, close to the audience, in which the use of an informal register plays an important role. This self-image contributes to the overall argumentative purpose of her farewell speech, which consists of positioning herself as a head of state who listens to the people, is close to them, and has worked to improve their lot while, at the same time, being willing to return to the presidency to correct the mistakes that will be made by Macri, who, she says, will end up betraying the people.

In keeping with this image, the analogy discussed above, comparing Fernández de Kirchner to a coach that will become a pumpkin at midnight, connects with the intimacy of family life through intertextuality with the popular children's story "Cinderella." Moreover, the farewell speech contains a number of locutions and lexemes that belong to an informal and colloquial register. This is the case with the locutions "to lend a hand" in the sense of "to support"; "with only the clothes on their backs," meaning "penniless"; and "spokes in the wheel," meaning "obstacles." It is also the case of the lexemes "mangos," slang for "pesos" or "money"; "we are tying ourselves up in knots," in the sense of "we are complicating matters unnecessarily"; and

"Chirolita," the name of a famous ventriloquist's doll and therefore someone who can be manipulated at will.

Fernández de Kirchner's farewell speech also includes intimate conversations with the audience marked by questions that she addresses: "Can you hear alright, are you sure everyone can hear alright?"; "Do you know why?"; "But you know what?"; "You know what?" This closeness to the audience is also constructed by referring to former president Néstor Kirchner only by his first name, "Néstor."

The conversational style and informal tone, however, are not exclusive to the former Argentine president. Rather, they are a feature of contemporary discourse that Norman Fairclough calls the conversationalization of public discourse.[39] This refers to the fact that discursive practices characteristic of the private sphere have been appropriated by the public sphere, which in turn leads to the informalization of identities. Mauricio Macri himself used an informal tone in his inauguration speech, delivered on December 10, 2015, one day after Fernández de Kirchner's farewell speech, when he simply called his vice president, Gabriela Michetti, by her first name, "Gabriela."

Conclusions

In her farewell speech Cristina Fernández de Kirchner uses a "rhetorical arsenal," similar to the one she used in her presidential speeches,[40] in order to construct a controversial ethos with pathos, a colloquial tone, and an informal register as its main features. This ethos polarizes the audience between "us" and "them" and associates "them" critically with Argentina's last military dictatorship and those people before whom she presents herself as a victim. The "we the Kirchnerists" positions in her favor the achievements of the government of Néstor Kirchner. However, her presidential speeches highlight the construction of an ethos that has been described as "pedagogical-expert,"[41] through which Fernández de Kirchner adopted the image of a teacher expounding to her audience, constructed asymmetrically as students, on various fields of knowledge such as economics and history. This pedagogical-expert ethos is no longer relevant in her farewell speech, in a context in which her confrontation with Mauricio Macri's government is central.

The vicissitudes of history have confirmed the argument that guided the analysis of Cristina Fernández de Kirchner's farewell speech, namely, that her farewell speech was predominantly intended to prepare the audience for her return. In fact, she ran for senator in the province of Buenos Aires in the primary elections of August 13, 2017, in which she beat Mauricio Macri's candidate by a small margin. Under Argentina's election system, the winning party in each Senate race gets two of the province's three seats, with the remaining seat going to the second-place finisher. Cristina Fernández de Kirchner tried to run again in the legislative elections held on October 22, 2017.

Although she was elected senator, the candidates supported by Macri won a 4 percent lead and two seats. In October 2019, she ran as vice president in the presidential election that defeated Macri, who aspired to be reelected. Alberto Fernández, a former cabinet chief and close colleague of Néstor Kirchner, ran for president with her. She had proposed him to replace her as presidential candidate in a bid to win votes from other sectors of Peronism that are not Kirchnerist, and because of her poor performance in opinion polls.

Beyond this factual information, Cristina Fernández de Kirchner's farewell speech contains clear indications that she was not prepared to withdraw from politics and that she would try to win back the presidency from Mauricio Macri at some future date. The conflict over the location where the presidential symbols—the sash and the baton—were to be handed over had a marked impact on the way she constructed a polemical and victim ethos, unlike what happens in United States within the rhetorical tradition of the presidential farewell speech. In short, Néstor Kirchner's widow inaugurated a genre; only time will tell if it will become an established or conventional genre in Argentina. In this respect, there is no doubt that, regardless of whether one shares her ideas, she was a good speaker who developed and enriched the genres of presidential rhetoric.

It should be noted that when she enumerates the alleged achievements of her government (and those of Néstor Kirchner; i.e., "we the Kirchnerists") the effect is not so much to construct a public memory of her administration, as Amos Kiewe claims is the case with presidential farewell speeches in the United States (he focuses on the case of Ronald Reagan).[42] Rather, her aim is to legitimize herself before her audience as a future opponent of Mauricio Macri who, in her view, will betray the vote of ordinary citizens.

In this sense, and bearing in mind Argentina's markedly controversial political culture, Cristina Fernández de Kirchner's farewell speech ratified rather than questioned the democratic process. Its rhetorical peculiarities, especially its aggressive tone and its closeness to the audience, reflect the particularities of democracy in Argentina: deep polarization and a lack of respect for institutions, in which the public favors direct communication between leaders and followers.

Finally, it should be remembered that Cristina Fernández de Kirchner's political rhetoric does not correspond to a liberal conception of democracy that focuses public debate on reaching consensus and *homonoia*. It is, instead, what Chantal Mouffe calls "agonistic democracy," which recognizes in the confrontation between the adversaries—"us" and "them"—the reality of democracy and accepts the inherently problematic nature of pluralism derived from the impossibility of reconciling all points of view.[43]

II

SPECTACULAR CRISIS: RHETORICS OF REPRESENTATION IN VENEZUELA

Abraham Romney

News coverage of Venezuela's economic decline has featured numerous reports of its citizens starving, suffering shortages of necessities, and fleeing to neighboring countries.[1] Once one of South America's richest nations, Venezuela has suffered a widespread economic downturn with the falling price and diminished production of its principal export, petroleum. The recession comes after more than a decade with a populist socialist government that had, under its charismatic leader Hugo Chávez Frías, successfully reduced poverty in much of the country. Venezuela's drastic economic demise has spurred worldwide debate. Is socialism itself to blame? Or, rather, were economic forces backed by imperialism set against Venezuela from the start? Because of its polarized politics, Venezuela presents numerous avenues for the study of the rhetoric of democracy. Chávez's populist rhetoric arguably aided him in gaining power and maintaining regional ties. Since Chávez's death in 2013, his successor, Nicolás Maduro, has been much less favored domestically and abroad. What Chávez called twenty-first-century socialism has long been opposed by the right-wing elite, and opposition politicians won a majority in the National Assembly in 2015 for the first time in sixteen years, gaining control of just one of five branches of government. But since that time, Maduro's rhetoric and political maneuvering has sought to circumvent the authority of the assembly to form the National Constituent Assembly, a move that, in 2017, sparked protest and drew consternation from allies and detractors alike, with some, citing corrupt polling, describing the National Assembly as the last remaining democratically elected governing body in Venezuela.

In the Venezuelan press and in reports about Venezuela, we see a clash of opposing narratives: official and quasi-official channels painting a more positive picture of the situation and faulting the opposition for the country's economic woes, critical sources from Venezuela and mainstream media sources in the United States and elsewhere pointing to a spectacular crisis. These rhetorics of crisis emerge in a turbulent and divided context in which both sides rely on what I call spectacular rhetorics to assert divergent claims about the reality of the crisis. I analyze representations of the crisis in Venezuela in terms of two concepts that I derive from the idea of the spectacle as theorized by Guy Debord: spectacle logic and what I call the spectacle image. Spectacle logic is the underlying global logic that reinforces the dominance of capital and commodity, often in visual ways. Spectacle image refers to the proliferation of visual representations that normalize notions of commodification. These images are commonplace and largely banal. However, in representations of economic crisis, images and reportage increasingly highlight a lack of commodity that appears to threaten spectacle logic, while the way it is highlighted actually tends to bolster it.

Spectacular rhetoric relates to but diverges from much of the thinking about spectacle in rhetorical studies by reemphasizing the role of media and capital present in the Debordian notion of spectacle. Rhetoricians have approached the idea of spectacle as an interplay between rhetor and audience. David E. Procter connects spectacle to salient events, using the term "dynamic spectacle" to designate "those spectacles which [have the power to] . . . become a touchstone for community-building."[2] The rhetor's role, for Procter, lies in interpreting these events for a community: "Their interpretations or accounts of the event are the spectacles" that symbolically frame events, connect them to a group's ideology, and drive community action.[3] More recently, rhetoricians discussing the concept of spectacle have been at pains to emphasize the importance of the audience in providing meaning. In analyzing pageantry, S. Michael Halloran even doubts the efficacy of the rhetor on the stage: "For every 'Gettysburg Address' or 'I Have a Dream' there are hundreds of banal drones whose significance lies more in the fact and the circumstances of their delivery than in their texts."[4] By contrast, in spectacle, the roles of rhetor and audience are blurred. Halloran argues that, unlike Guy Debord, who he says sees in the spectacle a negation or displacement of life, "a spectacle is itself a lived experience."[5] Jonathan Mark Balzotti sees disruptive potential in the visual nature of spectacles that can "run counter to the script," where even monumental displays can serve as "an aesthetic resource for thinking and exploring alternate possibilities."[6] Discussing personal accounts of interpretations of the Ferris wheel at the 1893 World's Colombian Exhibition, he suggests that such spectacles do not simply present a dominant message but are opportunities for individual interpretation. Like Halloran, he emphasizes spectacle as a "rhetorical expression experienced by actual people."[7] For Balzotti, "Spectacle defined as a tool of hegemony is a pale reflection of a much more interesting and rich concept."[8] It is right to note that audience engagement and participation can play an important role in spectacular events or displays. A rich concept, however, should not lead us to overlook dominant modes in media representations of poverty being discussed in this chapter.

While the foregoing rhetorical theories of spectacle can be useful for analyzing the impact of events, pageants, or monumental displays, and could be of service in analyzing government ceremonies, a different type of spectacle unfolds in media reports that have accumulated over the last several years about Venezuela. Although such a lens does not necessarily provide a rosy view of rhetorical agency, Guy Debord's theories elaborated in *Society of the Spectacle* prove useful in understanding the rhetoric of everyday mass media representation in this context.

My emphasis on news media as spectacle is much closer to the way the term is used by Murray Edelman, who suggests that "the spectacle constituted by news reporting continuously constructs and reconstructs social problems, crises, enemies, and leaders and so creates a succession of threats and reassurances."[9] In Edelman's view, political life as shaped by this reporting is "hyperreal,"[10] raising explanations for persistent problems that "are notable for the diversity of causes and of ideologies to which they point, not for their rigor, verifiability, or explanatory power."[11] Edelman points out that the traditional distinction between problems as chronic, recurring issues "resistant to facile solutions" and crisis as an acute moment that "heralds instability" and deprivation, is one that usually turns out to be arbitrary. Rather, "more often than not a crisis is an episode in a long sequence of similar problems."[12] Edelman thus views a crisis, "like all news developments," as "a creation of the language used to depict it."[13] In this way, events do not amount to a crisis until they are represented as such in the language of the political spectacle, with an inconsistent relationship between representation and reality. Such depictions, however, are based not just in language; instead, as in the case of the present study, images play a supporting role in forwarding narratives of crisis.

Seeming to anticipate the age of Instagram, Debord's now classic neo-Marxian theory, in contrast to the theories of spectacle that emphasize rhetorical agency, sees image and commodity as dominating social relationships within the spectacle. Debord describes mass media operating in a system in which "social relationship[s]" are "mediated by images."[14] While the spectacle is actually "subordinate" to "social practice," it asserts itself as the "apparent goal" of social practice.[15] The relationship between spectacle and commodity is central to this theory. For Debord, capitalism has led to a world mediated by images. In that world, the appearance of commodity reigns. The selling of labor had initially resulted in an abundance that "liberates societies from the natural pressures occasioned by their struggle for survival," but this very abundance of commodities reduces human pursuits to "no more than an *augmented survival*."[16] A major aspect of this shift, according to Debord, is an emphasis on appearance. Whereas, previously, bourgeois society was driven by the accumulation of wealth and capital, the spectacle seeks to make commodities visible to such an extent that society's focus shifts from having to *appearing*. As Debord puts it, the commodity is now "all there is to see," and for that reason, in the context of economic crisis, the absence of commodity becomes unsettling, something that threatens to disrupt spectacle commodity. Paradoxically, when lenses are trained on the crisis in Venezuela, and frequently on the commodity's conspicuous absence, this disruption of the spectacle itself becomes commodified in international media representation.

Still, the application of this theory does not point us only to a critique of, say, the neoliberal right. In Debord's theory, different logics compete within the spectacle: "Just as the logic of the commodity reigns over capitalists' competing ambitions . . . so the harsh logic of the spectacle controls the abundant diversity of media extravagances."[17] Analyzing media representations of Venezuela reveals starkly divided accounts between opposition outlets and government-sponsored news. The more the crisis has been publicized, the more Western mainstream media sources have become disenchanted with Maduro and the throes of Chavismo's populism. Narratives of crisis, however, can also be sensationalized. Such a narrative is precisely what consumers of Western media have come to expect from Latin American politics—exactly the kind of rhetorics that reinforce the logic of the spectacle. The crisis narrative, for example, has been used by election strategy consultants from the United States in Latin America, as in the case of the Bolivian election of 2002, the subject of the 2005 documentary *Our Brand Is Crisis*.[18] Still, Venezuela's fall from economic grace has been particularly striking, making this habituated narrative framing seem all the more fitting. To better understand the rhetoric of spectacle in the current crisis, I briefly situate it within the historical context, including the attempted coup in 2002 that nearly ended Chávez's presidency. With this discussion of media representation in mind, I then turn to media representations of the more recent economic downturn and unrest under Maduro to show the way that media representations pro and contra make use of logics of the spectacle. As of the date of this writing, Maduro remains in power, as these competing narratives result in the paradox of Maduro's prolonged presidency despite images of a bumbling leader besieged by crisis.

Chavismo and Protest

Maduro should be understood both in his context in the legacy of Chavismo and in the shifting dynamics of regional politics. Coming as part of what some dubbed a "pink tide" of leftist leaders influenced by Marxist principles, Chavismo entered the scene with popular support at its outset and during much of Chávez's presidency from 1999 until his death in March 2013.[19] A former military leader who headed a failed coup in 1992, Chávez was released from prison two years later and emerged as a populist hero. As an early item of business in 1999, and backed by popular referendum, he supported a newly written constitution to replace the constitution of 1961. Purportedly based on the philosophical ideals of the South American liberator Simón Bolívar, this new constitution changed the official name of the country from República de Venezuela to the República Bolivariana de Venezuela. In subsequent years, Chávez managed to solidify power by nationalizing various industries, including much of the oil industry under Petróleos de Venezuela (PDVSA), which allowed him to develop social programs aimed at reducing poverty and rewarding his supporters.

Chávez became famous for a fiery rhetoric that countered US hegemony and sought to unify Latin American countries. Chávez famously spoke at the United Nations in 2006, holding Noam Chomsky's *Hegemony or Survival*, which he said all Americans should read. He then referred to President George W. Bush as *el diablo*, stating that the podium from which Bush had spoken the day before smelled of sulfur.[20] In March of that year, he dedicated a portion of his weekly television show *Alo Presidente* to critiquing Bush's imperialism through US involvement in Iraq. He called Bush a "donkey" and "Mr. Danger," along with a string of other insults, complaining "You messed with me, little bird" (*Te metiste conimgo, pajarito*).[21] The next year, Chávez undertook the nationalization of various parts of the economy, including communications and electricity industries and the Central Bank. He attempted but failed to remove term limits in a constitutional referendum and began to draw negative attention from abroad from organizations like Human Rights Watch, which issued a critical report in 2008. That same year, as a show of solidarity with Bolivia, he expelled the US ambassador from Venezuela and withdrew Venezuela's ambassadors from the United States, shouting to a crowd "Go to hell, shitty Yankees!" (*Váyanse al carajo, yanquis de mierda!*).[22] While Chávez tended to ramble, he was undeniably charismatic. In contrast, Chávez's handpicked successor, Nicolás Maduro, lacked his predecessor's charm and was ridiculed for uttering absurdities. In what seems a better fit for magic realism, Maduro claimed on camera to a group of supporters during his campaign that Chávez had appeared to him in a chapel as a small *pajarito* that flew into the building and circled above him before flying away, giving Maduro the blessing to continue the revolution.[23] Maduro took the helm after narrowly defeating Henrique Capriles by a margin of less than 1 percent, and detractors cried foul. With a drop in oil prices beginning in 2014, Maduro has faced recurring protests but has yet to yield. Critics point to economic mismanagement while the government blames an "economic war" waged by opposition leaders, something that has been echoed repeatedly in the pro-government press.[24]

The biggest existential threat to the Chávez government came in the form of an attempted coup in April 2002 when, after antigovernment protesters in Caracas were killed by gunfire, the military arrested Chávez, and the opposition set up a short-lived interim government that was quickly recognized as legitimate by the United States. The opposition government took sweeping measures to dismantle institutions, but just days later Chávez was back in power. The interpretation of April 2002 continued long after the events transpired, and I review some of that interpretation to show a transition to what I call spectacular rhetorics in the current crisis. An analysis of spectacular rhetorics can critique the way that such representations uphold or resist systems of power and production. The spectacle engages in representation of real events but also in falsification, what Debord calls the spectacle's "real unreality."[25] My own experience of the attempted coup came while I was living as a missionary in the small town of El Tigrito, hours from Caracas, where most of the action was occurring. Apolitical as a rule, missionaries for the Church of Jesus Christ of Latter-Day Saints avoided political topics and did not keep abreast of current events during their two-year service. Our only knowledge of events came from what the people of the town related to us and from their television sets, perpetually turned on during the ordeal. The momentum for the coup had relied largely on certain images presented in a sequence that made it appear that shots had been fired by military and pro-Chávez supporters on a crowd of peaceful protesters. People I spoke to were condemning the violence allegedly done under Chávez's direction. During those few days everyone seemed to believe what they were hearing and seeing on television. However, on the evening when he returned to power, walking home to my apartment, I found myself suddenly surrounded by an impromptu sea of red berets (the signature military headwear of Chávez and his supporters) as they took to the streets to celebrate his return to Miraflores by loyal members of the military. I mention my own experience then because, during current events surrounding Maduro and purportedly grassroots protests against him, I am reminded of the difficulty of finding what is really happening at a distance and through media outlets.

The attempted coup has been the subject of documentaries that have tried to untangle the story of what exactly happened. Some blame the 2002 events on media manipulation. In his documentary praising Chávez and other leftist Latin-American leaders, Oliver Stone recounts the events as a media ploy.[26] Stone's account of the attempted coup paints the opposition movement as largely fueled by private media. When pro- and antigovernment protest began to converge, shots were fired from rooftops. Chávez supporters on a bridge fired back at someone shooting at them from a building, and, according to Stone's analysis in *South of the Border*, opposition media cut the scenes together to make it appear that Chávez supporters had opened fire on a peaceful crowd below.[27] Stone then focuses on the way the opposition leaders were too quick to appoint a wealthy businessman, Pedro Carmona, as interim president and to abolish the National Assembly. As a response, many people took to the streets to demand that Carmona step down. Loyal members of the military rescued Chávez and returned him to power at the presidential palace in Miraflores. *South of the Border* marks this event as a moment in which Chávez's enmity against the US government was solidified. In his interview with Stone, Chávez argues that the whole plot was orchestrated by the United States and fueled by their desire to control petroleum production, the same motivation Chávez attributes to the subsequent US invasion of Iraq.

Others disagree with some of the accusations of media manipulation. Francisco Toro, who marched with the opposition during that protest in 2002, argues that many of the details about the shootings have been obscured by "Chavista mythmaking."[28] As he puts it, "The April Crisis was pressed into service as a kind of Myth of Origin for the Bolivarian Revolution's radicalization: a tale of C.I.A. conspiracy, shadowy agents and provocateur sharpshooters planted by the opposition to fire on its own supporters." One early source arguing along the lines critiqued by Toro was *The Revolution Will Not Be Televised*, a documentary distributed in 2003 and made by a crew from Ireland's national broadcaster Raidió Teilifís Éireann (RTE).[29] The filmmakers were in Venezuela at the time of the attempted coup filming a documentary about Chávez. *The Revolution* shows the opposition and pro-Chávez groups poised for a clash in front of Miraflores, with the military attempting to "act as a buffer." When the gunfire began, the voice-over declares, "We couldn't tell where the shots were coming from, but people were being hit in the head. Soon it became clear that we were being shot at by snipers." A quick montage of handheld shots flash images of high-rise buildings, insinuating the location of the shooters. In response, the documentary *Radiografía de una mentira* (X-ray of a lie) sought to disprove the claims in *The Revolution* and criticize its manipulation of the story.[30] Another documentary, *Claves de una massacre* (Keys to a massacre), concludes that Chávez's supporters firing from the Puente Llaguno overpass were doing so in self-defense and much later than the shooting that wounded members of the opposition.[31]

This review of contradictory claims points to the history of US involvement in Venezuelan politics and to the ways protests in the country have been staged and interpreted. With rising oil prices after 2002, Chávez was able to pursue a more radical vision of twenty-first century socialism, only running into trouble as economic difficulties began to set in. Kirk A. Hawkins, who studies populist movements, suggests that Maduro's current low popularity provides an opportunity to look at ways of effectively opposing "strongly populist" movements through "patient efforts by the opposition."[32] Hawkins suggests that populist movements come as a response to "widespread failures of democratic governance such as corruption and inequality," making voters willing to support a populist candidate.[33] And, while Hawkins credits Chávez's initial democratic appeal, he suggests that the second phase of Chavismo (from 2004 to 2013) was fueled not so much by democratic support as by rising global oil prices.[34] In response to sharp declines in the price of oil as Maduro took office, he enacted policies that would solidify his military support by giving members of the military more control and resources such as subsidized housing, but at the cost of democratic support.[35] Hawkins's analysis shows that most of the means of resistance were ineffective against Chávez's removal of human rights protections and stacking of the judiciary, especially given his ability to use oil revenues. Ultimately, he suggests, effective resistance requires a patiently organized opposition that reaches the electorate broadly.[36] A common critique of the opposition in recent years has been that it lacks coherence. Julia Buxton mockingly credits the disorganized opposition as the "stalwart ally" responsible for keeping Maduro in power: "Certainly the opposition has enjoyed major electoral success and demonstrated a capacity to convoke large-scale protests. Yet it has never maintained the momentum of political change."[37] Buxton acknowledges electoral gains by the opposition but suggests that a diffuse message, division over tactics (protests vs. signatures, for example), and a lack of attention to social issues mire the opposition's progress.[38]

Venezuela's contemporary milieu of protests, often staged for media outlets or for social media, echoes the earlier media event of the attempted coup. The visual nature of the representation of protests and scarcity may call for thinking in terms of the theory of the image event, a concept some have used to understand protest and spectacle in the age of television. Notably, John W. Delicath and Kevin Michael Deluca define image events as "staged acts of protest intended for media dissemination . . . understood as a form of argumentative practice."[39] They see image events as "a form of oppositional argument" capable of "generating social controversy" and increasing the opportunity for argumentation and debate. As opposed to the "spectacles" staged by corporation and nations to affirm status before publics, image events are performed by "subaltern counterpublics" to gain publicity and "hold corporations and nations accountable."[40] Their analysis draws on the way environmental groups like Greenpeace use protests as opportunities to create striking images that, through audience interpretation, can serve as "inventional resources for future argumentation and deliberation."[41] Delicath and Deluca work to recognize these kinds of protest as arguments that have greater access to the public through television as opposed to more formal, traditional contexts for debate. Galia Yanoshevsky, however, argues that "the picture of image events" as they really occur "is more complex than the one depicted by Delicath and Deluca."[42] As she points out, the image event also speaks to the power of media to spread, constrain, and even create "simulated images" by reframing other types of photographs or footage. She further questions the extent to which new arguments are possible in a context where certain images become recognizable as stereotypes of protest, such as a man standing in protest before a machine. Yanoshevsky's attempt to update the term is useful and, as I see it, relevant to the Debordian notion of the spectacle that I have been forwarding in that it breaks the tidy separation between spectacle and image event present in Delicath and Deluca's theory and accounts for the process of dissemination.

As the opposition has continued to rely on protests, the most troubling ways that Maduro's government has held onto power involve violence against protestors and journalists and the taking of political prisoners like Leopoldo Lopez, who was in prison or under house arrest for organizing protests in 2014 that turned violent. After the opposition gained control of the legislature in 2015, Maduro called for the election of a new congressional body to bypass the one controlled by the opposition, a move that sparked protest.[43] As a result, angry protests led to violent altercations with the National Guard and police. And during the time in which this chapter was revised, the opposition, in an effort to challenge Maduro's move to bypass them and control elections, forwarded the president of the National Assembly, Juan Guaidó, as the interim president, with recognition coming quickly from the United States and numerous other countries in the region. During this time, however, Maduro has not yielded, leading to continued increasing inflation. Guaidó's attempts to usher in regime change through protest have largely proven ineffective, and the United States has proposed a transitional government that would involve both men stepping aside. Still, Maduro continues efforts to consolidate power despite pressure and sanctions from abroad, even recently taking over control of opposition political parties.[44]

Representation of the Crisis Under Maduro

With such polarized positions, battled over in the streets and in the media, the Venezuelan government has attempted to manage media representations by being less friendly to opposition and foreign journalism. In the aftermath of the coup attempt in 2002, Chávez blamed the media and especially television stations, calling them a "laboratory of lies" without which the coup would not have been able to take place.[45] It was no secret that private television stations had wealthy owners who opposed Chávez. Since then, however, the Venezuelan government has greatly expanded its own media offerings and control, going as far as to refuse to renew the license of Radio Caracas Television (RCTV) in 2007. By such actions, the government has aimed at "media hegemony" by expanding its media production, putting much more pressure on outlets deemed critical of the government, and reducing coverage of the crisis. Maduro has even called investigative journalism about food shortages "war propaganda."[46] Since taking over, Maduro has clearly seen much of his battle as taking place in the media, announcing in 2013 that he would do battle in social media against those who oppose him.[47] Promotional videos on Maduro's webpage speak openly about encouraging supporters to join the "communication battle in social media" (*batalla comunicacional en las redes sociales*).[48] Denied foreign currency required to buy imported paper, traditional print sources have had to reduce circulation, moving much of the negative reporting to independent sources leveraging social media.[49] The government has also occluded facts by refraining from publishing negative statistics and reports.[50]

The state crackdown on journalists has suppressed critical representation. At the same time, elements of the opposition continue to turn to social media to spread criticism of the government. In recent years some journalists have been imprisoned, intimidated, and robbed of equipment.[51] The government has also denied visas to some foreign reporters. In an interview, Nick Casey of the *New York Times* details the way the government refused interviews with the press and eventually barred him from entering the country after the paper covered the poor conditions people were living in and the sorry state of health facilities. According to Casey, no one working for the *Times* had had access to a visa since he was barred from entering in 2016.[52] As Casey points out, local journalists face an even grimmer situation. For example, Braulio Jatar was arrested for publishing a video of hungry Venezuelans banging pots and pans while chasing President Maduro.

The government's lack of transparency has not quelled concern over the crisis, and its silence on some issues has shaped the way the crisis is represented by Western media outlets. Australian foreign correspondent Eric Campbell and producer Matt Davis, for example, clandestinely visited to report on the crisis in Venezuela, smuggling cameras into the country and posing as tourists to sidestep government suppression of foreign journalists while filming *Post-Chavez Venezuela Has Become a Failed State*.[53] The documentary shows the difficulties faced by those trying to get their hands on everyday necessities with money that is "worth less than the paper it's printed on." Venezuela has "more oil than Saudi Arabia," they say, but the populist government "has blown the lot." Interviewing individuals in the poorest sectors of Caracas who live at the top of the city's hills, they reveal a disillusioned demographic, some of whom were faithful to Chávez but have found little inspiring in either Maduro or the opposition. In addition, they interview opposition protesters and leaders, including Maria Corina Machado, who argue that their cause is for all of Venezuela, not just the wealthy. A shocking part of the documentary includes an interview with well-armed, masked gang members who participate in organized crime with apparent impunity. When asked if they must worry about the police, the young leader says that he has good contacts, hinting at corrupt law enforcement. Campbell places the blame squarely on the lingering effects of the Bolivarian revolution: "Chávez destroyed the market economy, leaving the country entirely dependent on oil." Later they observe, "And that is Venezuela's conundrum: people clinging to a dream as it becomes a nightmare." He sardonically concludes, "The revolution really is creating a more equal society in which almost everyone is poor." After interviewing a Venezuelan historian about the dangers of populism, Campbell draws a broader conclusion: "Having chosen a populist savior, Venezuelans are finding it impossible to shake his legacy, and some say it's a warning to the world."

The crisis narrative in Venezuela has been commonplace, as are arguments that place the blame on socialism. For example, in 2014, Juan Carlos Hidalgo wrote an opinion piece titled "How Socialism Has Destroyed Venezuela," declaring that "socialism has turned Venezuela into an authoritarian basket case that thousands try to escape every year," and warning that the worst was still to come.[54] Tom Worstall, in July 2016, blamed the shortages on the government's meddling with food pricing, declaring that "the price system works."[55] News outlets have reported the increasingly dire nature of the crisis, sometimes in apocalyptic terms depicting imminent disaster or collapse. Many reports since Maduro's tenure began to paint a lurid picture of a failed state, particularly in opinion pieces. For example, as early as 2014, Moisés Naím, former minister of trade and industry, declared Venezuela a tragedy, calling it "the world champion of inflation, homicide, insecurity, and shortages of essential goods."[56] Raúl Stolk writing in 2016 describes Venezuela as a "starvation state" presided over by an inept Maduro refusing to solve the country's problems. The government fails to fix the situation, he concludes, "because they can't. And the reason is part incompetence, part thuggery, and a big part, the dead man himself, Chávez."[57] In 2016, *The Atlantic* featured a piece titled "Venezuela Is Falling Apart," by Moisés Naím and Francisco Toro, which discussed the "anatomy of a collapse," pointing to government corruption. Venezuela's "garish implosion," the authors argue, preceded falling oil prices and can be blamed on Chavismo and its propensity for mismanagement and corruption, often in the form of business regulations and fixed prices that make it difficult to do business.[58]

The commonplace narrative that blames socialism alone for the current economic crisis, however, oversimplifies the way spectacle logics work to impose themselves globally.[59] The opposition, the government, media sources both sympathetic and critical—all can contain elements of the rhetoric of the spectacle. Because of this, coverage of the crisis is also not the same as the colloquial "media circus" offering oversized coverage to a minor event. Instead, the framing of the crisis from opposing media sources frequently serves to reinforce spectacle logics from differing perspectives.

Crisis and the Spectacle

The winner of the 2018 World Press Photo contest was "Venezuela Crisis," a profile view of a young male protestor wearing a gas mask, running from an explosion, his body engulfed in flames. The image was taken in 2017 by Venezuelan photographer Ronaldo Schemidt, working for Agence France-Presse, who captured a moment when a motorcycle gas tank exploded during a protest, catching the young man, who escaped with his life, on fire.[60] Many images of protests since Maduro took office have been equally striking, with Molotov cocktails exploding, tear gas, and clouds of smoke. Photographs and video depict the young people facing off against police lines, tanks, and fire-trucks. Because of the use of tear gas to suppress the protestors, many have taken to wearing gas masks or wrapping their T-shirts around their faces to help them breathe and to hide their identity. Since the government worked to suppress images of the protests, many relied on social media to spread them. With the protest in 2014, sources such as CNN vetted images submitted to them since supporters of Maduro claimed photo manipulation.[61] But the image of the protestor on fire is certainly arresting. The *Washington Post* described it as "spine-tingling," and the jury chair for the photo contest said it produced in her "an instantaneous emotion."[62] The image is clearly an emotional one. At the same time, its close-cropped nature reveals little of its context: a graffitied brick wall in the background, a closed store front catching fire. Devoid of context, the image is visually striking but does not tell its own story. Could the protestor be a criminal, as the Venezuelan government might claim? The state-funded, pro-government news source TeleSUR produced its own infographic of the 124 deaths associated with the protests by August 2017, color-coding and dividing them into Chavistas, bystanders, those shot by various law-enforcement entities, and those still being investigated. Thirteen of the individuals, colored in black, they claim, were "killed during looting."[63] It is noteworthy that, in this infographic, the government highlights looting, an obvious violation of the commodity system.

Recently, the opposition attempted to stage an image event in which the self-proclaimed interim president Juan Guaidó planned to bring truckloads of humanitarian aid into the country at the border with Colombia. The move aimed to put Maduro in the position of either being outdone by the opposition in taking care of Venezuelans or of refusing to allow his people access to life-saving aid. The result was unbelievable: the military blocked and set fire to the trucks transporting the aid materials, a story quickly picked up by international news and by the US government. Vice President Mike

Pence tweeted that while "the tyrant danced" at a celebration in Caracas, his "henchmen murdered civilians & burned food & medicine."[64] However, the *New York Times* later issued a story, sharing video that shows it was likely that the conflagration was caused by a flaming rag that fell from a Molotov cocktail lobbed by a protestor, not by the soldiers.[65] The speed with which the story had spread suggests a predisposition to accept a certain illogic in the Venezuelan government from the perspective of spectacle commodity.

And consumption is a conspicuous part of documenting the crisis. Those pointing to crisis and those denying its cruelest aspects both rely on normal attitudes toward commodity in the society of the spectacle for their appeals. The spectacle, as engaged by state media, presents Venezuelans appearing to have access to commodity. Government propaganda surrounding CLAP (a government program for supplying and producing food through local organizations) shows images of cheerful Venezuelans distributing produce to one another, reminiscent of community-supported agriculture programs.[66] According to some reports, however, the program merely redistributes imported and purchased dry goods like flour, rice, and sugar from companies inside and outside of Venezuela.[67] TeleSUR, which began creating English-language news content on the web in 2014 and by broadcast in 2015, launched a series called *Empire Files*, hosted by Abby Martin, a former host of *Breaking the Set* from RT (a state-funded Russian network). In an episode published just three weeks before the July 30, 2017, vote that Maduro called to replace the National Assembly, Martin attacks the main claims of the opposition.[68] Touring a few supermarkets, she shows shelves almost completely stocked but admits that some items like toilet paper could not be found, a fact she blames entirely on opposition businessmen whom she curiously also blames for causing inflation by tracking the price of the dollar. Even in this way, both sides accuse the other of disrupting the logic of spectacle and commodity.

Images of empty refrigerators and the sparse supermarket shelves appearing in other reportage, however, have become a trope to signal a crisis of spectacle itself. In other words, the appearance of supposed ruptures in the spectacle become part of the rhetoric that enacts and reinforces the logic of the spectacle. As a representative example from state-funded media from the United States, consider the following headline from Voice of America in May 2017: "Venezuela Full of Strife with Empty Refrigerators."[69] The article is accompanied by a simulated rendering of a point-of-view image looking out of an empty fridge at the colors of the Venezuelan flag, as if asking the viewer to see Venezuela from the perspective of the absent commodity. An individual quoted in the article claims that soon Venezuelans will "eat whatever we see." If the full supermarket shelf presented by pro-government sources plays a role in the spectacle's emphasis on appearing to have, then the opposition's signaling of empty shelves and refrigerators attempts to disrupt that narrative as proof of crisis and the need for intervention.

The idea of indiscriminate hunger signals a rupture of the commodity system. The crisis becomes a crisis when it appears as a threat to the spectacle itself; however, rather than actually improve situations, most often such images and ideas simply reinforce one group's adherence to the spectacle in the assurance that their system is correct. Such is the function of recent articles depicting Venezuelans scavenging for food in the trash, for example.[70] Headlines, largely from international sources, continue to focus on such topics: "In Venezuela, They Were Teachers and Doctors: To Buy Food, They Became Prostitutes"[71] or "Venezuelans Eating Dogs, Zoo Animals as Economy Collapses"[72] or "In Venezuela, Hungry Child Gangs Use Machetes to Fight for 'Quality' Garbage."[73] These reports represent the crisis in Venezuela from its most extreme outcomes. Such reportage has the potential to rely on stereotypes and presumptions. At its worst, even serious reportage often takes part in the representation of crisis as spectacle for Western consumption. The fact is ridiculed in a parody from the sketch comedy television program *Portlandia* in which devoted NPR listeners hold a tailgating party outside of the *Prairie Home Companion* live show.[74] During a montage, Malcom (played by Fred Armisen, whose mother is Venezuelan) and his friends listen to NPR news bites as if they were listening to sports radio announcers. As an NPR reporter discusses the bankruptcy of Brazilian billionaire Eike Batista and a bleak economic future for Brazil, Malcom shakes his head, lamenting "Wow, it's South America. . . . That will never change." What this sketch gets right in its ironic presentation is the tendency of news media to provide narratives that fit a sense of never-ending South American struggle and crisis as a foil for US economic stability. In this way, ever more extreme accounts of penury or of dictatorial abuses do not disrupt expectations but rather solidify the logic that produces them. And yet, in the case of Venezuela, the actions of Maduro's government and the gravity of people's suffering no doubt make such narratives seem like the most obvious choice for reporters—to wit, a rash of headlines like "Let Them Eat Rabbit" in response Maduro's so-called *plan conejo* aimed at reducing hunger by getting Venezuelans to see rabbits as food commodities rather than pets.[75] In this case, however, reporters can be forgiven for grasping at such low-hanging fruit; Maduro and his staff themselves laughed on camera when discussing the proposal.[76]

Maduro's Prolonged Crisis

Many images of Maduro have emerged during coverage of the crisis: the cruel dictator oblivious to his people's plight, a delusional leader caricatured as being guided by a little bird with the head of Chávez, and more recently a reincarnation of past dictators, particularly Stalin, to whom even Maduro, with his mustache, has admitted he bears a passing resemblance. Though support for Maduro seems to have waned, some intellectuals still defend the revolution. George Ciccariello-Maher, for example, suggests that "rather than abandon the Bolivarian Process by echoing mainstream denunciations of the government of Nicolás Maduro as undemocratic, repressive, and even authoritarian, it is precisely in this most difficult of moments that revolutionaries must think clearly and carry the fight forward."[77] Ciccariello-Maher, a professor of political science and expert on Chavismo, says that the opposition party cannot claim "any great popular legitimacy." He also blames the perception of the Venezuelan crisis on the mainstream media: "The international media has played its role, framing the question as simply a matter of time: when will the democratically elected and legitimate president step down?"[78] Ciccariello-Maher claims, "The situation that prevails is not the result of too much socialism, but too little, and any path that attempts to split the difference between socialism and capitalism will endure the worst of both worlds."[79] The idea of increasing socialism seems counterintuitive to the logic of most media framing of the conflict, but it could also refer to an increase in the bottom-up efforts and labor organizing in Venezuela's communal counsels and communes, rather than official government action, which has sometimes supported but sometimes co-opted grassroots efforts, elements that are often overlooked in the international press.[80] Other scholars have voiced criticisms of Maduro, citing concerns over human rights violations. In April 2017, the leadership of the Latin American Studies Association (LASA) issued a statement expressing concern over Venezuela's Supreme Tribunal of Justice's decision to invalidate the democratically elected National Assembly and urging the leaders of Venezuela to respect the Constitution and release political prisoners.[81] A subsequent open letter from LASA members, however, took issue with the statement and dismissed it as "highly misleading" because it offered no criticism of the opposition and furthered the opposition narrative about political prisoners, arguments the letter referred to as the "Cold War framing" one might expect "from Fox News or the *New York Times*."[82] Political scientists Barry Cannon and John Brown, in reviewing activity in the country in 2016, concluded that Venezuela's crisis has resulted from the tactics of both the government and the opposition.[83] They see a government whose "actions have done little to alleviate and much to aggravate" the problem, combined with an opposition that has primarily sought destabilization by seeking the president's removal rather than bringing policy changes that could be agreed on by both sides.

Defending Maduro's government from accusations of human rights violations appears more difficult at this point. In August 2017, the United Nations issued a report on human rights violations in Venezuela, with the UN high commissioner declaring that democracy in Venezuela was "barely alive, if still alive."[84] Similarly, Freedom House has ranked Venezuela as "not free" in its "Freedom in the World" and "Freedom of the Press" 2017 reports.[85] In its "World Report, 2017," Human Rights Watch cited a number of grave issues in Venezuela, including the jailing of political opponents, violent crackdown on protests, tortured confessions from protestors, and extrajudicial killings and disappearances.[86] The report also cited political discrimination in government jobs and in food distribution as a concern, as well as the ongoing shortages of food and medicine. In a 2016 documentary produced by Human Rights Watch and embedded in the report, footage and interviews show the long lines in which people wait for food and the dire situation of those suffering from acute and chronic conditions without access to medicine. The documentary also includes brief interviews of individuals detained for protesting and health professionals who have lost their jobs for voicing concerns about medical conditions.[87] The Americas director for Human Rights Watch, José Miguel Vivanco, closes by encouraging international actors to pressure Maduro to address the crisis and stop repressing political opponents. In a follow-up video to accompany its 2018 report, Human Rights Watch concluded that there was sufficient evidence to suggest systematic oppression of political opponents and even torture, crimes for which, Vivanco suggests in the video, perpetrators should be brought to justice.[88] Human Rights Watch's position on Venezuela under Chávez was controversial in 2008, but these criticisms increasingly appear justified.[89]

While the economy of Venezuela has continued to falter, plagued by inflation, these arguments against Maduro have still not cost him his presidency. Despite the claims in 2019 of an interim president recognized by the United States, Maduro remains in control. After an April 30, 2019, uprising that failed to materialize as planned, Mauricio Claver-Carone, senior director of the White House National Security Council, described Maduro as backed into a corner, paranoid, weak, and unable to run his country.[90] Such a description is reminiscent of a political cartoon published early in 2019 in

We're Magazine featuring a cowering Maduro, sweating in fear before a little blue bird with Trump's head, his combover drawn like an exaggerated beak, saying "I'm going to remove you" (*Te voy a quitar*).[91] The repeated spectacle image of Maduro in crisis has so far proved ineffective in actually producing the end of his leadership. As Nicholas Casey argues, although "Maduro appears in constant crisis," the "portrait of vulnerability" that often appears in the media may miss the fact that Maduro is empowered by the crisis.[92] Such an observation invites rhetoricians to consider both the accuracy and effects of framing even corrupt leaders as constantly in crisis, especially when such narratives reinforce a logic of the spectacle.

Conclusion: Looking for Something Else

My aim in describing the logic and image of the spectacle is not to critique concern over either the plight of Venezuelans or scarcity. Rather, my main point is to critique the way the logic behind the narrative distances the crisis, denying the human effects in ways that simply affirm one logic of the spectacle. Such a perspective is insufficient, not least because it attempts to localize the problem and its actors. The Venezuelan crisis has spilled out of its borders as refugees have sought opportunities elsewhere. While it is no secret that, initially, many from the wealthy and middle classes fled Chavismo, since Maduro has taken power, "a second diaspora is underway—much less wealthy and not nearly as welcome."[93] Tomás Paez, who has studied the exodus of Venezuelans to numerous countries around the globe, writing in 2015, suggested that increasingly those who had emigrated within the previous six years cited political and economic factors in their decision.[94] At that time, he placed 2015 estimates of Venezuelans living abroad as high as 1.2 million, an exponential increase since the beginning of Chavismo.[95] This exodus has only increased, with estimates now at well over 4.5 million.[96] In many places, like Peru, educated Venezuelans from the middle class get by selling arepas in the streets, often because they do not have the papers that would allow them to be part of the formal economy.[97] In a departure from mainstream narratives of the crisis, the photographer Felipe Jácome has documented the lives of individuals crossing the border into Colombia on foot, photographing them, and superimposing their image onto sheets of paper made from now worthless Venezuelan currency. These haunting images, almost spectral in their appearance, work as a palimpsest that disrupts and points to the ongoing logic of the spectacle.[98]

The staggering impact of such a diaspora means that many stories have yet to be told. Even among my own acquaintances, I can count Venezuelans who have emigrated to Peru, Ecuador, Panama, Argentina, Spain, Colombia, Mexico, Brazil, and the United States. The Venezuelan band Desorden Público (Public Disorder), which has a history of political critique that predates Chavismo, comments on the crisis in their 2016 album *Bailando sobre las ruinas*.[99] Their song "Los que se Quedan" asks after friends who have left the country to live in places as far flung as Panama, Switzerland, Argentina, Colombia, and Japan, declaring that "someday they will return" (*algún día volverán*). In "Estoy Buscando Algo en el Caribe," the lyrics proclaim, "I'm looking for something in the Caribbean. I'm looking for something else." They ask, "Why does the political regime matter? We are still Latin Americans even if they put up barriers because many things unite us. The crisis has no borders" (*Que importa el régimen político Democracia, dictadura o socialismo. Seguimos siendo latinoamericanos aunque sigan poniendo barreras porque muchas cosas nos unen. La crisis no tiene fronteras*). This identification as Latin American rather than just Venezuelan resists the caricature of Venezuela as a country in crisis.

Reducing a country and its citizens to a simplistic narrative based on their access to commodity reinforces the logic of the spectacle itself, which plays a role in the rhetoric of democracy. In the case of the spectacle image, the distinction between traditional spectacle and the image event appears to be blurred now in that both can proliferate and reinforce the logic of the spectacle. In the image-mediated spectacle, representation supersedes and inscribes itself on daily reality, its logics difficult to avoid. For this reason, media reportage should focus not only on sensational claims but on the human beings involved in crises. Certainly, narratives of crisis should be critiqued when the underlying logic is that the greatest victim of such a crisis is the market system itself. Likewise, narratives of crisis used to justify interventions and interference should also be thoroughly questioned. Despite the competing logics of the spectacle, the way out of the persistent problems faced by Venezuelans must be otherwise, between defense of the state made by propagandists and the opposition-fueled narrative of penury. Venezuela needs narratives that can unite the country politically and resist facile representations.

NOTES

INTRODUCTION

1. Christa J. Olson, "Review of *Rhetoric in South America*," *Rhetoric Society Quarterly* 44 (2014): 394.

2. See María Alejandra Vitale and Philippe-Joseph Salazar, eds., *Rhetoric in South America* (Cape Town: AfricaRhetoric, 2013); see also Damián Baca and Victor Villanueva, *Rhetorics of the Americas, 3114 BCE to 2012 CE* (New York: Palgrave Macmillan, 2010); and "La Idea de la Retórica Americana / The Idea of American Rhetoric," special issue, *Rhetoric Society of America* 45 (2015).

3. Christa J. Olson and René Agustín De los Santos, "Expanding the Idea of América," in "La Idea de la Retórica Americana / The Idea of American Rhetoric," special issue, *Rhetoric Society Quarterly* 45 (2015): 193–94.

4. Walter Mignolo, *The Idea of Latin America* (Malden, MA: Blackwell, 2005), x.

5. Boaventura de Sousa Santos, "Epistemologies of the South and the Future," *From the European South* 1 (2016): 18.

6. D. Robert DeChaine, "Introduction: For Border Studies," in *Border Rhetorics: Citizenship and Identity on the US-Mexico Frontier* (Tuscaloosa: University of Alabama Press, 2012), 2, 8.

7. Bernadette Marie Calafell and Fernando P. Delgado, "Reading Latina/o Images: Interrogating *Americanos*," *Critical Studies in Media Communication* 21 (2004): 1.

8. Darrel Wanzer-Serrano, *The New York Young Lords and the Struggle for Liberation* (Philadelphia: Temple University Press, 2015), 12.

9. De Sousa Santos, "Epistemologies," 20.

10. Boaventura de Sousa Santos, *Una epistemología del Sur* (Mexico City: Siglo XXI, 2009); Walter Mignolo, "Delinking," *Cultural Studies* 21 (2007): 449–514; and Anibal Quijano, "Colonialidad del poder y clasificación social," *Contextualizaciones Latinoamericanas* 3 (2011): 1–33.

11. See Yoshitaka Miike, "An Anatomy of Eurocentrism in Communication Scholarship: The Role of Asiacentricity in De-Westernizing Theory and Research," *China Media Research* 6 (2010): 1–11, and Molefi Kete Asante, "Paradigmatic Issues in Intercultural Communication Studies: An Afrocentric-Asiacentric Dialogue," *China Media Research* 9 (2013): 1–19.

12. Lisa A. Flores, "Between Abundance and Marginalization: The Imperative of Racial Rhetorical Criticism," *Review of Communication* 16 (2016): 5.

13. Michelle Colpean and Rebecca Dingo, "Beyond Drive-By Race Scholarship: The Importance of Engaging Geopolitical Contexts," *Communication and Critical/Cultural Studies* 15 (2018): 307.

14. Wanzer-Serrano, *New York Young Lords*, 26 (italics in the original).

15. Karrieann Soto Vega and Karma Chávez, "Latinx Rhetoric and Intersectionality in Racial Rhetorical Criticism," *Communication and Critical/Cultural Studies* 15 (2018): 320.

16. Breny Mendoza, "La epistemologia del sur la colonialidad de genero y el feminismo latinoamericano," in *Aproximaciones críticas a las prácticas teórico-políticas del*

feminismo latinoamericano, ed. Yuderkys Espinosa Miñoso (Buenos Aires: En la Frontera, 2010), 1:34.

17. Josiah Ober, "The Original Meaning of 'Democracy': Capacity to Do Things, Not Majority Rule," *Constellations* 15 (2008): 8.

18. Octavio Paz, *Ideas y costumbres: La letra y el cetro*, 2nd ed. (Mexico City: Fondo de Cultura Económica USA, 1995), 51.

19. David M. Timmerman and Todd F. McDorman, "Introduction: Rhetoric and Democracy," in *Rhetoric and Democracy: Pedagogical and Political Practices*, ed. Todd F. McDorman and David M. Timmerman (East Lansing: Michigan State University Press, 2008), xiii.

20. Benedetto Fontana, "Rhetoric and the Roots of Democratic Politics," in *Talking Democracy: Historical Perspectives on Rhetoric and Democracy*, ed. Benedetto Fontana, Cary J. Nederman, and Gary Remer (University Park: Pennsylvania State University Press, 2004), 29.

21. Robert Asen, "A Discourse Theory of Citizenship," *Quarterly Journal of Speech* 90 (May 2004): 191.

22. These are not topics covered directly in this volume; rather, they have received important attention elsewhere. Consider John Jones, "Compensatory Division in the Occupy Movement," *Rhetoric Review* 33 (2014): 148–64; Joshua Atkinson, "Networked Activists in Search of Resistance: Exploring an Alternative Media Pilgrimage Across the Boundaries and Borderlands of Globalization," *Communication, Culture, and Critique* 2 (2009): 137–59; and Dave Zirin, *Brazil's Dance with the Devil: The World Cup, the Olympics, and the Fight for Democracy* (Chicago: Haymarket Books, 2014).

23. Geoff Dyer, "A Bolsonaro Victory Will Put Brazil's Democracy to the Test," *Financial Times*, October 25, 2018, https://www.ft.com/content/e98b545c-d844-11e8-ab8e-6beodcf18713; Vincent Bevins, "Can Brazil's Democracy Withstand Jair Bolsonaro?," *The Atlantic*, October 29, 2018, https://www.theatlantic.com/international/archivev/2018/10/brazil-democracy-jair-bolsonaro/574258/; and Matt O'Brien, "Democracy Is in Danger All over the World: Brazil Is Just the Latest Example," *Washington Post*, November 2, 2018, https://www.washingtonpost.com/business/2018/11/02/democracy-is-danger-all-over-world-brazil-is-just-latest-example.

24. Europe is not our focus in this book, yet it is important to note the influence of nationalism around the world. For more on this, see Katya Adler, "Is Europe Lurching to the Far Right?," BBC News, April 28, 2016, https://www.bbc.com/news/world-europe-36150807; and Gideon Rachman, "Donald Trump Leads a Global Revival of Nationalism," *Financial Times*, June 25, 2018, https://www.ft.com/content/59a37a38-7857-11e8-8e67-1e1a0846c475.

25. "¿Primavera Latinoamericana? 2019, un año de protestas en la region," CNN Español, November 22, 2019, https://cnnespanol.cnn.com/2019/11/22/primavera-latinoamericana-2019-un-ano-de-protestas-en-la-region.

26. Will Grant and Boris Miranda, "'Evo Morales debe responder a la justicia porque se fue de la manera más cobarde': Jeanine Áñez, presidenta interina de Bolivia," BBC Mundo, November 22, 2019, https://www.bbc.com/mundo/noticias-america-latina-50431076.

27. Joe Parkin Daniels, "Colombia: Thousands Take to the Streets in Third National Strike in Two Weeks," *The Guardian*, December 4, 2019, https://www.theguardian.com/world/2019/dec/04/colombia-protest-duque-bogota.

28. Hillary Rodham Clinton, "American Democracy Is in Crisis," *The Atlantic*, September 16, 2018, https://www.theatlantic.com/ideas/archive/2018/09/american-democracy-is-in-crisis/570394.

29. On the electoral college, see Jonathan Freedland, "US Democracy Is in Crisis: But Trump Is Only the Symptom," *The Guardian*, November 9, 2018, https://www.theguardian .com/commentisfree/2018/nov/09/us-democracy-trump-white-rural-minority-majority; and Ezra Klein, "The Rigging of American Politics," *Vox*, October 16, 2018, https://www .vox.com/policy-and-politics/2018/10/16/17951596/kavanaugh-trump-senate -impeachment-avenatti-democrats-2020-supreme-court; on racial capitalism, see Michael C. Dawson, "Racial Capitalism and Democratic Crisis," *Items: Insights from the Social Sciences*, December 4, 2018, https://items.ssrc.org/race-capitalism/racial-capitalism-and -democratic-crisis/.

30. Shasta Darlington, "A Momentous Election in Brazil: What's at Stake?," *New York Times*, October 28, 2018, https://www.nytimes.com/2018/10/28/world/americas /brazil-presidential-election-news.html.

31. Arturo Sarukhan, "What Mexico's Next President Means for Trump," *Washington Post*, July 2, 2018, https://www.washingtonpost.com/news/theworldpost/wp/2018 /07/02/lopez-obrador.

32. Joe Parkin Daniels, "Iván Duque Wins Election to Become Colombia's President," *The Guardian*, June 18, 2018, https://www.theguardian.com/world/2018/jun/18 /ivan-duque-wins-election-to-become-colombias-president.

33. Alex Boutilier, "Rise of Right-Wing Extremists Presents New Challenge for Canadian Law Enforcement Agencies," *Toronto Star*, October 7, 2018, https://www.thestar .com/news/canada/2018/10/07/rise-of-right-wing-extremists-presents-new-challenge -for-canadian-law-enforcement-agencies.html.

34. Octavio Paz, "América Latina: Las desventuras de la democracia," *Los Libros de Vuelta* 123 (1987): 43–52.

35. Ignacio Walker, *La democracia en América Latina: entre la esperanza y la desesperanza* (Santiago: Uqbar Editores, 2009).

36. Everett Rogers, *Diffusion of Innovations* (New York: Free Press of Glencoe, 1962).

37. Octavio Paz, *Fundación y disidencia: Dominio hispánic* (Mexico City: Fondo de Cultura Económica USA, 1998), 16.

38. Daniel Lerner, *The Passing of Traditional Society: Modernizing the Middle East* (New York: Free Press of Glencoe, 1958).

39. Ricardo Dello Buono, "Technology and Development in Latin America: Urgent Challenges for the 21st Century," *Perspectives on Global Development* 11 (2012): 341–51.

40. Paz, "América Latina."

41. Inés Nercesian, "Ideas, pensamiento y político en Argentina, Brasil, Chile y Uruguay entre los 50 y los 60," *Trabajo y Sociedad* 19 (2012): 393–415.

42. Dello Buono, "Technology and Development"; Armand Mattelart, *La mundialización de la comunicación* (Barcelona: Paidós, 1998); Nercesian, "Ideas, pensamiento y político."

43. Walker, *La democracia en América Latina*.

44. Andrés Solimaro, Vito Tanzi, and Felipe del Solar, *Las terminas del estado: Ensayos sobre corrupción, transparencia y desarrollo* (Santiago: Fondo de Cultura Económica).

45. Manuel Antonio Garretón, *Neoliberalismo corregido y progresismo limitado: Los gobiernos de la concertación en Chile, 1990–2010* (Santiago: Editorial Arcis / CLACSO, 2012).

46. Dello Buono, "Technology and Development."

47. David Harvey, *A Brief History of Neoliberalism* (New York: Oxford University Press, 2005), 3.

48. Ernesto Laclau and Chantal Mouffe, *Hegemony and Socialist Strategy: Towards a Radical Democratic Politics*, 2nd ed. (London: Verso, 2001).

49. Wendy Brown, *Undoing the Demos: Neoliberalism's Stealth Revolution* (New York: Zone Books, 2015), 28.

50. Mark Goodale and Nancy Postero, eds., *Neoliberalism, Interrupted: Social Change and Contested Governance in Contemporary Latin America* (Stanford, CA: Stanford University Press, 2009), 3.

51. Susan Eckstein, "Power and Popular Protest in Latin America," in *Power and Popular Protest: Latin American Social Movements*, ed. Susan Eckstein (Berkeley: University of California Press, 2001), 3.

52. Juan Carlos Moreno-Brid and Igor Paunovic, "What Is New and What Is Left of the Economic Policies of the New Left Governments of Latin America?," *International Journal of Political Economy* 37 (2009): 82–108.

53. Luiz Carlos Bresser-Pereira, "O Paradox o da Izquierda no Brasil," *Novos Estados* 74 (2006): 25–45; Amy Kennemore and Gregory Weeks, "Twenty-First Century Socialism? The Elusive Search for a Post-Neoliberal Development Model in Bolivia and Ecuador," *Bulletin of Latin American Research* 30 (2011): 267–81; Thomas Muhr, "(Re)constructing Popular Power in Our America: Venezuela and the Regionalization of 'Revolutionary Democracy' in the ALBA-TCP Space," *Third World Quarterly* 33 (2012): 225–41; Verónica Pérez, "Los desafíos de gobernar por izquierda cuando la economía se contrae," *Revista de Cincia Politica* 36 (2015): 339–63.

54. "Chile Election: Conservative Piñeda Elected President," BBC News, December 18, 2017, https://www.bbc.com/news/world-latin-america-42388019.

55. For a summary of the agreement, see Heather Long, "U.S., Canada, and Mexico Just Reached a Sweeping New NAFTA Deal," *Washington Post*, October 1, 2018, https://www.washingtonpost.com/business/2018/10/01/us-canada-mexico-just-reached-sweeping-new-nafta-deal-heres-whats-it.

56. Aside from shocking the global diplomatic community, this decision also alienated military leadership within the United States, contributing to the resignation of Secretary of Defense Jim Mattis. For more on this, see Helene Cooper, "Jim Mattis, Defense Secretary, Resigns in Rebuke of Trump's Worldview," *New York Times*, December 20, 2018, https://www.nytimes.com/2018/12/20/us/politics/jim-mattis-defense-secretary-trump.html. On concerns about Trump's responses to Iran, see David D. Kirkpatrick, "In Trump's Iran Response, Some See a Dangerous Ambiguity," *New York Times*, June 21, 2019, https://www.nytimes.com/2019/06/21/world/middleeast/trump-iran-retaliation.html.

57. There is much to be said about war culture in the United States, especially in light of the nation's responses to 9/11 and the subsequent "war on terror." For an overview, see Paul Achter, "Rhetoric and the Permanent War," *Quarterly Journal of Speech* 102 (2016): 79–94; Jeremy Engels and William O. Saas, "On Acquiescence and Ends-Less War: An Inquiry into the New War Rhetoric," *Quarterly Journal of Speech* 99 (2013): 225–32; Stephen John Hartnett and Laura Ann Stengrim, *Globalization and Empire: The U.S. Invasion of Iraq, Free Markets, and the Twilight of Democracy* (Tuscaloosa: University of Alabama Press, 2006); and Robert L. Ivie and Oscar Giner, *Hunt the Devil: A Demonology of US War Culture* (Tuscaloosa: University of Alabama Press, 2015).

58. For more on Obama and drone policy, see James Downie, "Obama's Drone War Is a Shameful Part of His Legacy," *Washington Post*, May 5, 2016, https://www.washingtonpost.com/opinions/obamas-drone-war-is-a-shameful-part-of-his-legacy/2016/05/05/a727eea8-12ea-11e6-8967-7ac733c56f12_story.html.

59. Laura Macdonald and Arne Ruckert, "Post-Neoliberalism in the Americas: An Introduction," in *Post-Neoliberalism in the Americas*, ed. Laura Macdonald and Arne Ruckert (London: Palgrave Macmillan, 2009), 2.

60. For examples, see Bill McKibben, "Stop Swooning over Justin Trudeau. The Man Is a Disaster for the Planet," *The Guardian*, April 17, 2017, https://www.theguardian .com/commentisfree/2017/apr/17/stop-swooning-justin-trudeau-man-disaster-planet; and Alan Freeman, "Canadians' Love Affair with Justin Trudeau Is Over," *Washington Post*, March 29, 2018, https://www.washingtonpost.com/news/worldviews/wp/2018/03 /29/canadians-love-affair-with-justin-trudeau-is-over.

61. David McGuffin, "Justin Trudeau Wins Reelection in Canadian Election," NPR, October 22, 2019, https://www.npr.org/2019/10/22/772170458/justin-trudeau-wins -reelection-in-canadian-election.

62. For more on party affiliations and differences, see Dan Balz and Jon Cohen, "Big Gulf Between Parties, Divisions Within," *Washington Post*, August 18, 2012, http://www.washingtonpost.com/politics/big-gulf-between-parties-divisions-within /2012/08/18/f5ee15d4-e31a-11e1-ae7f-d2a13e249eb2_story.html.

63. Gregory Wallace, "Voter Turnout at 20-Year Low in 2016," CNN, November 30, 2016, https://www.cnn.com/2016/11/11/politics/popular-vote-turnout-2016/index .html.

64. Carroll Doherty, "Key Findings on Americans' Views of the U.S. Political System and Democracy," *Pew Research Center Fact Tank*, April 26, 2018, http://www.pewresearch .org/fact-tank/2018/04/26/key-findings-on-americans-views-of-the-u-s-political-system -and-democracy. For more on the growth of partisanship among citizens in the United States, see Lilliana Mason, *Uncivil Agreement: How Politics Became Our Identity* (Chicago: University of Chicago Press, 2018).

65. For more on the "rhetoric of shared beliefs," see Vanessa B. Beasley, "A Presidential Rhetoric of Shared Beliefs," in *You, the People: American National Identity in Presidential Rhetoric* (College Station: Texas A&M University Press, 2004), 46–67.

66. John Locke, *Second Treatise of Government*, ed. C. B. Macpherson (Indianapolis: Hackett, 1980).

67. Walker, *La democracia en América Latina*; and Jorge Carpizo, *Concepto de democracia y sistemas de gobierno en América Latina* (Bogotá: Universidad Externado de Colombia, 2009).

68. Barry Holden, *Understanding Liberal Democracy* (Oxford, UK: Philip Allan, 1988).

69. Manuel Alcántara, "La escala de la izquierda," *Nueva Sociedad* 217 (2008): 72–85; André Borges, "The Political Consequences of Center-Led Redistribution in Brazilian Federalism: The Fall of Subnational Party Machines," *Latin American Research Review* 47 (2011): 21–45; Alain Touraine, "Entre Bachelet y Morales ¿Existe una izquierda en América Latina?," *Nueva Sociedad* 205 (2006): 46–56.

70. Giulio Alinolfi, "Las estructuras de los populismos: Diferenciación funcional en el populismo latinamericao," *Nómadas* 25 (2010): 455–71; Sebastián Barros, "Populismo, pueblo y liderazgo en América Latina," *Colombia Internacional* 82 (2014): 297–302.

71. Adriana Angel, "La construcción retórica de la corrupción," *Chasqui* 132 (2016): 309–27.

72. José del Tronco, "Desconfianza y accountability: ¿Las causas del populismo en América Latina?," *Latin American Research Review* 48 (2013): 55–78; Walker, *La democracia en América Latina*.

73. Borges, "Political Consequences"; Carpizo, *Concepto de democracia*.

74. Russell L. Hanson, "The Rhetoric of Democracy," in *The Democratic Imagination in America: Conversations with Our Past* (Princeton, NJ: Princeton University Press, 1995), 22–53; Robert L. Ivie, "Rhetorical Deliberation and Democratic Politics in the Here and Now," *Rhetoric and Public Affairs* 5 (2002): 277–85; Gerard A. Hauser, "Rhetorical

Democracy and Civic Engagement," in *Rhetorical Democracy: Discursive Practices of Civic Engagement*, ed. Gerard A. Hauser and Amy Grim (Mahwah, NJ: Lawrence Erlbaum, 2004), 1–14.

75. Flores, "Between Abundance and Marginalization," 6.

76. Olson and De los Santos, "Expanding the Idea of América," 197.

CHAPTER I

1. For example, see Ralph Cintrón, "Democracy and Its Limitations," in *The Public Work of Rhetoric: Citizen-Scholars and Civic Engagement*, ed. John M. Ackerman and David J. Coogan (Columbia: University of South Carolina Press, 2010), 98–116; Karma R. Chávez, "Beyond Inclusion: Rethinking Rhetoric's Historical Narrative," *Quarterly Journal of Speech* 101, no. 1 (January 2015): 162–72; J. David Cisneros, "Rhetorics of Citizenship: Pitfalls and Possibilities," *Quarterly Journal of Speech* 100, no. 3 (2014): 375–88; and Darrel Enck-Wanzer, "A Radical Democratic Style? Tradition, Hybridity, and Intersectionality," *Rhetoric and Public Affairs* 11, no. 3 (2008): 459–65.

2. Cintrón, "Democracy and Its Limitations," 100.

3. Ibid., 100.

4. For more on the links between land, place, and social life within Indigenous knowledges, see Heather Davis and Zoe Todd, "On the Importance of a Date, or Decolonizing the Anthropocene," *ACME* 16, no. 4 (2017): 761–80; Vanessa Watts, "Indigenous Place-Thought and Agency Amongst Humans and Non-Humans (First Woman and Sky Woman Go on a European World Tour!)," *Decolonization: Indigeneity, Education and Society* 2, no. 1 (2013): 20–34; and Kyle Powys Whyte, "Our Ancestors' Dystopia Now: Indigenous Conservation and the Anthropocene," in *The Routledge Companion to the Environmental Humanities*, ed. Ursula K. Heise, Jon Christensen, and Michelle Niemann (New York: Routledge, 2017), 206–15.

5. Latin American republics have had complicated relationships with democracy, but appeals to "America" as particularly democratic (especially those emerging from the United States) have consistently absorbed and elided Latin America. When I invoke "America" here, I conjure that sense of a hemisphere that exceeds yet remains tethered to the United States. When I intend to reference only the United States, I will be explicit. All references to "America" intentionally invoke the national-hemispheric slippage.

6. See, for example, Gregory Clark, *Rhetorical Landscapes in America: Variations on a Theme from Kenneth Burke* (Columbia: University of South Carolina Press, 2004); and Barbara E. Willard, "Rhetorical Landscapes as Epistemic: Revisiting Aldo Leopold's *A Sand County Almanac*," *Environmental Communication* 1, no. 2 (November 2007): 218–35.

7. Caroline Gottschalk Druschke, "Watershed as Common-Place: Communicating for Conservation at the Watershed Scale," *Environmental Communication* 7, no. 1 (March 2013): 80–96; Christa J. Olson, *Constitutive Visions: Indigeneity and Commonplaces of National Identity in Republican Ecuador* (University Park: Pennsylvania State University Press, 2014), 92; Samantha Senda-Cook, "Materializing Tensions: How Maps and Trails Mediate Nature," *Environmental Communication* 7, no. 3 (September 2013): 356.

8. Gabriela Mistral of Chile and Benjamín Carrión of Ecuador wrote prolifically about *tropicalismo*, drawing on José Vasconcelos's *La Raza Cósmica* to articulate the movement's social significance. See, for example, Gabriela Mistral, "Palabras que hemos manchado: Tropicalismo," in *Toda Gabriela Mistral en repertorio americano*, ed. Francisco González Alvarado, Marybel Soto Ramírez, and Mario Oliva Medina (Costa Rica: Editorial Universidad Nacional, 2011), 1:87–88; Benjamín Carrión, *Cartas al Ecuador* (Quito:

Editorial Gutenberg, 1943); José Vasconcelos, *The Cosmic Race: A Bilingual Edition*, ed. Didier Tisdel Jaén (Baltimore: Johns Hopkins University Press, 1997).

9. Druschke, "Watershed as Common-Place," 93.

10. Diane M. Keeling and Jennifer C. Prairie, "Trophic and Tropic Dynamics: An Ecological Perspective of Tropes," in *Tracing Rhetoric and Material Life: Ecological Approaches*, ed. Bridie McGreavy et al. (New York: Palgrave Macmillan, 2018), 54; Caroline Gottschalk Druschke, "A Trophic Future for Rhetorical Ecologies," *Enculturation* 28 (2019): ¶ 20.

11. Druschke, "Trophic Future," ¶ 35 (italics in the original). Marisol de la Cadena, *Earth Beings* (Durham, NC: Duke University Press, 2015); Eduardo Viveiros de Castro, "The Transformation of Objects into Subjects in Amerindian Ontologies," *Common Knowledge* 10, no. 3 (2004): 463–84.

12. The Spanish word *criollo*, rendered in English as "creole," has varied meanings by context, though it generally refers to American-born people. Here, I use it to identify American-born elites, usually white, who align themselves with European heritage while staking claims to American identity.

13. For background on the idea of "worlds and knowledges otherwise," see Arturo Escobar, "Worlds and Knowledges Otherwise: The Latin American Modernity/Coloniality Research Program," *Cultural Studies* 21, nos. 2–3 (March–May 2007): 179–210; Walter D. Mignolo, "Epistemic Disobedience, Independent Thought and Decolonial Freedom," *Theory, Culture and Society* 26, nos. 7–8 (2009): 159–81; and Aníbal Quijano, "Coloniality and Modernity/Rationality," *Cultural Studies* 21, nos. 2–3 (March–May 2007): 168–78.

14. Latin Americans typically imagine a single American continent while people in the United States habitually distinguish North from South.

15. For more on water as connecting and dividing, see Tiara R. Na'puti, "Archipelagic Rhetoric: Remapping the Marianas and Challenging Militarization from 'A Stirring Place,'" *Communication and Critical/Cultural Studies* 16, no. 1 (2019): 4–25.

16. For more on how North and South America cast shadows and shade on each other, see Elizabeth Millán-Zaibert, "A Great Vanishing Act? The Latin American Philosophical Tradition and How Ariel and Caliban Helped Save It from Oblivion," *CR: The New Centennial Review* 7, no. 3 (Winter 2007): 152.

17. Nancy Fraser, "Rethinking the Public Sphere: A Contribution to the Critique of Actually Existing Democracy," *Social Text*, nos. 25–26 (1990): 56–80.

18. Thomas Jefferson, *Notes on the State of Virginia*, ed. William Peden, 2nd ed. (Chapel Hill: University of North Carolina Press, 2011), https://muse.jhu.edu/book/43979; Lee Alan Dugatkin, *Mr. Jefferson and the Giant Moose: Natural History in Early America* (Chicago: University of Chicago Press, 2009); Dustin A. Gish and Daniel Klinghard, *Thomas Jefferson and the Science of Republican Government: A Political Biography of Notes on the State of Virginia* (Cambridge, UK: Cambridge University Press, 2017), 136–67.

19. Dawn Ades, "Nature, Science and the Picturesque," in *Art in Latin America: The Modern Era, 1820–1980* (New Haven, CT: Yale University Press, 1989), 63–99; Antonio Lafuente, "Enlightenment in an Imperial Context: Local Science in the Late-Eighteenth-Century Hispanic World," *Osiris* 15 (2001): 155–73; Christa Olson, "Casta Painting and the Rhetorical Body," *Rhetoric Society Quarterly* 39, no. 4 (October 2009): 307–30.

20. James Monroe, "Monroe Doctrine (1823)," Our Documents, accessed June 25, 2020, https://www.ourdocuments.gov/doc.php?flash=true&doc=23&page=transcript.

21. Ibid., ¶ 2.

22. Ibid., ¶ 4.

23. Ibid., ¶ 1.

24. Walt Whitman, "Disunion," *Brooklyn Daily Eagle*, May 22, 1847.

25. Monroe, "Monroe Doctrine," ¶ 4.

26. Simón Bolívar, "The Cartagena Manifesto: Memorial Addressed to the Citizens of New Granada by a Citizen from Caracas (15 December 1812)," in *El Libertador: Writings of Simón Bolívar*, ed. David Bushnell, trans. Frederick H. Fornoff (Oxford, UK: Oxford University Press, 2003), 3–11.

27. Simón Bolívar, "The Jamaica Letter: Response from a South American to a Gentleman from This Island," in *El Libertador: Writings of Simón Bolívar*, ed. David Bushnell, trans. Frederick H. Fornoff (Oxford, UK: Oxford University Press, 2003), 13. Bolívar nominally wrote the "Carta de Jamaica" in response to an inquiry about the state of South American politics from Henry Cullen, a British gentleman living in Jamaica. In 1819, it was published for a broader, English-speaking audience in the *Jamaica Quarterly Journal and Literary Gazette*. The letter's original audience was British, not Latin American, and it was only published in Latin America and in Spanish in 1833, three years after Bolívar's death.

28. Ibid., 18.

29. Ibid., 23.

30. Ibid., 25.

31. Ibid., 27.

32. Ibid., 30.

33. Simón Bolívar, "The Bolivian Constitution," in *El Libertador: Writings of Simón Bolívar*, ed. David Bushnell, trans. Frederick H. Fornoff (Oxford, UK: Oxford University Press, 2003), 58.

34. "El mundo sabe que el Alto-Perú ha sido, en el continente de América, el ara adonde se vertió la primera sangre de los libres, y la tierra donde existe la tumba del último de los tiranos." "Acta de la Independencia de Bolivia (6 de agosto de 1825): Acta de Independencia de las Provincias Alto Peruanas," in *Los Vascos en las Independencias Americanas*, ed. Francisco de Abrisketa Iraculis (Bogota: Fundación Centro Vasco Euskal Etxea / Editorial La Oveja Negra, 2009), 100.

35. Baron de Montesquieu, *The Spirit of Laws*, trans. Thomas Nugent, vol. 1 (London: Colonial Press, 1900), bk. 1, chap. 3, p. 6.

36. Alexis de Tocqueville, *Democracy in America*, trans. Henry Reeve (New York: Adlard and Saunders / George Dearborn, 1838), 12.

37. Donald E. Pease, "José Martí, Alexis de Tocqueville, and the Politics of Displacement," in *José Martí's "Our America,"* ed. Jeffrey Grant Belnap and Raul A. Fernandez (Durham, NC: Duke University Press, 1998), 42.

38. Carrión, *Cartas al Ecuador*, 14–15.

39. Ibid., 19.

40. Ibid., 82.

41. Cintrón, "Democracy and Its Limitations," 106.

42. Carrión, Cartas al Ecuador, 81.

43. María Josefina Saldaña-Portillo, "Critical Latinx Indigeneities: A Paradigm Drift," *Latino Studies* 15, no. 2 (July 2017): 141.

44. For scholarship illuminating contemporary examples in Latin America, see, for example, Bret Gustafson, "Manipulating Cartographies: Plurinationalism, Autonomy, and Indigenous Resurgence in Bolivia," *Anthropological Quarterly* 82, no. 4 (Fall 2009): 985–1016; and Patricia Rodriguez and David Carruthers, "Testing Democracy's Promise: Indigenous Mobilization and the Chilean State," *European Review of Latin American and Caribbean Studies* 85 (October 2008): 3–21. For select historical examples, see Marc Becker, *Indians and Leftists in the Making of Ecuador's Modern Indigenous Movements* (Durham, NC: Duke University Press, 2008); Casey Ryan Kelly, "Détournement, Decolonization, and the American Indian Occupation of Alcatraz Island (1969–1971)," *Rhetoric Society Quarterly* 44, no. 2 (March 2014): 168–90; and Scott Richard Lyons, "Rhetorical

Sovereignty: What Do American Indians Want from Writing?" *College Composition and Communication* 51, no. 3 (February 2000): 447–68.

45. Leanne Betasamosake Simpson, *As We Have Always Done: Indigenous Freedom Through Radical Resistance* (Minneapolis: University of Minnesota Press, 2017), 160.

46. Ibid.

47. Emiliano Zapata, "Plan de Ayala (1911)," doc. no. 6, chap. 3, *Modern Latin America* web supplement for 8th ed., ¶ 2, accessed June 26, 2020, https://library.brown .edu/create/modernlatinamerica/chapters/chapter-3-mexico/primary-documents-with -accompanying-discussion-questions/document-6-plan-de-ayala-emilio-zapata-1911/.

48. Ibid., ¶ 10, 11.

49. Ibid., ¶ 11.

50. Rigoberta Menchú Tum, "Nobel Lecture," Nobel Prize, December 10, 1992, https://www.nobelprize.org/nobel_prizes/peace/laureates/1992/tum-lecture.html.

51. Ibid.

52. Ibid.

53. Ibid.

54. Confederación de Nacionalidades Indígenas del Ecuador, "Declaration of Quito," Native Web, July 1990, last modified June 5, 2019, http://www.nativeweb.org /papers/statements/quincentennial/quito.php; Kelly, "Détournement."

55. Gabriela Raquel Ríos, "Mestizaje," in *Decolonizing Rhetoric and Composition Studies: New Latinx Keywords for Theory and Pedagogy*, ed. Iris D. Ruiz and Raúl Sanchéz (New York: Palgrave Macmillan, 2016), 113.

56. Vidal Guato and Elvio Sosa, "Paraguay: Por El Derecho a La Tierra y Territorio," Enlace Indígena," Enlace Indígena, March 19, 2015, https://www.movimientos.org/es /content/paraguay-por-el-derecho-la-tierra-y-territorio.

57. Gustafson, "Manipulating Cartographies," 1003.

58. Joy Harjo, "Conflict Resolution for Holy Beings," in *Conflict Resolution for Holy Beings* (New York: W. W. Norton, 2015), 77.

59. Organización Nacional Indígena de Colombia, "Mensaje de los pueblos indígenas de Colombia al Papa Francisco: El camino de la paz es la armonización y liberación de la Madre Tierra," Enlace Indígena, September 8, 2017, https://www.movimientos.org /es/content/el-camino-de-la-paz-es-la-armonización-y-liberación-de-la-madre-tierra.

60. "Nunca más las Américas, sin los pueblos indígenas!" Enlace Indígena, April 24, 2007, https://www.movimientos.org/es/enlacei/show_text.php3%3Fkey%3D9783.

61. I am far from the first to make this point. See, for example, Malea Powell et al., "Our Story Begins Here: Constellating Cultural Rhetorics," *Enculturation* 18 (2014), http://enculturation.net/our-story-begins-here; Eve Tuck and Wayne K. Yang, "Decolonication Is Not a Metaphor," *Decolonization: Indigeneity, Education and Society* 1, no. 1 (2012): 1–40; and Davis and Todd, "On the Importance of a Date."

62. Qwo-Li Driskill, "Doubleweaving Two-Spirit Critiques: Building Alliances Between Native and Queer Studies," *GLQ: A Journal of Lesbian and Gay Studies* 16, nos. 1–2 (January 2010): 71.

CHAPTER 2

1. Alberto Moreiras, *The Exhaustion of Difference: The Politics of Latin American Cultural Studies* (Durham, NC: Duke University Press, 2001), 135. In these pages I engage this question at the register of Latinamericanism, which Moreiras defines as "the set or sum total of engaged representations providing a viable knowledge of the Latin American object of enunciation" (32). Although my analysis covers the engaged representations

of Latin America produced in the field of US-American scholarship (by US-American authors), I contend, following Moreiras, that the location from which one produces critical reflection does not formally determine what can be said or thought about Latin America. By Latinamericanism, I refer to any study that takes Latin America as an object of study, regardless of location. I make no distinction, in other words, between Latin Americans and US-Americans studying the object of Latin America.

2. Walter Mignolo, "Delinking: The Rhetoric of Modernity, the Logic of Coloniality, and the Grammar of De-coloniality," *Cultural Studies* 21, no. 2 (2007): 449–514.

3. Cristina Ramírez, *Occupying Our Space: The Mestiza Rhetorics of Mexican Women Journalists and Activists, 1875–1942* (Tucson: University of Arizona Press, 2015), 21, 52.

4. Damián Baca, "Te-Ixtli: The 'Other Face' of the Americas," in *Rhetorics of the Americas: 3114 BCE to 2012 CE*, ed. Damián Baca and Victor Villanueva (New York: Palgrave Macmillan, 2010), ix.

5. Ibid., 3; Damián Baca, *Mestiz@ Scripts: Digital Migrations and the Territories of Writing* (New York: Palgrave Macmillan, 2008), 3.

6. Giorgio Agamben, *Homo Sacer: Sovereign Power and Bare Life*, trans. Daniel Heller-Roazen (Stanford, CA: Stanford University Press, 1998).

7. Moreiras, *Exhaustion of Difference*, 32.

8. José Manuel Cortez, "Of Exterior and Exception: Latin American Rhetoric, Subalternity, and the Politics of Cultural Difference," *Philosophy and Rhetoric* 51, no. 2 (2018): 124–50.

9. Emma Pérez, *The Decolonial Imaginary: Writing Chicanas into History* (Bloomington: University of Indiana Press, 1999), 11.

10. Ibid., xvi–xvii.

11. Homi Bhabha, *The Location of Culture* (New York: Routledge, 1994), 53.

12. Ibid., 122–23.

13. Pérez, *Decolonial Imaginary*, xii.

14. Ibid., 5.

15. Ibid.

16. Chela Sandoval, *Methodology of the Oppressed* (Minneapolis: University of Minnesota Press, 2000), 183.

17. Pérez, *Decolonial Imaginary*, 25.

18. Ibid. Mestizaje, of course, is not the felicitous discourse of hybridity that produces the consciousness of a supposedly smooth space because it is grounded within and presupposes the foundational exclusion of yet another part of the social text: the unrepresentable alterity of blackness.

19. Ibid., 26.

20. Gareth Williams, *The Other Side of the Popular: Neoliberalism and Subalternity in Latin America* (Durham, NC: Duke University Press, 2002), 30–32.

21. Moreiras, *Exhaustion of Difference*, 32.

22. *The Decolonial Imaginary* emerged in close proximity to several other projects across the fields of Latino and Latin American cultural studies at the turn of the century that sought to rethink the role of critical thought in relation to fundamental shifts in contemporary social, political, and scholarly formations in the wake of free trade global capital, including John Beverley, *Subalternity and Representation: Arguments in Cultural Theory* (Durham, NC: Duke University Press: 1999); José David Saldívar, *Border Matters: Remapping American Cultural Studies* (Berkeley: University of California Press, 1997); Moreiras, *Exhaustion of Difference*; Juan Poblete, *Critical Latin American and Latino Studies* (Minneapolis: University of Minnesota, 2003); Sandoval, *Methodology of the Oppressed*; and Williams, *Other Side of the Popular*.

23. Moreiras, *Exhaustion of Difference*, 20.

24. Ibid., 107.

25. Jacques Rancière argues that "politics exists simply because no social order is based on nature, no divine law regulates human society" (*Disagreement: Politics and Philosophy*, trans. Julie Rose [Minneapolis: University of Minnesota Press, 1999], 16). If "sheer contingency," or a lack of grounding in divine law, is the first and primary condition of possibility for any social order, then hegemony is the name for a mode of power operating via the rhetorical process of attempting to fuse signifier to signified in absolute fashion, of managing subjectivities, or, "parts," proper to their place in society, and of circulating "the lie that invents some kind of social nature in order to provide community with an *arkhê*" (16).

26. Williams, *Other Side of the Popular*.

27. Ibid., 1.

28. Ibid., 8.

29. George Yúdice, "Civil Society, Consumption, and Governmentality in an Age of Global Restructuring," *Social Text*, no. 48 (1995): 1–25.

30. Ibid., 4.

31. Michael Hardt, "The Withering of Civil Society," *Social Text*, no. 48 (1995): 40.

32. Antonio Gramsci, *Selections from the Prison Notebooks of Antonio Gramsci*, ed. and trans. Quintin Hoare and Geoffrey Nowell Smith (New York: International Publishers, 1971), 238.

33. Gilles Deleuze, "Postscript on the Societies of Control," *October* 59 (1992): 3–7.

34. Williams, *Other Side of the Popular*, 149.

35. Moreiras, *Exhaustion of Difference*, 46.

36. Baca, *Mestiz@ Scripts*, 64.

37. Guillermo Gómez-Peña, *Dangerous Border Crossers: The Artist Talks Back* (New York: Routledge, 2000), 220.

38. Franny Howes, "Imagining a Multiplicity of Visual Rhetorical Traditions: Comics Lessons from Rhetoric Histories," *ImageTexT* 5, no. 3 (2008), http://imagetext.english.ufl.edu/archives/v5_3/howes/.

39. Kat Austin and Carlos-Urani Montiel, "Codex Espangliensis: Neo-Baroque Art of Resistance," *Latin American Perspectives* 39, no. 3 (2012): 99.

40. Cruz Medina, *Reclaiming Poch@ Pop: Examining the Rhetoric of Cultural Deficiency* (New York: Palgrave Macmillan, 2015), 123.

41. Guillermo Gómez-Peña, *Warrior for Gringostroika* (St. Paul, MN: Graywolf Press, 1993), 220. I am citing the performance poem "Califas," an excerpt of which appears as the narrative core in *Codex Espangliensis*, for accuracy. The text is nearly identical in its reproduction in *Codex*, with the exception of sentence casing, spacing, the replacement of "misunderstandings" for "misconceptions."

42. Coco Fusco, "The Other History of Intercultural Performance," *Drama Review* 38, no. 1 (1994): 143–67.

43. Rancière, *Disagreement*, 30.

44. Ibid., 30.

45. Eduardo Mendieta and Guillermo Gómez-Peña, "A Latino Philosopher Interviews a Chicano Performance Artist," *Napantla: View from the South* 2, no. 3 (2001): 548–49.

46. Slavoj Žižek, *The Puppet and the Dwarf: The Perverse Core of Christianity* (Cambridge, MA: MIT Press, 2003), 96.

47. Michel Foucault, *The Order of Things: An Archaeology of the Human Sciences* (New York: Vintage, 1970), xix.

48. Denarrativization, as Moreiras writes, is the name for "the moment when a narrative, any narrative, breaks into its own abyss" and "a moment of flight in which

subjectivity registers as noncapturable; indeed, it is a moment of pure production with-out positivity that will not let itself be exhaustively defined in the name of any heteroge-neity." Moreiras, *Exhaustion of Difference*, 56.

49. Žižek, *Puppet and the Dwarf*, 413.

CHAPTER 3

1. Greg Grandin, "A Voter's Guide to Hillary Clinton's Policies in Latin America," *The Nation*, April 15, 2016, https://www.thenation.com/article/a-voters-guide-to-hillary -clintons-policies-in-latin-america.

2. Suzanne Gamboa, "Clinton to Latinos at LULAC: 'You Are Not Intruders,'" NBC News, July 14, 2016, https://www.nbcnews.com/news/latino/clinton-latinos-lulac -you-are-not-intruders-n609476.

3. Lucinda Shen, "The U.S. Was Just Downgraded from a 'Full' to a 'Flawed' Democracy," *Fortune*, January 25, 2018, http://fortune.com/2017/01/25/us-democracy -downgrade.

4. George F. Will, "Vote Against the GOP This November," *Washington Post*, June 22, 2018, https://www.washingtonpost.com/opinions/vote-against-the-gop-this -november/2018/06/22/a6378306-7575-11e8-b4b7-308400242c2e_story.html.

5. Amy N. Heuman and Alberto González, "Trump's Essentialist Border Rhetoric: Racial Identities and Dangerous Liminalities," *Journal of Intercultural Communication Research* 47 (2018): 326–42.

6. Michael Calvin McGee, "The 'Ideograph': A Link Between Rhetoric and Ideol-ogy," *Quarterly Journal of Speech* 66 (1980): 1–16.

7. For a summary of this issue, see Aaron Hegarty, "Timeline: Immigrant Children Separated from Families at the Border," *USA Today*, June 27, 2018, https://www.usatoday .com/story/news/2018/06/27/immigrant-children-family-separation-border-timeline /734014002.

8. J. David Cisneros, *The Border Crossed Us: Rhetorics of Borders, Citizenship, and Latina/o Identity* (Tuscaloosa: University of Alabama Press, 2014), 5, 6.

9. J. David Cisneros, "Contaminated Communities: The Metaphor of 'Immigrant as Pollutant' in Media Representations of Immigration," *Rhetoric and Public Affairs* 11 (2008): 569–602; Anne Demo, "Sovereignty Discourse and Contemporary Immigra-tion Politics," *Quarterly Journal of Speech* 91 (2005): 291–311; Kent A. Ono and John M. Sloop, *Shifting Borders: Rhetoric, Immigration, and California's Proposition 187* (Philadel-phia: Temple University Press, 2002).

10. McGee, "Ideograph," 7.

11. Casey Ryan Kelly, "'We Are Not Free': The Meaning of <Freedom> in American Indian Resistance to President Johnson's War on Poverty," *Communication Quarterly* 62 (2014): 457.

12. Richard D. Pineda and Stacey K. Sowards, "Flag Waving as Visual Argument: 2006 Immigration Demonstrations and Cultural Citizenship," *Argumentation and Advo-cacy* 43 (2007): 167.

13. Scott Horsley, "Fact Check: Trump, Illegal Immigration, and Crime," NPR, June 22, 2018, https://www.npr.org/2018/06/22/622540331/fact-check-trump-illegal -immigration-and-crime.

14. Tal Kopan, "Trump Admin Drops Asylum Protections for Domestic Violence Victims," CNN, June 11, 2018, https://www.cnn.com/2018/06/11/politics/jeff-sessions -asylum-decision/index.html.

15. These are drawn from Ono and Sloop, *Shifting Borders*.

16. "Transcript: Donald Trump's Full Immigration Speech Annotated," *Los Angeles Times*, August 31, 2016, http://www.latimes.com/politics/la-na-pol-donald-trump-immigration-speech-transcript-20160831-snap-htmlstory.html.

17. Lily Moore-Eissenberg, "Small Area Farms Feel Effect of Labor Shortage," *Toledo Blade*, June 23, 2018, https://www.toledoblade.com/business/2018/06/23/Labor-shortages-cost-small-area-farms.html.

18. See the Victims of Immigration Crime Engagement Office, which operates under the Department of Homeland Security, at https://www.ice.gov/voice.

19. Vivian Salama, "Trump to Mexico: Take Care of 'Bad Hombres' or US Might," AP News, February 2, 2017, https://www.apnews.com/0b3f5db59b2e4aa78cdbbf008f27fb49; Amy Tennery, "Trump's 'Bad Hombres' and 'Nasty Woman' Stoke Online Outrage," Reuters, October 20, 2016, https://www.reuters.com/article/us-usa-election-debate-socialmedia-idUSKCN12KoI4.

20. Alex Dobuzinskis, "Illegal Immigrant Acquitted of Murder in San Francisco, Trump Slams Verdict," Reuters, November 30, 2017, https://www.reuters.com/article/us-california-crime-immigrant/illegal-immigrant-acquitted-of-murder-in-san-francisco-trump-slams-verdict-idUSKBN1DV3CR.

21. Horsley, "Fact Check."

22. Z. Byron Wolf, "Trump Blasts 'Breeding' in Sanctuary Cities: That's a Racist Term," CNN, April 24, 2018, https://www.cnn.com/2018/04/18/politics/donald-trump-immigrants-california/index.html.

23. The tweets from Donald J. Trump (@realDonaldTrump) quoted in this paragraph are dated September 19, 2014; October 14, 2014; July 6, 2015; April 18, 2018; and June 19, 2018.

24. Brett Samuels, "Sessions Unveils 'Zero Tolerance' Policy at Southern Border," *The Hill*, April 7, 2018, http://thehill.com/homenews/administration/386634-sessions-illegal-border-crossers-will-be-prosecuted-families-may-be.

25. "U.S. Strategy for Central America," US Department of State, accessed June 1, 2020, https://www.state.gov/p/wha/rt/strat/index.htm.

26. Dana L. Cloud, "'To Veil the Threat of Terror': Afghan Women and the <Clash of Civilizations> in the Imagery of the U.S. War on Terrorism," *Quarterly Journal of Speech* 90 (2004): 287.

27. Demo, "Sovereignty Discourse," 292.

28. Jenna Johnson, "Trump in Texas: 'I'm the Builder President, Remember That,'" *Washington Post*, October 25, 2018, https://www.washingtonpost.com/news/post-politics/wp/2017/10/25/trump-in-texas-im-the-builder-president-remember-that/?utm_term=.4134e902f862.

29. Dartunorro Clark, "Trump Visits California to See Wall Prototypes near Mexico Border," NBC News, March 13, 2018, https://www.nbcnews.com/politics/white-house/trump-visits-california-see-wall-prototypes-near-mexico-border-n854836.

30. Mairead McArdle, "Report: Trump Threatens Government Shutdown over Border-Wall Funding," *National Review*, June 19, 2018, https://www.nationalreview.com/news/donald-trump-border-wall-funding-government-shutdown.

31. Donald J. Trump (@realDonaldTrump), Twitter, June 25, 2018.

32. Kate Linthicum, "Mexico's Foreign Minister Calls Trump's Wall 'a Hostile Act,'" *Los Angeles Times*, April 26, 2017, http://www.latimes.com/politics/washington/la-na-essential-washington-updates-mexico-s-foreign-minister-calls-trump-s-1493217935-htmlstory.html.

33. Ylan Q. Mui, "Withdrawal from Trans-Pacific Partnership Shifts U.S. Role in the World's Economy," *Washington Post*, January 23, 2017, https://www.washingtonpost.com/business/economy/withdrawal-from-trans-pacific-partnership-shifts

-us-role-in-world-economy/2017/01/23/05720df6-e1a6-11e6-a453-19ec4b3d09ba
_story.html.

34. Timmons Roberts, "One Year Since Trump's Withdrawal from Paris Climate Agreement," Brookings Institution, June 1, 2018, https://www.brookings.edu/blog/planetpolicy/2018/06/01/one-year-since-trumps-withdrawal-from-the-paris-climate-agreement.

35. Mark Landler, "Trump Abandons Iran Nuclear Deal He Long Scorned," *New York Times*, May 8, 2018, https://www.nytimes.com/2018/05/08/world/middleeast/trump-iran-nuclear-deal.html.

36. Luis Sanchez, "Trump Refuses to Endorse G-7 Communique, Threatens Canada with More Tariffs," *The Hill*, June 9, 2018, http://thehill.com/homenews/administration/391516-trump-refuses-to-endorse-g7-communique.

37. Donald J. Trump (@realDonaldTrump), Twitter, August 27, 2017.

38. Ibid., January 18, 2018.

39. Damian Paletta, "Trump Aims to Split Up NAFTA Negotiations, Deal with Canada and Mexico Separately," *Washington Post*, June 5, 2018, https://www.washingtonpost.com/news/business/wp/2018/06/05/trump-aims-to-split-up-nafta-negotiations-deal-with-canada-and-mexico-separately.

40. Donald J. Trump (@realDonaldTrump), Twitter, April 23, 2018.

41. Laignee Baron, "Hundreds Protest on Father's Day Against a Tent City for Immigrant Children near Texas Border," *Time*, June 18, 2018, http://time.com/5314596/tornillo-texas-tent-city-protest.

42. Daniel Borunda, "Hundreds Protest in Tornillo Against Separation of Immigrant Children, Family Detention," *El Paso Times*, June 24, 2018, https://www.elpasotimes.com/story/news/immigration/2018/06/24/protesters-separation-children-detention-families-tornillo-trump-zero-tolerance-policy-immigration/728948002.

43. Matthew Haag and Jess Bidgood, "Governors Refuse to Send National Guard to Border, Citing Childhood Separation Practice," *New York Times*, June 19, 2018, https://www.nytimes.com/2018/06/19/us/national-guard-trump-children-immigration.html.

44. Bart Jansen, "American, Frontier, Southwest and United Airlines Refuse to Transport Immigrant Children Separated from Parents for Government," *USA Today*, June 20, 2018, https://www.usatoday.com/story/news/2018/06/20/airlines-refuse-fly-immigrant-children-separated-parents/718654002.

45. Mahita Gajana, "American Airlines Doesn't Want to Fly Migrant Children Separated from Their Families," *Time*, June 20, 2018, https://time.com/5317471/american-airlines-migrant-children/.

46. "The Latest: ACLU Says Government Wrong to Detain Families," Associated Press, June 29, 2018, https://apnews.com/4eeea36a363a40a0879d1b8a80a2de9c/The-Latest:-ACLU-says-government-wrong-to-detain-families.

47. Ibid.

48. Meagan Flynn, "Kirstjen Nielsen Heckled by Protestors at Mexican Restaurant: Other Diners Applauded Them," *Washington Post*, June 20, 2018, https://www.washingtonpost.com/news/morning-mix/wp/2018/06/20/kirstjen-nielsen-heckled-by-protesters-at-mexican-restaurant-if-kids-dont-eat-in-peace-you-dont-eat-in-peace.

49. Gregory Krieg, "The Movement to 'Abolish ICE' Is Heating Up—and Going Mainstream," CNN, July 2, 2018, https://www.cnn.com/2018/06/30/politics/abolish-ice-movement-gaining-support-democrats/index.html.

50. "The Latest: ACLU Says Government Wrong to Detain Families," Associated Press, June 29, 2018, https://apnews.com/4eeea36a363a40a0879d1b8a80a2de9c/The-Latest:-ACLU-says-government-wrong-to-detain-families.

51. Christopher Ingraham, "Republican Lawmakers Introduce Bills to Curb Protesting in at Least 18 States," *Washington Post*, February 24, 2017, https://www.washingtonpost.com/news/wonk/wp/2017/02/24/republican-lawmakers-introduce-bills-to-curb-protesting-in-at-least-17-states.

52. Donald J. Trump (@realDonaldTrump), Twitter, June 17, 2018.

53. Michelle Goldberg, "We Have a Crisis of Democracy, Not Manners," *New York Times*, June 25, 2018, https://www.nytimes.com/2018/06/25/opinion/trump-sarah-huckabee-sanders-restaurant-civility.html.

54. Azam Ahmed, "U.S. Ambassador to Mexico to Quit amid Tense Relations Under Trump," *New York Times*, March 1, 2018, https://www.nytimes.com/2018/03/01/world/americas/us-ambassador-mexico.html.

55. Hannah Dreier, "I've Been Reporting on MS-13 for a Year: Here Are the 5 Things Trump Gets Most Wrong," ProPublica, June 25, 2018, https://www.propublica.org/article/ms-13-immigration-facts-what-trump-administration-gets-wrong.

56. Zamira Rahim, "Trump Overheard Saying 'Get Me Out of Here' as He Suddenly Walks Off Stage at G20 Summit," *Independent*, December 2, 2018, https://www.independent.co.uk/news/world/americas/trump-g20-video-watch-stage-hot-mic-mauricio-macri-summit-argentina-buenos-aires-a8663486.html.

57. Andreas Wiseman, "Donald Trump Talks 'Talented' Kim Jong-un and New North Korea 'Bond': 'Adversaries Can Become Friends,'" Deadline, June 12, 2018, https://deadline.com/2018/06/donald-trump-north-korea-kim-jong-un-singapore-nuclear-1202408503.

58. Jessica Donati, "U.S. Withdrawing from U.N. Human Rights Council," *Wall Street Journal*, June 19, 2018, https://www.wsj.com/articles/u-s-poised-to-withdraw-from-u-n-human-rights-council-1529430908.

59. WashPostPR, "*Washington Post* Publisher and CEO Fred Ryan Statement on Jamal Khashoggi," *WashPost PR Blog*, November 20, 2018, https://www.washingtonpost.com/pr/2018/11/20/washington-post-publisher-ceo-fred-ryan-statement-jamal-khashoggi.

60. Jennifer Bendery, "Mitch McConnell Reaps the Benefits of His Stolen Supreme Court Seat," *Huffington Post*, June 26, 2018, https://www.huffingtonpost.com/entry/mitch-mcconnell-neil-gorsuch-conservative-court_us_5b326aabe4b0cb56051c92d6.

CHAPTER 4

I want to thank the editors of this volume and my two anonymous reviewers for their insights and feedback on my drafts.

1. I use the term "Mexican migrant civil society" as a broad umbrella term to describe this population. I do so with the knowledge that such a wide umbrella is imperfect at best for capturing the full diversity and experiences of the many Mexican migrant civic societies in existence today.

2. Rebecca Vonderlack-Navarro and William Sites, "The Bi-National Road to Immigrant Rights Mobilization: States, Social Movements and Chicago's Mexican Hometown Associations," *Journal Ethnic and Racial Studies* 38, no. 1 (2015): 144.

3. Jonathan Fox and Xóchitl Bada, "Migrant Civic Engagement" (Research Paper Series on Latino Immigrant Civic and Political Participation, no. 3, June 2009), https://www.wilsoncenter.org/sites/default/files/media/documents/publication/Fox%20%26%20Bada%20-%20Migrant%20Civ%20Engagement%202008.pdf.

4. Luis Eduardo Guarnizo, "The Fluid, Multi-Scalar, and Contradictory Construction of Citizenship," *Comparative Urban and Community Research* 10 (2012): 1.

5. Hector Amaya, *Citizenship Excess: Latinos/as, Media, and the Nation* (New York: New York University Press, 2013); Ana Milena Ribero, "Citizenship," in *Decolonizing Rhetoric and Composition Studies: New Latinx Keywords for Theory and Pedagogy*, ed. Iris D. Ruiz and Raúl Sánchez (New York: Palgrave Macmillan, 2016), 31–45.

6. Guarnizo, "Fluid, Multi-Scalar, and Contradictory Construction," 18.

7. Ibid.

8. Ibid.

9. Ibid.

10. Christa J. Olson, "Places to Stand: The Practices and Politics of Writing Histories," *Advances in the History of Rhetoric* 15 (2012): 84.

11. Formally known as the Border Protection, Antiterrorism, and Illegal Immigration Control Act of 2005 (H.R. 4437), this piece of legislation passed by the US House of Representatives would have criminalized the status of undocumented immigrants as well as actions by citizens to assist them.

12. Vonderlack-Navarro and Sites, "Bi-National Road to Immigrant Rights Mobilization," 143. Growth has ballooned especially in the last twenty years: "Between 1998 and 2006, the total number of HTAs registered nationwide almost doubled from 441 to 815." In Chicago, the growth of HTAs has been even more dramatic, growing in number from thirty-five in 1995 to over 340 in 2008. See Xóchitl Bada, "Mexican Hometown Associations in Chicago: The Newest Agents of Civic Participation," in *¡Marcha! Latino Chicago and the Immigrant Rights Movement*, ed. Nilda Flores-González and Amalia Pallares (Urbana: University of Illinois Press, 2010), 147.

13. Vonderlack-Navarro and Sites, "Bi-National Road to Immigrant Rights Mobilization," 143.

14. Ibid., 147.

15. The winner, Felipe Calderón from the conservative National Action Party (Partido Acción Nacional, PAN), prevailed with less than 1 percent of the votes cast (that is, 243,000 of the 41 million ballots) over his rival, Andrés Manuel López Obrador.

16. Bada, "Mexican Hometown Associations in Chicago," 156.

17. Josue David Cisneros, "Review Essay: Rhetorics of Citizenship: Pitfalls and Possibilities," *Quarterly Journal of Speech* 100, no. 3 (2014): 375–76.

18. Ibid., 376.

19. Christian Kock and Lisa Villadsen, "Introduction: Rhetorical Citizenship as a Conceptual Frame: What We Talk About When We Talk About Rhetorical Citizenship," in *Contemporary Rhetorical Citizenship*, ed. Christian Kock and Lisa Villadsen (Leiden: Leiden University Press, 2014), 13, 10, 11.

20. Cisneros, "Review Essay," 376.

21. Ibid., 377.

22. Josue David Cisneros, *The Border Crossed Us: Rhetorics of Borders, Citizenship, and Latina/o Identity* (Tuscaloosa: University Alabama Press, 2014), 84.

23. Hector Amaya, *Citizenship Excess: Latino/as, Media, and the Nation* (New York: New York University Press, 2013), 17.

24. Ribero, "Citizenship," 32, 41.

25. Cisneros, "Review Essay," 386.

26. Vonderlack-Navarro and Sites, "Bi-National Road to Immigrant Rights Mobilization," 143.

27. Ibid., 151.

28. Ibid., 149.

29. Cisneros, *Border Crossed Us*; Ribero, "Citizenship."

30. Vonderlack-Navarro and Sites, "Bi-National Road to Immigrant Rights Mobilization," 147.

31. Robert Asen, "A Discourse Theory of Citizenship," *Quarterly Journal of Speech* 90 (2004): 189–211.

32. Guarnizo, "Fluid, Multi-Scalar, and Contradictory Construction," 18.

33. Cisneros, *Border Crossed Us*, 135.

34. As a reminder, those questions were: What does it mean to behave publicly? Who, when, and how can individuals participate publicly? Where, when, how does a *public* begin and end? Where does citizenship, and our ability to act as a citizen, begin and end?

35. This is not a new phenomenon. The Mexican Revolutionary era (1906–40) provides an earlier example of a phenomenon that has not been explored in rhetorical scholarship.

36. Guarnizo, "Fluid, Multi-Scalar, and Contradictory Construction," 1.

37. Vonderlack-Navarro and Sites, "Bi-National Road to Immigrant Rights Mobilization," 147.

38. I wish to thank one of my anonymous reviewers for bringing this insight to my attention.

39. Guarnizo, "Fluid, Multi-Scalar, and Contradictory Construction," 1.

40. Ibid., 11.

41. Walter Mignolo, "Cultural Studies: Geopolitics of Knowledge and Requirements/Business Needs," *Revista Iberoamericana* 69 (2003): 401–15.

42. Guarnizo, "Fluid, Multi-Scalar, and Contradictory Construction," 20.

43. Ibid., 12.

44. Ibid., 8.

45. Ibid., 20.

CHAPTER 5

1. Richard Lapchick, *The 2019 Racial and Gender Report Card: Major League Baseball* (Orlando, FL: Institute for Diversity and Ethics in Sport, 2019), https://docs.wixstatic.com/ugd/7d86e5_e943e1c08a514661a86b449dea5bcfd2.pdf.

2. Samantha Schmidt, "Jose Altuve's World Series Triumph Gives Shattered Venezuela Something to Celebrate," *Washington Post*, November 2, 2017, https://www.washingtonpost.com/news/morning-mix/wp/2017/11/02/jose-altuves-world-series-triumph-gives-shattered-venezuela-something-to-celebrate/?utm_term=.2190a88c7804.

3. The American Dream myth commonly portrays the United States as a place of unlimited opportunity for natives and immigrants alike, but only to the extent that they embrace national values and demonstrate an obvious commitment to work. Among the rhetorical effects of this myth, of course, is that individuals who are unable to succeed are commonly blamed for their own failures and cultural or structural are minimized. For more on this in the context of sport, see Robert Elias, ed., *Baseball and the American Dream: Race, Class, Gender, and the National Pastime* (Armonk, NY: M. E. Sharpe, 2001).

4. For more on the history of these stereotypes, see Samuel O. Regalado, *Viva Baseball! Latin Major Leaguers and Their Special Hunger*, 3rd ed. (Urbana: University of Illinois Press, 2008). For more on the perceptions of Puig, see Andy McCullough, "Yasiel Puig Left Behind a Complicated Dodgers Legacy," *Los Angeles Times*, April 14, 2019, https://www.latimes.com/sports/dodgers/la-sp-yasiel-puig-dodgers-legacy-reds-20190414-story.html.

5. Quoted in Peter Keating, "Diving into the Walks Gap Between U.S.-Born and Latin American Players," ESPN, September 16, 2017, http://www.espn.com/mlb/story/_/id/20778736/diving-walks-gap-us-born-latin-american-players.

6. Jorge L. Ortiz, "Yasiel Puig's Latest Episode Another Test of Dodgers' Patience," *USA Today*, June 14, 2017, https://www.usatoday.com/story/sports/mlb/2017/06/14/dodgers-yasiel-puig-has-history-behaving-badly/102856818.

7. Josue David Cisneros, *The Border Crossed Us: Rhetorics of Borders, Citizenship, and Latina/o Identity* (Tuscaloosa: University of Alabama Press, 2013).

8. Scott Eden, "No One Walks Off the Island," *ESPN The Magazine*, April 17, 2014, http://www.espn.com/espn/feature/story/_/id/10781144/no-one-walks-island-los-angeles-dodgers-yasiel-puig-journey-cuba; Jesse Katz, "Escape from Cuba: Yasiel Puig's Untold Journey to the Dodgers," *Los Angeles Magazine*, April 14, 2014.

9. Dan Gartland, "The Story of How Jose Fernandez Got to the United States on His Fourth Try," *Sports Illustrated*, September 25, 2016, https://www.si.com/mlb/2016/09/25/jose-fernandez-marlins-cuba-united-states-defection-story.

10. Jules Tygiel, "Our National Spirit," in *Baseball as America: Seeing Ourselves Through Our National Game*, ed. John Odell (Washington, DC: National Geographic, 2002), 27; David Q. Voigt, *American Baseball: From Gentleman's Sport to the Commissioner System* (Norman: University of Oklahoma Press, 1966), xxvii.

11. Louis A. Pérez, "Between Baseball and Bullfighting: The Quest for Nationality in Cuba, 1868–1898," *Journal of American History* 81 (September 1994): 512.

12. For more on baseball as a symbol of democracy, see Michael L. Butterworth, *Baseball and Rhetorics of Purity: The National Pastime and American Identity During the War on Terror* (Tuscaloosa: University of Alabama Press, 2010); for more on baseball's invented mythology, see Charles Fruehling Springwood, *Cooperstown to Dyersville: A Geography of Baseball Nostalgia* (Boulder, CO: Westview Press, 1996).

13. Peter Baker, "U.S. to Restore Full Relations with Cuba, Erasing a Last Trace of Cold War Hostility," *New York Times*, December 17, 2014, https://www.nytimes.com/2014/12/18/world/americas/us-cuba-relations.html.

14. Peter Kornbluth, "Normalization of Relations with Cuba Is All but Irreversible Now," *The Nation*, October 19, 2016, https://www.thenation.com/article/obamas-new-directive-probably-assures-the-irreversibility-of-normalization-with-cuba.

15. Robert L. Ivie and Oscar Giner, "American Exceptionalism in a Democratic Idiom: Transacting the Mythos of Change in the 2008 Presidential Campaign," *Communication Studies* 60 (September–October 2009): 359–75.

16. See Deborah L. Madsen, *American Exceptionalism* (Jackson: University Press of Mississippi, 1998).

17. John F. Kennedy, "Address to a Joint Convention of the General Court of the Commonwealth of Massachusetts," American Rhetoric, January 9, 1961, http://americanrhetoric.com/speeches/jfkcommonwealthmass.htm; Ronald Reagan, "Farewell Address to the Nation," American Rhetoric, January 11, 1989, http://americanrhetoric.com/speeches/ronaldreaganfarewelladdress.html.

18. Jason Gilmore, "American Exceptionalism in the American Mind: Presidential Discourse, National Identity, and U.S. Public Opinion," *Communication Studies* 66 (July–August 2015): 304.

19. Alexis de Tocqueville, *Democracy in America and Two Essays on America*, ed. Isaac Kramnick, trans. Gerald E. Bevan (1835; repr., London: Penguin Books, 2003), 525.

20. Seymour Martin Lipset, *American Exceptionalism: A Double-Edged Sword* (New York: W. W. Norton, 1996), 18.

21. David Weiss and Jason A. Edwards, "Introduction: American Exceptionalism's Champions and Challengers," in *The Rhetoric of American Exceptionalism: Critical Essays*, ed. Jason A. Edwards and David Weiss (Jefferson, NC: McFarland, 2011), 1.

22. David Zarefsky, "The United States and the World: The Rhetorical Dimensions of Obama's Foreign Policy," in *The Rhetoric of Heroic Expectations: Establishing the Obama*

Presidency, ed. Justin S. Vaughn and Jennifer R. Mercieca (College Station: Texas A&M University Press, 2014), 111.

23. Donald E. Pease, *The New American Exceptionalism* (Minneapolis: University of Minnesota Press, 2009), 16.

24. For more on the embargo and other acts of legislation over the years, see John O'Brien, "Political Balk: Opening the Door for U.S.-Cuba Policy Reform via Diplomatic Blunder at the World Baseball Classic," *Villanova Sports and Entertainment Law Journal* 15 (2008): 135–74.

25. William J. Clinton, "Inaugural Address," American Presidency Project, January 20, 1997, https://www.presidency.ucsb.edu/documents/inaugural-address-12.

26. Pease suggests that "irreconcilable rifts within U.S. political culture" emerged between the Cold War and the "war on terror" (*New American Exceptionalism*, 1). Meanwhile, several books attend to the United States' diminished global standing after the Bush presidency. A representative recent example is Jean Edward Smith, *Bush* (New York: Simon & Schuster, 2016). In addition, helpful rhetorical studies that explain how American exceptionalism exacerbated tensions after 9/11 include Stephen John Hartnett and Laura Ann Stengrim, *Globalization and Empire: The U.S. Invasion of Iraq, Free Markets, and the Twilight of Democracy* (Tuscaloosa: University of Alabama Press, 2006); and Robert L. Ivie, *Democracy and America's War on Terror* (Tuscaloosa: University of Alabama Press, 2005).

27. Ivie and Giner, "American Exceptionalism in a Democratic Idiom," 363.

28. Jason A. Edwards, "Resetting America's Role in the World: President Obama's Rhetoric of (Re)Conciliation and Partnership," in *The Rhetoric of Heroic Expectations: Establishing the Obama Presidency*, ed. Justin S. Vaughn and Jennifer R. Mercieca (College Station: Texas A&M University Press, 2014), 133.

29. Jay P. Childers, "A Lighthouse at the Crossroads: Barack Obama's Call for Agonistic Democracy," in *The Rhetoric of Heroic Expectations: Establishing the Obama Presidency*, ed. Justin S. Vaughn and Jennifer R. Mercieca (College Station: Texas A&M University Press, 2014), 45.

30. Robert E. Terrill, "An Uneasy Peace: Barack Obama's Nobel Peace Prize Lecture," *Rhetoric and Public Affairs* 14 (2011): 764, 775.

31. Robert L. Ivie and Oscar Giner, *Hunt the Devil: A Demonology of US War Culture* (Tuscaloosa: University of Alabama Press, 2015), 130.

32. Barack Obama, "Full Transcript: President Obama's Sept. 10 Speech on Syria," *Washington Post*, September 10, 2013, http://www.washingtonpost.com/politics/running-transcript-president-obamas-sept-10-speech-on-syria/2013/09/10/a8826aa6-1a2e-11e3-8685-5021e0c41964_story.html?tid=pm_politics_pop.

33. Vladimir V. Putin, "A Plea for Caution from Russia: What Putin Has to Say to Americans About Syria," *New York Times*, September 11, 2013, http://www.nytimes.com/2013/09/12/opinion/putin-plea-for-caution-from-russia-on-syria.html?pagewanted=all&_r=0.

34. See Rico Neumann and Kevin Coe, "The Rhetoric in the Modern Presidency: A Quantitative Assessment," in *The Rhetoric of American Exceptionalism: Critical Essays*, ed. Jason A. Edwards and David Weiss (Jefferson, NC: McFarland, 2011), 11–30.

35. Dick Cheney and Liz Cheney, *Exceptional: Why the World Needs a Powerful America* (New York: Threshold Editions, 2015), 260.

36. For more on this, see M. Scott Mahaskey, "How White Nationalists Learned to Love Donald Trump," *Politico Magazine*, October 25, 2016, https://www.politico.com/magazine/story/2016/10/donald-trump-2016-white-nationalists-alt-right-214388; Evan Osnos, "The Fearful and the Frustrated: Donald Trump's Nationalist Coalition Takes Shape—For Now," *New Yorker*, August 31, 2015, https://www.newyorker.com

/magazine/2015/08/31/the-fearful-and-the-frustrated; and Jon Wiener, "Eric Foner: White Nationalists, Neo-Confederates, and Donald Trump," *The Nation*, August 16, 2017, https://www.thenation.com/article/eric-foner-white-nationalists-neo-confederates-and-donald-trump.

37. See J. David Cisneros, "Contaminated Communities: The Metaphor of 'Immigrant as Pollutant' in Media Representations of Immigration," *Rhetoric and Public Affairs* 11 (2008): 569–602; and Kent A. Ono and John M. Sloop, *Shifting Borders: Rhetoric, Immigration, and California's Proposition 187* (Philadelphia: Temple University Press, 2002).

38. Donald Trump, "Full Text: Donald Trump Announces a Presidential Bid," *Washington Post*, June 16, 2015, https://www.washingtonpost.com/news/post-politics/wp/2015/06/16/full-text-donald-trump-announces-a-presidential-bid/?utm_term=.e4e73d0694f5.

39. Jeffrey D. Sachs, *A New Foreign Policy: Beyond American Exceptionalism* (New York: Columbia University Press, 2018), 2.

40. Jake Sullivan, "What Donald Trump and Dick Cheney Got Wrong About America," *The Atlantic*, January/February 2019, https://www.theatlantic.com/magazine/archive/2019/01/yes-america-can-still-lead-the-world/576427.

41. Stephen Wertheim, "Trump Against Exceptionalism: The Sources of Trumpian Conduct," in *Chaos in the Liberal Order: The Trump Presidency and International Politics in the Twenty-First Century*, ed. Robert Jervis, Francis J. Gavin, Joshua Rovner, and Diane Labrosse (New York: Columbia University Press, 2018), 126.

42. Jason A. Edwards, "Make America Great Again: Donald Trump and Redefining the U.S. Role in the World," *Communication Quarterly* 66 (2018): 189.

43. Edwards, "Resetting America's Role in the World," 140.

44. Christa J. Olson, "'But in Regard to These (the American) Continents': U.S. National Rhetorics and the Figure of Latin America," *Rhetoric Society Quarterly* 45 (2015): 273.

45. For more on neoliberalism and US influence, see Leonardo Avritzer, *Democracy and the Public Space in Latin America* (Princeton, NJ: Princeton University Press, 2002); and Mark Goodale and Nancy Postero, *Neoliberalism, Interrupted: Social Change and Contested Governance in Contemporary Latin America* (Stanford, CA: Stanford University Press, 2013).

46. Declarations of American superiority were commonplace in the newly revived Olympic Games. For example, see S. W. Pope, *Patriotic Games: Sporting Traditions in the American Imagination, 1876–1926* (New York: Oxford University Press, 1997). Domestically, baseball was routinely upheld as a democratic exemplar. For examples, see Butterworth, *Baseball and Rhetorics of Purity*; and Robert Elias, *The Empire Strikes Out: How Baseball Sold U.S. Foreign Policy and Promoted the American Way Abroad* (New York: New Press, 2010).

47. Elias, *Empire Strikes Out*, 40.

48. For a particularly good discussion about Cuban players in baseball, see Brad Snyder, *Beyond the Shadow of the Senators: The Untold Story of the Homestead Grays and the Integration of Baseball* (New York: McGraw-Hill, 2003).

49. Given space constraints, I have simplified this issue. For more explanation, see especially Alan Klein, *Sugarball: The American Game, the Dominican Dream* (New Haven, CT: Yale University Press, 1991); and Arturo J. Marcano Guevara and David P. Fidler, *Stealing Lives: The Globalization of Baseball and the Tragic Story of Alexis Quiroz* (Bloomington: Indiana University Press, 2002).

50. Peter C. Bjarkman, *A History of Cuban Baseball, 1864–2006* (Jefferson, NC: McFarland, 2007), 312.

51. Michael L. Butterworth, "Saved at Home: Christian Branding and Faith Nights in the 'Church of Baseball,'" *Quarterly Journal of Speech* 97 (2011): 326.

52. Debra Hawhee, *Bodily Arts: Rhetoric and Athletics in Ancient Greece* (Austin: University of Texas Press, 2005), 15–16.

53. Stuart Murray, "The Two Halves of Sports-Diplomacy," *Diplomacy and Statecraft* 23 (2012): 577.

54. Quoted in ibid., 578.

55. Justin W. R. Turner, "1970s Baseball Diplomacy Between Cuba and the United States," *Nine: A Journal of Baseball History and Culture* 19 (Fall 2010): 67.

56. Milton H. Jamail, *Full Count: Inside Cuban Baseball* (Carbondale: Southern Illinois University Press, 2000).

57. Afsheen J. Nomai and George N. Dionisopoulos, "Framing the Cubas Narrative: The American Dream and the Capitalist Reality," *Communication Studies* 53 (Summer 2002): 98.

58. Turner, "1970s Baseball Diplomacy Between Cuba and the United States," 79.

59. Joseph S. Nye, *Soft Power: The Means to Success in World Politics* (New York: Public Affairs, 2005).

60. Craig Hayden, "Promoting America: U.S. Public Diplomacy and the Limits of Exceptionalism," in *The Rhetoric of American Exceptionalism: Critical Essays*, ed. Jason A. Edwards and David Weiss (Jefferson, NC: McFarland, 2011), 193–94.

61. Daniel Añorve, "The Role of Baseball in the Normalization of Cuba-US Relations," *Journal of Sports Management and Commercialization* 7 (2016): 2.

62. Kornbluth, "Normalization of Relations with Cuba Is All but Irreversible Now."

63. Gregory Korte, "Obama Brings Baseball Diplomacy to Havana," *USA Today*, March 22, 2016, http://www.usatoday.com/story/news/politics/2016/03/22/obama-goes-game-does-wave-castro/82126632; Dan Roberts, "Obama Embraces Cuba's Pastime with a Spot of Baseball Diplomacy," *The Guardian*, March 22, 2016, https://www.theguardian.com/world/2016/mar/22/obama-cuba-baseball-diplomacy; S. L. Price, "Baseball Diplomacy: How a Changing World Will Change the Game," *Sports Illustrated*, March 22, 2016, http://www.si.com/mlb/2016/03/22/cuba-united-states-barack-obama-rays.

64. Nolan D. McCaskill, "Obama Defends Attending Baseball Game in Cuba After Brussels Attacks," *Politico*, March 22, 2016, https://www.politico.com/story/2016/03/barack-obama-cuba-baseball-game-brussels-attacks-221107; Obama White House, "The First Family Takes in a Baseball Game in Havana, Cuba," YouTube, uploaded March 23, 2016, https://www.youtube.com/watch?v=klG6Q7daivc.

65. Derrick Goold, "MLB Concern: Will Trump Presidency Affect Cuban, International Markets?" *St. Louis Post-Dispatch*, November 10, 2016, http://www.stltoday.com/sports/baseball/professional/birdland/mlb-concern-will-trump-presidency-affect-cuban-international-markets/article_1eeb0ad9-3e4c-5eef-91d5-2c47e0e3da69.html.

66. Clark Spencer, "MLB Commissioner Rob Manfred: 'Cuba Is a Great Market for Us,'" *Miami Herald*, March 10, 2015, http://www.miamiherald.com/sports/mlb/miami-marlins/article13202399.html.

67. Adam Kilgore, "Normalized Relations Between Cuba and the United States Could Have 'Drastic' Impact on MLB," *Washington Post*, December 17, 2014, https://www.washingtonpost.com/news/sports/wp/2014/12/17/normalized-relations-between-cuba-and-united-states-could-have-drastic-impact-on-mlb/?utm_term=.bd36ba3a7a34.

68. Añorve, "Role of Baseball in the Normalization of Cuba-US Relations," 13.

69. See Hilary Andersson, "Living in Fear of President Trump's Deportation Drive," BBC News, July 17, 2017, http://www.bbc.com/news/world-us-canada-40600552; Clark Mindock, "Immigrants Fear Harassment in Trump's America So Much It's Started to

Damage the Economy," *Independent*, August 24, 2017, http://www.independent.co.uk /news/business/trump-hispanic-immigrants-us-economy-damage-fear-deportation -staying-at-home-a7910941.html; Amy Taxin, "Immigrants Fear Loss of Humanitarian Program Under Trump," *U.S. News and World Report*, October 30, 2017, https:// www.usnews.com/news/best-states/california/articles/2017-10-30/central-americans -fear-trump-may-ax-immigration-program.

70. Jeff Passan, "White House Scuttles MLB's Cuban Agreement," ESPN, April 9, 2019, http://www.espn.com/mlb/story/_/id/26472986/white-house-scuttles-mlb -cuban-agreement.

71. Will Fischer, "Cuban Players Helped Build the Modern MLB: America Doesn't Want to Help Them," *New York Magazine*, April 19, 2019, http://nymag.com /intelligencer/2019/04/trump-administration-cancels-mlb-agreement-with-cuba.html.

72. David Waldstein and Michael Tackett, "Trump Ends Deal Between MLB and Cuban Baseball Federation," *New York Times*, April 8, 2019, https://www.nytimes.com /2019/04/08/sports/mlb-cuba-donald-trump.html.

73. Quoted in Karen DeYoung, "Trump Administration Cancels Major League Baseball Deal with Cuba," *Washington Post*, April 8, 2019, https://www.washingtonpost.com /world/national-security/trump-administration-cancels-mlb-deal-with-cuba/2019/04 /08/99c7d9be-5a2f-11e9-842d-7d3ed7eb3957_story.html?utm_term=.436401e7dc68.

74. Passan, "White House Scuttles MLB's Cuban Agreement."

75. Brian Schwartz, "MLB Hires Trump-Allied Lobbyist for Guidance on 'Trafficking' of Cuban Baseball Players," CNBC, May 13, 2019, https://www.cnbc.com/2019/05 /13/mlb-hires-trump-allied-lobbying-firm-over-cuban-baseball.html.

76. Murray, "Two Halves of Sports-Diplomacy," 587.

CHAPTER 6

I want to thank undergraduate students Juliana Villanueva and Juan Pineda who helped to assemble and analyze the collection of data that made this study possible.

1. Martín Rodríguez, "Sí, en Guatemala está empezando la primavera," *Estudios de Política Exterior* 168 (2015), http://www.politicaexterior.com/articulos/politica-exterior /si-en-guatemala-esta-empezando-la-primavera; Edelberto Torres Rivas, "Guatemala: La corrupción como crisis de gobierno," *Nueva Sociedad* 258 (2015), http://nuso.org/articulo /guatemala-la-corrupcion-como-crisis-de-gobierno.

2. See the Corruption Perception Index by Transparency International, available at https://www.transparency.org/en/cpi.

3. The results of the first phase of this study were published in Spanish, in 2016, in the journal *Chasqui*. That publication focused on the political construction of corruption in Guatemala. The current chapter describes, compares, and analyzes the rhetorics of corruption of Guatemalan politicians, citizens, and judicial investigators. The examination of the rhetorics of these three agents made it possible to suggest three different levels through which corruption manifests itself rhetorically in democratic contexts. The reflection on this diversity of agents and the discursive levels lead me to present a series of recommendations about the discursive deconstruction of corruption.

4. Juan Paullier, "Iván Velásquez, el colombiano que precipitó la renuncia de Pérez Molina," BBC Mundo, September 3, 2015, https://www.bbc.com/mundo/noticias /2015/08/150825_guatemala_corrupcion_cicig_perfil_ivan_velasquez_jp.

5. Juan Hernández, "Una situación extraordinaria: Miles contra la corrupción," *Envío*, no. 399 (June 2015), http://www.envio.org.ni/articulo/5019.

6. Torres Rivas, "Guatemala."

7. Helge Rønning, "The Politics of Corruption and the Media in Africa," *Journal of African Media Studies* I (2009): 1–17; Nubia Ureña, *Corrupción y ética: Polos opuestos de la misma realidad* (Bogotá: Tercer Mundo Editores, 1997).

8. Ignacio Walker, *La democracia en América Latina: Entre la esperanza y la desesperanza* (Santiago: Uqbar Editores, 2009), 27–62.

9. José Vargas, "The Multiple Faces of Corruption: Typology, Forms and Levels," *Contemporary Legal and Economic Issues* 3 (2009): 269–90.

10. Andrés Solimano, Vito Tanzi, and Felipe del Solar, *Las termitas del estado: Ensayos sobre corrupción, transparencia y desarrollo* (Santiago: Fondo de Cultura Económica, 2008), 23–56.

11. Arvind Jain, *The Political Economy of Corruption* (New York: Routledge, 2001).

12. Pranab Bardhan, "Corruption and Development: A Review of Issues," *Journal of Economic Literature* 35 (1997): 1320–46; José Gamarra, *Pobreza, corrupción y participación política: Una revisión para el caso colombiano* (Bogotá: Banco de la República de Colombia, 2006); Luminita Ionescu, "The Economics of Anti-Corruption," *Contemporary Readings in Law and Social Justice* I (2011): 116–21; Umbreen Javaid and Faruq Saadat Faruq, "Corruption Pervades Poverty: In Perspective of Developing Countries," *South Asian Studies: A Research Journal of South Asian Studies* 30 (2015): 175–87; Muhammad Yusha'u, "Investigative Journalism and Scandal Reporting in the Nigerian Press," *African Journalism Studies* 30 (2009): 155–74.

13. Kenneth Burke, *A Rhetoric of Motives* (1945; repr., Berkeley: University of California Press, 1969), 19–23.

14. Sighard Neckel, "Political Scandals: An Analytical Framework," *Comparative Sociology* 4 (2005): 101–11; Juan Restrepo, "El escándalo: Una construcción social y política de la corrupción en los medios de comunicación," *Escribanía* 15 (2005): 69–77; Elizabeth Stein and Marisa Kella, "Programming Presidential Agendas: Partisan and Media Environments That Lead Presidents to Fight Crime and Corruption," *Political Communication* 31 (2014): 25–52; Howard Tumber and Silvio Waisbord, "Political Scandals and Media Across Democracies," *American Behavioral Scientist* 47 (2004): 1031–39.

15. Eric Breit, "On the (Re)construction of Corruption in the Media: A Critical Discursive Approach," *Journal of Business Ethics* 92 (2010): 619–35; Pier Paolo Giglioli, "Political Corruption and Media: The Tangentopoli Affair," *International Social Science Journal* 48 (1996): 381–94.

16. Luis Pásara, "El conflicto entre medios de comunicación y justicia," *Revista Mexicana de Justicia* 3 (2013): 79–91.

17. Tumber and Waisbord, "Political Scandals and Media Across Democracies."

18. James F. Jarso, "The Media and the Anti-corruption Crusade in Kenya: Weighing the Achievement, Challenges, and Prospects," *International Law Review* 26 (2010): 33–88.

19. Adriana Angel and Benjamin Bates, "Terministic Screens of Corruption: A Cluster Analysis of Colombian Radio Conversations," *KB Journal* 10 (2014), http://kbjournal.org/angel_bates_terministic_screens_of_corruption.

20. I did not study newspapers because they did not offer a space for politicians, judicial authorities, and citizens to communicate their versions, analyses, and opinions regarding the different corruption cases. The newspaper articles were simple accounts of the facts that did not include interviews with or the direct voice of the mentioned agents. Likely because of their low rates of literacy and education, audiences prefer listening to the radio and watching television over reading newspapers and magazines. Unfortunately, it is difficult to find studies that support this claim, as media scholarship on Guatemala is emerging rather than established.

21. Multivex Sigma Dos Guatemala, "Medición de diciembre radio," December 2015, http://www.multivexsigmados.com/uploads/5/8/4/4/5844261/medici%C3%B3n _de_diciembre_2015.pdf.

22. Kenneth Burke, *Attitudes Toward History* (1937; repr., Los Altos, CA: Hermes, 1959).

23. Carol Berthold, "Kenneth Burke's Cluster-Agon Method: Its Development and an Application," *Central States Speech Journal* 27 (1976): 302–9; Sonja Foss, "Women Priests in the Episcopal Church: A Cluster Analysis of Establishment Rhetoric," *Religious Communication Today* 7 (1984): 1–11; John Lynch, "Race and Radical Renamings: Using Cluster Agon Method to Assess the Radical Potential of 'European American' as a Substitute for 'White,'" *Journal of Kenneth Burke* 2 (2006), http://www.kbjournal.org/lynch.

24. Quoted in Adriana Angel and Benjamin Bates, "Terministic Screens of Corruption: A Cluster Analysis of Colombian Radio Conversations," *Journal of Kenneth Burke* 10 (2014), http://kbjournal.org/angel_bates_terministic_screens_of_corruption.

25. Ibid.; Adriana Angel and Julio Valencia, "Construcción retórica de la crisis organizacional," *Opción* 76 (2015): 117–40.

26. Federico de la Riva, "Entrevista a Baldetti en Radio Sonora," YouTube, uploaded May 11, 2015, https://www.youtube.com/watch?v=nI5gQON2ONs. Original voices are in Spanish, the native Guatemalan language. All English translations were performed by the author of this chapter.

27. Canal Antigua, "A las 7AM: Entrevista completa sobre reacción ciudadana ante corrupción en el Congreso," YouTube, uploaded August 14, 2015, https://www.youtube .com/watch?v=9CrrM-mxK5A.

28. Ibid.

29. Producción Audiovisual, "03 09 15 SN, Entrevista con el Presidente República Otto Pérez Molina con relación a su renuncia," YouTube, uploaded September 3, 2015, https://www.youtube.com/watch?v=rozM9eqcAC4.

30. Producción Audiovisual, "23 08 15 N7, Mensaje a la nación del Presidente Otto Pérez Molina," YouTube, uploaded August 23, 2015, https://www.youtube.com/watch?v =htmgrSk66Fc.

31. Ibid.

32. Jonathan Potter, *Representing Reality: Discourse, Rhetoric and Social Construction* (London: Sage, 1996).

33. De la Riva, "Entrevista a Baldetti en Radio Sonora."

34. Producción Audiovisual, "03 09 15 SN, Entrevista con el Presidente República Otto Pérez Molina."

35. Canal Antigua, "A las 8:45: Entrevista completa sobre el aspecto filosófico y ético en la corrupción," YouTube, uploaded July 10, 2015, https://www.youtube.com/watch?v =7KoqsQWvQxM.

36. Producción Audiovisual, "03 09 15 SN, Entrevista con el Presidente República Otto Pérez Molina."

37. Mark Ruhl, "Political Corruption in Central America: Assessment and Explanation," *Latin American Politics and Society* 53 (2011): 33–58.

38. De la Riva, "Entrevista a Baldetti en Radio Sonora."

39. Barry Brummett, "Burke's Representative Anecdote as a Method in Media Criticism," *Critical Studies in Mass Communication* 1 (1984): 161–76.

40. Richard Weaver, "Language Is Sermonic," in *The Rhetorical Tradition: Readings from Classical Times to the Present*, ed. Patricia Bizzell and Bruce Herzberg (Boston: Bedford / St. Martin's, 2016), 1348.

41. Canal Antigua, "A las 8:45: Entrevista completa con Iván Velázquez, de la CICIG," YouTube, uploaded July 27, 2015, https://www.youtube.com/watch?v=MnemkA36hG8.

42. Burke, *Rhetoric of Motives*.

43. Dana Cloud, "The Materiality of Discourse as Oxymoron," *Western Journal of Communication* 58 (1994): 141–63.

CHAPTER 7

1. The concept of *feminicidio* (feminicide) was coined and theorized initially by Dr. Julia Monárrez, a local feminist researcher, after the murders in Ciudad Juárez. Accordingly, it is not a parallel to homicide, as in femicide. It expands on the notion of *femicide*, in that it refers to the murder of women because of their gender, therefore considering power relations. It is associated with the local, state, and federal authorities' participation in action or omission based on a long history of impunity. For more on the concept of *feminicidio*, see Julia Monárrez Fragoso, "La cultura del feminicidio en Ciudad Juárez (1993–1999)," *Frontera Norte* 12 (2000): 87–117.

2. In this text, I enunciate as a Juarense feminist scholar in a process of "unlearning the privilege" of my social and cultural capital in order to listen, better comprehend, and politically engage with local women grassroots activists. I grew up in a middle-class Mexican family. I had the privilege of a Spanish-English bilingual education. I went to the National Autonomous University of Mexico in Mexico City during the 1970s, where I was awarded a bachelor's degree in political journalism. I was formed within a Marxist, mainly Gramscian milieu common in many Latin American public universities during the 1970s. In my late thirties, I went back to graduate school and obtained my master's in communications studies (University of Texas in El Paso) and my doctorate in rhetoric and communication (New Mexico State University in Las Cruces) in the United States. I position myself as a postcolonial and decolonial feminist who lives and works in a neocolonial country.

3. For more information about the feminicides and the social protests, I suggest the following sources, which include local perspectives: Gaspar de Alba and Georgina Guzmán, eds., *Making a Killing: Femicide, Free Trade, and La Frontera* (Austin: University of Texas Press, 2010); Clara E. Rojas, "The Rhetoric of Dismissal: Theorizing the Political Activism of the Juarense/Fronterizas' from a Feminist Rhetorical Perspective" (PhD diss., New Mexico State University, 2006); Clara E. Rojas, "La retórica de la tragedia y el feminicidio en Ciudad Juárez," in *Rhetoric in South America*, ed. Alejandra Vitale and Joseph-Philippe (Cape Town: AfricaRhetoric, 2013), 19–31; Clara E. Rojas, "Voces que silencian y silencios que enuncian," *Nóesis: Revista de Ciencias Sociales y Humanidades* 15 (2005): 15–32; Julia Monárrez, *Trama de una injusticia: Feminicidio sexual sistémico en Ciudad Juárez* (Tijuana: El Colef, Miguel Ángel Porrúa, 2009); Martha Estela Pérez, *Luchas de arena: Las mujeres en Ciudad Juárez* (Juárez: Publicaciones UACJ, 2011); Rita Sagato, *La escritura en el cuerpo de las mujeres asesinadas en Ciudad Juárez territorio, soberanía y crímenes de segundo estado* (Mexico City: Universidad del Claustro de Sor Juana, 2006); Melissa W. Wright, *Disposable Women and Other Myths of Global Capitalism* (New York: Routledge, 2006); and Melissa W. Wright, "The Paradox of Protests: The Mujeres de Negro of Northern Mexico," *Gender, Place and Culture* 12 (2005): 277–92.

4. I understand agonism, within contemporary rhetorical theory, as an intrinsic characteristic of public or political rhetoric, especially in social protests or confrontations. For more on agonism, see Kenneth Burke, *Grammar of Motives* (1945; repr., Berkeley: University of California Press, 1969), xv–xxiii; and Robert A. Cathcart, "Movements: Confrontation as Rhetorical Form," in *Readings on the Rhetoric of Social Protest*, ed. Charles E. Morris and Stephen H. Browne (State College, PA: Strata, 2001), 95–103.

5. See Kenneth Burke, *Language as Symbolic Action: Essays on Life, Literature, and Method* (Berkeley: University of California Press, 1966).

6. Rojas, "Rhetoric of Dismissal," 4.

7. Most of the local activists had a long experience in community-based activism. They have a close-knit network with low-income women in the community.

8. Juarense grassroots women activists were always present in the public protests, close to the victims' mothers, but they did not make the calls or become part of the organizing feminist group. On the contrary, they distanced themselves from the feminist group making the calls. The public events were organized by the Grupo Feminista 8 de Marzo (March 8 Feminist Group), who were from the capital city of Chihuahua. This group had several participants in Ciudad Juárez, among them the main voice, Esther Chavez Cano. Most of them occupied a professional middle-class position, mainly teachers and lawyers, and had a long history as feminist activists in the capital. This group can be described within what is known in the United States as liberal or reformist feminists; at that point they did not recognize the importance of difference among women, in terms of location, experience, and epistemology.

9. See the Instituto Municipal de las Mujeres Facebook page at https://www.facebook.com/MujerJuarense.

10. I use their real names because they agreed to let me do so, and because I hope this text foregrounds the potential of intentionally opening rhetorical spaces for those whose voice and knowledge has been dismissed as unimportant. Plus, they are currently public figures, so I can share their public Facebook links. They grew up in different barrios and participated in different CEBs. They met in Casa Promoción Juvenil (Youth Promotion and Advising Center), in 2001, where they worked as social promoters with low-income youth. Verónica was born in Juárez. She is currently forty-seven years old, divorced, and has two daughters (fifteen and nineteen years old). Verónica was part of the founders of the nonprofit civil association Casa Promoción Juvenil AC (Youth Promotion and Advising Center). She has dedicated the last ten years to learning, teaching, and promoting art and cultural activities in low-income communities. Sandra was about to continue her bachelor's degree in graphic design when she was invited to be director of the Women's Municipal Institute of Ciudad Juárez, where she was born. She is currently forty-one years old. She is a single mother of two daughters (twelve and fifteen years old). She is currently a senior studying psychology at the Universidad Autónoma de Ciudad Juárez (UACJ).

11. For the past fifteen years, Verónica and Sandra, as well as several other local activists, have attended multiple workshops related to gender, power, and public policy. Among these, I have taught several on rhetorical agency as it relates to gender and power. So, they have an idea of how to make sense of their rhetorical agency.

12. Gayatri Chakravorty Spivak, *The Spivak Reader: Selected Works of Gayatri Chakravorty Spivak*, ed. Donna Landry and Gerald MacLean (New York: Routledge, 1996), 292.

13. See Jan Svennevig, "Abduction as a Methodological Approach to Spoken Interaction," *NORskrift* (2001): 3–22.

14. My account of activists' rhetorical agency formation is informed by an ongoing conversation and series of interviews since 2008, when I began a register of talks with several grassroots local women as part of a personal book project, in process, tentatively titled *La genealogía de la conciencia feminista en Ciudad Juárez* (The Genealogy of the Feminist Consciousness in Ciudad Juárez). This project is also part of a wider collective project titled "Prácticas culturales y emancipación de la lengua," coordinated by Dr. Rossana Cassigoli, from the Universidad Autónoma de México. In this case, I focus on my conversations with Verónica and Sandra because their current political position gave me the opportunity to locate what I believe is a visible outcome of their struggle to construct

their rhetorical agency. I conducted recent interviews with Verónica and Sandra, during 2017, specifically for this chapter.

15. For an initial local academic account of the murders, see Martha E. Pérez and Héctor Padilla, "Interpretaciones locales sobre la violencia en contra de las mujeres en Ciudad Juárez," *Revista de Estudios de Género a Ventana* 15 (2002): 195–230.

16. This was happening during an important national political conjuncture. In 2000, the hegemonic PRI party, in power for more than seventy years, had lost the elections to the right-wing PAN party. This produced a rupture between the federal and the state government, still controlled by the PRI party. The civil society organizations and other civil associations in Juárez appealed to the federal government and were able to produce and position the Juárez Agenda.

17. I was a participant observer in this assembly for several years, during my doctoral research (2001–4), thus my questions are informed registers. I revisit these registers in this text, which are closer to my ongoing personal and academic interests. At that point in time, I knew something was happening, but I focused my doctoral research on the rhetoric of the women's public protests as the most salient events of the femicide crisis. In the deliberations within this assembly, I witnessed and documented the emergence of what at that point in time I thought was a feminist consciousness among local grassroots women activists.

18. I intentionally use the concept of civil society as it is commonly employed in Ciudad Juárez, in Mexico, and Latin America to refer to issues of governance and citizenship, as these relate to the civil society associations' demands for justice vis-à-vis the state. In this sense, I understand civil society or civil space as it refers to "the people." The "public sphere"—in Jürgen Habermas's terms—is commonly used as a theoretical approach in political science. The concept of the public sphere, as a limited approach to understand the complexity of multiple public deliberations, has for long been questioned by feminist critical thinkers such as Nancy Fraser. For more on this see Jean L. Cohen and Andrew Arato, *Civil Society and Political Theory* (Cambridge, MA: MIT Press, 1994); and Nancy Fraser, "Rethinking the Public Sphere: A Contribution to the Critique of Actually Existing Democracy," *Social Text*, nos. 25–26 (1990): 56–80.

19. Lorraine Code, *Rhetorical Spaces: Essays on Gendered Locations* (New York: Routledge, 1995), ix.

20. Ibid., x.

21. *Pinole* refers to finely ground dried corn with added sugar, which is usually dissolved in water or milk, but it is also eaten without any liquid.

22. Barbara Biesecker, "Rethinking the Rhetorical Situation from Within the Thematic of *Différance*," *Philosophy and Rhetoric* 22 (1989): 110–30.

23. Larry Grossberg, "Identity and Cultural Studies: Is That All There Is?" in *Questions of Cultural Identity*, ed. Stuart Hall and Paul Du Gay (London: Sage, 1996), 99.

24. Karlyn Kohrs Campbell, "Agency: Promiscuous and Protean," *Communication/Critical Studies* 2, no. 1 (March 2005): 1–19.

25. Ibid., 1–2.

26. Ibid., 5.

27. Pierre Bourdieu, *Language and Symbolic Power*, trans. Gino Raymond and Matthew Adamson (Malden, MA: Polity Press, 1991), 107.

28. Ibid.

29. Code, *Rhetorical Spaces*, x.

30. Ibid., xi.

31. I use *represent* for lack of a better word to refer to the translation process. I believe that whenever we translate, we are representing others, in another language. As we all know, we are born in language, so translation is never innocent. For instance,

Spanish is a very emotional language; intonations, silences, and body language are an intrinsic part of speaking and understanding colloquial Spanish. Unavoidably we lose a lot in translation, in this case I tried to be as precise as possible, to represent them through their experience as best I could. I consider this part of my text a context-based cultural translation, underlined by the power of language. I claim this, not only because I am writing for an English-speaking audience, but also because in many ways I have always occupied a privileged position as an insider in terms of *social, cultural and economic capital*; in terms of *race* I am *morena*, or a dark-skinned Mexican woman, which is always already a trope.

32. For more on liberation theology, see Gustavo Gutiérrez, *A Theology of Liberation* (London: SCM Press, 1974).

33. For more on ecclesial-based communities in Ciudad Juárez, see Alfredo Limas Hernández, "Memorias, fronteras y utopías: Paso del Norte 1995: Proceso utópico en comunidades eclesiales de base, organización popular independiente y El Paso Inter-religious Sponsoring Organizations: Ciudad Juárez-El Paso" (master's thesis, Instituto Mora, 1997), https://mora.repositorioinstitucional.mx/jspui/handle/1018/194.

34. See http://www.casapromocionjuvenil.org/quienes-somos.

35. See https://www.facebook.com/LaPromesaCiudadJuarez/ and https://www.facebook.com/elarteyculturaesunderechohumano.

36. In this particular case, I did consider the way social constructions of gender and class intersect with racial identities, because throughout our conversations Verónica and Sandra refer mainly to class and gender structures, although they are aware that Mexico is a profoundly racist country. Racist practices are recognized in Mexico, but its theorization is still relegated to academia; it has not been openly discussed in civil deliberations. In the 2018 presidential election, racial insults were constantly manifested through social media; these are always overdetermined by class. See "Estudio del Inegi revela racismo en México," *El Informador*, June 20, 2017, https://www.informador.mx/Economia/Estudio-del-Inegi-revela-racismo-en-Mexico-20170620-0091.html.

CHAPTER 8

1. Corte Constitucional, "Democracia participativa-alcance/participación ciudadana," Sentencia No. C-180/94, http://www.corteconstitucional.gov.co/relatoria/1994/C-180-94.htm.

2. "Polarización del país, reflejada en resultados del escrutinio," *El Tiempo*, October 2, 2017, http://www.eltiempo.com/politica/proceso-de-paz/resultados-plebiscito-2016-42861.

3. For the influence of religious rhetoric on American presidential campaigns, see, for example, Christopher B. Chapp, *Religious Rhetoric and American Politics: The Endurance of Civil Religion in American Electoral Campaigns* (Ithaca, NY: Cornell University Press, 2012).

4. Sonia Correa, "Gender Ideology: Tracking Its Origin and Meaning in Current Gender Politics," *Engenderings* (blog), December 11, 2017, https://blogs.lse.ac.uk/gender/2017/12/11/gender-ideology-tracking-its-origins-and-meanings-in-current-gender-politics.

5. The peace agreement refers to this group with the term LGBT.

6. Judith Butler, "The Backlash Against Gender Ideology Must Stop," *New Statesman of America*, January 21, 2019, https://www.newstatesman.com/2019/01/judith-butler-backlash-against-gender-ideology-must-stop.

7. Michelle Gallo, "'Gender Ideology' Is a Fiction That Could Do Real Harm," Open Society Foundation, August 29, 2017, https://www.opensocietyfoundations.org/voices/gender-ideology-fiction-could-do-real-harm.

8. Veronica Smink, "Aborto en Argentina: Por qué pese a sus leyes progresistas el aborto sigue siendo intocable en el país sudamericano," BBC Mundo, August 10, 2018, https://www.bbc.com/mundo/noticias-america-latina-45137418.

9. John Poulakos, "Towards a Sophistic Definition of Rhetoric," *Philosophy and Rhetoric* 16, no. 1 (1983): 36.

10. Susan C. Jarratt, *Rereading the Sophists: Classical Rhetoric Refigured* (Carbondale: Southern Illinois University Press, 1998), 11.

11. Anne Carson, "Simonides Painter," in *Innovations of Antiquity*, ed. Ralph Hexter and Daniel Selden (New York: Routledge, 1992), 51–68.

12. Poulakos, "Towards a Sophistic Definition," 37.

13. Robert L. Scott, "Rhetoric Is Epistemic: What Difference Does That Make?," in *Defining the New Rhetorics*, ed. Theresa Enos and Stuart C. Brown (Newbury Park, CA: Sage, 1993), 120–36.

14. Nola J. Heidlebaugh, *Judgment, Rhetoric, and the Problem of Incommensurability: Recalling Practical Wisdom* (Columbia: University of South Carolina Press, 2001), 42.

15. Jarratt, *Rereading the Sophists*.

16. Erika Pluhar et al., "Understanding the Relationship Between Religion and the Sexual Attitudes and Behaviors of College Students," *Journal of Sex Education and Therapy* 23 (1998): 4.

17. Amy Adamczyk and Brittany E. Hayes, "Religion and Sexual Behaviors: Understanding the Influence of Islamic Cultures and Religious Affiliation for Explaining Sex Outside of Marriage," *American Sociological Review* 77 (2012): 5.

18. "British Muslim Parents Oppose LGBT Lessons in Primary School," *Economist*, March 7, 2019, https://www.economist.com/britain/2019/03/07/british-muslim -parents-oppose-lgbt-lessons-in-primary-school.

19. Anne Harding, "Religious Faith Linked to Suicidal Behavior in LGBQ Adults," Reuters, April 13, 2018, https://www.reuters.com/article/us-health-lgbq-religion -suicide/religious-faith-linked-to-suicidal-behavior-in-lgbq-adults-idUSKBN1HK2MA. See also Diane Richardson, "Sexuality and Citizenship," *Sociology* 32, no. (1998): 83–100.

20. "¿Cuál es el lío con las cartillas del Ministerio de Educación?," *El Espectador*, August 9, 2017, https://www.elespectador.com/noticias/educacion/cual-el-lio-cartillas -del-ministerio-de-educacion-video-648283.

21. Ruben Rivera, "No a la paz en Colombia, gana el sector más reaccionario," *La Izquierda Socialista*, August 4, 2016, http://www.laizquierdasocialista.org/a-la-paz-en -colombia-gana-sector-reaccionario.

22. Heidlebaugh, *Judgment, Rhetoric, and the Problem of Incommensurability*, 42.

23. Javier Barragán, "Fue mentiroso decir que le iba a entregar el país a las Farc: Santos," RCN Radio, July 13, 2018, https://www.rcnradio.com/politica/fue-mentiroso -decir-que-le-iba-entregar-el-pais-las-farc-santos.

24. "Los sermones incendiarios del Pastor Miguel Arrázola," *Las 2 Orillas*, October 4, 2016, https://www.las2orillas.co/miguel-arrazola-el-pastor-que-volvio-su-pulpito-la -tribuna-del-no-en-cartagena.

25. Los Ángeles de Juan, "'Yo no soy homofóbico': Alejandro Ordóñez," YouTube, uploaded September 19, 2014, https://www.youtube.com/watch?v=efD_6eOsj5g.

26. Ibid.

27. MCM Presencia De Reino Yumbo, "Ideología de género Apóstol Eduardo Cañas," YouTube, uploaded August 28, 2016, https://www.youtube.com/watch?v =ammENSP1LF0.

28. "Ideología de género: Una estrategia para ganar adeptos por el 'No' al plebiscito," *Revista Semana*, August 17, 2016, http://www.semana.com/nacion/articulo/ideologia -de-genero-una-estrategia-para-ganar-adeptos-por-el-no-al-plebiscito/488260.

29. "'Rechazamos implementación de la ideología de Género': Cardenal Rubén Salazar," *El País*, August 9, 2016, http://www.elpais.com.co/colombia/rechazamos -implementacion-de-la-ideologia-de-genero-cardenal-ruben-salazar.html.

30. "'En el centro de la negociación no está Jesucristo,' polémico mensaje de futbolista a Santos," *El País*, September 28, 2016, http://www.elpais.com.co/proceso-de -paz/en-el-centro-de-la-negociacion-no-esta-jesucristo-polemico-mensaje-de-futbolista-a -santos.html.

31. Bryan Camacho, "Decirle No a esta az es lo que Dios Quiere," *Las 2 Orillas*, September 15, 2016, https://www.las2orillas.co/decirle-no-a-esta-paz-es-lo-que-dios-quiere.

32. "Por qué ganó el No," *Revista Semana*, March 10, 2016, https://www.semana .com/nacion/articulo/por-que-gano-el-no-en-el-plebiscito-por-la-paz-2016/496636.

33. Barbara Rosenwein, *Emotional Communities in the Middle Ages* (Ithaca, NY: Cornell University Press, 2006), 24.

34. Ibid., 25.

35. Ibid., 84.

36. Frank Biess, "Feelings in the Aftermath: Toward a History of Postwar Emotions," in *Histories of the Aftermath: The Legacies of the Second World War in Europe*, ed. Frank Biess and Robert G. Moeller, 30–48 (New York: Berghahn Books, 2010), 40.

37. Ibid., 199.

38. Ibid.

39. Barrera García, Boris. "¡Los Cristianos seguimos decididos y votaremos No en el Plebiscito!" *Las 2 Orillas*, September 16, 2016, https://www.las2orillas.co/los-cristianos -seguimos-decididos-y-votaremos-no-en-el-plebiscito.

40. Kenneth Burke, *The Rhetoric of Religion: Studies in Logology* (1961; repr., Berkeley: University of California Press, 1970), 184.

41. Ibid., 183.

42. Roger Scruton cited by Andrew Gilbert, *British Conservatism and the Legal Regulations of Intimate Relationships* (London: Bloomsbury, 2018), 31–32.

43. "Leviticus 2," Bible Study Tools, n.d., https://www.biblestudytools.com/com mentaries/jamieson-fausset-brown/leviticus/leviticus-2.html.

44. MCM Presencia De Reino Yumbo, "Ideología de género Apóstol Eduardo Cañas."

45. Ibid.

46. Poulakos, "Towards a Sophistic Definition of Rhetoric," 39.

47. Heidlebaugh, *Judgment, Rhetoric, and the Problem of Incommensurability*, 47.

48. Miguel Arázola, "Ganamos, ganamos, de dios nadie se burla . . . gobernantes," *Revista Semana*, October 4, 2016, https://www.semana.com/nacion/multimedia/pastor -miguel-arrazola-publica-video-por-el-triunfo-del-no-en-el-plebiscito/496718.

49. David Osorio, "Pastor acusa al presidente santos de ser el anticristo," *De Avanzada* (blog), September 6, 2016, http://de-avanzada.blogspot.com.co/2016/09/Santos -anticristo.html.

50. Cynthia Enloe, *Bananas, Beaches, and Bases: Making Feminist Sense of International Politics* (Berkeley: University of California Press, 2014), 12.

51. "Acuerdo final para la terminación del conflicto y la construcción de una paz estable y duradera," November 24, 2016, https://draftable.com/compare /FeKDSvYWDAREgnvq.

52. "Ordóñez y la purga de la ideología de género," *El Espectador*, October 11, 2016, https://www.elespectador.com/noticias/politica/ordonez-y-purga-de-ideologia-de -genero-articulo-659858.

53. Viridiana Molinares, Carlos Andrés Orozco, and Julia Bernal, "Identidades suspendidas por el silencio, la opacidad, la vergüenza y los tabúes," *Revista de Derecho*

43 (January–June 2015), http://rcientificas.uninorte.edu.co/index.php/derecho/article /view/7476/7334.

54. Natalio Cosoy, "¿En qué se diferencia el nuevo acuerdo de paz entre el gobierno de Colombia y las FARC del que fue rechazado en el plebiscito?" BBC Mundo, November 14, 2016, http://www.bbc.com/mundo/noticias-america-latina-37965382.

55. "Acuerdo final para la terminación del conflicto."

56. Poulakos, "Towards a Sophistic Definition of Rhetoric," 42.

57. Ibid., 42–43.

58. Ibid., 215.

59. Ibid., 38.

60. Richardson, "Sexuality and Citizenship."

61. Génica Mazzoldi, Irina Cuesta, and Eduardo Álvarez, "'Gender Ideology': A Spoiler for Peace?" Open Democracy, October 26, 2016, https://www.opendemocracy .net/en/democraciaabierta/gender-ideology-spoiler-for-pe.

62. "Así son los Colombianos frente a la religión y la política," *Revista Semana*, January 7, 2017, https://www.semana.com/nacion/articulo/colombianos-consideran-a -la-religion-muy-importante-en-sus-vidas/530679.

63. "Constitución Política de Colombia," 2016, http://www.corteconstitucional.gov .co/inicio/Constitucion%20politica%20de%20Colombia.pdf.

64. Pedro Mercado, "Falacia Laicista," *El Tiempo*, April 29, 2017, http://www.eltiempo .com/opinion/columnistas/pedro-mercado-cepeda/falacia-laicista-colombia-como -estado-laico-82792.

65. Laura Aguilera, "Colombia: Victims Must Be at the Centre of the Public Agenda," International Committee of the Red Cross, March 1, 2018, https://www.icrc .org/en/document/colombia-victims-must-be-centre-public-agenda.

CHAPTER 9

1. This scheme reproduces hierarchies typical of a colonial mentality. This mentality has already been object of criticism from the postcolonial perspective. For examples, see Edward W. Said, *Orientalism* (New York: Vintage, 1979); and Gayatri Chakravorty Spivak, "Can the Subaltern Speak?" in *Marxism and the Interpretation of Culture*, ed. Cary Nelson and Lawrence Grossberg (London: Macmillan, 1988), 271–316.

2. Jack Goody, *The Domestication of the Savage Mind* (Cambridge, UK: Cambridge University Press, 1977).

3. This period was particularly prolific in the production of Brazilian media texts about Lula's public speeches. In 1989, he disputed the presidential elections for the first time. Between 2011 and 2012 there was the diagnosis and cure of his laryngeal cancer.

4. Michel Foucault, *The Archaeology of Knowledge*, trans. A. M. Sheridan Smith (New York: Harper and Row, 1972), 19.

5. Arlette Farge, *Essai pour une histoire des voix au XVIIIème siècle* (Paris: Bayard, 2009), 199, 202.

6. Ibid., 206.

7. Jean-Michel David, "*Eloquentia popularis* et conduites symboliques des orateurs à la fin de la République," *Quaderni Storici* 12 (1980): 170.

8. Ibid. For more on the relationship between rhetoric and social trials, see Robert Hariman, "Status, Marginality, and Rhetorical Theory," *Quarterly Journal of Speech* 72, no. 1 (1986): 38–54.

9. David, "*Eloquentia popularis*," 177.

10. Ibid., 182.

11. Ibid., 70.

12. Ibid., 72.

13. Jean-Jacques Courtine and Carlos Piovezani, eds., *História da fala pública: Uma arqueologia dos poderes do discurso* (Petrópolis: Vozes, 2015).

14. See Silvia Montiglio, "Falar em público e ficar em silêncio na Grécia clássica" (25–52) and Jacques Guilhamou, "Falas democráticas e poderes intermediários na Revolução Francesa" (57–184), both in ibid.

15. Friedrich Nietzsche, *Da retórica* (Lisbon: Veja, 1999), 27.

16. See Montiglio, "Falar em público"; see also Hariman, "Status, Marginality, and Rhetorical Theory."

17. Fernando Collor was the main candidate against Lula in the Brazilian presidential elections in 1989. Deriving from an aristocratic family in the northeast region of the country, he had been the governor in the state of Alagoas. His speech was traditionally embedded with attacks presented with the use of a far-fetched style, which was based on the use of rare words; "Lula Tries to Calm Down the Middle Class," *Folha de São Paulo*, November 30, 1989, 6.

18. "Lula Uses Moderate Discourse as an Electoral Strategy," *Folha de São Paulo*, December 15, 1989, B2.

19. Leonel Brizola was the president of PDT, the Democratic Labour Party (Partido Democrático Trabalhista) and former governor of Rio de Janeiro. He and Lula were the two main candidates for the left in the 1989 election.

20. Adverbs in Portuguese are not flexible in number or gender. Gender bending in *menos* is a stereotype of stigmatized popular speech.

21. "Debates: Cenas secretas," *Veja* 22, no. 49 (December 13, 1989): 54, 59.

22. "A arrancada de Lula," *Veja* 22, no. 46 (November 22, 1989): 54.

23. Ibid., 62.

24. José Simão, "Lula e seu estilo francês," *Folha de São Paulo*, September 17, 1989, B4. In this case, my translation has sought to preserve the original's humorous tone.

25. The *s* is the prototypical mark in Portuguese for plural expression in the names, and the omission of it is a stigmatized feature of popular speech.

26. Gilberto de Mello Kujawski, "O linguajar de Lula," *Estado de São Paulo*, February 17, 2005, A2.

27. Marli Quadros Leite, *Preconceito e intolerância na linguagem* (São Paulo: Contexto Press, 2008).

28. See Carlo Ginzburg, *Miti, emblemi, spie: Morfologia e storia* (Torino: Einaudi, 1989).

29. For more information on the relationship between the outer and inner zones of the body, see Jean-Jacques Courtine and Claudine Haroche, *Histoire du visage* (Paris: Payot, 1988); and Alain Corbin, Jean-Jacques Courtine, Georges Vigarello, *Histoire du corps* (Paris: Seuil, 2006).

30. Michel de Certeau, Dominique Julia, and Jacques Revel, "A Beleza do Morto: O Conceito de Cultura Popular," in *A invenção da sociedade*, by Jacques Revel (Lisboa: DIFEL, 1989), 49–75.

31. Kujawski, "O linguajar de Lula," A32.

32. I performed an analysis of these speeches about Lula's voice produced by the Brazilian media during his treatment for laryngeal cancer and soon after the announcement of his recovery; see Carlos Piovezani, "Discursos sobre a voz de lula na mídia brasileira," *Linguagem em (Dis)curso* 15 (2015): 33–46.

33. Ruth de Aquino, "A voz de Lula," *Época*, March 30, 2012, 26.

34. Fernando Henrique Cardoso had been minister of finance between May 1993 and July 1994, when he left the ministry to run for president. Before that, he was

nationally and internationally known as a Brazilian intellectual. The "all *s*'s and *r*'s" metaphorically indicate speech that corresponds perfectly to the standard norm; "Teste: Monte você mesmo O Anti-Lula," *Carta Capital*, August 1994, 31, 34.

35. See William Labov, *Sociolinguistic Patterns* (Philadelphia: University of Pennsylvania Press, 1972).

36. See Marc Angenot, *O discurso social e as retóricas da incompreensão* (São Carlos: EdUFSCar, 2015), 101–4.

37. Aldo Lins e Silva, "Painel do leitor," *Folha*, December 15, 1989, A3.

38. Carlos Piovezani, "Falar em público na política contemporânea: A eloquência pop e popular brasileira na idade da mídia," in Courtine and Piovezani, *História da fala pública*, 324–30.

CHAPTER 10

1. On Cristina Fernández de Kirchner's speeches, see Irene Lis Gindin, "El poder de legitimar: El campo en el discurso de Cristina Fernández (2007–2011)," *Razón y Palabra: Primera Revista Electrónica en Iberoamérica Especializada en Comunicación* 93 (2016): 694–708; Ana Laura Maizels, "Argumentación e imagen de sí de la Presidenta argentina, Cristina Fernández, en el marco de la crisis con el sector agropecuario," *Rétor* 4, no. 2 (2014): 153–81; Alejandro Raiter, "'Hablo y entiendan': Creencias, presuposición e interdiscurso en los actos de Cristina Fernández de Kirchner," *Oralia* 12 (2009): 73–96; Sara Isabel Pérez, "Genre et discours politique en Argentine: La construction du leadership de Cristina F. de Kirchner," in *Discours, identité et leadership présidentiel en Amérique latine*, ed. Morgan Donot, Christian Le Bart, and Yeny Serrano (Paris: L'Harmattan, 2017), 43–61; María Alejandra Vitale, "Legitimizing Leadership: Argentine President Cristina Fernández De Kirchner's 2007 Inaugural Address," *Rhetoric Society Quarterly* 45 (2015): 250–63; and María Alejandra Vitale, "El ethos en la 'conversacionalización' del discurso público: Las alocuciones de asunción de la presidente argentina Cristina Fernández de Kirchner," *Langage et Societé* 149 (2014): 49–67.

2. These are speeches that Cristina Fernández de Kirchner gave regularly to young Kirchnerist militants from the balconies overlooking the various internal courtyards of the Government House. They were reproduced by newspapers that endorsed her government and were occasionally reported in those that did not.

3. Cambiemos is an Argentine national political coalition founded in 2015, based on an agreement between the ARI Civic Coalition, Republican Proposal (PRO, the party founded by Mauricio Macri in 2005), the Radical Civic Union, and other political forces. It contested the presidential elections for the first time in 2015 and won, elevating Macri to the presidency.

4. See Karlyn Kohrs Campbell and Kathleen Hall Jamieson, *Presidents Creating the Presidency: Deeds Done in Words* (Chicago: University of Chicago Press, 2008); and Amos Kiewe, "Framing Memory Through Eulogy," in *Framing Public Memory*, ed. Kendall Phillips (Tuscaloosa: University of Alabama Press, 2004), 248–66.

5. Argentine law allows each candidate to be president for only two consecutive periods, as happened with Fernández de Kirchner; however, it does not prevent the same person running again for the presidency after a different person has been in office for at least one term.

6. See Vitale, "Ethos en la 'conversacionalización'"; and Vitale, "Legitimizing Leadership."

7. The constitutions of many Latin American countries require their citizens to vote. In Argentina, those wishing not to choose among the available candidates may

return their ballot empty (a "blank vote"), include a statement of protest in their ballot (an "impugned vote"), or refuse to comply with compulsory suffrage (an "abstention").

8. ALIANZA was formed in 1997 in opposition to the neoliberal government of Carlos Menem (president for two consecutive periods, 1989–95 and 1995–99). The two main parties within ALIANZA were the Radical Civic Union (UCR) and FREPASO (Frente País Solidario, Front for a Country in Solidarity). FREPASO was itself a confederation of opposition parties established in 1994 that included the PAIS Alliance (of Peronist extraction), the Socialist Unity Coalition, and the Christian Democratic Party (PDC). Both ALIANZA and FREPASO dissolved after the crisis of 2001. For more on ALIANZA and FREPASO, see Marcos Novaro and Vicente Palermo, *Los caminos de la centroizquierda: dilemas y desafíos del Frepaso y de la Alianza* (Buenos Aires: Losada, 1998).

9. Néstor Kirchner's Front for Victory included sectors of the Justicialist Party (PJ), the Radical Civic Union (UCR), the Communist Party (PC), and the Humanist Party (PH), among others. Presidential elections were held on April 27, 2003. In the first round of the election, Néstor Kirchner received the second-highest percentage of the electorate with 22.24 percent (after Carlos Menem, who took 24.25 percent). Since neither candidate exceeded 40 percent and the difference between them was less than 10 percent, Argentine law called for a runoff election. That election was scheduled for May 18, but Menem withdrew his candidacy in the face of certain and resounding defeat, leaving the presidency to Kirchner. See Isidoro Cheresky, "Autoridad política debilitada y presencia ciudadana de rumbo incierto," *Revista Nueva Sociedad* 179 (2002): 112–29.

10. See Isidoro Cheresky, ed., *La política después de los partidos* (Buenos Aires: Prometeo, 2006).

11. See Juan Carlos Torre, "La operación política de la transversalidad: El presidente Kirchner y el partido justicialista," in *Argentina en perspectiva: Reflexiones sobre nuestro país en democracia*, ed. Eduardo Baistrocchi (Buenos Aires: Universidad Torcuato Di Tella, 2005), 75–88.

12. See Gerardo Aboy Carlés, "El declive del kirchnerismo y las mutaciones del peronismo," *Nueva Sociedad* 249 (2014): 4–15.

13. Ibid.

14. See Marisella Svampa, "Argentina, una década después: Del 'que se vayan todos' a la exacerbación de lo nacional-popular," *Nueva Sociedad* 235 (2011): 17–34.

15. This is a monthly payment that domestic workers, workers in the informal economy, and the unemployed receive for each unmarried child younger than eighteen years of age.

16. See Gabriel Vommaro, "La centroderecha y el 'cambio cultural' argentino," *Nueva Sociedad* 270 (2017): 4–13.

17. See Sergio Morresi, "'Acá somos todos democráticos': El PRO y las relaciones entre la derecha y la democracia en Argentina," in *Hagmos equipo: PRO y la construcción de la nueva derecha en Argentina*, ed. Gabriel Vommaro and Sergio Morresi (Los Polvorines: Ediciones UNGS, 2015), 163–201.

18. See Dominique Maingueneau, "Problèmes d'ethos," *Pratiques* 113–14 (2002): 55–67; and Ruth Amossy, *La présentation de soi: Êthos et identité verbale* (Paris: Presses Universitaires de France, 2010).

19. See Christian Plantin, *Les bonnes raisons des émotions: Principes et méthode pour l'étude du discours émotionné* (Berne: Peter Lang, 2011).¶

20. See Eliseo Verón, "La palabra adversativa: Observaciones sobre la enunciación política," in *El discurso político: Lenguajes y acontecimientos*, ed. Eliseo Verón et al. (Buenos Aires: Hachette, 1986), 11–26.

21. Campbell and Jamieson, *Presidents Creating the Presidency*.

22. Elisabet Gerber, *Comunicación y política: Análisis de la campaña presidencial de Michelle Bachelet* (Santiago: Friedrich-Ebert-Stiftung en Chile, 2006).

23. See José Natanson, "Límites y desafíos del peronismo en la oposición: Un terminator de metal líquido," *Nueva Sociedad* 266 (2016): 45–56.

24. "Denuncian a Eugenio Zaffaroni por 'apología del delito,'" *Perfil*, January 22, 2018, http://www.perfil.com/politica/denuncian-a-zaffaroni-por-apologia-del-delito.phtml.

25. See "Puede pasar algo parecido a lo de 2001," *Política*, February 23, 2018, http://www.telam.com.ar/notas/201802/253401-zaffaroni-2001-preocupado-gobierno-macri.html.

26. In her first opening address on December 10, 2007, Fernández de Kirchner wore a white dress. In her second opening address, however, which she gave on December 10, 2011, she wore a black dress since she was in mourning for her husband and former president, Néstor Kirchner, who died in 2010.

27. See "Cristina Kirchner dijo que Macri le 'exigió' con 'gritos' que el traspaso sea en la Casa Rosada," *La Nación*, December 6, 2015, https://www.lanacion.com.ar/1851988-cristina-kirchner-dijo-que-macri-le-exigio-con-un-elevado-tono-de-voz-que-el-traspaso-sea-en-la-casa-rosada.

28. Perelman and Olbrechts-Tyteca describe analogy as a type of argument that presupposes a similarity of structures and whose general formula is A is to B as C is to D. A and B together are the elements of the theme, which contains the conclusion, and C and D are the elements of the *phoros*, which serve to support the reasoning. In the speech of Fernández de Kirchner the elements of the *phoros* are the carriage, which becomes pumpkin at midnight, and the elements of the theme are Fernández de Kirchner herself, who will lose her power at midnight. See Chaïm Perelman and Lucie Olbrechts-Tyteca, *The New Rhetoric: A Treatise on Argumentation* (Notre Dame, IN: University of Notre Dame Press, 1969).

29. "Cristina en la última Plaza de su segundo período presidencial," Sitio Oficial de Cristina Fernández de Kirchner, December 9, 2015, https://www.cfkargentina.com/discurso-de-cristina-kirchner-en-la-ultima-plaza-de-su-segundo-periodo-presidencial/.

30. See Helena Beristain Diaz, *Diccionario de retórica y poética* (Mexico City: Porrúa, 1995).

31. See Aristotle, *On Rhetoric: A Theory of Civic Discourse*, trans. George Kennedy (New York: Oxford University Press, 2007); and Marc Angenot, *Dialogues de sourds: Traité de rhétorique antilogique* (Paris: Mille et une Nuits, 2008).

32. The Law on Audiovisual Communication Services was passed on October 10, 2009. Popularly known as the "Media Law," it was widely panned by the Argentine press, who were mostly critical of Cristina Fernández de Kirchner.

33. See Plantin, *Les bonnes raisons des émotions* (2011); and Ruth Amossy, *Discours politique, littérature d'idées, fiction: Comment peut-on agir sur un public en orientant ses façons de voir, de penser?* (Paris: Nathan Université, 2000).

34. Mauricio Macri was prosecuted in 2010 for illegal wiretapping while serving as chief of government of Buenos Aires. The case, which was still unresolved when Macri became president, was dismissed shortly afterward, on December 30, 2015. The dismissal was upheld several months later by the federal court.

35. See Andrea Balbo, "Alcuni esempi di interazione oratore-pubblico a Roma trail I secolo a. C. e il I d.C.," *Cahiersdu Centre Gustave Glotz* 18 (2007): 375–88.

36. The change from "each one of you" to "each of those forty-two million Argentines" gives rise to a grammatically ambiguous sentence in which Fernández de Kirchner switches from "you" to generic "him" and "he." I have tried as far as possible to preserve her original style.

37. The "Mothers" refers to the Mothers of Plaza de Mayo, a group that arose during the last military dictatorship in Argentina (1976–83) to claim and search for their missing children. The Grandmothers of Plaza de Mayo also emerged during the last military dictatorship with the aim of locating all the missing children born in clandestine detention

centers while their mothers were detained, and restoring them to their legitimate families. The group HIJOS, an acronym that in Spanish stands for "Sons and Daughters for Identity and Justice Against Forgetfulness and Silence," was formed in 1994 and is composed mainly of the children of the disappeared, who defend the political struggle of their parents in the 1970s and call for the perpetrators to be tried and punished. The Kirchners' human rights policy was based on the annulment in 2003, during the presidency of Néstor Kirchner, of the laws of Full Stop and Due Obedience, which had left most of the military involved in crimes against humanity unpunished. It is true that Raúl Alfonsín, who took office in 1983 as the first democratic president after the 1976–83 military dictatorship, promoted the so-called Trial of the Juntas, which imprisoned the military leadership that installed state terrorism. But under pressure from a still powerful military establishment, he was forced to pass the amnesty laws already mentioned. The repeal of those laws led to the prosecution of many of those who participated in state terrorism for crimes against humanity. Some of these cases continue to be heard.

38. See Plantin, *Bonnes raisons des émotions*.

39. Norman Fairclough, *Discourse and Social Change* (Cambridge, UK: Polity Press, 1992); Norman Fairclough, *Critical Discourse Analysis: The Critical Study of Language* (London: Longman, 1995); Norman Fairclough, *Analysing Discourse: Textual Analysis for Social Research* (London: Routledge, 2003).

40. See note 1.

41. See Alejandra Vitale, "Ethos y legitimidad política."

42. See Kiewe, "Framing Memory."

43. Agonistic confrontation differs from antagonistic confrontation because the opponent is not considered an enemy to be destroyed, but an adversary whose existence is considered legitimate. In agonistic democracy, the antagonistic dimension is always present, but domesticated or regulated by democratic procedures. See Chantal Mouffe, *On the Political* (New York: Routledge, 2005); and Chantal Mouffe, *Agonistics: Thinking the World Politically* (London: Verso, 2013).

CHAPTER 11

1. "Latin-America's Worst-Ever Refugee Crisis: Venezuelans," *Washington Post*, February 23, 2018, accessed April 13, 2019, https://www.washingtonpost.com/opinions/global-opinions/the-collapse-in-venezuela-is-creating-a-refugee-crisis/2018/02/23/68b85c7e-1807-11e8-8b08-027a6ccb38eb_story.html.

2. David E. Procter, "The Dynamic Spectacle: Transforming Experience into Social Forms of Community," *Quarterly Journal of Speech* 76, no. 2 (May 1990): 119.

3. Ibid., 120.

4. S. Michael Halloran, "Text and Experience in a Historical Pageant: Toward a Rhetoric of Spectacle," *Rhetoric Society Quarterly* 31, no. 4 (September 2001): 15.

5. Ibid., 8.

6. Jonathan Mark Balzotti, "Rhetoric, Spectacle, and Mechanized Amusement at the World's Columbian Exposition," *Studies in Visual Arts and Communication: An International Journal* 3, no. 2 (2016): 4.

7. Ibid., 4–5.

8. Ibid., 5.

9. Murray Edelman, *Constructing the Political Spectacle* (Chicago: University of Chicago Press, 1988), 1.

10. Ibid., 6.

11. Ibid., 17.

12. Ibid., 31.

13. Ibid., 31.

14. Guy Debord, *The Society of the Spectacle*, trans. Donald Nicholson-Smith, rev. ed. (New York: Zone Books, 1995), 12.

15. Ibid., 13.

16. Ibid., 28.

17. Guy Debord, *Comments on the Society of the Spectacle*, trans. Malcolm Imrie (London: Verso Books, 1991), 7.

18. Rachel Boynton, *Our Brand Is Crisis*, documentary, 2005, http://www.imdb.com/title/tt0492714.

19. Although Chávez was unquestionably popular, scholars have recently conducted analyses that suggest irregularities in voting patterns that began in the referendum in 2004 and continued in subsequent elections. See Raúl Jiménez and Manuel Hidalgo, "Forensic Analysis of Venezuelan Elections During the Chávez Presidency," *PLOS ONE* 9, no. 6 (June 27, 2014), https://doi.org/10.1371/journal.pone.0100884.

20. "2006: Chavez Calls Bush 'the Devil,'" CNN, 2013, https://www.youtube.com/watch?v=lOsABwCrn3E.

21. "Otros dardos de Hugo Chávez," BBC Mundo, November 12, 2007, http://news.bbc.co.uk/hi/spanish/latin_america/newsid_7091000/7091825.stm.

22. "Chávez expulsa al embajador de EEUU en solidaridad con Bolivia," *El Mundo*, December 9, 2008, http://www.elmundo.es/elmundo/2008/09/12/internacional/1221177561.html.

23. EL HERALDO, "Chávez se me apareció en forma de pajarito: Maduro," YouTube, uploaded April 2, 2013, https://www.youtube.com/watch?v=qv5dAqSSoXU.

24. Tulio Moreno Alvarado, "Socialism Hasn't Failed Venezuela: Economic War Has," TeleSUR, October 2, 2017, https://www.telesurtv.net/english/opinion/Socialism-Hasnt-Failed-Venezuela.-Economic-War-Has.-20171002-0007.html.

25. Debord, *Comments on the Society of the Spectacle*, 13.

26. Oliver Stone, *South of the Border*, documentary, 2009, https://www.imdb.com/title/tt1337137/.

27. Ibid.

28. Francisco Toro, "Remembering a Massacre," *Latitude* (blog), April 10, 2012, https://latitude.blogs.nytimes.com/2012/04/10/remembering-the-2002-chavez-coup/.

29. Kim Bartley and Donnacha O'Briain, *The Revolution Will Not Be Televised*, documentary, 2003, http://www.imdb.com/title/tt0363510.

30. Wolfgang Schalk, *Radiografía de una mentira*, documentary, 2004, http://www.imdb.com/title/tt0479810.

31. Ángel Palacios, *Claves de una masacre*, documentary, 2004, http://www.imdb.com/title/tt0463676.

32. Kirk A. Hawkins, "Responding to Radical Populism: Chavismo in Venezuela," *Democratization* 23, no. 2 (February 2016): 243.

33. Ibid.

34. Ibid., 245.

35. Ibid., 246.

36. Ibid., 257.

37. Julia Buxton, "Situation Normal in Venezuela: All Fouled Up," *NACLA Report on the Americas* 49, no. 1 (January 2017): 2.

38. Ibid., 2–4.

39. John W. Delicath and Kevin Michael DeLuca, "Image Events, the Public Sphere, and Argumentative Practice: The Case of Radical Environmental Groups," *Argumentation* 17, no. 3 (September 2003): 317.

40. Ibid., 321.

41. Ibid., 328.

42. Galia Yanoshevsky, "6.2: The Possibility and Actuality of Image Events," *Enculturation* 6, no. 2 (2009), http://enculturation.net/6.2/yanoshevsky.

43. Harold Trinkunas, "Why Venezuela's Opposition Has Been Unable to Effectively Challenge Maduro," Brookings Institution, January 8, 2018, https://www.brookings.edu/blog/order-from-chaos/2018/01/08/why-venezuelas-opposition-has-been-unable-to-effectively-challenge-maduro.

44. Associated Press, "AP Explains: Options Narrowing for Venezuela's Opposition," *New York Times*, July 8, 2020, https://www.nytimes.com/aponline/2020/07/08/world/americas/ap-lt-ap-explainsvenezuela-party-takeover.html.

45. Michael Isikoff, "Hugo's Close Call," *Newsweek*, April 28, 2002, http://www.newsweek.com/hugos-close-call-143197.

46. "A Crackdown in Venezuela," *Economist*, October 19, 2013, https://www.economist.com/news/americas/21588083-nicol-s-maduro-continues-hugo-ch-vezs-campaign-against-media-news-thats-fit-print.

47. "Maduro: Vamos a dar la batalla en las redes sociales," Ministerio del Poder Popular para la Comunicación e Información, September 19, 2013, http://minci.gob.ve/maduro-vamos-a-dar-la-batalla-en-las-redes-sociales.

48. Nicolás Maduro Moros, "Sigueme por todas mis Redes Sociales oficiales," YouTube, uploaded August 30, 2017, accessed September 5, 2017, https://www.youtube.com/watch?v=1YowRowEgR8&feature=youtu.be.

49. "How the Venezuelan Government Made the Media into Its Most Powerful Ally," *Foreign Policy*, March 11, 2014, https://foreignpolicy.com/2014/03/11/how-the-venezuelan-government-made-the-media-into-its-most-powerful-ally.

50. "Maduro's Muzzle," *Economist*, April 4, 2015, https://www.economist.com/news/americas/21647645-not-content-harassing-press-regime-censors-itself-maduros-muzzle.

51. "Journalists Detained, Attacked, and Threatened amid Unrest in Venezuela," Committee to Protect Journalists, July 31, 2017, https://cpj.org/2017/07/journalists-detained-attacked-and-threatened-amid-.php.

52. Meg Dalton, "Q&A: *NYT*'s Nick Casey on Getting Barred from Venezuela amid Chaos," *Columbia Journalism Review*, August 10, 2017, https://www.cjr.org/q_and_a/nick-casey-new-york-times-venezuela.php.

53. Journeyman Pictures, "Post-Chavez Venezuela Has Become a Failed State," YouTube, uploaded March 27, 2017, https://www.youtube.com/watch?v=MlGlBUckqCw.

54. Juan Carlos Hidalgo, "How Socialism Has Destroyed Venezuela," *CityAM*, February 25, 2014, http://www.cityam.com/article/1393351308/how-socialism-has-destroyed-venezuela.

55. Tim Worstall, "Congratulations to Bolivarian Socialism: 35,000 Venezuelans Leave the Country to Feed Themselves," *Forbes*, July 17, 2016, https://www.forbes.com/sites/timworstall/2016/07/17/congratulations-to-bolivarian-socialism-35000-venezuelans-leave-the-country-to-feed-themselves.

56. Moisés Naím, "The Tragedy of Venezuela," *The Atlantic*, February 25, 2014, https://www.theatlantic.com/international/archive/2014/02/the-tragedy-of-venezuela/284062.

57. Raúl Stolk, "Venezuela Has Become a Starvation State," *The Daily Beast*, May 25, 2016, https://www.thedailybeast.com/venezuela-has-become-a-starvation-state.

58. Moisés Naím and Francisco Toro, "Venezuela Is Falling Apart," *The Atlantic*, May 12, 2016, https://www.theatlantic.com/international/archive/2016/05/venezuela-is-falling-apart/481755.

59. Debord argues that the spectacle operates freely in Western nations like the United States where apparent market freedom allowed for a "diffuse" spectacle. In nations with dictatorial bureaucracy, the spectacle simply existed in a more "concentrated" form. In *Comments on the Society of the Spectacle*, he suggests that the "integrated" spectacle combines aspects of both and has been the means by which the spectacle has "imposed itself globally."

60. James Estrin, "World Press Photo of the Year: A Tale Told Twice," *New York Times*, April 12, 2018, https://www.nytimes.com/2018/04/12/lens/world-press-photo-of -the-year-a-tale-told-twice.html.

61. Mariano Castillo, "Searching for Truth in Venezuela," CNN, February 21, 2014, https://www.cnn.com/2014/02/21/world/americas/venezuela-fact-from-fiction/index .html.

62. Olivier Laurent, "Photo of Venezuela Unrest Wins World Press Photo Contest," *Washington Post*, April 12, 2018, https://www.washingtonpost.com/news/in-sight /wp/2018/04/12/world-press-photo-harrowing-photograph-of-a-man-on-fire-wins-top -photo-prize/.

63. "Here's Your Guide to Understanding Protest Deaths in Venezuela," teleSUR, August 8, 2017, https://www.telesurenglish.net/news/Heres-Your-Guide-to-Understand ing-Protest-Deaths-in-Venezuela-20170422-0016.html.

64. Vice President Mike Pence (@VP), Twitter, February 25, 2019.

65. Nicholas Casey, Christoph Koettl, and Deborah Acosta, "Footage Contradicts U.S. Claim That Nicolás Maduro Burned Aid Convoy," *New York Times*, March 11, 2019, https://www.nytimes.com/2019/03/10/world/americas/venezuela-aid-fire-video .html.

66. "Ediciones de Revistas CLAP," Ministerio del Poder Popular para la Comunicación e Información, last modified April 25, 2020, http://www.minci.gob.ve/ediciones -de-revistas-clap/.

67. Luisana Córdova, "En revolución: Productos de la caja CLAP son importados," *El Billuyo*, January 22, 2017, http://elbilluyo.com/esto-es-lo-que-hay/productos-la-caja -clap-importados.

68. TeleSUR English, "Supermarkets to Black Markets, Empire Files," YouTube, uploaded July 11, 2017, https://www.youtube.com/watch?v=YUYWrPiUeWY.

69. Betty Endara and Carol Guensburg, "Venezuela Full of Strife with Empty Refrigerators," Voice of America, May 5, 2017, https://www.voanews.com/americas /venezuela-full-strife-empty-refrigerators.

70. J. M. Lopez, "Scavenging to Survive in Venezuela," Al Jazeera, October 16, 2017, http://www.aljazeera.com/indepth/inpictures/2017/09/scavenging-survive-venezuela -170903073024026.html.

71. Jim Wyss, "In Venezuela, They Were Teachers and Doctors: To Buy Food, They Became Prostitutes," *Miami Herald*, September 22, 2017, http://www.miamiherald.com /news/nation-world/world/americas/venezuela/article174808061.html.

72. Frances Martel, "Venezuelans Eating Dogs, Zoo Animals as Economy Collapses," *Breitbart*, September 5, 2017, http://www.breitbart.com/national-security/2017 /09/05/venezuelans-eating-dogs-zoo-animals.

73. Eduard Freisler, "In Venezuela, Hungry Child Gangs Use Machetes to Fight for 'Quality' Garbage," *Miami Herald*, March 27, 2018, http://www.miamiherald.com/news /nation-world/world/americas/venezuela/article206950449.html.

74. Jonathan Krisel, "Pull-Out King," *Portlandia*, March 20, 2014, https://www.imdb .com/title/tt3585364/.

75. Philip Reeves, "Let Them Eat Rabbit Is Venezuelan President's Response to Food Shortages," NPR, September 14, 2017, http://www.npr.org/sections/parallels

/2017/09/14/551026492/let-them-eat-rabbit-is-venezuelan-presidents-response-to-food
-shortages.

76. Univision Noticias, "'Plan Conejo,' La Insólita Iniciativa Del Gobierno Maduro Para Combatir El Hambre En Venezuela," YouTube, uploaded September 14, 2017, https://www.youtube.com/watch?v=MFFVPZBl9dE.

77. George Ciccariello-Maher, "Which Way Out of the Venezuelan Crisis?" *Jacobin*, July 29, 2017, http://jacobinmag.com/2017/07/venezuela-elections-chavez-maduro
-bolivarianism.

78. Ibid.

79. Ibid.

80. For more on labor and the Venezuelan communes, see Dario Azzellini's work in which he traces efforts from below that work both in cooperation with and in conflict with the state. See *Communes and Workers' Control in Venezuela: Building 21st Century Socialism from Below* (Boston: Brill, 2016).

81. Joanne Rappaport, "Statement on the Situation in Venezuela," Latin American Studies Association, April 2017, https://lasa.international.pitt.edu/members/news
/venezuela_04032017.asp.

82. "An Open Letter to the LASA Executive Committee on the Situation in Venezuela," Venezuela Analysis, May 12, 2017, https://venezuelanalysis.com/analysis/13121.

83. Barry Cannon and John Brown, "Venezuela 2016: The Year of Living Dangerously Venezuela," *Revista de Ciencia Política* 37, no. 2 (2017): 628.

84. "Democracy 'Barely Alive' in Venezuela, U.N. Rights Chief Says," Reuters, August 30, 2017, https://www.reuters.com/article/us-venezuela-politics-un-zeid
/democracy-barely-alive-in-venezuela-u-n-rights-chief-says-idUSKCN1BA173.

85. "Venezuela: Pro-Maduro Assembly to Take Powers of Opposition-Led National Assembly," Freedom House, August 17, 2017, https://freedomhouse.org/article/vene
zuela-pro-maduro-assembly-take-powers-opposition-led-national-assembly.

86. "World Report, 2017: Venezuela," Human Rights Watch, January 12, 2017, https://www.hrw.org/world-report/2017/country-chapters/venezuela.

87. Human Rights Watch, "Venezuela: Medicine and Food Crisis Demands Action Now," YouTube, uploaded October 24, 2016, https://www.youtube.com/watch?v
=zZSQPGRiFGQ&feature=youtu.be.

88. Human Rights Watch, "Venezuela: Systematic Abuse of Opponents," YouTube, uploaded November 28, 2017, https://www.youtube.com/watch?v=GehozIx7rtM
&feature=youtu.be.

89. "Taking Human Rights Watch to Task on the Question of Venezuela's Purported Abuse of Human Rights: Over 100 U.S. and Foreign Scholars Take Issue with the Head of HRW's Latin American Division," Council on Hemispheric Affairs, December 18, 2008, http://www.coha.org/taking-human-rights-watch-to-task.

90. Jim Wyss, "U.S. Official Describes Venezuela's Maduro as Paranoid, Weak, Isolated," *Miami Herald*, May 14, 2019, https://www.miamiherald.com/news/nation-world
/world/americas/venezuela/article230392499.html.

91. Mayo Sapiens, "El Pajarito de Maduro," *We're Magazine*, February 11, 2019, http://weremag.com/2019/02/10/el-pajarito-de-maduro.

92. Nicholas Casey, "Venezuela Is in Crisis but Its President Might Be Stronger for It," *New York Times*, August 6, 2018, https://www.nytimes.com/2018/08/06/world
/americas/venezuela-maduro-crisis.html.

93. Nicholas Casey, "Hungry Venezuelans Flee in Boats to Escape Economic Collapse," *New York Times*, November 25, 2016, https://www.nytimes.com/2016/11/25
/world/americas/hungry-venezuelans-flee-in-boats-to-escape-economic-collapse.html.

94. Tomás Páez Bravo, *La voz de la diáspora venezolana* (Madrid: Los Libros de la Catarata, 2015), 232.

95. Ibid., 138.

96. "Latin America Extends Sympathy to Venezuelans, but Little Else," Bloomberg News, September 7, 2018, https://www.bloomberg.com/news/articles/2018-09-07/latin -america-extends-sympathy-to-venezuelans-but-little-else. For more updated figures, see the UNHCR website at https://www.unhcr.org/en-us/venezuela-emergency.html.

97. AmaruTv, "¿A QUÉ TE DEDICABAS EN VENEZUELA? GUARDIA NACIONAL BOLI-VARIANA; MUJERES VENEZOLANAS EN PERÚ," YouTube, uploaded July 7, 2017, https://www.youtube.com/watch?v=vCHZj9oLSYQ.

98. Felipe Jácome and Chloe Coleman, "When Money in Venezuela Stopped Functioning as Currency, This Photographer Turned It into Art," *Washington Post*, May 24, 2019, https://www.washingtonpost.com/photography/2019/05/24/when-money -venezuela-stopped-functioning-currency-this-photographer-turned-it-into-art.

99. Desorden Público, *Bailando sobre las ruinas* (Santander, Spain: Fak Records, 2016).

CONTRIBUTORS

Adriana Angel is a former Fulbright scholar and an associate professor at the School of Communication at Universidad de la Sabana, in Chía, Colombia. She focuses on the study of rhetoric, specifically in relation to Latin American social and political phenomena. Her publications include *Delinking Rhetorics of Neoliberalism: An Analysis of South American Presidents' Speeches* and *Terministic Screens of Corruption: A Cluster Analysis of Colombian Radio Conversations.*

Michael L. Butterworth is the Governor Ann W. Richards Chair for the Texas Program in Sports and Media, Professor of Communication Studies and Director of the Center for Sports Communication and Media in the Moody College of Communication at the University of Texas at Austin. His research explores the connections between rhetoric, democracy, and sport, with particular interests in national identity, militarism, and public memory. He is the author of *Baseball and Rhetorics of Purity: The National Pastime and American Identity During the War on Terror*, coauthor of *Communication and Sport: Surveying the Field*, editor of *Sport and Militarism: Contemporary Global Perspectives*, and coeditor of *Sport, Rhetoric, and Political Struggle*. His work has appeared in the *Journal of Communication*, the *Quarterly Journal of Speech*, and *Rhetoric and Public Affairs*, as well as other journals in communication and sport studies.

José M. Cortez is Assistant Professor in the Department of English at the University of Oregon. His research on critical theory, comparative rhetoric, and cultural studies appears in *Rhetoric Society Quarterly*, *Philosophy and Rhetoric*, and *Decolonizing Rhetoric and Composition Studies: New Latinx Keywords for Theory and Pedagogy*, and is forthcoming in *College Composition and Communication*.

Linsay M. Cramer is Assistant Professor in the Department of Communication, Media, and Culture at Coastal Carolina University. Her research is situated at the intersection of rhetoric and critical intercultural communication with a specific focus on whiteness, race, gender, and popular media. She also examines whiteness and pedagogy. Her recent work has been published in *Communication Studies*, *Communication & Sport*, *Howard Journal of Communications*, and *Communication Education* and has also been published in the edited volume *Critical Intercultural Communication Pedagogy*.

René Agustín De los Santos is an independent scholar. His publications on the rhetorical legacies of and about Latin America include *Expanding the Idea of América* (with

Christa J. Olson), *The Specter of Nuestra América: Barack Obama, Latin America, and the 2009 Summit of the Americas*, and *La Ola Latina: Recent Scholarship in Latina/o and Latin American Rhetorics*.

Pamela Flores is Associate Professor and Coordinator of the PhD Program in Communication at Universidad del Norte, Barranquilla, Colombia. In 2019, she published *Testimoniando el testimonio: Estrategias identitarias para resignificar la memoria común* (Witnessing the testimony: Identity strategies to resignify the common memory).

Nancy R. Gómez is a professor in gender and communication topics in the Department of Communication and Journalism at Universidad Del Norte in Barranquilla, Colombia. Among her research interests are the questioning of gender violence in media discourses, gender inequality in private and public spaces, women's resistance and identity, and embodied memories.

Alberto González is Distinguished University Professor in the School of Media and Communication at Bowling Green State University. He is a co-editor of *The Rhetorical Legacy of Wangari Maathai: Planting the Future* and *Our Voices: Essays in Culture, Ethnicity, and Communication*, 6th ed.

Amy N. Heuman is Associate Professor in the Department of Communication Studies at Texas Tech University. Dr. Heuman researches the centrality of communication in negotiations of identity and culture. She has examined cultural dynamics along the US-Mexico border and the racially essentialist border rhetoric of President Donald J. Trump and his administration. Her latest research regarding border dynamics can be found in the *Journal of International and Intercultural Communication* and the *Journal of Intercultural Communication Research*.

Christa Olson is a rhetorical historian focusing on trans-American visual cultures. She is the author of *Constitutive Visions: Indigeneity and Commonplaces of National Identity in Republican Ecuador* and has published articles on visual culture, historiography, and American rhetoric. Olson's current research examines the visual history of US–Latin American relations in order to understand how US publics came to see themselves as particularly American among Americans. She is a regular contributor to *Reading the Pictures*, an online venue dedicated to public-facing analysis of photojournalism.

Carlos Piovezani is Associate Professor of Linguistics and Discourse Analysis at the Federal University of São Carlos and the coordinator of the research group "Discourse Analysis and History of Linguistic Ideas." Among others, he is the author of *Verbo, corpo e voz: A fala pública e o discurso político* (Verb, body, and voice: Public speech and political discourse), *História da fala pública* (History of public speech) (with Jean-Jacques Courtine), and *A voz do povo: Uma longa história de discriminações* (The voice of the people: A long history of discrimination).

Clara Eugenia Rojas Blanco is Associate Professor in the Department of Social Science at the Universidad Autónoma de Ciudad Juárez, México. Her research examines the relationship between rhetoric, power, and gender with particular focus on local feminist rhetorical formations in Mexico. Her work appears in international journals and books such as *Comunicación Vivat, La Ventana, Revista de Estudios de Género, Noésis, Rhetoric in South America/African Yearbook of Rhetoric*, and *Making a Killing: Femicide, Free Trade, and La Frontera*.

Abraham Romney is Associate Professor of Rhetoric and Composition. He is the Director of Composition and Director of the Multiliteracies Center at Michigan Technological University. He studies histories and theories of rhetoric, comparative cultural rhetorics, digital rhetorics, and writing pedagogy. He is currently finishing a book on criollo and indigenous rhetorics in Latin America during the long nineteenth century.

María Alejandra Vitale is a professor and researcher at the Institute of Linguistics at Universidad de Buenos Aires. She has taught graduate seminars at several universities in Argentina, Brazil, and Spain and has been invited to give lectures at Universities in Mexico, Peru, Chile, Brazil, Portugal, Italy, the United States, Poland, and China. She is the director of the electronic journal *Rétor*, published by the Argentine Association of Rhetoric, of which she has been president. Currently she serves as General Secretary of the Argentine Society of Linguistic Studies. Vitale has directed and participated in international research projects with several universities worldwide.

INDEX

abortion laws, 145
Abreu, José, 101
absolutism, 62
See also immigration
academic tourism, 3
acclamatio, 189
accreditation, 113, 118, 123
See also corruption
accusation of third parties, 113, 116–17,
118–19, 123
"Acta de Independencia" (Bolivia, 1825), 33
activism. *See* social movements and
resistance; women's activism
Acts of the Apostles, 155
Adamczyk, Amy, 147
addressees, 184, 187, 189
See also oratorical performances
"Address to the Constituent Congress"
(Bolívar, 1826), 31, 32–33
Afghanistan, 12
Africentricity, 3
agency. *See* rhetorical agency
aggression, 18, 163, 166, 167, 168–69,
171, 176
See also popular speech
agonism, 125, 239n4
agonistic democracy, 195, 250n42
agons, 117
See also cluster analyses
agriculture, 65–66, 182, 188
Alcatraz, Occupation of, 37
Alfonsín, Raúl, 249n36
Alliance for Progress, 9
Alliance for Work, Justice and Education
(ALIANZA), 181, 248n8
Alo Presidente (Venezuela), 200
Alto Perú, 33
See also Bolivia
Altuve, Jose, 88
Álvarez, Eduardo, 158–59
Amaya, Hector, 77
America, use of term, 91, 220n5
American Airlines, 66–67

American Dream, 59, 88, 89, 99, 102,
231n3
American exceptionalism. *See*
exceptionalism, American
American hemisphere. *See* democratic
hemisphere
Amossy, Ruth, 183, 184
amplification, 187
See also oratorical performances
analogy, 186, 192, 249n27
anaphora, 187, 189, 191, 192
Andean Indigenous communities, 38
Angel, Adriana, 17–18, 107–24
anger, 146, 152–53, 155, 163
Añorve, Daniel, 100, 101–2
apagoresis, 150
See also classical sophistic rhetoric
apatê, 146, 148–49
aposiopesis, 149
appearances, 199
See also spectacular rhetorics
archaeology, 41, 43
Argentina
abortion laws in, 145
democracy and election system in, 194
farewell speeches in, 180
inauguration ceremonies in, 185–86
political context of, 181–83
political discourse analysis in, 183–85
political power of, 185
presidential terms in, 247n5
right-wing resurgence in, 11
See also Fernández de Kirchner, Cristina
argumentum ad verecundiam, 150–51
See also classical sophistic rhetoric
Aristotle, 157
Armisen, Fred, 210
Arrázola, Miguel, 149, 150, 156
art production, 138–39, 140, 141
Asen, Robert, 5–6, 76
Asiacentricity, 3
Athens, 26
The Atlantic, 6, 207

atopics, politics of, 40, 54–55, 56
audience vs. rhetor, roles of, 197, 198
  See also spectacular rhetorics
Audiovisual Communication Services Law
    (Argentina), 182, 183, 188, 249n31
augmented survival, 199
  See also capitalism
Austin, Kat, 51
authority, appeals to, 150–51
  See also classical sophistic rhetoric

Baca, Damián, 39–40, 50
Bachelet, Michelle, 11
Bada, Xóchitl, 75
Bailando sobre las ruinas (album), 214
Baldetti, Roxanna, 107, 109, 115, 117, 118–19,
    121
Ballard, Brian, 103
Baltimore Orioles, 99
  See also baseball diplomacy
Balzotti, Jonathan Mark, 197–98
baseball diplomacy
  exceptionalism and, 17, 99, 101–2
  exploitation and, 97
  limitations of, 103–4
  overview, 88–89, 90–91
  rhetorical promise of, 97–98, 101
  US-Cuban relations and, 89–90, 96–97,
    98–99, 100–104
Base Ecclesial Communities (CEBs), 126,
    132, 133–35, 138, 140, 141, 240n10
Bastille Day military parade, 70
Bates, Benjamin, 111
Bay of Pigs invasion, 92
beauty of the dead, 172
  See also popular speech
binationalism, 79–81, 84
  See also citizenship
Bjarkman, Peter, 97
black corruption, 110, 119, 123
  See also corruption
body, outer and inner zones of, 170–71, 174,
    175–76
  See also oratorical performances
Bolívar, Simón, 30–33, 200
Bolivarian Revolution, 11, 206, 211
  See also Venezuela
Bolivia, 6, 10, 31, 32–33, 199, 201
Bolsonaro, Jair, 6, 7
Bolton, John, 102
Border Protection, Antiterrorism, and
    Illegal Immigration Control Act (US,
    2005), 74, 75, 78, 82, 230n11

borders
  citizenship and, 2, 76, 82–83, 87
  cultural difference and, 46
  essentialism and, 58
  globalization and, 49
  hybridity and, 51
  identity and, 2, 59
  mestizaje and, 44
  rhetoric and, 1–2, 3
  US-Mexico, 2, 16, 58, 63–64, 65–66
Bosniak, Linda, 76
Bouden, Tom, 147–48
Bourdieu, Pierre, 131
Brazil, 6, 7, 11, 160, 164–65, 178, 210
  See also media, Brazilian
breeding, use of term, 62
  See also immigration
Britain, 28
Brizola, Leonel, 166, 246n19
Brouwer, Dan, 76
Brown, John, 211–12
Brown, Wendy, 10
Buenos Aires, 185
  See also Argentina
Buffon, Georges-Louis Leclerc, 28, 33
Bull, Hedley, 98
Burke, Kenneth, 25, 111, 113, 117, 122, 153
Bush, George W., 12, 92, 93, 200, 233n26
Butler, Judith, 145
Butterworth, Michael L., 17, 88–104
Buxton, Julia, 203–4

Calafell, Bernadette, 2
Calderón, Felipe, 230n15
Cambiemos (Argentina), 180, 183, 247n3
Campbell, Eric, 206–7
Campbell, Karlyn Kohrs, 130–31, 140, 184
La Cámpora (Argentina), 183
Canada, 7, 12, 65
Cañas, Eduardo, 155
Cannon, Barry, 211–12
capitalism, 2, 7, 197, 198–99, 209–10, 211,
    214
Capriles, Henrique, 201
Cardoso, Germán, 145
Carlés, Aboy, 182
Carmona, Pedro, 202
Carpizo, Jorge, 13
Carrión, Benjamín, 34, 35
Carta Abierta (Argentina), 182
Carta Capital (Brazil), 161, 174–75
"Carta de Jamaica" (Bolívar, 1815), 31,
    222n27

"Cartas al Ecuador" (Carrión, 1943), 34
CASA Promoción Juvenil AC (Mexico),
    136–37, 138, 240n10
Casa Rosada (Argentina), 185, 186
Casey, Nicholas (Nick), 206
Castro, Fidel, 9, 90, 92, 97
Castro, Julian, 66
Catholicism, 13, 136, 145, 150
Central America, 60, 63, 65, 69, 107, 117
    See also Latin America
Central Bank (Guatemala), 109
Central Bank (Venezuela), 200
centralism, 13
Centro de Asesoria y Promocion Juvenil AC
    (CASA), 136–37, 138, 240n10
Centro Democrático Movement
    (Colombia), 144, 151
Chapman, Aroldis, 103
Chávez, Karma, 4
Chavez Cano, Esther, 240n8
Chávez Frías, Hugo
    coup of 2002 and, 19, 199, 201–3
    criticism of, 200, 206–7
    impact of, 11
    Maduro and, 201
    on media, Venezuelan, 205
    oil prices and, 203
    presidency of, 200–201, 251n19
    socialism and populism of, 196
Chavismo, 200–205, 207, 213
Cheney, Dick, 94
Chicago hometown association (HTA), 73,
    74, 75, 79
    See also migrant civil societies
Childers, Jay, 93
child separations, 58, 61, 62–63, 66–67, 68
    See also immigration
Chile, 10, 11, 184–85
China, 98
Chomsky, Noam, 200
Choquhuanca, David, 38
Christianity, 133, 144, 150–51, 152–55
    See also liberation theology
Ciccariello-Maher, George, 211
Cicero, Marcus Tullius, 162–63, 177
"Cinderella," 186, 192
Cintrón, Ralph, 35
Cisneros, Josue David, 59, 76–77, 83
Citizens' Assembly for a Social Agenda
    (Mexico), 128–29, 136, 137–38, 139
    See also women's activism
citizenship
    borders and, 2, 76, 82–83, 87

democratic engagement and, 5–6, 8, 13
H. Clinton and, 57
land rights and, 27
migrant civil society and, 17, 72–74, 78,
    80–81, 84–86
rhetorical studies and, 5
rhetorics of, 76–77
sexuality and, 158
topoi and, 16, 51
white settler control of, 30
Citizenship Excess (Amaya), 77
Ciudad Juárez (Mexico), 18, 125, 128, 133,
    134–35, 241n16
    See also women's activism
civil deliberations, 127, 128–29, 132, 137–38
"Civil Society, Consumption, and
    Governmentality" (Yúdice), 48–49
civil society, usage of term, 129, 241n18
CLAP (Venezuela), 209
Clarín Group (Argentina), 182, 188
class
    and language, policing of, 172
    popular speech and, 160–65, 167–70,
        173–74, 176–79
    rhetorical agency and, 140–42
    transculturation and, 45
class consciousness, 133–34, 135, 141, 142
    See also women's activism
classical sophistic rhetoric
    apagoresis, 150
    apatê or illusion, 148–49
    aposiopesis, 149
    argumentum ad verecundiam, 150–51
    dynaton, 154–55, 157
    explanation of, 145
    kairos, 155–56
    No campaign and, 145–46
    pathos, 151–54, 156
    to prepon, 156
    reality construction and, 147
Claver-Carone, Mauricio, 212
Claves de una massacre (documentary), 203
clientelism, 9, 13, 110
climate policy, 64
Clinton, Bill, 93
Clinton, Hillary Rodham, 7, 57
Clinton administration, 65
Cloud, Dana, 63
cluster analyses, 108, 112–17
CNN, 208
Code, Lorraine, 129, 131, 132
Codex Espangliensis (Gómez-Peña), 40,
    50–55

Cold War, 90, 92, 233n26
Colectiva Comunidad, Arte y Equidad, 127,
    139, 141
collective imagination, 59
Collor, Fernando, 166, 168, 246n17
Colombia
    Bolívar on freedom of, 32
    Constitution of, 159
    corruption in, 111–12
    Iván Duque, election of, 7
    land rights in, 38
    neoliberalism in, 11
    protests and demonstrations in, 6
    Venezuelan refugees and, 213
    See also peace agreement, Colombia
colonialism
    baseball and, 89
    citizenship and, 77
    Codex Espangliensis and, 50–51, 54–55
    corruption and, 110
    decolonial imaginary and, 42, 44
    democracy in Americas and, 8, 9, 13, 24,
        31–32
    global South as metaphor for, 2
    hierarchy and, 245n1
    hybridity and, 51–52
    land and, 25–27, 28
    racial science and, 28–29
    rhetoric of resistance and, 39
Colpean, Michelle, 3
Comisión Internacional contra la
        Impunidad en Guatemala (CICIG),
        108–10, 112, 120, 121
commodities, 197, 198–99, 208, 209–10
commonplaces. See topoi
communes, 211, 254n80
Communication and Critical/Cultural
        Studies (Colpean), 3
communism, 92, 99, 148, 153
Community, Art, and Equality Collective
        (Mexico), 127, 139, 141
Comunidades Eclesiales de Base (CEBs),
        126, 132, 133–35, 138, 140, 141, 240n10
conquest. See colonialism
Consejo Ciudadano por una Agenda Social
        (Mexico), 128–29, 136, 137–38, 139
    See also women's activism
Constitutional Court (Colombia), 143
Constitution of Colombia, 159
Constitution of Venezuela, 200, 211
Constitution Square (Guatemala), 107, 109
consumption, 209, 210
    See also capitalism
conversationalization, 192–93

See also oratorical performances
Corchado, Verónica, 127–28, 132–34, 135,
        136–42, 240nn10–11, 240n14
Corina Machado, Maria, 206
corruption, 9, 14, 110, 111, 203, 207
corruption in Guatemala
    defense for and accusations of, 118–20
    discursive levels of, 121–22
    "La Línea" case, 108–9
    programs of action and, 112, 113–14,
        120–21, 123–24
    rhetorics of, overview, 17–18, 107–8,
        236n3
    vocabulary and terministic screens of,
        112–17, 122–23
Cortez, José, 16, 39–56
counter-addressees, 184, 187, 189
    See also oratorical performances
counterhegemony, 39, 40, 41–44, 49,
        50–51, 55, 126
coups
    in Argentina, 187, 189
    soft, in Guatemala, 114, 116–17, 120
    in Venezuela, 19, 199, 200, 201–3, 205
courtyard speeches, 180, 247n2
    See also Fernández de Kirchner,
        Cristina
Cramer, Linsay M., 16–17, 57–71
criminality, 60, 61
criollo, 26, 221n12
crisis narratives
    disruption of, 213–14
    images and, 208
    media and, 201–3, 206–7
    sensationalization and, 199
    spectacle and, 197, 198, 208–10, 212, 213
critical pedagogy, 136–37
Cruz, Ted, 61
Cuba, 7, 17, 89–91, 92, 95–97, 98–104
    See also baseball diplomacy
Cuban Baseball Federation, 102
Cuban Missile Crisis, 92
Cuban Revolution, 9
Cubas, Joe, 99
Cuesta, Irina, 158–59
customs fraud, 108, 109, 112, 121
    See also corruption in Guatemala

David, Jean-Michel, 163, 164
Davis, Matt, 206
de Blasio, Bill, 68
Debord, Guy, 197, 198–99, 201, 253n59
DeChaine, Robert, 2
Declaration of Quito, 37

The Decolonial Imaginary (Pérez), 41–44, 45–46, 224n22
decolonial option, 41, 56
decolonization
    citizenship and, 77
    and difference, discourse of, 54
    epistemology and, 2–3
    land and land rights and, 23, 25, 35–38
    mestiza rhetorics and, 39–40, 44–45
defection, 98–99, 101, 102
    See also baseball diplomacy
defense policy, 12, 218n56
Deferred Action for Childhood Arrivals (DACA), 62
degeneration, theory of, 28, 29
de la Cadena, Marisol, 25
Delgado, Fernando, 2
Delicath, John W., 204
de los Santos, René Agustín, 1, 17, 72–87
Deluca, Kevin Michael, 204
Demo, Anne, 63
democracy
    in Americas, history of, 8–14, 24
    citizen engagement and, 5–6, 13, 14
    citizenship and migration and, 17, 72–87
    in contemporary moment, 6–8
    corruption in Guatemala and, 17–18, 107–24
    diverse perspectives on, 16
    editorial approach to, 2–5, 14–16
    exceptionalism and baseball diplomacy and, 17, 88–104
    Fernández de Kirchner in Argentina and, 19, 180–95
    immigration and Trump and, 16–17, 57–71
    land and rhetorical construction of, 16, 23–38
    in Latin America, key features of, 14
    Latinamericanism and posthegemony and, 16, 39–56
    media in Brazil and, 18–19, 160–79
    neoliberalism and, 10–12
    religion and human rights in Colombia and, 18, 143–59
    and rhetoric, importance of, 5
    spectacular rhetorics in Venezuela and, 19, 196–214
    transnational approaches to study of, 3–5
    women's activism in Mexico and, 18, 125–42
"Democracy and Its Limitations" (Cintrón), 35
Democracy in America (de Tocqueville), 91

democratic engagement
    alternative models of, 5–6
    citizenship and, 76
    Cuban-US relations and, 90, 100, 103, 104
    grassroots women activists and, 126, 129, 132–33
    land and, 27–28
    in Latin America, 8, 14
    mestizaje and, 53
    migrant civil societies and, 72–73, 75, 77, 78, 79, 82, 83–87
    religious rhetoric and, 147, 157, 159
    rhetorical agency and, 130–31
    rhetoric and, 5, 8
    spectacular rhetorics and, 198
    US and, 13, 71
    See also social movements and resistance
democratic exceptionalism, 90, 93–95, 100, 103–4
    See also exceptionalism, American
democratic hemisphere
    colonialism and construction of, 28–29
    contradictions and political implications of, 34–35
    elitism and, 30–31
    history and rhetorical construction of, 26–27
    land rights and, 27–28, 35–38
    Latin American tensions in, 31–32
    overview, 23–25
    racial science and, 28–29
    as telluric and topographically determinant, 29–30, 32–34
    tropicalismo and, 34
Democrats (US), 13, 62
denarrativization, 55, 225n48
Department of Homeland Security (DHS), 61, 62–63, 69
dePauw, Cornelius, 28, 33
deportation, 60
    See also immigration
desafió (defiance), 79–80, 81
    See also social movements and resistance
Desorden Público (band), 214
de Sousa Santos, Boaventura, 2
de Tocqueville, Alexis, 33, 91
development models, 9
    See also socialism
diaspora. *See* immigration; migrant civil societies
dichotomies, 160, 169, 171, 173–74, 175
    See also media, Brazilian
dictatorships, 8, 9, 107, 182, 185, 249n36

difference, cultural, 41–44, 45–47, 49,
    53–54, 59, 60
    See also identity
Dingo, Rebecca, 3
Dionisopoulos, George, 99
diplomacy, 98, 103
    See also baseball diplomacy
Dirty War (Argentina), 182
discourse analysis, 183–84
disease metaphors, 60, 61–62
    See also immigration
disgust, 146, 152–53, 155
    See also *pathos*
divine law, 155
    See also religious rhetoric
"Doctrine" (Monroe, 1823), 27, 29–30, 96
Dodgers, Los Angeles, 89
Dominican Republic, 97
Driskill, Qwo-Li, 38
drug-trafficking, 109
Druschke, Caroline Gottschalk, 25
dual-citizenship, 72, 73–74
    See also citizenship
Due Obedience law (Argentina), 182,
    249n36
duplicity, 167, 169, 173, 176
    See also Lula da Silva, Luiz Inácio
Duque, Iván, 6, 7
dynamic spectacle, 197
    See also spectacular rhetorics
dynaton, 154–55, 157
    See also classical sophistic rhetoric

Ebola, 61
economic crises, 10, 196–97, 199, 201,
    206–12
Economist, 147
Ecuador, 34, 35
Edelman, Murray, 198
Eden, Scott, 89
Edwards, Jason, 91, 93, 95, 96
elections, 5, 6, 7, 71, 78–79, 194, 199
electoral colleges, 7, 32, 57
electoral democracies, 14
elitism
    democratic hemisphere and, 30–31
    in Latin America, 13
    popular speech and, 18–19, 162, 163–64,
        172, 174, 176–79
    racial science and, 28–29
    telluric democracy and, 27, 38
    in Venezuela, 196
eloquentia popularis, 162–63, 173, 177
    See also popular speech

El Salvador, 69
embezzlement, 109
emotions or *pathos*, 146, 151–52, 156,
    183–84, 189, 192, 193
Empire Files (series), 209
engagement. *See* democratic engagement
Enlightenment, 174
Enloe, Cynthia, 156
enthymemes, 184, 188
entrepreneurs, 119
epistemologies, 2–3
Época (Brazil), 161
Equal Marriage Law (Argentina), 183
Escobar, Veronica, 66
ESPN The Magazine, 89
essentialism, 58–59, 68–69
    See also Trump, Donald
O Estado de São Paulo (*Estadão*, Brazil), 161,
    169–70
"Estou Buscando Algo en el Caribe"
    (Desorden Público), 214
ethics vs. religion, 146, 159
    See also religious rhetoric
ethos, 183, 187–89, 190, 192, 193
Eurocentrism, 3, 39–40, 48
Europe
    American exceptionalism and, 91–92
    in colonial history of Americas, 28–29
    democracy in Americas and, 8–9, 13
    popular speech and, 164
    right-wing nationalism in, 6, 216n24
    telluric democracy and, 35
evidence, use of, 113, 118, 119–20, 123
exceptionalism, American
    baseball and, 90, 99, 101–2
    Cuban relations and, 92
    global critiques of, 93
    history of, 91–92, 96
    military intervention and, 12
    Obama administration and, 93–94, 100
    Trump and, 95–96, 103
    US diplomatic strategy and, 17, 99–100
    US influence and, 8, 13
The Exhaustion of Difference (Moreiras), 44

facial expressions, 170–71
    See also oratorical performances
Fairclough, Norman, 193
Fajardo, Sergio, 144
families, traditional, 145, 146, 147, 148, 150,
    152–54, 158
    See also religious rhetoric
farewell discourses, 180, 184, 193–94
    See also Fernández de Kirchner, Cristina

Farge, Arlette, 162
farmers' revolt (Argentina), 182
fascism, 6
fear, 146, 152–53, 155
Federación Agraria Argentina, 182
feelings and thoughts, 170–71
　See also *pathos*
feminicide
　definition, 239n1
　Juárez Agenda and, 129, 137–38
　rhetorical responses to, 125, 130
　social conditions and, 128
　and women's activism, development of,
　　18, 125–26, 128, 132, 142
feminist consciousness, 142
　See also women's activism
Fernández, Alberto, 194
Fernández, José, 89, 104
Fernández de Kirchner, Cristina
　bills of, controversial, 187–88
　courtyard speeches of, 180, 247n2
　democracy and, 19, 194–95
　farewell speech, overview and purpose,
　　180–81, 193–94
　farmers' revolt and, 182
　inaugural speeches of, 186, 249n25
　inauguration ceremonies and,
　　185–86
　informal register, use of, 192–93
　legislative races after presidency, 194
　political context, 181–83, 185
　rhetorical strategies of, 184, 186–87,
　　188–92, 193, 194, 249n27
　symbolic clothing of, 186
financial crises, 10, 196–97, 199, 201,
　206–12
Financial Times, 6
First Amendment (US), 68
flexible accumulation, 49, 54
　See also posthegemony
Flores, Lisa, 3, 15
Flores, Pamela, 18, 143–59
fluidity, 73–74, 81, 82–83, 84
　See also migrant civil societies
Folha de São Paulo (Brazil), 161, 166
Fontana, Benedetto, 5
Foreign Assistance Act (US, 1961), 92
foreign policy, 8, 12, 92, 218n56
forgiveness, 153–54, 155
Fortune, 57
Foucault, Michel, 41, 43, 55, 161
Fraser, Nancy, 241n18
fraud, 18, 108, 113–15, 116, 121–22
　See also corruption in Guatemala

freedom
　democracy and, 5, 9
　democratic hemisphere and, 26–27, 30,
　　32, 34
　Fernández de Kirchner on, 189, 190, 191
　gender ideology and, 145
　human rights in Venezuela and, 212
　land and, 31–32, 33, 36, 37
　mestizaje and, 44
　of religion, 159
　of speech, 164, 165
　US narratives of, 66, 94, 99
Freedom House, 212
free markets and trade, 10, 11–12, 253n59
Freire, Paulo, 136
French Revolution, 162
Frente País Solidario (FREPASO), 248n8
Frente Renovador, 185
Friedman, Milton, 10
Front for a Country in Solidarity
　(FREPASO), 248n8
Front for Victory Party (Argentina), 181,
　248n9
Frontier Airlines, 66–67
Fuerzas Armadas Revolucionarias de
　Colombia (FARC)
　government conflict with, 143–44
　peace agreement with, 6, 7, 18, 143, 149,
　　152
　religious rhetoric and, 145, 148
Full Stop law (Argentina), 182, 249n36

G7 Summit Communique, 64
G20 Summit, 69
gang territories, 134–35
gender consciousness, 128, 141–42
　See also women's activism
gendered spaces, rhetorical, 131–33, 141
gender ideology
　Colombian context of, 147–48
　Colombian peace agreement and, 18,
　　144, 145–46, 148–53, 156–57
　explanation of, 144–45
gender violence, 125, 126, 129, 137, 138
Genesis, 152
geopolitics, 27
gerrymandering, 71
gestures, 170–71
　See also oratorical performances
Gillibrand, Kirsten, 67
Giner, Oscar, 90, 93, 94, 100
Ginzburg, Carlo, 171
Global Campus of Human Rights, 141
globalization, 12, 14, 46, 48–49, 54, 55

Global South, 2, 3
Goldberg, Michelle, 68
Gómez, Nancy R., 18, 143–59
Gómez-Peña, Guillermo, 40, 50–52, 53–54
González, Alberto, 16–17, 57–71
Goodale, Mark, 10
Gorgias (sophist), 146
Gorsuch, Neil, 68, 71
Gramsci, Antonio, 48, 49
Gran Colombia, 31
Grandmothers of Plaza de Mayo, 191, 249n36
La Gran Marcha, 74
    See also immigration
grassroots movements. See women's activism
Greece, 24, 26, 84, 164
Greek philosophy, 174
Greenpeace, 204
Grossberg, Larry, 130
Grupo Feminista 8 de Marzo (Mexico), 240n8
Guaidó, Juan, 71, 205, 208
Guantanamo Bay, 92
The Guardian, 100
Guarnizo, Luis, 73, 81, 83, 86, 87
Guatemala, 17–18, 37
    See also corruption in Guatemala
Guatemalan Public Prosecutor's Office, 109
guerrilla groups, 9
    See also Fuerzas Armadas
        Revolutionarias de Colombia (FARC)
Gustafson, Bret, 38

Habermas, Jürgen, 241n18
Halloran, S. Michael, 197, 198
Hanson, Russell, 14
Hardt, Michael, 49
Harjo, Joy, 38
Hauser, Gerard, 14
Havana, 90, 99
    See also Cuba
Hawkins, Kirk A., 203
Hayden, Craig, 100
Hayes, Brittany, 147
hegemony
    Chávez and, 200
    decolonial imaginary and, 41
    globalization and, 48–49
    identity and reinstallation of, 40, 44–46, 47
    language and, 171, 177–79
    media and, 205
    mestizaje and, 53

rhetoric and, 225n25
    spectacle and, 198
Hegemony or Survival (Chomsky), 200
Heidlebaugh, Nola, 149, 156
hemispheres, 26–27
    See also democratic hemisphere
Henrique Cardoso, Fernando, 175, 246n34
Heuman, Amy N., 16–17, 57–71
Hidalgo, Juan Carlos, 207
Histoire Naturelle (Buffon), 28
history, 41, 43, 44, 46, 130
hometown associations (HTAs). See migrant civil societies
homonoia, 195
Howes, Franny, 51
"How Socialism Has Destroyed Venezuela" (Hidalgo), 207
Huerta, Dolores, 66
human rights
    art production and, 141
    Fernández de Kirchner and, 249n36
    gender ideology and, 144–45
    religious rhetoric and, 18
    US and, 70–71
    in Venezuela, 203, 211, 212
    women and, 126, 129, 138–39
Human Rights Watch, 200, 212
human trafficking, 102, 103
    See also baseball diplomacy
Hurd, Will, 66
Hurtado, Paola, 121
hybridity, 39, 50–51, 53–54, 87
hyperreality, 198
    See also spectacular rhetorics

Iberian ethos, 13
    See also colonialism
identity
    anti-immigration rhetoric and, 60–61
    borders and, 2, 59
    citizenship and, 73, 76–77, 83
    colonial encounters and, 55–56
    of cultural difference, 45–46
    decolonial imaginary and, 41–44
    exceptionalism and, 91–92
    globalization and, 54–55
    hegemony and, 40
    hybridity and, 50–51
    informal discourse and, 193
    mestizaje and, 44–45, 52–53
    posthegemony and, 47, 49–50
    rhetorical agency and, 15, 130–31
    of speakers, construction of, 183

ideographs, 58, 59–60, 63, 69
   See also topoi
ideology of gender. *See* gender ideology
ignoratio elenchi, 149
illusion, 146, 148–49
   See also classical sophistic rhetoric
images and image events, 198–99, 201,
   204, 208, 214
   See also spectacular rhetorics
immigration
   baseball diplomacy and, 88, 89
   binational awareness and, 78–80
   criminalization of, 61, 62, 68, 74,
      230n11
   disease metaphors for, 61–62, 95
   economic worth and, 60–61
   H. Clinton and, 57
   ideographs and, 59
   NAFTA and, 64–66
   Trump administration and, 7, 58–60,
      61–63, 66–69, 95
   US-Mexico wall and, 63–64
Immigration and Customs Enforcement
   (ICE), 62, 67–68
imperialism, 8, 196, 200
   See also colonialism
independence, 31–33, 34
Indigenous communities, 23, 31
Indigenous land rights, 27, 35–38
inflation, 11, 205, 207, 209, 212
informal language, 192–93, 194
   See also Fernández de Kirchner, Cristina
Instagram, 198
   See also spectacular rhetorics
Instituto Municipal de las Mujeres de
   Ciudad Juárez, 127
International Commission Against
   Corruption in Guatemala (CICIG),
   108–10, 112, 120, 121
International Committee of the Red Cross,
   159
International Monetary Fund, 10
interpretation, 113, 170–71, 204
interventionism, 18, 108, 113–14, 116–17,
   120, 123
Iran, 12
Iran Deal, 64
Iraq, 12, 200, 202
irony, 187, 188
Israel, 70
Ivie, Robert, 14, 90, 93, 94, 100

Jacobsen, Roberta, 68
Jácome, Felipe, 213

"The Jamaica Letter" (Bolívar, 1815), 31,
   222n27
Jamieson, Kathleen Hall, 184
Jarratt, Susan, 146
Jatar, Braulio, 206
Jefferson, Thomas, 23, 28, 143
Joint Comprehensive Plan of Action, 64
journalism. *See* media; media, Brazilian;
   media, Venezuelan
Juárez Agenda, 129, 137–38, 139, 241n16
   See also women's activism

kairos, 146, 155–56, 168
   See also classical sophistic rhetoric
Katz, Jesse, 89
Kennedy, George A., 146
Kennedy, John F., 9, 91
Khashoggi, Jamal, 71
Kiewe, Amos, 194
Kim Jong-un, 70
Kirchner, Máximo, 183
Kirchner, Néstor, 181–82, 185–86, 193,
   248n9, 249n25, 249n36
   See also Fernández de Kirchner, Cristina
Kirchnerism, 181–83, 185, 186
Kissinger, Henry, 10
knowledge production, 131, 132, 136–37, 142
Kock, Christian, 76, 82
Kramer, Dora, 170, 172
Kujawski, Gilberto de Mello, 169–72
Kushner, Jared, 68

labor, 99, 101, 103, 199
labor organizing, 65, 211
laicism, 158, 159
Lake Amatitlán (Guatemala), 109
land, 16, 23–25, 26–28, 32–34
   See also democratic hemisphere
land rights, 27, 33, 35–38
language
   class discrimination and, 162–65, 167–70
   elitism and, 177
   informal, as rhetorical strategy, 192–93,
      194
   oral vs. written models of, 160, 173–74
   oratorical practices and, 160–61
   perception and, 111, 113
   physical body and, 170–71, 175, 176
   and reality, construction of, 146–47, 149,
      154
   rhetorical agency and, 126, 130, 135, 137,
      140, 141
   spectacular rhetorics and, 198
   translation and, 241n31

Latin, 163–64
Latin America
    Chávez and, 200
    Codex Espangliensis and, 51–52, 53
    colonialism, legacy of, 13–14
    corruption in, 9, 107, 110
    crisis narratives and, 199
    democracy in, 6, 8–14, 17, 220n5
    globalization and, 48
    human rights in, 145
    Major League Baseball and, 97
    neoliberalism in, 10–11
    Obama administration and, 96
    posthegemony and, 49–50
    rhetorical scholarship in, 4
    spectacular rhetorics and, 210
    telluric democracy and, 27, 30–32, 34
    tropicalismo and, 24
    Trump administration and, 58, 69–71
    US military action and, 12, 96
    voting in, 247n7
    See also democratic hemisphere; specific
        countries
Latinamericanism
    decolonial imaginary and, 41–44, 56
    definition, 223n1
    first- vs. second-order, 40, 44, 47
    identities of difference, 44–46, 54–55
    mestizaje and, 39–40, 51–52
    posthegemony and, 46–50
Latin American Network of
    Communitarian Feminisms, 126
Latin American Studies Association
    (LASA), 211
Latina/o and Latinx, use of terms, 4
Latina/o identities, 2, 59, 60, 61, 71, 77
Lehrer, Brian, 68
Leviticus, 154
LGBT rights, 144–45, 146, 147–50, 152,
    156–57, 158
Liberal Party (Canada), 12
liberation theology, 133, 134, 135, 136, 141
"La Línea," 108–9, 112, 115, 116, 119, 121
    See also corruption in Guatemala
Lipset, Seymour, 91
literacy, 160, 162, 173–74
    See also popular speech
Locke, John, 13, 14
logos, 146–47, 156
Lopez, Leopoldo, 204–5
Los Angeles Dodgers, 89
"Los que se Quedan" (Desorden Público),
    214

Lula da Silva, Luiz Inácio
    cancer diagnosis, 172–73
    elections, 165
    life and career of, 161
    media discrimination after presidency,
        173–74
    media discrimination during candidacy,
        166–69
    media discrimination during presidency,
        169–72
    media discrimination of, overview, 18–19,
        161–62, 165, 176–77, 178
    progressive media on, 174–76
    timeline, 245n3
Lynch, John, 113

Macri, Mauricio
    criminal prosecution of, 189, 249n33
    Fernández de Kirchner on, 19, 180–81,
        185, 188–92
    inauguration ceremonies and, 185–86,
        187
    informal register, use of, 193
    political context, 180, 183, 247n3
    senate and, 194
    Trump and, 69
Maduro, Nicolás
    baseball diplomacy and, 102
    democracy and, 11
    international criticism of, 199, 211–13
    on media and social media, 205
    media representation of, 19, 199–200,
        207, 210–11
    opposition to, 203–5, 208
    political context, 200
    popularity of, 196
    populism and, 203
    presidency of, 201, 209
Maingueneau, Dominique, 183
Major League Baseball (MLB), 88, 89–90,
    96–97, 98–99, 101–2, 103
Manfred, Rob, 101
maquiladora industry, 128, 133–34
Marrufo, Imelda, 138
Martí, José, 33–34
Martin, Abby, 209
Marx, Karl, 130
Marxism, 133, 200
Massa, Sergio, 185
Mattis, Jim, 218n56
Mazzoldi, Génica, 158–59
McConnell, Mitch, 71
McDorman, Todd, 5

McGee, Michael Calvin, 59
media
    on corruption, 111, 112, 117, 121
    in Guatemala, 237n20
    image events and, 204
    reality and falsification by, 201–3
    spectacle and crisis and, 198–99, 207,
        213, 214
    Trump administration and, 68, 69,
        70, 71
    on Venezuela, international, 205–7,
        208–9, 209–10, 211, 212–13
media, Brazilian
    elitism and impact of, 18–19
    Lula, criticism of, 161–62
    Lula, discrimination of, 165, 166–75,
        176–77
    oratorical practices and, 160–61, 170–71
    progressive, on Lula, 174–76
media, Venezuelan
    on coup in 2002, 201–3, 205
    crisis narratives in, 199, 207
    on economic decline, 196–97
    government control of, 205–6, 208
    on poverty, 198
    spectacular rhetorics and, 197, 199–200,
        209–10
Media Law (Argentina), 182, 183, 188,
    249n31
Medina, Cruz, 51
Menchú, Rigoberta, 36–37
Mendieta, Eduardo, 53–54
Mendoza, Breny, 4
Menem, Carlos, 181, 182, 248nn8–9
mestizaje
    Codex Espangliensis and, 50–53, 55
    counterhegemony and, 39–40, 44, 47–48
    democracy and, 53, 55–56
    hybridity vs., 224n18
Mexican hometown associations. See
    migrant civil societies
Mexico
    democracy in, 7
    identity and borders of, 2
    Mexican HTAs and, 85, 86–87
    NAFTA and, 12, 65
    racism in, 242n36
    telluric democracy and, 36
    Trump administration and, 68
    US border wall and, 64, 66
    voting and citizenship rights, 72, 75
    See also Ciudad Juárez
Mexico City, 138

Michetti, Gabriela, 186, 193
Mignolo, Walter, 2
migrant civil societies
    binational awareness and action of,
        79–80, 81–82, 85–87
    citizenship and, 17, 72–74, 76–77, 80–81,
        82–83, 84–86
    democracy and rhetorics of, 77–79,
        83–84, 86–87
    history and context of, 74–75, 230n12
    immigration rights and, 75, 78–79
    institutions and, 85
    overview, 72–73
military, 12, 92, 93, 94, 96, 218n56
mimicry, 42
Miraflores (Venezuela), 202, 203
Mi Vida en Juárez, 139
modernity and modernization, 9, 39
monarchies, 32, 33
Monárrez, Julia, 239n1
Monroe, James, 27, 29–30, 33, 35, 96
Montesquieu, Baron de, 33
Montiel, Carlos-Urani, 51
Morales, Evo, 6
Morales, Jimmy, 109–10
Moreiras, Alberto, 40, 44, 46–47, 55, 223n1,
    225n48
Morresi, Sergio, 183
Mothers of Plaza de Mayo, 191, 249n36
Mouffe, Chantal, 195
Movimiento Amplio de Mujeres de Ciudad
    Juárez, 126, 127
Movimiento Pacto por la Cultura, 138–39,
    141
MS-13 (gang), 69
multiscalarity. See migrant civil societies
murder of women and girls. See feminicide
Murray, Stuart, 98, 103

Naím, Moisés, 207
Natanson, José, 185
National Action Party (Mexico), 230n15
National Assembly (Venezuela), 196, 202,
    205, 209, 211
National Congress (Argentina), 185–86, 188
National Council for Reconciliation and
    Coexistence (Colombia), 157
National Guard (Venezuela), 205
National Institute of Sport, Physical
    Education, and Recreation (INDER), 97
nationalism, 6, 7, 10, 95
National Reorganization Process (PRN,
    Argentina), 182

national security, 59, 60, 63
National Woman's Party, 77
nation-states
    borders and, 2
    citizenship and, 77, 83, 84–85, 86
    democratic breakdown and, 16
    globalization and, 48–49
    identity and, 44–45, 46
nativism, 60, 62
neoliberalism, 10–12, 48, 95–96, 110,
        198–99
neo-Marxism, 198
neo-sophism, 146
New York Times, 7, 206, 209
Nielsen, Kirstjen, 62, 67, 68
Nietzsche, Friedrich, 164
9/11 attacks (2001), 233n26
Nobel Peace Prize, 93–94
No campaign (Colombia)
    apatê or illusion and, 148–49
    classical and religious rhetoric of, 18,
        144, 145–46, 148–51, 154–55, 158
    kairos and, 155–56
    pathos and, 151–54
    political power of, 156–57, 158–59
    to prepon and, 156
Nomai, Afsheen, 99
nomoi, 146
North America
    elitism in, 30
    Latin American democracy and, 9
    neoliberalism in, 11
    rhetoric and, 1, 3
    right-wing nationalism in, 6
    Trump administration and, 69
    US influence on, 13
    See also Latin America; Mexico
North American Free Trade Agreement
    (NAFTA), 12, 17, 50, 57, 58, 64–66, 70
North Korea, 71
Notes on the State of Virginia (Jefferson), 28
Nye, Joseph, 100

Obama, Barack
    Cuban relations, 17, 90, 100–101, 102,
        103–4
    democracy and, 12
    democratic exceptionalism of, 93–95, 96
    justice nominations, 68
    Operation United Assistance, 61
Obediencia Debida law (Argentina), 182,
        249n36
Ober, Josiah, 5
oblation and offerings, 154–55

Obrador, Andrés Manuel López, 7, 75, 230n15
Ocasio-Cortez, Alexandria, 67
Occupation of Alcatraz, 37
oceans, 26–27, 29
    See also democratic hemisphere
oil industry, 196, 200, 201, 202, 203, 206–7
Olbrechts-Tyteca, Lucie, 249n27
Old World. *See* Europe
Olson, Christa J., 1, 16, 23–38, 96
Olympic Games, 6, 97, 234n46
    See also baseball diplomacy
Open Letter (Argentina), 182
Operation United Assistance, 61
oratorical performances
    in Brazil, 160
    class and delegitimization of, 160–62,
        165–67
    eloquentia popularis and, 162–64
    ethos and, 183–92
    informal speech in, 192–93
    outer and inner zones of body and,
        170–71, 174, 175–76
    written word vs., 160, 173–74
The Order of Things (Foucault), 41
Ordoñez, Alejandro, 149, 157
organic intellectuals, 127
Organización Nacional de Aborígenes
        Independientes (Paraguay), 37
Organización Nacional Indígena de
        Colombia, 38
Organization of American States, 67
O'Rourke, Beto, 66
otherness, cultural, 41–44, 45–47, 49,
        53–54, 59, 60
Our Brand Is Crisis (documentary), 199

Pact for Culture Movement (Mexico),
        138–39, 141
Padilla, Alex, 66
Paez, Tomás, 213
para-addressees, 184
    See also oratorical performances
Paraguay, 11, 37
Paris Agreement (Climate Accord), 64
Parody, Gina, 147–48
participation, democratic. *See* democratic
        engagement
Partido Acción Nacional (PAN, Mexico),
        230n15, 241n16
Partido Revolucionario Institucional (PRI,
        Mexico), 241n16
pathos, 146, 151–52, 156, 183–84, 189, 192,
        193
patrimonialism, 9, 110

Paz, Octavio, 5, 9
peace agreement, Colombia
  gender ideology and, 18, 144–46, 147–51,
    152, 156–57
  overview, 143–44
  religious rhetoric and, 144, 146, 148–49,
    158–59
  women's rights in, 157
Pease, Donald, 34, 92, 233n26
pedagogy, critical, 136–37
Pena, Brayan, 101
Pence, Mike, 208–9
Perelman, Chaïm, 249n27
Pérez, Emma, 41–42, 43, 44, 46, 47
Perez, Louis, 89
Pérez, Otto, 107, 109, 112, 115, 116–17,
    118–20, 121
Peronism, 185, 194
  See also Argentina
persuasive strategies, 135, 137, 140, 141
  See also rhetorical agency
Peru, 213
Petróles de Venezuela (PDVSA), 200
petroleum industry, 196, 200, 201, 202,
    203, 206–7
phoros, 249n27
Pineda, Richard, 60
Piñera, Sebastián, 11
ping-pong diplomacy, 98
  See also baseball diplomacy
Pinochet, Augusto, 10
pinole, 129, 241n21
Piovezani, Carlos, 18–19, 160–79
"Plan de Ayala" (Zapata, 1911), 36
Plantin, Christian, 183, 189
Plaza de la Constitución (Guatemala), 107,
    109
Plaza de Mayo (Argentina), 191, 249n36
plebiscites. See peace agreement, Colombia
Pluhar, Erika, 147
pluralism, 195
"Poem of Many in One" (Whitman), 30
Poland, 145
popular speech
  contemporary place for, 178
  discrimination of, 160–62, 165, 167–74,
    176–77, 178–79
  elitism and, 18–19
  history of, 162–65, 177
  progressive media on, 174–76
populism
  in Argentina, 182
  in Brazil, 164
  global resurgence of, 6

  in Latin America, 9, 14
  Lula and, 170, 172
  Trump and, 95
  in Venezuela, 196, 200, 203, 206–7
Portlandia, 210
Portugal, 8, 9, 13
positionality, 4–5, 79, 119, 239n2
positivism, 9
Post-Chavez Venezuela Has Become a Failed
    State (documentary), 206–7
postcoloniality, 42, 44
Postero, Nancy, 10
posthegemony, 40, 46–50
Potter, Jonathan, 118, 120
Poulakos, John, 155, 156, 157, 158
poverty
  in Ciudad Juárez, 128, 129, 134
  class consciousness and, 135
  Kirchner and reduction of, 182
  in Latin America, 14
  liberation theology and, 133
  media representation of, 198
  popular speech and, 18
  in Venezuela, 196, 200, 206, 207
power, 129, 130, 131, 141–42
to prepon, 156
presidential discourse ##, 194
private property, 9, 110, 154
private sphere, 83, 193
privatization, 10, 11
privilege, 131
pro-addressees, 184
  See also oratorical performances
Proceso de Reorganización Nacional (PRN,
    Argentina), 182
Procter, David E., 197
Program for Mexican Communities
    Abroad, 82
programs of action, 111–12, 113–14
propriety, 156
protests. See social movements and
    resistance
public, rhetorical understandings of, 72,
    85–86
Public Disorder (band), 214
public sphere
  citizenship and, 76
  in Colombia, 18
  informal speech and, 193
  nation-state impact on, 83
  popular speech and, 164, 165, 172, 174
  religion and, 146–47, 158–59
  transculturation and, 44–45
  use of term, 241n18

Puerto Rico, 7
Puig, Yasiel, 88, 89, 104
Punto Final law (Argentina), 182, 249n36
The Puppet and the Dwarf (Žižek), 54
Putin, Vladimir, 94

Quijano, Anibal, 2
Quito Declaration, 37

race and racism, 2, 3, 242n36
racial logics, 58
racial purity, 44–45
racial science, 27, 28–29
Radio Caracas Television (RCTV,
    Venezuela), 205
Radiografía de una mentira (documentary),
    203
Radio Sonora (Guatemala), 113, 119
Raidió Teilifís Éireann (RTE, Ireland),
    202–3
Ramírez, Cristina, 39–40
Ramírez, Sandra, 127–28, 132–33, 134–36,
    137, 138–42, 240nn10–11, 240n14
Rancière, Jacques, 53, 225n25
Raynal, Guillaume Thomas-Francois, 28, 33
Reagan, Ronald, 91, 194
reality, construction of, 146–47, 149, 198,
    201–3, 204, 214
Reconstruction, 27
Red de Feminismos Comunitarios de
    Latinoamerica, 126
Red de Mesa de Mujeres de Ciudad Juárez,
    138, 139
refugees, 34, 58, 65, 213–14
    See also immigration
religious rhetoric
    apatê or illusion and, 148–49
    classical sophistic strategies of, 149–51
    and democracy, compatibility of, 146–47,
        158–59
    dynaton and, 154–55, 157–58
    gender ideology and, 18, 144–46
    kairos and, 155–56
    pathos and, 151–54
    political campaigns, impact on, 144
    to prepon and, 156
    sexual practices and rights, 147
repetition, 184, 187, 189, 191, 192
representation. *See* media
Republicans (US), 13, 71, 90
resistance. *See* social movements and
    resistance
Resolution 125 (Argentina), 188

Revista Semana, 151, 159
revolution. *See* social movements and
    resistance
Revolutionary Armed Forces of Colombia
    (FARC). *See* Fuerzas Armadas
    Revolucionarias de Colombia
The Revolution Will Not Be Televised
    (documentary), 202–3
rhetoric
    citizenship and migration and, 17, 72–87
    corruption in Guatemala and, 17–18,
        107–24
    definitions of, 111, 146
    and democracy, shaping of, 5
    and democracy in Americas, history of,
        8–14
    democratic potential of, 7–8
    editorial approach to, 2–5, 14–16
    exceptionalism and baseball diplomacy
        and, 17, 88–104
    Fernández de Kirchner in Argentina and,
        19, 180–95
    immigration and Trump and, 16–17,
        57–71
    land and democracy and, 16, 23–38
    Latinamericanism and posthegemony
        and, 16, 39–56
    media in Brazil and, 18–19, 160–79
    of Obama administration, 93–94
    religion and human rights in Colombia
        and, 18, 143–59
    spectacular rhetorics in Venezuela and,
        19, 196–214
    women's activism in Mexico and, 18,
        125–42
rhetorical agency
    community-based knowledge and,
        138–40, 141
    constraints to and resignification of,
        140–41
    construction of, 129, 132, 134, 140–41,
        240n14
    definitions and theory of, 130–31, 142
    gender consciousness and, 141–42
    overview, 127–28
    power and authority and, 131
    self-recognition and, 135, 136–37
    spectacle and, 198
rhetorical cluster analysis, 108, 112–17
rhetorical gendered spaces, 131–33, 141
rhetorical studies, 1–2, 3, 4–5, 27, 38
Rhetoric in South America (Vitale), 1
Rhetoric Society Quarterly, 1

rhetorics of democracy. *See* democracy; rhetoric
rhetor vs. audience, roles of, 197, 198
   See also spectacular rhetorics
Rhodes, Benjamin, 102
Ribero, Ana, 77
Ríos, Gabriela, 37
Ríos de Vida (Colombia), 149
Rojas Blanco, Clara Eugenia, 18, 125–42, 239n2
Romans, 162, 163–64, 177
Romney, Abraham, 19, 196–214
Roosevelt Corollary, 96
Rosenwein, Barbara, 151
Rousseau, Jean-Jacques, 14
RT (Russian network), 209
Rúa, Fernando de la, 181
Russia, 71
Ryan, Fred, 71

Salazar, Philippe-Joseph, 1
Salazar, Ruben, 150
salt, 154
Samuel, Juan, 88, 89
sanctuary cities, 62
Santos, Juan Manuel, 143, 147, 151, 156
Sarukhan, Arturo, 7
Saudi Arabia, 71
Schemidt, Ronaldo, 208
Scruton, Roger, 154
Secondat, Charles-Louis de (Baron de Montesquieu), 33
semiotics, 183
Sensenbrenner Bill (2005), 74, 75, 78, 82, 230n11
September 11th attacks (2001), 233n26
Servini de Cubría, Maria, 186
Sessions, Jeff, 62
settlers
   American distinction and, 28–29
   citizenship and, 86
   Indigenous land rights and, 35, 36, 37, 38
   land control and, 27, 30
   Western hemisphere and, 26
sexuality, 147, 149–50, 158
   See also gender ideology
shame, politics of, 111
Simpson, Leanne Betasamosake, 35–36
Sites, William, 73, 78
slavery, 33
   See also colonialism
socialism, 9, 11, 196, 203, 207, 211
social media, 198, 204, 205–6, 208

social movements and resistance
   baseball and, 99
   in Colombia, 6
   to corruption in Guatemala, 107–9, 111–12, 113, 120–21, 123–24
   democratic ideals and, 17
   to feminicide, 125–26, 137, 142
   globalization and, 48
   government limitations to, 68
   hybridity and, 51
   image events and, 204–5
   land and, 23–24, 25
   mestiza rhetorics and, 39–40, 44–45
   neoliberalism and, 10–11
   rhetoric, 15
   social media and, 206, 208
   spectacular rhetorics and, 19, 197, 209
   telluric democracy and, 26, 27, 35–37
   to Trump administration, 58, 66–68
   in Venezuela, 11, 196, 201–2, 203, 212
   See also democratic engagement; No campaign (Colombia)
social security, 183
Social Security Institute (Guatemala), 109
Sociedad Rural Argentina, 182
Society of the Spectacle (Debord), 198
soft power, 100, 103
   See also exceptionalism, American
"Song of Myself" (Whitman), 30
Sonora radio station (Guatemala), 113, 119
Sons and Daughters for Identity and Justice Against Forgetfulness and Silence (HIJOS, Argentina), 191, 249n36
sophism, 146–47, 149
   See also classical sophistic rhetoric
Southard, Belinda Stillion, 77
South of the Border (Stone), 202
Southwest Airlines, 66–67
Soviet Union, 92, 98
Sowards, Stacey, 60
Spafford, Horatio G., 143
Spain, 8, 9, 13, 28
Spanish-American War, 89, 96
Spanish language, 13, 241n31
speaking subjects, 127, 130–31, 134, 138, 140–41, 178–79
spectacle images, 197, 198–99, 213, 214
spectacle logic, 197, 207, 209, 213–14
spectacular rhetorics
   and audience, importance of, 197, 198
   capitalism and, 198–99
   crisis and, 19, 197, 208–10, 214
   disruption of, 213–14

spectacular rhetorics (*continued*)
  explanation and aspects of, 197
  global influence on, 207, 253n59
  image events and, 204
  interpretations of, 197–98
  media role in, 198, 210, 212–13
  reality, representation of, 201–2
The Spirit of Laws (Montesquieu), 33
Spivak, Gayatri, 127
sports diplomacy, 97–98, 103
  See also baseball diplomacy
Sports Illustrated, 100
Standing Rock, 37
State Department (US), 63
states of exception, 40
Steinle, Kate, 61
stereotypes, 69, 88–89, 183, 210
  See also ideographs
St. Louis Post-Dispatch, 101
Stolk, Raúl, 207
Stone, Oliver, 202
subalternity, 42, 43, 47, 56, 127, 204
subjectivity. *See* identity
suffrage. *See* voting
sujetas hablantes, 127, 130–31, 134, 138,
  140–41, 178–79
superiority, cultural, 59–60, 91, 95, 96
Supreme Court of Argentina, 182
Svampa, Marisella, 182
symbolic action, 126, 127, 130, 135, 141
Syria, 12, 94
system, use of term, 114–15, 120–21

Tampa Bay Rays, 100
  See also baseball diplomacy
tariffs, 10, 65
taxes, 10, 28, 115, 182, 188
tear gas, 208
TeleSUR (Venezuela), 208, 209
television, 204
the telluric
  decolonial resistance and, 35–37
  definition, 24
  democracy and, 25
  democratic hemisphere and, 26–27,
    29–30, 32–35
  land rights and, 37–38
terministic screens, 108, 112–13, 122–24
Terrill, Robert, 94
territory, 16, 23–25, 26–28, 32–34
  See also democratic hemisphere
third parties, accusation of, 113, 116–17, 118,
  123
  See also corruption in Guatemala

thoughts and feelings, 170–71
  See also oratorical performances
Timmerman, David, 5
Toledo Blade, 61
topography, 16, 23–25, 26, 29–35, 38
  See also democratic hemisphere
topoi
  and atopics, politics of, 55
  democracy and limitations of, 16, 23,
    25, 27
  globalization and, 48
  identity and, 50–51, 54, 56
  land rights and, 35–36, 37, 38
  Latinamericanism and, 39, 40
  mestizaje and, 52
  of spectacle, 197
  See also ideographs
Toro, Francisco, 202, 207
Torre, Joe, 101
Torres, Daniel, 151
Torres, Merlyn, 115
trade agreements, 64–65
  See also North American Free Trade
    Agreement
trafficking, human, 102, 103
  See also baseball diplomacy
transculturation, 44–45
translation, 241n31
transnationalism, 48, 82
Trans-Pacific Partnership Agreement, 64
travel bans, 71
  See also immigration
Tres por Uno program, 82
Trial of the Juntas (Argentina), 249n36
tropicalismo, 24, 34
Trudeau, Justin, 12, 64
Trump, Donald
  American exceptionalism and, 95
  anti-immigration and essentialism of,
    16–17, 58–63, 68–69, 95
  democracy and, 7, 57
  Latin America-US relations, 69–71
  NAFTA and, 12, 64–66
  public response to, 66–68
  US-Cuban relations and, 90–91, 102–4
  US-Mexico wall and, 63–64
truth, nature of, 146, 158, 159
Turner, Frederick Jackson, 33–34
Turner, Justin, 98, 99

United Airlines, 66–67
United Nations, 70, 93, 200, 212
United States
  citizenship and democracy in, 17

Cuba, relations with, 89–90, 92, 95, 96–97, 98–104
democracy in, 7, 8–9, 13
exceptionalism in, 17, 91–94
farewell discourse in, 184, 194
foreign policy and military of, 8, 12, 218n56
Guatemala and, 114, 116–17, 120
identity and borders of, 2
Latin America, impact on, 8, 9, 10, 16–17, 220n5
media of, on Venezuela, 197
migrant civil societies in, 73–74, 85
neoliberalism in, 11–12
North America, impact on, 13
spectacular rhetorics and, 210, 253n59
superiority, rhetorics of, 59–60
telluric democracy and, 27, 29–30, 33–34, 35
Venezuela, relations with, 200–201, 202, 203, 205, 212
See also Obama, Barack; Trump, Donald
United States-Mexico-Canada Agreement (USMCA), 12, 70
Universal Child Allowance (Argentina), 183, 248n15
universities, 48
urbanitas, 163, 177
See also popular speech
USA Today, 100
US-Mexico border, 2, 58, 59, 63–64, 65–66

Vargas, José, 110
Vega, Karrieann Soto, 4
Veja (Brazil), 161, 166, 168
Velázquez, Iván, 121
Venezuela
baseball diplomacy and, 102
commodification of, 199
coup in 2002, 201–3
economic crisis in, 11, 19, 196–97, 206–12
exodus from, 213–14
media control in, 205–6, 208
political context of, 200–205
See also spectacular rhetorics
Verón, Eliseo, 184
Victims of Immigration Crime Engagement (VOICE, US), 61
Videgaray, Luis, 64
Vietnam War, 93
Villadsen, Lisa, 76, 82
Vitale, Alejandra, 19, 180–95

Vitale, María Alejandra, 1
Vivanco, José Miguel, 212
Viveiros de Castro, Eduardo, 25
Voice of America (US), 209–10
Vommaro, Gabriel, 183
Vonderlack-Navarro, Rebecca, 73, 78
voting
in Argentina, 181, 247n7
in Colombia, 144
democracy and importance of, 5
in Latin America, 14
in Mexico, 36, 72, 75, 78
in US, 13, 71
women and, 77

Walker, Ignacio, 13
the wall (US-Mexico), 58, 59, 63–64, 65–66
Wall Street, 6
Wanzer-Serrano, Darrel, 2, 3
war culture, 94
war on terror, 12, 93, 218n57, 233n26
Washington Consensus, 10
Washington Post, 6, 7, 88, 101, 208
Watts, Vanessa, 23
Weaver, Richard, 120
Weiss, David, 91
We're Magazine (Venezuela), 213
Wertheim, Stephen, 95
West, concept of, 43–44, 45, 46
white corruption, 110, 119, 123–24
See also corruption in Guatemala
white nationalism, 95
Whitman, Walt, 30
Will, George F., 57–58
Williams, Gareth, 44–45, 48
Winthrop, John, 91
Wolf, Z. Byron, 62
Wolford, Lisa, 50
women's activism (Ciudad Juárez)
civil deliberations and, 128–29, 137–38
class consciousness and, 133–34, 135, 141, 142
community-based knowledge and, 137, 138–40, 141
feminicide and development of, 125–26, 128
gender consciousness and, 141–42
rhetorical agency and, 126–28, 129, 132, 138–39, 140–41
Women's Collective Movement of Ciudad Juárez, 126, 127, 139
Women's Municipal Institute of Ciudad Juárez, 127

women's rights, 77, 144–45, 157
Women's Table Network of Ciudad Juárez,
   139
Workers' Party, 171
World Bank, 10, 93
World Press Photo contest, 208
World's Colombian Exhibition (1983),
   197–98
Worstall, Tom, 207
writing vs. orality, 160, 173–74, 183

xenophobia, 95
   See also immigration

Yanoshevsky, Galia, 204

Yes campaign (Colombia), 148, 151, 155
   See also No campaign
Young Lords of New York, 2
Youth Promotion and Advertising Center
   (Mexico), 136–37, 138, 240n10
Yúdice, George, 48–49

Zaffaroni, Eugenio, 185
Zapata, Emiliano, 36
Zapatista movement, 6
Zarate, Garcia, 61
Zarefsky, David, 92
zero tolerance policy (US), 62–63, 66, 68
   See also immigration
Žižek, Slavoj, 54, 55

RHETORIC AND **DEMOCRATIC** DELIBERATION

Other books in the series:

Karen Tracy, *Challenges of Ordinary Democracy: A Case Study in Deliberation and Dissent* / Volume 1

Samuel McCormick, *Letters to Power: Public Advocacy Without Public Intellectuals* / Volume 2

Christian Kock and Lisa S. Villadsen, eds., *Rhetorical Citizenship and Public Deliberation* / Volume 3

Jay P. Childers, *The Evolving Citizen: American Youth and the Changing Norms of Democratic Engagement* / Volume 4

Dave Tell, *Confessional Crises and Cultural Politics in Twentieth-Century America* / Volume 5

David Boromisza-Habashi, *Speaking Hatefully: Culture, Communication, and Political Action in Hungary* / Volume 6

Arabella Lyon, *Deliberative Acts: Democracy, Rhetoric, and Rights* / Volume 7

Lyn Carson, John Gastil, Janette Hartz-Karp, and Ron Lubensky, eds., *The Australian Citizens' Parliament and the Future of Deliberative Democracy* / Volume 8

Christa J. Olson, *Constitutive Visions: Indigeneity and Commonplaces of National Identity in Republican Ecuador* / Volume 9

Damien Smith Pfister, *Networked Media, Networked Rhetorics: Attention and Deliberation in the Early Blogosphere* / Volume 10

Katherine Elizabeth Mack, *From Apartheid to Democracy: Deliberating Truth and Reconciliation in South Africa* / Volume 11

Mary E. Stuckey, *Voting Deliberatively: FDR and the 1936 Presidential Campaign* / Volume 12

Robert Asen, *Democracy, Deliberation, and Education* / Volume 13

Shawn J. Parry-Giles and David S. Kaufer, *Memories of Lincoln and the Splintering of American Political Thought* / Volume 14

J. Michael Hogan, Jessica A. Kurr, Michael J. Bergmaier, and Jeremy D. Johnson, eds., *Speech and Debate as Civic Education* / Volume 15

Angela G. Ray and Paul Stob, eds., *Thinking Together: Lecturing, Learning, and Difference in the Long Nineteenth Century* / Volume 16

Sharon E. Jarvis and Soo-Hye Han, *Votes That Count and Voters Who Don't: How Journalists Sideline Electoral Participation (Without Even Knowing It)* / Volume 17

Belinda Stillion Southard, *How to Belong: Women's Agency in a Transnational World* / Volume 18

Melanie Loehwing, *Homeless Advocacy and the Rhetorical Construction of the Civic Home* / Volume 19

Kristy Maddux, *Practicing Citizenship: Women's Rhetoric at the 1893 Chicago World's Fair* / Volume 20

Craig Rood, *After Gun Violence: Deliberation and Memory in an Age of Political Gridlock* / Volume 21

Nathan Crick, *Dewey for a New Age of Fascism: Teaching Democratic Habits* / Volume 22

William Keith and Robert Danisch, *Beyond Civility: The Competing Obligations of Citizenship* / Volume 23

Lisa A. Flores, *Deportable and Disposable: Public Rhetoric and the Making of the "Illegal" Immigrant* / Volume 24

Milton Keynes UK
Ingram Content Group UK Ltd.
UKHW010012221123
433005UK00007B/350